We beheld His glory!

John's Gospel: the master-key to Jesus's hidden identity

Andrew Wright

Cover design by ***Jake Bryant***

Typeset in 12pt Calibri, footnotes in TNRoman

Printed and bound in Great Britain by

www.p2dbooks.co.uk

Published by P2D Books Ltd

Westoning, Bedfordshire, UK

ISBN: 978-1-914458-50-7

Dedicated to

My fellow members of the CFM bible study, 2023-2024

But especially to

My wife, Sue, for her patience and encouragement!

INDEX

Preface:
Christ's glory, & our communion with Him

This book's aim is to help you find fresh joy, in discovering more deeply who Christ is; and so, entering into deeper fellowship with Him and His Father. It is for Christians, who already know their bible but also long for more.

John's aim in writing his gospel, many years after Matthew Mark and Luke, was to unveil Jesus's divine identity. His Jewish compatriots, despite all the miracles and teaching, had failed to grasp this. So he summarises his primary theme by saying, *"We beheld His glory!"*. Revealing Christ's glory was the key to others believing in Him, and believers experiencing His life[1].

To that end he picks out seven miracles, each demonstrating an aspect of Jesus's glory and grace. And he records a series of teachings in which Jesus urges His hearers to believe in Him as the Son of God. He portrays the cross as Christ drawing all men to Himself; and the ascension as the restoring of His pre-incarnate glory.

For him, the foundational truth of the gospel was that *'Jesus Christ has come in the flesh'*: that the eternal Word of God took flesh and dwelt among us. Accepting Christ's dual nature as both fully God and fully man (i.e. the incarnation) was absolutely central. It was the acid test by which anti-Christ spirits, such as drove the heresies in the early church, could be discerned.

Only John records Christ's teaching the disciples about living union with Him. Evangelicalism has largely lost any sense of the experiential nature of this union, having limited its application to our justification. But despite being in his nineties, in exile and confronting grievous heresies, John could still describe his spirituality thus: *'Our fellowship is with the Father and His Son!'* The thrill of knowing Jesus was still vivid, and a source of deep joy to him.

In the Upper Room, Christ had taught them that they need not fear losing Him. His death would bring them brief agony, but they would be joyfully reunited: not just for forty days, but for a lifetime's communion. And not just

1 (20:31)

with Him, but indwelt by the Spirit and knowing the Father. This experiential fellowship with all three of the Trinity, John said, was the essence of eternal life. And his gospel's stated aim was *'so that in believing, you may have life'*.

Like all commentaries, you'll find stuff about the social and political context of Jesus's time, geographical references, and key Greek words. But to avoid blunting the impact of the prologue, I've placed background on the gospel's authorship, date, themes and purpose in an appendix; and studies of the symbolic meanings of some key words, in a second appendix. Finally, there are some questions to help you reflect once you've finished.

Unlike other commentaries, however, I hope you'll find you can see a bigger picture, especially in Christ's teaching at the Last Supper. It can seem hard to follow Jesus's train of thought, because:-

- John's gospel was the result of a lifetime's worship and meditation on the person of Christ. His memory has filtered out all irrelevant details, leaving a condensed but logically integrated record.
- In the context of the disciples' dread, Christ was teaching stuff so new that He had to use an iterative approach: returning to the same themes repeatedly but going a little deeper each time round.

But it all makes sense, and flows naturally, when seen as the disciples' entry point into a new dimension of life: *zoe* life, eternal life, life communing with the Father, the Son and the Holy Spirit.

This Upper Room discourse is the basis for all the New Testament teaching about being *'in Christ'*. For example, Paul takes it as read whenever he says things like, *'I live; nevertheless not I, but Christ lives in me'*. Or again, *'If any man be in Christ, he is a new creation'*. Beyond His death and resurrection, our union with Christ extends to His ascension. He prays for us to be with Him in the heavenlies, to gaze on His glory, and be changed into His likeness!

Each chapter of this book is about a fifteen-minute read. The final chapter is longer however, being a summary of John's major insights about Christ. Chapter headings refer to the relevant section of the gospel's text: so read with your bible beside you, and a heart open to what the Holy Spirit is saying.

Enjoy!

Jesus's hidden identity; Almighty God (1:1-18)

In his awesome prologue, John summarises everything about Jesus's hidden identity as the Son of God.

John's prologue is like the DNA in the nucleus of a living cell. It completely specifies everything needed for that cell. But if you only had the DNA, it would be hard to imagine the cell itself. Only once you had seen the cell would you fully understand the significance of each gene.

Likewise, the full significance of each phrase in John's prologue only emerges once you have studied the whole Gospel. But given that manuscript copies would have been rare, and memorisation the norm, John summarises his key points down into these few verses.

Interwoven with these truths, are verses about what it meant for Jesus to become man. We'll look at those, in chapter two. Then in chapter three we'll look at John the Baptist's role in announcing Christ's coming.

Within the eternal Godhead (1:1,2)

'In the beginning was the Word. And the Word was with God, and the Word was God'.[1]

John's opening words convey powerful and mysterious mood music. We are looking back through the mists of time, back beyond Creation itself into Eternity Past. Before the beginning of time and space, the Word - the ultimate expression of God's heart and mind - already was. This 'Word' was, somehow, both inherently God *and* distinct from God.

Jesus is the living Word of God. He has always been, is always, and will always be the embodiment of the mind of God. *'In Him are hidden all the treasures of wisdom and knowledge'*.

He is the Alpha and the Omega, the beginning and the end. There has never been a time when He did not exist. He had no birthday. He is *'a priest*

[1] (See Appendix 1)

forever, having neither beginning of days nor end of life; after the order of Melchizedek, through the power of an endless life'.[2]

He is the Word of God. His *logos* is the *torah*, the teaching, of God.

> *Break thou the bread of life, O Lord, to me,*
> *as thou didst break the loaves beside the sea.*
> *Beyond the sacred page I seek thee Lord;*
> *my spirit longs for thee, O living Word!*

Those who continue in His Word know the truth, and are set free by it[3]. In Him, *'all the promises of God are 'Yes!', and 'Amen!'*[4]. He Himself is the New Covenant[5], made in His blood. He speaks, and His sheep hear His voice. Like Mary at the tomb, we recognise His voice, and respond with joy and adoration, 'Rabboni!'

His word has ultimate authority. He spoke, and worlds came into being. He speaks, and the paralysed walk, and demons obey. One day *'the dead will hear the voice of the Son of God; and they that hear, shall live'*[6]. He has authority to pronounce judgement on every living being.[7]

He is and has always been face-to-face with God: or as v18 puts it, *'in the bosom of the Father'*. Closer than a nursing infant to its mother. Closer than a lover to their beloved. In intimate communion such that each immediately knows the other's mind.

Tozer says, *"When the Son of God walked the earth as the Son of Man, He spoke often to the Father and the Father answered Him again.... The dialogue involving the Father and the Son recorded in the scriptures is always to be understood as being between the Eternal Father and the Man Christ Jesus. That instant, immediate communion between the Persons of the Godhead which has been from all eternity, knows not sound nor effort nor motion".*

---

[2] (Heb 7:16,17)
[3] (8:31,32)
[4] (2 Cor 1:20)
[5] (Isa 42:6)
[6] (5:25)
[7] (5:22,27)

Though He was *with* God, He also *was* God: a separate Person, yet *'of one substance with the Father'*.[8] This is the mystery of the Trinity, which was such a stumbling block to the Jews.[9] Raised to repeat the mantra that *'The Lord our God, the Lord is One'*[10], the idea of a separate Person in the Godhead (with equal authority to give or take life, to judge, to raise the dead, to give life to those He wills) was anathema.

The disciples themselves struggled to grasp this truth; that though fully man, Jesus was also fully God. When Peter confessed, *'You are the Christ, the Son of the Living God'*, Jesus told him that knowledge of this truth could only come by revelation[11]. It is the foundational truth on which the Church is built, and the distinguishing feature that separates true belief from antiChrist heresy[12]. But even at the Last Supper, the disciples' understanding was limited. Phillip asked Jesus, *'Show us the Father, and that will suffice'*.

Jesus replied, *"I and the Father are One ...Have I been with you so long, and yet you have not known Me? Do you not believe, that I am in the Father and the Father in Me? The words that I speak to you I do not speak on My own. The Father who dwells in Me does the works."*

Our sovereign Creator (1:3,10,11)

'All things were made through Him, and without Him nothing was made that was made... the world was made through Him'.

We are blessed to live in a place with big skies, rushing clouds, changing tides, and a backdrop of mountains. The whole landscape is vibrant with life; from the tiniest lichen clinging to a wall, through all the myriad forms of life great and small. Migrating geese flying overhead, curlews calling, sheep bleating. All declaring the glory of God! Of Christ!

"The world is charged with the grandeur of God. It will flame out, like shining from shook foil; it gathers to a greatness, like the ooze of oil crushed ... nature

---

[8] (The Nicene Creed)
[9] (Isa 8:14)
[10] (Deut 6:4)
[11] (Matt 16:15-19)
[12] (1 Jn 4:1,2)

is never spent. There lives the dearest freshness deep down things".

(Gerard Manley Hopkins)

An art critic can recognise an artist's work without a signature. The brushstrokes, the colours, the composition all speak of the creator's identity, skill, and care. Similarly, *'the heavens are telling the glory of God: day to day pours forth speech, night to night declares knowledge'* of Christ's wonderful handiwork[13].

Everything we can now see, touch, or feel, was made by Christ. Initially this planet was covered with ocean from pole to pole, and in pitch darkness. But He created a boundary between the seas and the dry land. Then He created a firmament; an atmosphere that could sustain life. He made all the different lifeforms, from microscopic bacteria to giant sequoia trees. Finally He made the first human, Adam; modelling his body out of clay, then breathing the breath of life into him. And He created a perfectly-matched life-partner, so that together they could 'fill the earth, and subdue it'.

A creator has authority over his work. The clay cannot say to the potter, *"Why did you make me like this?"*.[14] But our fallen nature rebels at the thought that we are created; that we are not independent of Him, not our own yardstick of truth, not meant to hate how He made us. Hence when Christ entered the world, *"The world was made through Him, and the world did not know Him. He came unto His own, and His own received Him not."*

Christ's creator-ship is a theme throughout John's gospel. John's seven signs all attest that He is *'the firstborn over all Creation'*[15], in the sense of having full-blown authority over it. He is not, as some say, a 'divine clockmaker'; who makes a clock, winds it up and then leaves it to run. He is continuously active in His creation, healing seven days a week, turning water into wine, multiplying loaves and fishes, subduing storms, making blind eyes see.

---

[13] (Ps 19:1,2)
[14] (Rom 9:20,21)
[15] (Col 1:15,16)

If He is our Creator (and He is!) then we need to come to terms with that. We need to accept His sovereign authority, and learn to give thanks in every circumstance. But it also means there is *nothing* we cannot pray for!

Wellspring of life (1:4)

'In Him was life'

Jesus has life in a different dimension from our bodily, mental or social lives[16]. John uses three different words for life, depending on whether he is referring to bodily life (Gk: 'bios'), soul life (Gk: 'psyche') or spiritual life (Gk: 'zoe'). Christ has *zoe* life: God-life, life inherent within Himself, just as Almighty God has[17]. This life is un-ageing, endless, spiritual, and pure. His life challenged all the darkness in mankind by its transformative energy. But though this life-light shone into our darkness, we could neither grasp it nor extinguish it.

In a desert, even SAS soldiers cannot last longer than three days without water. During the Exodus, Israel was followed through Sinai from campsite to campsite by a huge boulder which Moses had broken open with the rod of God[18]. Out of it, flowed all the water needed to sustain two million people in the middle of the desert! That rock was Christ, says Paul.[19] And at the Feast of Tabernacles Jesus cries out, *"If anyone is thirsty, let him come to Me; and let him drink, if he believes in Me. For as the scripture has said, 'Out of His belly shall flow rivers of living water'"*[20]

He offers this water of life to the woman at the well: *"Whoever drinks of the water that I will give him will never thirst. But the water that I shall give him, will become in him a fountain of water springing up into everlasting life."*[21]

In his later Letter, John says, *"This is the testimony, that God has given us eternal life, and this life is in His Son. He who has the Son has life; he who does not have the Son of God does not have life."*[22]

---

[16] (See Appendix Two for more about the different words for different forms of life)

[17] (5:26)

[18] (Ex 17:1-7)

[19] (1 Cor 10:4)

[20] (7:37-38). See explanatory note on this translation, on p.112)

[21] (4:14)

[22] (1 Jn 4:11,12)

Just as the Universe would cease to exist without God's sustaining power, we believers cannot exist without an ongoing supply of this water of life. Unlike Jesus, we don't have this life inherent in us. Unless we abide in Christ, we become like a withered branch of a vine, fruitless and dead.[23]

This is the truth Jesus was teaching, when He spoke about us abiding in Him. Just as the branches of the vine will become fruitless and wither, without life-giving sap from the vine itself, so it is with us. It is through our union with Him, that we receive His Spirit. There is a sense in which, as He says to the Samaritan woman, when you've drunk once, a permanent fountain opens in your heart. But it is also true that the ongoing flow depends on our abiding.

Living light (1:4,5,9)

'His life was the light of men ... The light shines in the darkness, and the darkness has never over come it .. the true light which, by coming into the world, gives light to every man'.[24]

In the material world, light and life go together. Sunlight powers the growth of all vegetation, and thereby provides food for animals to grow. Though light can be thought of as particles, they have no mass, no substance. Light is energy in transit, as we see with lasers.

Genesis records that the earth was chaotic and void, despite the Spirit of God hovering over it, until God said, "Let there be light"[25]. It was that act that created the rhythm of day and night, which underpins all our 'biological clocks'.

To a Jew, especially at the Feast of Tabernacles, Jesus's claim to be the light would speak of the shekinah glory that hovered over Israel during the Exodus. It gave them light at night, as well as shade by day. And it guided them when to travel and when to rest. It also lit the altar fire, enabling sacrifices and offerings for sin. But it demonstrated God's awful holiness, when Aaron's sons tried to substitute it with 'strange fire'.

---

[23] (15:5,6)
[24] (1:4,5,9)
[25] (Gen 1:2,3)

But light also has various symbolic meanings. In 'Star Wars', the Jedi can turn from the light to the dark side of their nature. 'Bringing things to light' means exposing what is hidden. 'Light-hearted' means joyful.

So what did John mean by saying that Christ's *zoe* life was the light of men?

Some have previously interpreted this light as intellectual enlightenment. We refer to 'the Dark Ages' being followed by 'the Enlightenment'. But this verse cannot be referring to human reason. Nicodemus was the top theologian of his time - *the* teacher of Israel - and yet Christ told him, no-one can see the Kingdom of God unless they're born again. The message of the cross seems foolish to the cleverest of minds.[26]

Jesus says that natural man walks in darkness: even the holiest leader in Judaism was a child of Satan[27]. And He teaches the disciples that there is a spiritual power behind every societal structure, which He called 'the World'. That power structure is ruled by the Prince of darkness.

It hardly needs saying that Christ's *earthly* life, His example of love, humility, grace and purity, has probably had a much greater effect on the human race, than any other single life. Until recently, it was the chief formative influence on Western civilisation and its values. So, many read this verse as referring to this general moral influence of Christ's life down through history. And in that sense, the darkness has never overcome it.

But the aspect of Christ's life which John is speaking of, is not Christ's biological life, or His example of how to live well as a social being. It's about His *zoe* life - His God-life, eternal life, spiritual life. This light-giving life is communicable, but only to disciples: *"I am the Light of the world. He who follows Me shall not walk in darkness, but shall have the light of life"*[28]

John later says, *"This is the message which we have heard from Him and declare to you, that God is light and in Him is no darkness at all."*[29] When Christ uses God's eternal name, *'I AM the light of the world'*, He is saying that the living God of the burning bush is a consuming fire. The gospel in a

---

[26] (1 Cor 1:18,19)
[27] (8:44)
[28] (8:12)
[29] (1 Jn 1:5)

nutshell, is that in His very essence God is holy. So this light is the light of God's holiness. And it is inseparable from His *zoe* life. One cannot claim to have communion with God, whilst continuing to walk in darkness.

But lest we should think that such light is unapproachable for us who are steeped in sin, the context of Christ's claim is His astonishing grace towards the woman caught in adultery: *"I do not condemn you; go and sin no more"*[30]. If John had to choose only two words to describe God, they would be *light* and *love*[31]. Somehow this light, the light of Christ, is full of grace as well as truth. Given that no-one can say they have no sin, or that they have never sinned, 'walking in the light' is primarily about accepting God's definition of sin and confessing our sin, so that we can be continuously cleansed by the blood of Christ.[32]

Only-begotten Son of God (1:14)

"Glory as of the only-begotten Son of the Father"

Jesus's only-begottenness does not refer to His unique conception and birth, but to His unique relationship to His Father.

Jesus is *unique* in His glory. He is the *only* way to the Father. He is the *only* gate for the sheep. Many may come, claiming to be the Son of God: but Jesus is uniquely the Son of the Father. All this would still be true, if Jesus was just God's only Son. So why does John call Him only-*begotten*?

In human terms Abraham 'begat' two sons, Ishmael & Isaac: yet Isaac is called 'only-begotten'.[33] The difference is that unlike Ishmael, Isaac was continuously fathered for seventy-five years, until Abraham's eventual death. Throughout that time, Abraham and Isaac lived together in Hebron.[34]

The Nicene Creed of AD325 states that we believe *"in one Lord Jesus Christ, the Son of God, the Only-begotten, begotten of the Father before all ages;*

---

[30] (8:11)
[31] (1 Jn 4:8)
[32] (1 Jn 1:6-2:2)
[33] (Heb 11:17)
[34] ((Gen 35:27))

Light of Light, true God of true God; begotten, not made; of one essence with the Father, by whom all things were made."

The Son of God was begotten 'before all ages'. He never had a birthday. There never was a time when He was not the Son, or when His Father was not His Father. His incarnation came *'at just the right time'* in history[35]; but His begottenness had no beginning. This continual Father-Son relationship, going back before time began, is the essence of His Personhood within the Trinity.

In *Healing the Masculine Soul*, Gordon Dalby talks about 'the brown ooze'. By this he means something indefinable but vitally important, that flows from father to son. As a child grows into adulthood, it establishes their identity as a man-to-be. For Jesus, this flow from Father to Son has continued throughout eternity. *'The Father loves the Son, and shows Him all things that He Himself does'*.[36]

And Jesus's loving obedience as a son, His honouring of His Father, has also been continual, even before His incarnation[37]. *'I come to do Thy will'* has always been His motto. *'The Son can do nothing except what the Father shows Him'*.[38] This perfect Father-Son relationship within the Godhead, is why He teaches us to pray, *'Our Father ... Thy will be done'*.

This continual begottenness, says John, is the source of Jesus's unique glory. It is why He so perfectly displays God's character, that He can say, *'He who has seen Me has seen the Father'*[39]. He is '*the brightness of God's glory and the exact image of His Person'*[40]; God's Word in these last days.

The glory which Peter, James and John saw at the Transfiguration, was what Jesus calls *"the glory which I had with You before the world began"*[41]. But all twelve had seen His glory manifested in each of the seven signs John records.

---

[35] (Gal 4:4)
[36] (5:20)
[37] (Heb 10:5-7)
[38] (5:19)
[39] (14:9)
[40] (Heb 1:1-3)
[41] (17:5)

The One who baptises in Holy Spirit 1:33

"This is He who baptises with the Holy Spirit"

When Israel crossed the Red Sea, they were baptised *into* Moses. Baptism, in Jewish thought, joined baptiser and baptised. And when John came baptising with water, His followers became disciples.

When Jesus's followers began baptising, at first it was similar to John's baptism: a baptism of repentance for the forgiveness of sins. But the dove had identified Jesus as the One who had been given the Spirit measurelessly[42], and who would baptise in Holy Spirit: the Son of God.

During His earthly ministry, the Holy Spirit was present with the disciples in Christ. But after He ascended, He said, the Father would authorise Him to pour out the Spirit; and they would be *filled*. As a sponge dunked in a bucket comes out filled! They would receive power to be His witnesses[43].

The same Spirit that filled Jesus, had been promised by the Father centuries earlier. We receive, simply by asking; believing that just as earthly fathers know how to give their children good gifts, our heavenly Father will give the Holy Spirit to those who ask in faith.

Just as Peter and Andrew, James and John, Phillip and Nathanael made the trek from Galilee to be baptised in the Jordan, seeking to make way for Messiah to come into their lives, we come to Jesus as our Baptiser, longing for *'the Spirit of life in Christ Jesus'*. His Spirit flows into us, joining us with Him and producing the fruit of His character: love, joy, patience, kindness, goodness, gentleness, faithfulness, self-control.

Thank you Lord Jesus, for baptising us into the Holy Spirit! Thank you for joining us into Your body! Thank you for all your wonderful gifts, Holy Spirit! Thank you for glorifying Christ to us!

---

[42] (3:34)

[43] (14:17; Acts 1:8)

The Lord of Glory (1:14)

"We beheld His glory."

John chooses each of the seven miraculous 'signs' in his gospel, because they demonstrated something of Jesus's glory - in the sense of His authority over Creation, His ability to heal, His glorious grace etc. The other gospels also record Peter, James and John seeing Jesus physically transfigured. And of course Revelation records John seeing Jesus's heavenly glory in detail, up close. But whilst it does refer to the miracles and the physical glory of Jesus's divine nature, this verse primarily points to the glory of Christ's *character,* 'full of grace and truth'.

In the Upper Room, Jesus addressed the disciples' separation anxiety by revealing the blessings they would gain from His returning to the Father. It would open up a new realm of Christian experience. Their sadness and fear would be replaced by permanent joy. Jesus would re-appear to them, and they would be united with Him in a far deeper way than ever before: they in Him, and He in them. The Father would love them, making His home with them[44]. They would have direct personal access to Him, with authority to pray in Jesus's Name[45]. The Holy Spirit within them, would unpack everything they hadn't yet grasped.

The incarnation was only the outward portion of a return ticket: Jesus's ascension was the other half. Having preached in hell, He began His return to the Father, pausing en route for a forty-day stopover to teach the disciples about the Kingdom. But His final destination was to be restored to the glory which He'd had with His Father, before the foundation of the world.

Jesus prayed for all His followers to be able to see this glory[46]. His prayer for went like this: *"Father I desire that they also who You gave Me, may be with Me where I am, that they may behold My glory which You gave Me in Your love, before the foundation of the world".*[47]

---

[44] (14:23)
[45] (16:26,27)
[46] (17:24)
[47] (17:24)

Paul describes God's response to this prayer as a normative Christian experience.[48] *"We all, with unveiled face, beholding as in a mirror the glory of the Lord, are being transformed into the same image from glory to glory, just as by the Spirit of the Lord".*[49]

Meditating on His glory causes our faces to shine. And the love within the Godhead, somehow becomes etched more deeply on our hearts.

Glorious Grace (1:14)

"Glory ... full of grace and truth"

Moses knew God's glory better than anyone in Israel. He'd been up Mount Sinai, when the holy fire of God's Presence was on it. He'd received from God's hand the tablets of the Law, and the blueprints for the Tabernacle. Yet before the ink was dry (so to speak) the Israelites broke the first commandment, by making an idol, a golden calf. The Law said nothing about how God would respond; nevertheless Moses prayed for their forgiveness, even if it meant him dying in their place. Then, astonishingly, he prays, *"Show me now Your glory"*![50]

How did God respond? How does *He* define the essence of His glory?

The Lord passed before him and proclaimed, *"The Lord, the Lord God, merciful and gracious, long-suffering, and abounding in goodness and truth, keeping mercy for thousands, forgiving iniquity and transgression and sin, by no means clearing the guilty, visiting the iniquity of the fathers upon the children and the children's children to the third and the fourth generation." So Moses made haste and bowed his head toward the earth, and worshiped. Then he said, "If now I have found grace in Your sight, O Lord, let my Lord, I pray, go among us, even though we are a stiff-necked people; and pardon our iniquity and our sin, and take us as Your inheritance."*[51]

The essence of God's glory is His grace. Without objective truth, there is no definition of sin. But as soon as we accept God's truth about ourselves, we

---

[48] (2 Cor 3:18)
[49] (2 Cor 3:18)
[50] (Ex 33:18)
[51] (Ex 34:6-9)

know we need grace. And in Christ, is *'grace upon grace'*. Abundant forgiveness, yet without compromising God's holiness: because He has visited our sins on His only Son.

Glory, glory, glory! Our God is a God of glorious grace. Grace sufficient for all our sin. Merciful, patient, good; forgiving iniquity, transgression and sin. Willing to live amongst us, even though we are stiff-necked. Glory to Him!

Fully human, yet fully divine (1:14-18)

When John calls Jesus ''the Only-Begotten Son of the Father', he is referring to their Father-Son relationship within the Trinity, not the Incarnation.

Jesus was fully human and fully divine. His deity was in no way inferior to the Father's; nor was it diminished in any way when He 'took flesh'.

Believing this is absolutely central to true Christian faith in Him.

The Jesus of history, the real man who lived in a real place at a real point in history, was and is Almighty-God-become-man. Grasping this truth is absolutely central to true Christian faith, according to John.[1] It is the acid test of whether someone claiming to speak for God, is genuine or not.

As John aged, he realised that this wonderful truth about Jesus was being undermined. The eternal Word of Life whom he had seen, heard, and touched - the Word who had been with the Father and had been made manifest to him, and with whom he experienced continual joyful fellowship - was being denied by heretics within the church.[2] Many others' faith in Jesus was being rocked or even destroyed.

The heresies fell into two categories.

- One group taught that Jesus was not truly human but rather, some sort of emanation from God who took on a human appearance. Not being fully man, he didn't really die on the cross, and wasn't actually raised from the dead[3].

- Some of them thought that God existed in different states at different times, and that Jesus was just the form He took for that particular period. Others believed that Jesus was merely a man - but a man who was possessed by the Spirit of God from his baptism until just before the cross.

As Bishop of Ephesus, John wrote three pastoral letters to the churches under his care, about this issue. You'll find them near the end of the New Testament. The first addresses believers who've been shocked by some of

---

[1] (1 John 4:2)
[2] (1John 1:1-3)
[3] (1 Cor 15:12)

their friends leaving the church, claiming they have superior new revelation. John writes to reassure them that what they were taught about Jesus is still true; and he gives them three ways of testing whether people claiming to have new revelation were right or wrong. The second letter was addressed to a specific church which was weighing up whether to join the new teaching, or to stay in fellowship with John. And the third was to encourage an individual whose church had broken with John's teachings.

This battle over the truth of the incarnation, has continued down through the centuries and still rages today. To quote just a few examples:-

- Jehovah's Witnesses say Jesus was 'a god', inferior to the One True God.
- Unitarians (some, at least) deny that Jesus was the Son of God
- Orthodox Jews still deny that Jesus was their Messiah, & came in the flesh
- Muslims believe Jesus was a prophet, but that Allah has no sons

But unless we believe in Jesus as the Son of God, truly God and truly man, John says we have no salvation.[4] We have not got eternal life, and cannot have fellowship with the Father and with His Son.

John's gospel, and its teaching about Christ's dual identity as Son of God and Son of Man, was the foundation on which all his subsequent pastoral teaching was built. For us, if Christ was not both God and man, His sacrifice on the cross would either be irrelevant or inadequate. And if He was not truly raised from the dead, 'we are of all men the most to be pitied' - for having believed a spiritual lie. The doctrine of the incarnation is also the foundation for all Paul's teaching about us being 'in Christ', as we shall see when we look at Jesus's Upper Room teaching about our union with Him.

Believing in the incarnation logically requires that we believe that there is more than one Person within the Godhead. But Jesus taught that 'I and the Father are One'. We are about to explore the mystery of the Trinity, as we assemble John's teachings about Jesus's identity into a coherent whole. We'll do this by asking a series of questions to clarify what John is saying.

---

[4] (1 Jn 5:11-12)

What does John mean when he calls Jesus 'the Son of the Father'?

Nowadays we usually use the words 'son' or 'father' to mean genetic relationship, or perhaps adoption. But in tribal cultures such as Uganda, its meaning is quite different. 'Father' means anyone who you look up to, who looks out for you, teaches you, protects you, provides for you. 'Son' means anyone you provide for, protect, teach, etc. There is usually an implication of family likeness, whatever culture one looks at.

Scripture often uses the phrase 'son of' in the non-genetic sense. When Jesus calls His Jewish detractors, 'sons of Satan', He wasn't denying their Abrahamic lineage[5]. And He gives those who believe in Him, the authority to become children of God[6] - but that doesn't make us gods!

When John calls Jesus the Son of God, he is not talking about Jesus's virgin birth, or a genetic connection. He is not talking about the incarnation, or the Christmas story. We've already seen that Jesus was God's Son, before ever Creation occurred. Their Father-Son relationship is eternal, not temporal.

In using this phrase, John definitely means to indicate likeness. The Son of God is 'the Word', the expression of God's heart and purposes towards us. He is full of grace and truth, just like His Father. In fact He is the exact image of the invisible God[7] and anyone who has seen Him has seen the Father[8].

But 'Son of God' goes beyond likeness, to *identity*.

John says the Son of God is co-eternal with the Father: He existed before time began.[9] He is co-Creator with the Father, of everything that was made at Creation.[10] He has the same divine life[11] inherent in Himself, unlike any other human being. He knows everything about everyone[12] - He is omniscient. He

---

[5] (Jn 8:44)
[6] (1:12-13))
[7] (Heb 1:3)
[8] (14:9)
[9] (1:1)
[10] (1:3)
[11] (5:26)
[12] (2:24,25; 21:17; Col 2:1-3)

has been given all authority to judge.[13] He is indwelt with all the fullness of the Godhead[14] and one in Being with the Father[15].

This is the mystery which we call 'the Trinity'!

Some think of the Trinity as three Persons united by mutual love. But though the Father loves the Son, and the Son loves the Father, their unity is not primarily social in nature. Some think of it as consisting of mutual respect and honouring, but it is more than that. Some see it as down to the complete submission of Jesus to His Father's will: but it goes deeper than complete agreement. Rather, even though Father and Son are distinct persons (*the Word was with God*), they are of the same essence, of one substance' (*the Word was God*).

So in what sense is Jesus 'begotten'?

The word 'begat' appears frequently in biblical genealogies, and clearly there it means physical generation. However though Abraham begat Isaac after Ishmael, scripture nevertheless refers to Isaac as only-begotten.[16] The word therefore carries the idea of generation, but also of ongoing relationship and ultimately, the right to all that the Father possesses.[17]

John's usage is clearly the latter: for the begotten Son is 'in the bosom of the Father'[18], where He has been since eternity past. In other words, the Son of God had no birthday! His being *'begotten'* can't refer to His *'becoming flesh'.*

How then *should* we understand His begotten-ness?

As with human fathering, there is both causing-to-be *and* relationship; but unlike human fathering, it is not an event in time, but an eternal relationship. There has never been, and never will be, a time when God was not Father God; and there never was and never will be a time when Christ was not God the Son. God's Father-heart is eternal, as is Christ's Sonship: their relationship

---

[13] (5:22)
[14] (3:34; Col 1:17)
[15] (10:30)
[16] (Heb 11:17)
[17] (Gen 21:10)
[18] (1:18)

has never had a beginning. Throughout all eternity, God continually begets His Son. (Theologians call this 'eternal filiation')

Father and Son (and Holy Spirit) do not have distinct roles, for they collaborate in everything: in Creation, in providence, in redemption, in pouring out the Spirit, and in the final judgement. Nor are they distinct in historical dispensations, for all Three are active throughout history. Their distinctness as Persons stems from their eternal relationship to each other.

Jesus's being *begotten* expresses God's missional father-heart. The Father continually sends the Son, and the Son continually *proceeds from* the Father[19]. *'Man shall not live by bread alone, but by every word that proceeds out of the mouth of God'*[20]. He is the Living Bread that came down from heaven. The same Father-heart that eternally begets His Son, seeks to Father you, too.

<u>Why does John call Jesus *only*-begotten</u>?

'Only-begotten' (*monogenes*) is a term used almost exclusively by John: but he uses it four times.[21] It cannot refer to Jesus being God's only child, for John says anyone can become a child of God.[22] Nor does it relate to Jesus's rank as *'firstborn over all creation'*[23]; firstborn in Greek is *prototokos*, not *monogenes*, and refers to the right to inherit leadership of a family.

Modern paraphrases of the Bible often translate *monogenes* as 'unique', 'one-of-a-kind'.

- Jesus is unique in His continuous father-son relationship with God. We have previously noted how Isaac is referred to Abraham's only-begotten son, despite Ishmael also being Abraham's child.
- He is uniquely perfect in being the image of God. Which of us, even the most saintly of Christians, can describe ourselves as full of grace and truth?!

---

19 (6:57;7:29; 8:42)
20 (Matt 4:4)
21 (1:18; 3:16,18;1Jn 4:9)
22 (1:12)
23 (Col 1:15)

- And He is unique in the degree of His intimacy with the Father

We know that in the last days, many false Christs will arise, and will try if possible to deceive even God's elect people. But Jesus is 'one-of-a-kind'. They may be able to perform great miracles, signs and wonders; but the key test will be, are they full of grace and truth? Do they sound like Jesus? Do they manifest His character?

If begotten-ness and incarnation are different,

What did John mean, that Jesus took flesh?

"The Word became flesh, and dwelt among us" *1:9,10,14*

John is spectacularly uninterested in the details of Jesus's conception, birth and upbringing, as recorded in the other gospels. He just says that the Word, though being God Himself, veiled His glory in flesh, and took the form of a man. He *dwelt* among us: the word means He camped among us, just as God's shekinah glory dwelt in the Tabernacle during the Exodus. His body was the antitype of which the Tabernacle spoke; the true Temple, the place where man can meet with God.

Those of you who enjoy camping will agree that you get to know people quickly, when you camp with them! Jesus was fully man, yet fully God too. The glory of His character shone out in the signs He performed; His miracles were the Father's works; His words were the Father's words; His character was the Father's character. He shone with the Father's holiness and grace. He demonstrated the Father's love, laying down His life for His friends. And yet His divine glory was 'veiled in flesh': just as we often fail to recognise the significance of someone's life until after they're gone, and 'a prophet is without honour in his own home'.

Paul tells us Christ made Himself of no reputation; He was born into a working class family; took up a manual trade; and became the Suffering Servant.[24] He came and took the body His Father had prepared for Him, knowing it was to be used as a sacrifice on the cross.[25] He identified Himself

[24] (Phil 2:5-8)

[25] (Heb 10:5-10)

as the Son of Man, or in Hebrew, the Son of Adam. He was tempted just like us: everything we struggle with, He has faced Himself - yet without sin. He was the One who would pick up the tab for Adam's original sin: and instead of bringing death to all men, grace would reign through His righteousness, giving us eternal life[26].

The fact that Jesus 'took flesh' and became incarnate, is absolutely central to the atonement. If He was not truly man, if there had been no flow of blood when the centurion pierced His side, then His death could not have made atonement for our sins.

But His humanity is also central to His ministry as our High Priest. It is because He has been tempted in every possible way that we are, and come through, that He sympathises with our weaknesses and is our advocate in heaven when we sin[27]

During His earthly ministry, only three of the disciples ever saw Him transfigured. His dual identity is still hidden from most, except those who believe. But veiled in that human body, was *'all the fullness of the Godhead'*.[28] God was *in Christ, reconciling the world to Himself.*[29] He was filled with the Holy Spirit *'without measure'*.[30] Even while talking with Nicodemus, He was in continuous communion with His Father,[31] operating with split-screen vision as it were.

This was the fulfilment of Isaiah's prophecy six hundred years earlier: *"the Lord Himself will give you a sign: Behold, the virgin shall conceive and bear a Son, and shall call His name Immanuel"*[32] (God with us). Transcendent God has made Himself known to us, becoming immanent in our Lord. The Kingdom of Heaven is at hand (within touching distance) in the Person of Christ.

---

[26] (Rom 5:21)
[27] (1 Jn 2:1; Heb 4:14-16)
[28] (10:30; Col 2:9)
[29] (2 Cor 5:19)
[30] (3:34)
[31] (3:13)
[32] (Isa 7:14)

John's wonder at this, that he had actually seen and touched the eternal Word of God, was still fresh in his mind sixty years after Jesus's death. He writes, *"That which was from the beginning, which we have heard, which we have seen with our eyes, which we have looked upon, and our hands have handled, concerning the Word of life - the life was manifested, and we have seen, and bear witness, and declare to you that eternal life which was with the Father and was manifested to us - that which we have seen and heard we declare to you, that you also may have fellowship with us; and truly our fellowship is with the Father and with His Son Jesus Christ"*[33].

Though Christ had long since ascended, John was still in communion with Him, still experiencing the reality of His Presence: and he longs for all his readers to share that wonderful reality, of intimate communion with Immanuel. Christ's promise is that *"If anyone loves Me, he will keep My word; and My Father will love him, and We will come to him and make Our home with him"*[34]. Whilst it's true that we are to walk by faith, not by sight, it's also true that Jesus wants us to know Him, at a real, experiential level.

So when John talks about Jesus having 'taken flesh', as well as the wonder of God becoming man and entering His own Creation, and the wonder of His experiencing everything we experience and becoming just the High Priest we need, there is also something about His accessibility and ongoing Presence, or immanence, with us. He is still 'God with us'!

Was Jesus *made* flesh? Or did He volunteer?

'Flesh' has various meanings in scripture: it can mean:-

- physical muscle & connective tissues (vs bone)
- Human weakness and frailty [35]
- the fallen nature; our bodies and souls
- a collective term for humanity; or
- 'flesh and blood' as distinct from spirit[36]

---

[33] (1 Jn 1:1-3)

[34] (14:23)

[35] (Isa 40:6)

[36] (Lk 24:39)

Here, it is this latter sense that John is using. Jesus was not 'made man' in the sense of being created. Rather, He 'was manifested *(revealed, shown plainly)* in the flesh'[37], and He 'came in the flesh'[38] - made his appearance.

John knew that for Jesus to be the Lamb of God, the atoning sacrifice for our sins, He had to take flesh. *'The wages of sin is death'*, and for Jesus to die, He had to be made man. Only a substitutionary sacrifice would suffice[39].

Jesus too, knew this was why He had to take flesh. *"Sacrifice and offering You did not desire, but a body You have prepared for Me. In burnt offerings and sacrifices for sin You had no pleasure. Then I said, 'Behold, I come—in the volume of the book it is written of Me—to do Your will, O God.' "*[40].

In English, we only have two 'voices' for verbs: active and passive. *"I did something"* (active) or *"Something was done to me"* (passive). But Greek has a third voice and here the Greek word for 'became' is in this *middle voice*. So the incarnation was something Jesus actively chose, but God did too. Father God prepared a body for Him; but Jesus chose to occupy it.

In fact, all three Persons of the Trinity were involved in the incarnation. *"God so loved the world, that He gave His only-begotten Son"*[41]. The incarnation was the supreme sacrifice of the Father's agape love, the clearest evidence of His missional heart towards us. God the Father brought His Son into the world; the Holy Spirit came upon Mary; but Jesus chose to accept the role of 'Lamb of God' for you and me. It was His active choice - a supremely costly choice - to take flesh and become a human sacrifice for you and me.

Did the incarnation make Jesus any less than fully divine?

Paul says that though Christ was in the form of God, He didn't count equality with God as something to cling to, but made Himself a nonentity; took the role of a 'doulos' or bond-servant; and came in the likeness of men. And

---

[37] (1Tim 3:16)
[38] (1Jn 4:2)
[39] (Lev 17:11)
[40] (Heb 10:5)
[41] (John 3:16)

then, as a Man, He humbled Himself, gave up His right to life, and suffered the shame of crucifixion.[42]

John records Jesus praying to His Father, asking for things that He seemingly could not do for Himself. To our way of thinking, father and son relationships imply an undertone of authority and submission;, and Hebrews records that *In the days of His flesh, when He had offered up prayers and supplications, with vehement cries and tears to Him who was able to save Him from death, and was heard because of His godly fear, though He was a son, yet He learned obedience by the things which He suffered; and having been perfected, he became the author of eternal salvation, to all who obey Him.*[43]

Some take this as showing that Jesus was somehow diminished by being incarnate. And John records Jesus asking the Father to restore the glory He'd had before the world was made[44], implying that He had had to shed that glory to be incarnate.

However, John is quite clear that as the Word of God, Christ was in no way less than God: He was with God, but He also was God.[45] He existed before Creation, way back before Abraham was born.[46] Like His Father, He has been and still is, continuously active in Creation.[47] This was evidenced in the miracles He did.[48] He was filled with the Spirit, 'without measure'.[49] Paul says '*all the fullness of the Godhead dwells in Him in bodily form*'[50]. And John says, '*of His fullness have we all received*'[51].

---

[42] (Phil 2:5-8)
[43] (Heb 7:5-9)
[44] (17:1-5)
[45] (1:1)
[46] (9:58)
[47] (1:3; 5:17)
[48] (3:2)
[49] (3:34)
[50] (Col 2:9)
[51] (1:16,17)

John records Jesus claiming to be Messiah[52], equal with God[53], pre-existent Son of Man[54], Judge of all mankind, the source of resurrection life[55], worshipped by Abraham[56], Son of God[57], and One with the Father[58]. Though He chose to only do what He saw the Father do, He had authority to give life to whomever He chose: His Father had given Him autonomy.[59] It's significant that to the Jews, claiming to be the Son of God was the same as claiming to be God Himself.[60]

John clearly testifies that despite being incarnate, Jesus remained fully God.

This question of whether Christ was in some way less than God, was at the heart of the heresies John found himself confronting. So it was important then, and remains important today, to have a clear understanding of what the incarnation actually meant.

<u>One Person, two natures</u>

The Creed describes Jesus's dual nature like this: *His will as the Son of Man, must be distinguished from His will as the Son of God. As to the latter, His will and His Father's will are one and the same: they are of one substance. But as to the former, He learned obedience through what He suffered.*

A W Tozer says, *"When the Son of God walked the earth as the Son of Man, He spoke often to the Father and the Father answered Him again.... The dialogue involving the Father and the Son recorded in the scriptures is always to be understood as being between the Eternal Father and the <u>Man</u> Christ Jesus. That instant, immediate communion between the Persons of the Godhead which has been from all eternity, knows not sound nor effort nor motion".*[61]

---

52 (4:26)
53 (5:17,18)
54 (6:62)
55 (5:19-31)
56 (8:56-58)
57 (9:35-38)
58 (10:30)
59 (5:21)
60 10:32-33)
61 (Tozer, 'Knowledge of the Holy', ch 4)

My computer enables me to watch more than one Internet video at once, should I choose to do so. But I would probably not be paying full attention to either of them; or else my brain would get scrambled! Jesus however was able to live a split-screen existence; fully God and fully aware of what was happening in His Father's Presence, at the very same time as He was engaging with folk such as Nicodemus.[62]

It was essential that Jesus be both fully man, and fully God.

He had to be fully God,

- for His disclosure of the Father's mind and heart to be perfect & final;
- for His death to be the supreme evidence of God's love towards sinners;
- to guarantee the permanence, perfection & efficacy of His sacrifice; and
- to conquer Satan, 'dispossess the strong man' & free his captives.

At the same time, it was essential that He be fully Man, because

- only so could He mediate between God and men
- only so could He die for our sins
- only so could He supply 'the life of the flesh which is in the blood'
- only so could He be the Second Adam, representing the whole human race

Once we are joined to Christ, we too have two natures: our flesh, and the Holy Spirit. We become one spirit with Christ, and His Spirit within us continually battles with the fleshly desires[63] of our souls. He steadily forms the new man within us, so that eventually when Christ appears, we shall be like Him!

The effects of this union with Christ, form the basis of John's later teaching about how to discern true believers from heretics. He takes the puzzled and confused believers back to Christ's nature, and the touchstone of the Incarnation. This gives three tests of whether someone is truly saved:-

Morally, anyone who walks in darkness whilst claiming to be in the Light, is deceiving themselves and others about God's nature: Christ is Light, and in Him is no darkness at all.

---

62 (3:13)

63 (Jas 4:1-6; Gal 5:16,17; Rom 8:10-14)

Relationally, God is love: and anyone who says they love God but is not willing to love his brother as Christ has loved him, is still in darkness.

Theologically, anyone who denies that who denies that Jesus is fully God and fully man, is led by antiChrist rather than the Spirit of Christ.[64]

The next chapter will look at John-the-Baptist's role in pointing out Jesus to the Jews as their Messiah. Then we'll get into how the gospel hammers this message home, first by recounting seven key 'signs' Jesus gave, and then describing His debates with the Judaeans and His 'I AM' statements.

---

64 (1Jn 4:1-3)

John The Baptist:
warm-up, witness, wingman

(1:6f,19f; 3:22f)

John-The-Baptist's role was key in preparing the Jews to receive Messiah:
first, by preaching repentance and baptism, and
secondly, by clearly identifying Jesus as 'the Lamb of God'.

Once Jesus became known, John gladly made way for Him.

The first week of Jesus's ministry

After the Prologue, the rest of John 1 covers the first week of Jesus's ministry. John gives a detailed chronology, evoking the seven days of Creation:

- Day 1: John-the-Baptist's interrogation by the Jerusalem authorities, just as Jesus arrives back from His temptation[1]
- Day 2: John sees Jesus again, & hails Him as 'Lamb of God', & the One who baptises with the Holy Spirit[2]
- Day 3: He points Jesus out to two of his disciples (Andrew & ?John); and they spend the rest of the day with Him[3]
- Day 4: Andrew brings his brother Simon Peter to Jesus saying, 'We have found Messiah!'[4]
- Day 5: Jesus calls Philip, who then ropes in Nathanael, saying that Jesus is 'the fulfilment of the Law and the Prophets'[5]. They set off for Galilee.
- Day 6: Depending on John-the-Baptist's location, this could have been a forty mile trek. Or if he was on the lower Jordan, maybe eighty.
- Day 7: (The 'third day' in Jewish terms, counting from the day they set off). They reach Cana and are invited to a wedding[6]

---

[1] (1:19-28)
[2] (1:29-34)
[3] (1:35-39)
[4] (1:40-42)
[5] (1:43-51)
[6] (2:1,2)

John the Baptist's 'warm-up act'

At every pop concert, the star or headline act will be preceded by a warm-up act. John-the-Baptist was appointed by God for the sole purpose of preparing Israel for the arrival of their Messiah. He was to Israel, what the star was to the Magi. Whilst waiting for Christ to appear, John prepared the way by calling people to repentance, telling them that the Kingdom of Heaven was imminent.[7]

The location where he baptised people, is hard to be sure of. Elsewhere it is called 'Bethany-beyond-Jordan', presumably to distinguish it from the Bethany where Lazarus lived, just outside Jerusalem. But John calls it Bethabara-beyond-Jordan. It's possible of course that these were two different venues. But the traditional site is at the southern end of the Jordan, which would be eighty miles from Cana-in-Galilee. There is another possible site further north, only forty miles from Cana. The fact that Jesus and his team could walk to Cana in three days suggests the latter.

John demanded personal repentance before he would baptise anyone. If they were in any doubt as to what that meant, he gave them specific instructions[8]. It had to be a radical change of life, not just a verbal confession. He was particularly challenging to the Pharisees, who thought that simply being descended from Abraham was enough to guarantee salvation.[9] He warned them that when Messiah baptised them, it would be with Holy Spirit and fire. There would be a winnowing process, to separate the wheat from the chaff. And the chaff would then be destroyed by fire!

John's witness that Jesus was the Messiah (1:19-34)

John was born into a priestly family, living in Jerusalem.[10] His parents had longed for a child for many years, infertility being considered a shame. One day whilst serving in the Holy Place, his father Zachariah was told they would have a son, and to call him John. He would live as a Nazirite or holy man,

---

[7] (Mt 3:1-10)
[8] (Lk 3:10-14)
[9] (Mt 3:7-10)
[10] (Luke 1:3-23)

filled with the Holy Spirit even while still in his mother's womb. He would fulfil Malachi's prophecy four hundred years earlier, turning Israel back to God just as Elijah had done centuries earlier. But unlike Elijah, his work would prepare the way for Messiah's arrival.

The name John means "Yahweh is gracious". (In the Old Testament it's spelt Johanan or Jehohanan). Sadly, though Zachariah's own name means 'God remembers', in their family line there had never been a child called John.[11] And Zachariah found it impossible to believe that God was going to be so gracious to him and Elizabeth. So for nine months, until the moment when he had to name the baby, he was struck dumb.

Elizabeth was Mary's relative[12], probably her aunt, which would make Jesus John's 'first cousin once removed'. But John's parents lived in Jerusalem, whereas Jesus's family were from Nazareth. Though he had leapt for joy in his mother's womb when Mary visited[13], John says he had no prior knowledge that Jesus was the Messiah[14]. But one day a Galilean came forwards for baptism, whom John sensed was The One.

John knew he needed to be baptised by Jesus, not vice versa: but try as he would, Jesus insisted. And as Jesus emerged from the water, John saw heaven opened and a dove descending on Him. This was a pre-arranged, God-given sign that He would be the One who baptised in Holy Spirit.[15] As if that wasn't enough, the Father's voice affirmed His identity saying, *'This is My beloved Son, in whom I am well pleased'*[16].

By the time John had recovered from the shock, Jesus had disappeared into the wilderness. And for forty days, John was left wondering how he could fulfil his role, if the Messiah was nowhere to be found.

Just as Jesus returned from the temptation, a delegation of senior clergy arrived to investigate[17]. The Sanhedrin believed it was their role to discern

---

[11] (Luke 1:59-63)
[12] (Lk 1:36)
[13] (Lk 1:41)
[14] (1:31)
[15] (1:33)
[16] (Mt 3:13-17)
[17] (1:19)

who was the true Messiah, and to weed out the charlatans. Since John had attracted a huge following, they set up a Commission to investigate whether he might be the Messiah. But instead of seizing the opportunity for personal glory, John vehemently denied being the Messiah. Neither was he Elijah's reincarnation; nor the mysterious 'Prophet like me' that Moses had foretold.

Why then was John baptising? The commission seems to have taken it as given, that Messiah would baptise. In Jewish thought, baptism bound the person being baptised to their baptiser.[18] If John was merely clearing the way for Messiah, why was he baptising?

The Greek word 'baptizo' means more than just dipping; it's more like marinading. The medium in which something is baptised, changes the nature of the thing being baptised. John's baptism was *'a baptism of repentance, for the forgiveness of sins'*; and in that sense, it cleansed recipients' hearts ready to receive Messiah. But it was not enough. When Messiah came, they would need baptising all over again, this time into Christ, by the Holy Spirit.[19]

John's response must have stunned them. Jesus will later wash His disciples' feet as an object lesson in humility: but John counts himself unworthy even to touch Jesus's sandal straps. He has spotted Jesus, freshly back from the wilderness, mingling with the crowds and no doubt listening intently to the Commission's questions. Though they are supposed to be experts at identifying Messiah, He is right there among them, and they have no idea!

John seems to have left the clerics on tenterhooks; but to his disciples, he was quite clear about Jesus's identity. He declares Him to be:-

- *Pre-existent*, I.e. divine[20]
- *Worthy of ultimate honour*[21]
- *Lamb of God*, who takes away the sin of the world - Jews <u>and</u> Gentiles[22]
- *Anointed by the Spirit of God* (Messiah means anointed)[23]

---

[18] (1Cor 10:1,2)
[19] (Acts 19:1-7)
[20] (1:27)
[21] (1:27)
[22] (1:29)
[23] (1:32)

- The *Baptiser with the Holy Spirit*[24]
- The *Son of God*[25], meaning God Incarnate[26]

What a revelation John gave to Israel![27] And yet Jesus *'came unto His own, and His own received Him not'*. How sad that Judaism *still* denies that 'Jesus Christ is come in the flesh'. How Jesus must have wept, that His own people didn't recognise Him despite John's ministry, never mind all His signs.

John's role as Jesus's wingman (3:22-26)

In popular culture, a wingman is a friend who helps a young man in approaching potential romantic partners. The term originated amongst fighter pilots: planes were sent out in pairs, so that each could look out for the other one.

John-the-Baptist likens his role to that of the 'best man' at a wedding.[28] In Jewish weddings, when the groom is ready his friends go and fetch the bride. Their role is over, once the bride has been brought to the groom. The Baptist knew that his role was transient. Once he had identified and announced Jesus, from then on Jesus's following would grow whilst his own ministry would dwindle. His lack of personal ambition is a wonderful role model for all those involved in Christian ministry of any kind.

Jesus had moved out of Jerusalem into the Judaean countryside, spending time with His burgeoning group of disciples. He had taught His core team to baptise, even though He Himself didn't baptise anyone.[29] Such baptisms can't have been the same as the baptism He instructed them to do after His ascension[30], for the Holy Spirit hadn't yet been given. It couldn't have been Christian baptism *'in the name of the Father, the Son, and the Holy Spirit'*. Nor could it have been baptism into Christ. So it seems it was like John's

---

24 (1:33)
25 (1:34)
26 (Jn 10:32,33)
27 (1:31)
28 (3:28-30)
29 (4:2)
30 (Mt 28:19,20)

baptism, a baptism preparing the way of the Lord through repentance. In that sense His team were simply augmenting John's labours.

Summer had come and the Jordan's flow had dropped to a trickle, but there was one place where there was plenty of water left. The name *Aenon* means 'spring'. Much of the Judaean countryside is limestone karst, like the Yorkshire Dales. This means that rivers can flow underground then emerge as high-volume springs, rather like what happens at Malham Cove.

The only details John gives are that the site was within the Roman province of Judaea and near Salim - a place that hasn't yet been identified. The two most likely locations are both near Shechem, in Samaria. This would explain why Jesus's next encounter is at the well in Sychar.[31]

At this point, John the Baptist was still free. The lack of alternative baptismal sites meant that Jesus and John's teams were working very near each other. John's loyal followers couldn't help noticing that though Jesus Himself wasn't baptising, more people were coming to His team than to theirs.

The Pharisees got wind of this[32]; and perhaps to 'divide and conquer', sent a group to raise a query about purification[33]. They had previously stirred up trouble by questioning why Jesus's disciples didn't fast, when John's did.[34] And later, they would question Jesus Himself about why His disciples didn't wash their hands before eating.[35] All we know was that on this occasion, the 'gotcha' question had to do with purification.

John's disciples were hot on fasting and the like, whereas Jesus's disciples were much more laid back about details such as the Pharisees' handwashing rituals.[36] Their question painted Jesus's disciples in a bad light, fomenting hostility and rivalry from John's disciples. Though it must have touched John to see his team's concern for his reputation, he realises its origins and refuses to be defiled by their jealousy.

---

[31] (4:5)
[32] (4:1)
[33] (3:25)
[34] (Matt 9:11-17)
[35] (Mt 15:1-2)
[36] (Matt 15:2)

Firstly, he reminds his disciples that all true ministry is allotted by God. Knowing one's calling, and its limits, is vital. No-one should go beyond their allotted role. He'd always said his role was temporary, that of a forerunner.

Then he uses the analogy of the Best Man at a Jewish wedding. That role is important up to the point when the bride and groom are brought together. After that, the Best Man can heave a sigh of relief and join in the joyful celebrations. John found his joy and fulfilment in introducing others to Christ, and then quietly withdrawing so they could be together.

The church is the Bride of Christ, and Jesus is the Bridegroom.[37] Evangelism should never be about the evangelist, but always about the Bridegroom. But John's statement is also true on a personal level, as we struggle with the mismatch between our fallen human nature and Christ being formed within us: *"He must increase, and I must decrease"*!

John goes on to underscore many of the same themes that Jesus had taught Nicodemus. He says[38]:-

- Jesus is from heaven, whereas I am of this earth. Jesus is above all.
- Jesus is an eye-witness of heavenly truths; but no-one's listening.
- Anyone who accepts Jesus's teaching is accepting God's words as truth
- Jesus speaks God's own words, because the fullness of the Spirit is on Him
- Father God loves the Son, and treats Him as His equal in everything
- Believing *into* the Son brings everlasting, zoe life.
- Not believing means God's wrath hang over us, like a sword of Damocles.

This teaching was John's response to the Pharisees' controversy about purification. Their belief that this came through external rituals, is diametrically opposed to Jesus's message of grace. Cleansing comes not from anything we can do ourselves, but from accepting the Lamb of God as our sacrifice, and then being joined to Him in spirit and abiding in Him.

Jesus refers back to John's testimony about Him later[39], as one of the reasons they should believe in Him. We can perhaps learn from John's example, how

---

[37] (Eph 5:25-29)

[38] (3:31-36)

[39] (5:33,34)

to deal with hostile questioning when we are witnessing: focus not on the question which is designed to ridicule or demean, but on the Person of Christ.

John's closest disciples become the nucleus of Jesus's team (1:29-51)

Having had an overview of the different phases of John's ministry, let's come back to that first week of Jesus's ministry.

The day after the Sanhedrin's inquisition, John sees Jesus approaching him. He cannot contain his wonder, and says, *'Behold, the Lamb of God, who takes away the sin of the world!'* John challenges us to meditate deeply on Jesus's identity.

He would have had in mind Abraham's prophetic statement to Isaac, *'God will provide Himself the lamb!"*[40] He had identified Mount Moriah, where the Temple had later been built, as the place where God would provide: 'Jehovah-jireh'. Everything is of grace: it is by grace you have been saved, through faith; and even that is not of yourself, but is the gift of God.

He would also have had in mind Isaiah's prophecy of the Suffering Servant, on whom all our sins and iniquities were laid; and the twice-daily sacrifices in the Temple, to wash away Israel's sins. But remarkably, he speaks of sin rather than sins. He sees sin as a single entity rather than a multitude of individual acts or failures.

The following day would have been a sabbath, if we work backwards from the wedding in Cana. (The custom was for marriages to take place on a Wednesday). That might explain why there were only two disciples with John the Baptist[41] - no crowds. Andrew and (it is thought) John son of Zebedee, were presumably two of John's closest disciples. Jesus walked past, and though John is speaking to no-one in particular, he was so awestruck that he repeats, *"Behold, the Lamb of God!"*

The pair decided to find out where Jesus was staying, and began shadowing Him. Jesus noticed, and invited them to spend time with Him. (Though He was eager to get back to Galilee for a wedding, travel on the Sabbath was

40 (Gen 22:14)

41 (1:35)

forbidden). Unlike the traditional Jewish way of counting the hours from daybreak, John's gospel counts the hours as we do, from midnight: and he says it was about the tenth hour. This gave the two enquirers most of that day, for quality time with Jesus. By the end of the day they were convinced that *'We have found the Messiah'*. Each of them hurried off to tell their sibling. Andrew found Simon first, and brought him to Jesus.

As soon as they had made eye contact, Jesus spoke deep into Simon's identity, renaming him (like when Jacob became Israel). The name 'Simon' means 'He who hears'. But Jesus says he will now be known as Cephas: the Greek word for a stone, whose Latin equivalent is Petros or Peter. Later, Simon would be the first to hear the Spirit say that Jesus was *'the Christ, the Son of the living God'*. He was the first to grasp the truth of the incarnation! When that happened, Jesus said, *'You are Peter; and upon this rock I will build my church'*. This truth (the incarnation) would become the foundation stone of the Church.

With his usual self-deprecation, John didn't record what happened when he brought *his* brother James to Jesus. But by the end of that day, four men had bonded with Jesus.

The next day, Jesus personally called Philip to follow Him on His journey to Galilee. Philip was a neighbour of Andrew and Peter's. They lived in Bethsaida, a fishing port just east of the mouth of the Jordan on Lake Galilee.

Philip had a friend called Nathanael who came from Cana[42], their intended destination. He seems to have been having his morning quiet time, meditating in the shade of a fig tree, when Jesus and his entourage passed by. Philip knew him as someone well-versed in the scriptures. He perhaps knew Nathanael thought Nazareth would never produce anyone of note, and felt that a scriptural reference would help overcome his prejudice. So instead of simply referring to Jesus as the Messiah, he refers to Him as *'Him of whom Moses in the law, and also the prophets, wrote'*. When Nathanael reacted with predictable scorn, Philip challenged him to come and see for himself.

[42] (21:2)

As Nathanael came into earshot, Jesus once again revealed His supernatural intuition.[43] Instead of rebuking Nathanael for scepticism, He recognised his remark about Nazareth as honesty. Before Jacob was renamed Israel, he was a con-man, swindling his brother and tricking his father. But once he became Israel, all that guile went. So when Jesus said *'Behold, an Israelite indeed, in whom is no guile!'*, He completely demolished Nathanael's scepticism.

Embarrassed by this compliment from someone he has just dissed, Nathanael asked, *'How do You know me?'* Even his best friends wouldn't have known him well enough to brief Jesus to this depth. But Jesus knew him inside out, from one distant glance; and that knowledge told Nathanael that what Philip had said, was indeed true. Nathanael had just met the One he had been searching for all those years, as he pondered the scriptures. He was known, and now he knew. *'Rabbi, you <u>are</u> the Son of God! You <u>are</u> the King of Israel!'*.

We might think that Nathanael's words rival Peter's later testimony, *"You are the Christ, the Son of the Living God!"*[44] But we know that despite spending three years with Him, even by the Last Supper the disciples *still* hadn't grasped the reality that *'He who has seen Me has seen the Father'*[45]. Revelation had begun to dawn in Nathanael, perhaps accelerated by his knowledge of the scriptures; but he would go on unpacking the implications of his statement for many years to come.

Jesus tells Nathanael he is only at the very beginning of a wonderful journey. His faith, presently based solely on Jesus's knowledge of his heart, will be buttressed by witnessing many signs and wonders. Jacob had dreamt of a connection between heaven and earth, bringing angelic ministrations. Nathanael would observe that same divine favour resting upon the Son of Man[46]. Indeed, the Son of Man would Himself be the ladder between heaven and earth. In Jesus the original covenant promise to Abraham, *'In you shall all nations be blessed'*, would be fulfilled. And Jesus's Presence would be like Bethel - *'none other than the House of God, the Gate of Heaven'*.[47]

---

[43] (2:24,25)
[44] (Mt 16:13-16)
[45] (14:8,9)
[46] (Gen 28:10-17)
[47] (Gen 28:17)

<u>The wedding at Cana</u> (2:1-11)

Jesus re-purposes the massive water jars used for ritual cleansing, to hold wine instead. Those who celebrate with the Bridegroom will experience the joy of the Spirit for evermore.

In John's chronology of the first week of Jesus's ministry, this is day seven.

Jesus goes from Bethabara-beyond-Jordan[1] to Cana, arriving on the third day. Cana is about nine miles north of Nazareth, and Mary being first to notice the wine was running out, implies she was keeping an eye what was happening. She must have been involved in the wedding arrangements, since she had authority over the serving staff. Some suggest the groom's mother was Salome, Mary's sister: in other words, the groom was one of Jesus's cousins.

A wedding ceremony could last up to a week, and the whole village and dozens of relatives would have been invited. It was the groom's responsibility to pay for everything: not to provide enough food and drink brought shame. Mary realised a big problem was looming. What she thought Jesus could do, we don't know: just that she believed he could do something.

The Pharisees had very strict rituals about personal cleansing, to go with the *kosher* food laws. Your feet would be washed on arrival. You had to wash your hands in a specific way before eating, and repeat this between courses. Stone vessels were used to contain the needed water, because they were less likely to become ritually unclean than clay jars.

Though estimates vary, it is widely accepted that these jars held a huge volume of water: around a hundred and fifty gallons, or seven to eight hundred bottles of wine! Presumably they would have been hired for the occasion, to cope with the needs of so many guests.

At this point Jesus had just turned thirty, the age when one could become a rabbi. This means that for eighteen years after telling His parents He needed to *'be about My Father's business'*, He had worked as a carpenter. He had then left the family business and gone south to be baptised, before being tempted in the wilderness. Then He'd returned to John the Baptist, who had

---

[1] (1:28)

introduced Him to his inner circle. Over a few days Jesus had acquired five would-be disciples - Andrew and John, Peter and Phillip, and finally Nathanael - before returning to Galilee.

Jesus's response to Mary's request, seems rude. She probably hadn't seen Him for a couple of months, but would have quickly realised that something radical had changed. His response conveys His independence from her, as with all the other occasions when Mary seeks Him out during His ministry.[2]

Whether this form of address was in fact rude, is debated. Jesus used the same term when addressing Mary from the cross.[3] Some say it is formal: similar to our use of 'Lady', or 'Ma'am'. Whichever is correct, He is saying to her, 'Leave it to Me'. He can no longer be defined as Mary's son, or constrained by her agenda. Till Calvary, He was to plough a lonely path, even His immediate family thinking He was crazy at times.

His comfort and companionship, such as it was, came from those who journeyed with Him and hung on His every word. His followers were now His family. And yet, His continuing concern for His mother and siblings was real. Soon after this, He took them with Him when He relocated to Capernaum.

Was Mary asking Him to perform a miracle? We don't know. Elsewhere in John's gospel, Jesus's reply, *"My time has not yet come"*, always refers to the time of His coming glorification through the Cross. His siblings can choose what they do, and when[4], but He must stick precisely to His Father's schedule. We know that the knowledge of His eventual crucifixion was a massive burden for Him throughout these years: *"I came to send fire on the earth, and how I wish it were already kindled! But I have a baptism to be baptised with, and how distressed I am until it is accomplished!"*[5]

Though Jesus seems to rebuff Mary's initial overture, she shows her faith in Him by instructing the servants, *"Do whatever he tells you!"*. And Jesus responds, telling them to fill up the water jars: no mean task. Having obeyed,

---

[2] (Matt 12:46-50)

[3] (19:26)

[4] (7:6)

[5] (Lk 12:50)

they are then to take a sample to the master of ceremonies. Unaware of the problem, he compliments the groom on saving the best wine till last!

The meaning of the miracle

Initially the miracle remained private knowledge between the servants, Mary, Jesus and His disciples. But John states that this was the first occasion when the disciples saw who Jesus really was: the Son of God. The miracle *'manifested forth His glory'*. This miracle, with others such as the feeding of the five thousand and the calming of the storm, declare Jesus's sovereignty over Creation, and thus, His identity as Creator.

But there is something symbolic, too, in the use of the water jars. In Judaism there was an endless need for re-cleansing and ritual purification - whereas wine is a symbol of the joy of the Holy Spirit. For the rest of the wedding feast, there would have been no water for purification! It was no longer needed, for Jesus was there.

It also of course points forwards to the day when Jesus Himself will be the Bridegroom[6] at the Marriage Feast of the Lamb. The constant consciousness of our sinfulness will be replaced by the eternal joy of God's Presence. The whole mood will be one of grace!

---

[6] (3:27-31)

Cleansing the Temple (2:12-25)

Jesus bursts onto the scene in Jerusalem, de-monetising the Temple and reclaiming it as 'a House of Prayer for all nations'

The timing of this incident

John now skips over a significant time period, which is described in the Synoptic gospels. After the wedding, Jesus had embarked on a tour of Galilean synagogues, preaching the arrival of the Kingdom of Heaven. He did so in the power of the Spirit, and Luke says, *"He was glorified by all"*[1]. But when he announced His Messianic manifesto in the Nazareth synagogue, Mary's neighbours took offence and tried to kill Him. So Jesus relocated the family to Capernaum, a cosmopolitan fishing port on the Sea of Galilee. There, He officially called Peter, Andrew, James and John, to be 'fishers of men': evangelists, as we would say.

He then went off on a second evangelistic crusade round Galilee. By now His fame had grown such that crowds came from far and wide to hear and be healed. He taught them about the Kingdom of Heaven, in the Sermon on the Mount. Then He expanded His team of disciples to twelve, and sent them out in pairs to propagate His message.

Exactly where John's next section[2] interlocks with the Synoptic accounts, we can't be entirely sure. But it seems to have been an interlude in Jesus's Galilean ministry, in that

- John the Baptist is still at liberty[3], and
- near the end of this section, Jesus goes back to Cana in Galilee.

The other three gospels record Jesus cleansing the Temple shortly before He was crucified. But John here recounts a similar event, much earlier in Jesus's ministry. Were they two separate events, or one-and-the-same?

---

[1] (Lk 4:14-30)
[2] (2:13-4:54)
[3] (3:24)

Some of the details differ. In John the focus is on the desecration of what should have been a holy place, whereas in the Synoptics the focus is on the greed and corruption of those who trafficked the sacrificial lambs.

Some say the Synoptics are right and that John just recorded it at this point because it fitted the narrative he wanted to portray. Others think John was right and the Synoptics wrong. But it seems more natural to take the accounts at face value and conclude that Jesus in fact cleansed the Temple twice - once at the beginning and once at the end of His ministry. Though Matthew records Jesus cleansing the Temple just before being crucified[4], he also records that it is the words Jesus spoke at the *first* cleansing[5] which are eventually used to against Him when He was tried[6].

The cleansing of the Temple

Just as we might go to a travel money bureau before a trip abroad, a special currency was needed to pay the Temple tax. So a month before Passover money changers would fan out to the towns and cities across Israel. Then ten days later, they'd return to the Temple Court for three weeks before the Feast, to cash in on Jewish pilgrims who had come from abroad.

There were multiple currencies in common use at that time (Roman, Greek, Egyptian, Persian, Syrian, Tyrean) as well as Jewish shekels. Even then, Galilean shekels were worth only half a Jerusalem shekel! The agents' commission was 10-15%; but haggling was normal. The Temple tax was half a Jerusalem shekel. So two friends might jointly change their currency for a single Jerusalem shekel. This minimised the commission!

Pilgrims would also need to buy sheep or oxen for sacrifices, but the priesthood would reject any animal with the slightest blemish. So the only reliable course was to buy a pre-approved animal from the priests themselves! A significant proportion of the price then went into the High Priest's personal coffers, causing resentment at his greed and corruption.

---

[4] (Mt 21:12-17)
[5] (Jn 2:19)
[6] (Mt 26:59-65)

The Outer Court was supposed to be a *"House of Prayer for all nations"* (for Gentiles[7]) but instead it had been turned into *"a den of thieves"*.[8]

Some see this episode as Jesus being a prototype social revolutionary. But His team included Matthew the tax-gatherer, as well as Simon the Zealot. And Jesus was clear, when questioned later by Pilate, that *'My Kingdom is not of this world'*.

The disciples realised they were seeing an Old Testament prophecy being fulfilled.[9] Jesus's zeal for His Father's reputation was deeply offended by the merchandising of the Temple. It was making so many Jews skeptical, never mind the God-fearing Gentiles. It was zeal for His Father's honour, rather than social justice concerns, that drove Him to this radical action.

The prophets had foreseen this. Zechariah said that *'There will no longer be a merchant in the House of the Lord'*.[10] Malachi said, *'Suddenly the* LORD *will come to His Temple, purify the Levites, and refine them like gold and silver'.*[11]

It seems that at this point the Temple authorities made no attempt to stop Jesus. Perhaps they were too ashamed by what He said. Perhaps they knew that the crowd would back Him, out of contempt for 'Annas's bazaar' as it was known. Or maybe they were scared the Roman garrison in Fort Antonia, which overlooked the Temple, would intervene if a riot developed.

But they were so incensed by Jesus's teaching in the Temple, that they repeatedly sought to arrest or stone Him.[12] On each occasion, God's timing over-ruled man's; the crowd protected Him, the guards were overawed by His words, or He simply got away safely. But eventually Caiaphas, in his role as High Priest for that year, decided: Jesus was such a threat to national security that He must be killed, by whatever means.[13]

---

[7] (Isa 56.6,7)

[8] (Jer 7:11)

[9] (Ps 69:9)

[10] (Zech 14:26)

[11] (Mal 3:1-3)

[12] (7:30,32,44,45-46; 8:44,59; 10:31-39; 11:56-57)

[13] (Jer 7:11)

The true Temple

Jesus had claimed that the Temple was *'His Father's house'*. As they came to realise later, this was a direct claim that He Himself was God.[14] So they challenged Him to perform a miracle to validate His authority.

Jesus's reply shocked them: *"Destroy this Temple, and in three days I will raise it up!"* The temple had been the crowning glory of Herod the Great's fabled architectural legacy. In ten years or so he had doubled the size of the site by building huge retaining walls around the plateau of Mount Moriah. Various colonnades and other buildings were gradually added, such that work had been in progress for forty-six years at this point. It wasn't finally completed till AD65, long after Jesus's death. And then it was utterly destroyed five years later, when Emperor Titus destroyed Jerusalem.

You would think that the sheer craziness of Jesus's challenge would have made them wonder whether it might be meant symbolically, but no. Even had they been willing to put His challenge to the test, to them the Temple had by now become an idol, more important than God Himself. And any threat to it was inevitably seen as a threat to their power and wealth, by the High Priest and the Sadducees.

At His trial three years later, these very words of Jesus's were misquoted by two false witnesses, who twisted them into an allegation that He would destroy the Temple.[15] But His prophecy had been, *"If you destroy this Temple, I will rebuild it in three days"*. This would eventually be fulfilled in His crucifixion and resurrection. Only with hindsight and the teaching of the Holy Spirit, did the disciples realise: Jesus had been talking about His own human body as the Temple, the place where we should worship God.

The Body of Christ: our place of worship

As the Temple was originally intended as the dwelling place of God, so *'it pleased the Father that in Him (Jesus) all the fullness of God should dwell'.*[16]

---

[14] (10:30-33)
[15] (Mt 26:57-63)
[16] (Col 1:19)

The Father had given Him the Spirit 'without measure'.[17] And He *tabernacled* amongst us.

Just as the Temple had been where man was reconciled to God through sacrifice, now He has *'reconciled us to God in the body of His flesh through death, to present us holy, and blameless, and above reproach in His sight'*[18]. And the ripping of the Temple veil when Jesus died, indicated that the sacrifice of His body would enable us to enter the very Presence of God.[19]

When we believe into Jesus, the Holy Spirit baptises us into the Body of Christ.[20] As Peter meditated on this episode during the years after Jesus's death, he realised that we ourselves are being built into a new Temple, as 'living stones'.[21]. We become God's dwelling-place, both individually[22] and corporately![23]

At the individual level, there is something sacred about our human bodies as God's temple. We must keep our bodies and souls holy, staying away from everything that would defile us[24], not 'monetising the temple', if His glory is to reside in our lives. Otherwise, like the tabernacle, we become 'Ichabod'[25] (Hebrew, meaning 'the glory has departed').

At the corporate level, and especially when we meet to celebrate communion, we are to examine whether we have fully grasped this truth that we are part of His body. Jumping the food queue at a love feast, leaving others hungry while we get drunk, was how this manifested in Corinth.[26] But any selfishness, individualism or self-centredness is a denial that we belong to the Body of Christ.

---

17 (3:34)
18 (11:47-53)
19 (Heb 10:19-22)
20 (1 Cor 12:13)
21 (1Pet 2:4-5)
22 (14:23)
23 (1 Pet 2:4,5; 1 Cor 12:13; Eph 2:19-22; Eph 4:4)
24 (2Cor 6:14-18)
25 (1Sam 4:21)
26 (1 Cor 11:20-34)

The pilgrims' responses (2:23-25)

Though He had turned down the authorities' demand for a sign, Jesus went on to do many miracles in Jerusalem that Passover. We are not told what they were; but many of the Passover pilgrims *'believed in His name'* when they witnessed them. However, Jesus did not commit Himself to them, unlike with His disciples. Why was this?

Jesus knew that their acclaim would evaporate, and that soon they would be baying, *"Crucify! Crucify!"*. So some see this passage as teaching how self-deceptive we can be: *'The human heart is desperately wicked and deceitful. Who can know it? I, the* LORD, *search the heart and try the mind'*.[27]

But for example, what makes the difference between Peter's heart, which would give way and desert Jesus at the Cross, and Judas's heart, which betrayed Him for thirty pieces of silver? Why does Jesus pray for the one and not (as far as we know) for the other?

The Greek word for their *believing* and Christ's *committing* Himself, have the same root but different tenses. The pilgrims' belief was a single act: they would go home at the end of the feast, their lives unchanged by their 'belief'. Whereas the verb for Jesus committing Himself, implies an ongoing state. There was no real commitment from these pilgrims, whereas Peter had committed by leaving his home and business to follow Jesus. Christ commits to those who commit to Him.

---

[27] (Jer 17:9-10)

You must be born again (3:1-21)

Nicodemus, the most eminent theologian of his time, tries to make his own assessment of Jesus; but gets some puzzling answers!
His study of the Law will count for nothing
unless he is born again of the Spirit and believes in Christ.

Nicodemus secretly approaches Jesus

Nicodemus was highly respected as *the* Teacher of Israel.[1] He was also a senior politician in the Jewish Parliament (Sanhedrin), and an independent man, willing to go against the tide of his peers' opinion.[2] What his motives were, whether he came alone, and why he came by night, we can only guess. We assume he came secretly, on a private mission to find out more.

Opening the conversation respectfully, he acknowledged that Jesus's miracles proved God was with Him. In a sense therefore, he is representative of those who had seen Jesus's miracles and had some sort of faith, but not yet saving faith.[3] Later, he would help Joseph of Arimathea bury Jesus[4], suggesting that by that point he had become a secret believer.

As a person, Nicodemus reveals two negatives about finding our way to God.

Firstly, it's not about where one is born, or one's family origins or nationality, or one's social standing, or even one's studying of the scriptures. Secondly, it isn't about one's intelligence. No-one can reason their way to belief in Christ.[5]

Nicodemus's conversation with Jesus starts in a disjointed way. He doesn't actually ask a question; and then Jesus seems to immediately change the subject. However it makes perfect sense *if* we remember that the Sanhedrin held itself responsible for investigating any claims of Messiahship.

Jesus has just referred to the Temple as *'My Father's house'*: His first self-identification as the Son of God. The Pharisees' questions to John the Baptist had left them looking silly; so Nicodemus was trying a different approach.

---

[1] (3:10)
[2] (7:50-52)
[3] (2:23-25)
[4] (19:38-39)
[5] (1 Cor 1:18–24)

Nicodemus's use of the plural, *"We know ..."*, suggests he was coming on behalf of a wider group. It becomes clear later on that some of the Pharisees did believe that Jesus was from God, and that He was sinless.[6] So maybe he was coming unofficially on their behalf. Certainly he was respectful, addressing Jesus as a fellow rabbi even though He'd had no formal training.

We might expect Jesus to have responded eagerly with deference or flattery. This was a breakthrough: the top religious leader in Israel had sought Him out! But there is none of this; nor indeed irony, argumentativeness or superiority. His sole concern is for Nicodemus's salvation.

Nicodemus's conversation with Jesus

On the face of it, there seem to be a number of non-sequiturs in John's account. But if we read between the lines, knowing where Nicodemus was coming from, it all makes sense. The easiest way to convey this is with an amplified paraphrase, as follows.

Nicodemus: Rabbi, as a respected teacher myself, I and some of my colleagues recognise that your miracles prove God is with You, and validate your teaching. *But who are You? Are you the Messiah, Elijah, or the Prophet? Or if not, why do you call God your Father and claim the Temple as your family residence?*[7]

Jesus: *So you're really asking, Is this the arrival of the long-awaited Messianic kingdom, huh?*

Nicodemus would have known that the Old Testament identified Israel as God's *'kingdom of priests, and a holy nation'.*[8] The prophets had foretold that after the Babylonian Exile, one day God would restore the kingdom to Israel through a Spirit-anointed King[9], or Messiah. Daniel had gone even further, foreseeing that Messiah would reign not just over Israel but over the whole earth[10], and that after Messiah was killed on behalf of others' sin[11] there

---

[6] (9:13-16)
[7] (3:2)
[8] (Ex 19:6)
[9] (Acts 1:6)
[10] (Dan 7:23-27)
[11] (Dan 9:26)

would be a general resurrection of the dead, and judgement[12]. *So* Jews expected that they would all automatically be part of Messiah's kingdom just by virtue of being 'Abraham's seed'. Jesus immediately disabuses him:

Jesus: *You acknowledge Me as 'come from God' - from above - but you're questioning whether I am truly Messiah, come to reign. You assume that if I am, all Israel, and especially you as a respected Torah expert, will have places of honour in it. But - and this is really important - no-one can even see the Kingdom of God, unless he's born again from above.*[13]

Nicodemus, like all devout Jews, had been looking for the Kingdom for years. But he couldn't recognise it, unless God opened his eyes.

Faith is essential, to be able to see spiritual realities.[14] Faith enabled Abraham to see the Lamb of God Yahweh would provide, just as he was about to sacrifice his only child. Faith enabled him to continue searching for *'the city whose maker and builder is God'*, rather than abandoning his tent for the security of a house amongst the Canaanites like Lot. Faith enabled Moses to resist Pharoah's displeasure, and to endure *'as seeing Him who is invisible'*.

When Jesus said, *'You must be born again'*, he was deliberately using a double-entendre. The Greek word is *'anothen'*, which can mean either 'again' or 'from above'. Jews sometimes used the phrase 'born again' metaphorically, to describe major life changes such as Bar Mitzvah, marriage, coronation, or conversion to Judaism. But Nicodemus didn't realise Jesus was using a metaphor, and took it literally.

Nicodemus: *Are you saying you've found the elixir of life, that ageing can be reversed? How on earth could anyone climb back into their mother's womb?*[15]

Jesus: *You're asking how this regeneration happens. Listen very carefully, it's really important that you believe this. Unless you are born of water and spirit, you will never enter the Kingdom of God.* [16]

---

[12] (Dan 12:1-3)
[13] (3:3)
[14] (Heb 11:1)
[15] (3:4)
[16] (3:5)

<u>Detour: What is 'being born again'?</u> (3:5)

Jesus here talks about the new birth in three different ways: being born from above; being born of water and spirit; and being born of the Spirit as opposed to the flesh. (John has previously noted that the believer's authority to become a child of God, comes from being born *'not of blood, nor of the will of the flesh, nor of the will of man, but of God'*)

'Water and spirit' has been interpreted in various different ways, some more plausible than others:-

- simple parallelism: 'water, meaning the Spirit'
- physical birth (when a mother's waters break), and spiritual birth
- water baptism and Spirit baptism
- cleansing through repentance, and power through the Spirit

The first thing to note is that the Greek says, 'of water and spirit'; not 'of water and *the* Spirit'. Secondly, this phrase expands Jesus's first statement about being born from above: in other words, it refers to a single event, not two separate ones. Thirdly, Jesus expected Nicodemus to have known this already from the Jewish scriptures.[17] Fourthly, in Moses's writings water had to do with cleansing as well as life.

There are many Old Testament references to the Spirit being poured out like water, but much the closest comes from Ezekiel: *'"I will take you from among the nations, gather you out of all countries, and bring you into your own land. Then I will sprinkle clean water on you, and you shall be clean; I will cleanse you from all your filthiness and from all your idols. I will give you a new heart and put a new spirit within you; I will take the heart of stone out of your flesh and give you a heart of flesh. I will put My Spirit within you and cause you to walk in My statutes, and you will keep My judgments and do them.'*[18]

---

[17] (3:10)
[18] (Ezek 36:23-27)

So it seems that the new birth Jesus is speaking of, involves three elements:

- cleansing from sinfulness and idolatry
- renewal of the human heart and spirit, and
- the indwelling Holy Spirit, bringing obedience to the word of God

Without such a birth, not only will Nicodemus remain blind to the Kingdom, but he will never enter it.

Entering the Kingdom means coming under Messiah's rule, submitting to His Lordship and authority. *"At the Name of Jesus, every knee must bow".* We must become like little children, coming obediently whenever Jesus speaks to us.[19] All arrogance and intellectual pride must humble itself or be humbled. Not only must we be born again by the Spirit, we must walk by the Spirit and not rely on the works of the Law, such as being circumcised.[20]

<u>The conversation continues</u>. (3:6ff)

<u>Jesus:</u> *Fallen human nature can only beget fallen human nature. Spiritual life requires spiritual birth.*

This new life is *'a new creation'*[21], de novo, totally unrelated to our old sinful nature. But our old nature doesn't just disappear when we are born again. Just as Ishmael persecuted Isaac, mocking and belittling him, our old nature will always strive against the new. There is a continual conflict within us[22] and we need to *'cast out the bondwoman and her son'*.[23]

How do we do this? In various ways:

- By considering our old nature as dead[24] - we have been crucified with Christ, and yet are alive, Christ living in us.
- By feeding our new nature with the word of God, and starving the old[25] - by refusing to give it any houseroom in our behaviours.

---

19 (Mt 18:3,4)
20 (Gal 3:2-5)
21 (2Cor 5:17)
22 (Rom 7:18)
23 (Gal 4:21-31)
24 (Rom 6:11)
25 (1Pet 2:1-2)

- By living by the Spirit, rather than the flesh: developing love, joy, peace, patience, kindness, goodness, gentleness, faithfulness and self-control[26]

Jesus: *Don't be shocked by My insistence on this. It's essential that you, and all your fellow Jews, be born again from above.*[27]

The 'you' in 'You must be born again', is plural. Jesus may be referring to Nicodemus's 'We'[28]; in which case He is saying, "You and all your colleagues who sent you". Or He may be referring to all those Jews who had been impressed by the signs[29] but didn't yet have true faith.

There's a forcefulness in Jesus's words: it's a command. We can't avoid this.

Jesus: *The wind blows wherever it wants, and though you can hear it, you can't tell what drives it or what it is doing. The same is true of the Spirit's work in regeneration.*[30]

John is using a double-entendre again. The same Greek word for wind (pneuma) can also mean breath or spirit. Guest chambers in Jewish homes were usually built on the roof, and accessed by an external staircase. So if Jesus was maybe staying at John's house in Jerusalem[31], He and Nicodemus would have been very aware of the spring gusts around them.

Anyone who's sailed or windsurfed knows how capricious the wind can be. Meteorology can nowadays give us some idea, but it can't tell us why cyclones form when and where they do, or why a tornado follows the exact path it does, destroying one house whilst leaving its neighbour untouched. We can hear a gale howling and observe its effects, but the wind itself is invisible. We can harness its power, but we can't control its direction.

Note that Jesus is still answering Nicodemus's question, *'How can these things be?'* His point is, that new birth is not some mechanical, penny-in-the-slot process, guaranteed by saying the sinner's prayer. Salvation is entirely of God, utterly under His sovereignty. Why He chooses one and not another, we

---

[26] (Gal 5:16ff)
[27] (3:7)
[28] (3:2)
[29] (2:23-24)
[30] (3:8)
[31] (19:27)

cannot say. One thing is for sure, it's not because of any inherent merit in us who are saved: it's all of grace.

But while the wind is invisible, its effects are not. Ocean breakers crash into surf, trees bend and break. Likewise the Spirit will come and break a man, as He did with John Newton. Or He will enable ordinary Galilean fishermen to do astonishing miracles, and to preach with great power. There should be visible evidence of the Spirit's work, once we are born again.

Nicodemus: *I'm still having difficulty grasping what you're telling me.*[32]

Though Jesus has demolished Nicodemus's assumption of entitlement to enter the Kingdom, and then bypassed his tendency to concrete thinking, his scepticism remains unbroken.

Jesus's three-fold challenge to Nicodemus's scepticism

Jesus challenges Nicodemus head-on, with three arguments tailored to his Torah-based mindset:

- As an expert in the Law, he should recognise truth in what Jesus is saying[33]
- Jesus is the only eye-witness of heavenly truths[34]
- The story of Moses's bronze serpent prefigures what Christ is saying[35]

But as well as challenging his scepticism, Jesus is going on to teach him more about the New Birth: as well as being *of the Spirit*, it is also *by faith*, and *through the Cross*.

Jesus: *Every Jew regards you as the best bible teacher of your time, so how come you didn't already know this?*[36]

Jesus would have been thinking of scriptures such as the passage from Ezekiel about the valley of dry bones. Ezekiel is told to prophesy to the wind (or breath) and then, God says, *"I will put My Spirit in you, and you shall live"*.

For other references, see the footnote.[37]

---

32 (3:9)
33 (3:10)
34 (3:11-13)
35 (3:14-15)
36 (3:10)
37 (Ps 51:9,10; Isa 44:3; Joel 2:28-29; Ezek 37:1-14)

<u>Jesus:</u> *Seriously, I'm telling you that We are telling you heavenly truth, and you are rejecting it . No-one else has ever been an eye-witness in heaven.*[38]

Just as a midwife sees how a child is born, whereas the father waiting outside the delivery suite doesn't, Jesus is saying that in heaven He has watched rebirths happening. He is an eye-witness, in fact the only eye-witness; which in Jewish law was highly significant for validating testimony.

[The Jews believed Moses had been to heaven to receive the Torah, but he'd actually only been to the top of the mountain. Elijah went to heaven, but never came back again. Spiritualist mediums claim to communicate with the dead, but if so, the spirits they commune with are certainly not in heaven!]

Who are the '*We*' that Jesus is referring to? It cannot be the disciples, because they haven't ascended to heaven; nor is it likely to be an ironic response to Nicodemus's 'We'. It can only really make sense, if Jesus is speaking on behalf of Father, Son and Holy Spirit.[39] Later, He will go on to explain to His disciples in private that *'I and the Father are One'*. But at this point, Jesus's direct assertion of His divinity, and His authority to speak on behalf of the whole Godhead, must have been startling to Nicodemus.

His claim comes with an implicit warning: '*You do not receive our witness'*.[40] Nicodemus's unbelief amounts to rejecting God. No matter how righteous we pride ourselves on being, this is the ultimate sin: not to believe in Jesus and His words.[41]

Jesus now explains how new birth comes through His being lifted up on a cross, just as Moses erected the effigy of a bronze snake. The cross was essential, for a just God to justify sinners. But faith is essential too.

<u>Jesus's death brings us new life</u>

<u>Jesus:</u> *Do you remember the story of Moses nailing a bronze effigy of a snake, onto a pole? How anyone who looked at it would be healed from fatal*

---

[38] (3:11-13)
[39] (1Jn 5:7)
[40] (3:11)
[41] (3:18)

snake bites? That's a picture of what will happen to Me, and how I will bring life to the spiritually dead.[42]

In His struggle to bring him from scepticism to faith, Jesus refers Nicodemus back to the scriptures he has loved since birth. How gentle and loving Christ is, in handling this man who prided himself on knowledge of the scriptures!

In the story, the Israelites had been grumbling against God and His servant Moses. God's response was to bring a plague of venomous snakes, such that many of the people died.[43] They asked Moses to intercede, which he did. But instead of just removing the snakes, God told him to make an effigy of a snake, then nail it up on a high pole so that anyone could see it. Just looking at the effigy was enough to bring instant healing.

But it required faith, to look up and not down! After all, there were plenty more snakes around, as well as the one you'd been bitten by. And it took faith to believe that looking at the pole was more important than applying a tourniquet and sucking out the venom.

This story, Jesus says, prefigures

- What will happen to Him. He will be lifted up and nailed to a cross.
- How He will save people from death if they will only look to Him, by faith.

The serpent represents not Satan, but our old nature. Christ, who was sinless, would become sin for us - so that in Him, we might become righteous.

Yet again, John uses a double-entendre. Being 'lifted up' refers both to Jesus being physically hoisted, but also to His being glorified. The cross which was intended to utterly humiliate Him, will in fact bring Him such glory that it will draw people of every nation to Him[44]. What the enemy intended to kill Him, will instead bring judgement on the organised opposition to God built into fallen human society. And the ruler of this world will be cast out.

---

[42] (3:14,15)
[43] (Num 21:4-9)
[44] (12:31,32)

Here we have three great truths about the cross:

- *It is the means of eternal life, & salvation from sin, through atonement*
- *It is the place where the Devil, the Prince of this world, was defeated*
- *It is a worldwide magnet, drawing people from every nation to Christ*

Evangelical church traditions tend to focus on the first of these, whilst Eastern Orthodox churches focus on the second. And traditionally liberal Methodism has focussed on the third. But all three are true!

As we move on, verses 16 to 21 are written in the past tense, implying a post-Calvary viewpoint. Most commentators therefore agree that it represents John's retrospective reflection, rather than further dialogue between Jesus and Nicodemus.

The heart of the gospel (3:16-21)

God so loved the world, that He gave His only-begotten Son, that whosoever believeth in Him, should not perish but have everlasting life. For God did not send His Son into the world to condemn the world, but that the world through Him might be saved"

Many regard John 3:16-17 as the ultimate crystallisation of the gospel: but it must not be stripped of its context. It is sometimes portrayed as saying that God loves the sum total of fallen humankind, ignoring verses 15 & 18-21.

The argument goes like this: if Christ died for all, then either all will be saved, or Christ's death is not effective for some. Since God wants the whole world to be saved[45] and His Word never returns to Him void, the latter can't be true. Therefore, they conclude, the gospel is universalist: Christ's death avails for all.

Certainly this verse conveys God's compassionate heart and deep goodwill towards mankind.[46] He doesn't want any one of those He created, to perish.[47] And He didn't send Jesus into the world to condemn it, but rather

---

[45] (Jn 20:21)
[46] (Lk 2:14)
[47] (2Pet 3:9)

to bring men back to Him: to reconcile them and make peace. Jesus was actually the first missionary: *'As the Father sent Me, even so send I you'.*[48]

But the previous verse says that it is only those who believe in Him, who are saved from destruction and receive eternal life. And the subsequent verses say that those who do not believe in Jesus's hidden identity as the only-begotten Son of God, are condemned already by their unbelief.[49]

Jesus, the Light of the World, has been manifest in the flesh: but that light is intolerable for those who wish to continue living in darkness. Like the accusers of the woman caught in adultery, they slink away to plan their next attempt to discredit Him.

John develops this theme further in his first letter. Whilst God is love, He is also light. And light cannot fellowship with darkness. *"God is light and in Him is no darkness at all. If we say that we have fellowship with Him, and walk in darkness, we lie and do not practice the truth. But if we walk in the light as He is in the light, we have fellowship with one another, and the blood of Jesus Christ His Son cleanses us from all sin. If we say that we have no sin, we deceive ourselves, and the truth is not in us. If we confess our sins, He is faithful and just to forgive us our sins and to cleanse us from all unrighteousness. If we say that we have not sinned, we make Him a liar, and His word is not in us."*[50]

As the Teacher of Israel, Nicodemus's whole life had been lived with the aim of establishing his own righteousness. The idea of a new righteousness being revealed, a righteousness from God through Christ's atonement and to be received by faith alone, would have been deeply challenging.

Fallen man's default response is to hate the light of Christ, because our deeds are evil and we don't want to be exposed.[51] But those who come to Christ and practice His commandments, approach God without fear. They have sought to live Jesus's way: all their deeds are *'done in God'*. Their deep union

---

[48] (Jn 20:21)
[49] (3:18)
[50] (1 Jn 1:5-10)
[51] (3:19,20)

with Christ has led to a state of consistent through-and-through love of God, and they can approach His throne boldly.[52]

'Doing truth'[53] doesn't mean that we completely overcome our sinful nature, but rather, that we *'walk in the light'*, being honest about our sins and confessing them to God. Walking in the light means we don't have to hide from God or our fellow believers any more: as we confess our sins, the blood of Jesus continuously cleanses us from all their resulting defilement. If we live in this way, we will be happy to give God all the credit. We'll acknowledge that anything and everything good we've done, has been solely down to God's grace at work in us.[54]

Given man's natural aversion to the Light, Jesus's incarnation forces us to make a judgement about Him. We can either 'walk in the light', acknowledging our sins to Him and claiming His blood to cover our sins. Or we can reject Him[55] and His words[56], die whilst still living in our sins, and face His judgement after death. There is no reincarnation, no second chance to make a better choice.[57] All judgement has been committed to Him[58], and we will be judged by the standards He set: of loving one another as He loved us.

We see then that the Cross, the means of eternal life, springs from the agape love of God. We are saved *from* His wrath - but saved *by* His love. His holiness cannot leave sin unpunished, for *'the wages of sin is death'*. But it is quite wrong to see Jesus and God as the movie duo of 'good guy, bad guy'. Both suffered at the cross: *'God was in Christ reconciling the world to Himself'*.

God shows us the *breadth* of His love, in that *whoever* believes will not perish, but have eternal life. Salvation is available to all. He shows the incredible *length* His love went to for us, in that while we were yet sinners, Christ died for us.[59] He shows the *depth* of His love in that He gave His only

---

[52] (1Jn 4:18)
[53] (3:21)
[54] (3:21)
[55] (8:24)
[56] (12:48)
[57] (Heb 9:27)
[58] (5:22)
[59] (Rom 5:6-8)

child, His continuously-being-fathered Son, His beloved Son to whom He had always been so utterly close. And He shows us its *height* at Calvary, as Jesus is lifted up naked, flayed, thorn-crowned, feet and hands nailed to the Cross.

What does it mean, to believe *into* Jesus?

Greek has two separate words for 'in': 'en' meaning position, and 'eis' meaning direction of movement. 'Eis' is more equivalent to our word 'into' but is often just translated as 'in'.

When John talks about believing 'in' Jesus, as in this passage, he almost always uses 'eis'. Zoe life is only given to those who believe *into* Jesus. Those who don't believe, or don't believe in a way that produces movement and change in them, will perish.

There are three key implications about true faith here:

Firstly, we must believe that Jesus is fully God, become fully man. Our response to Christ's incarnation settles our future fate. For how we respond to His incarnation, and whether we believe that *'Jesus Christ is come in the flesh'*, determines whether we are condemned or forgiven on Judgement Day. John sees belief in Christ's divinity as even more central than belief in Him being our atonement - for without the former, the cross could not be effective; Jesus could not be 'the Lamb of God' for us.

Secondly, we must live in the light; being real with God and man, not living in hypocrisy and pretence. Because Jesus is the Light of the world, showing up our sins and sinfulness, most will choose to avoid coming into His Presence. But believing *into* Him requires that we walk in His light. *'Doing truth'* doesn't mean that we immediately become sinless, but rather, that we promptly agree with Jesus whenever His Spirit convicts us. That way His blood cleanses us from all defilement, while He intercedes for us in heaven.

But thirdly, this phrase 'believing *into* Jesus' foreshadows all Jesus's teaching in the Upper Room, about our union with Him after His resurrection and ascension. We are joined to Him just as its branches are joined to a vine. We become one spirit with Him: His sap flows through us, producing the lovely fruit of love, joy, peace, patience and so on. Together, we are the body of

Christ, each individual serving the others, under the headship of Christ. Someone who hates other members of the body, or who ignores their needs, probably never believed *into* Christ.

John will go on to apply these three tests of true faith, when he writes his pastoral letter to the churches under his bishopric in south Turkey. When people claim to have deeper revelation and cause division and schism within local churches, the test is, have they believed *into* Christ? Do they accept the truth of the incarnation, that 'Jesus Christ is come in the flesh'? Have they surrendered all pretensions to their own righteousness, and are they walking in the light? And do they manifest the same love and grace they claim to have received, in their fellowship with other believers?

Having previously looked at the rest of John chapter three, we'll now take a minor detour. Jesus's split-screen reality of being *'in the bosom of the Father'* whilst also present in our material world, challenges our limited expectations of Christian experience.

Then we'll look at the spiritual significance of Jacob's well and its location in Samaria, before looking at the Samaritan woman's encounter with Christ.

Split-screen reality

Being both God and man, Jesus was continually aware of what His Father was doing and saying, as well as His earthly surroundings.

Whereas we are continually aware of the world around us, but need our eyes opened to see spiritual realities, by faith.

When Nicodemus says, "You are a teacher come from God", Jesus tacitly accepts it. But though He has come from God, He is still with God[1], as He has been from all eternity!

*"No-one has ascended into heaven but He who came down from heaven, that is, the Son of Man who **is in heaven**. We speak what we know, and testify what we have seen, and you do not receive our witness. If I have told you earthly things and you do not believe, how will you believe when I tell you heavenly things?"*[2]

Because He is both God and man, Jesus lived in a **split-screen reality**, continually aware of what His Father was doing and saying, but also fully aware of His earthly surroundings.

Just as He had copied Joseph's woodworking techniques in every detail, so with His Heavenly Father: *"The Son can do nothing of Himself, but only what He **sees** the Father do".*[3] And like any true prophet, He speaks only what He hears the Father say: *"I have not spoken on My own authority, but the Father told Me what I should say".*[4]

A W Tozer says, *"When the Son of God walked the earth as the Son of Man, He spoke often to the Father and the Father answered Him again.... The dialogue involving the Father and the Son recorded in the scriptures is always to be understood as being between the Eternal Father and the <u>Man</u> Christ Jesus. That instant, immediate communion between the Persons of the Godhead which has been from all eternity, knows not sound nor effort nor motion".*

---

[1] (3:13)
[2] (3:11-12)
[3] (5:19)
[4] (12:49)

We too live in a split-screen reality: but of a different sort. We are continuously aware of the things of this world, but cannot conceive the things God has prepared for us[5], the '*things which are above, where Christ is, seated at the right hand of the Father'*[6]. Materialism sets our eyes on the newest must-have, or the latest fashions: especially in the West. Our spiritual eyes are blinded by Adam's sin, and our own. But Jesus came *'to open the eyes of the blind'*.[7]

You might think, it requires special grace for a Gehazi to see the armies of God, or a Saul to see Jesus on the Damascus Road. But the promise of God is, that when He pours out His Spirit on all flesh, *"Your old men shall dream dreams, and your young men shall see visions".*[8] It is God's will to give all of us a spirit of revelation, to enlighten our hearts' eyes to know the hope of our calling, (that Jesus will return one day); the wealth of glory He has invested in His saints; and the incredible power He exerts on our behalf.[9]

God does not give us a 'third eye' or chakra - indeed He abhors all divination. But at its simplest, Christians often experience seeing a picture as they pray. Sometimes we may have dreams in which we prophetically 'see' things in our spirits. Sometimes we may have waking visions, in which God takes us up into His Presence. Both Paul and John record such experiences: indeed it was a prolonged and complex vision through which Jesus revealed to John, what was to happen in the Last Days.

This does not obviate the need for faith - to walk by faith, and not by sight: *"Faith is confidence in what we hope for, and assurance about what we do not see ... By faith Abraham lived in the Promised Land like a nomad, because he was looking forward to the heavenly city built by God ... By faith Abraham offered up his only-begotten son ... By faith, Moses endured Pharoah's anger, as seeing Him who is Invisible"* [10]

---

5 (1Cor 2:9)
6 (Col 3:2)
7 (Lk 4:18)
8 (Joel 2:28)
9 (Eph 1:17-19)
10 (Heb 11:1,9-10,17,27)

Law or Grace? (4:5)

Samaria, *the location of Jacob's well, is very significant spiritually. It speaks of our destiny - blessing or curse, heaven or hell - being determined by God's Law. But the well itself speaks of God's grace.*

The geography of Jacob's well

In Jesus's time, Samaria referred to an area between Judea and Galilee: the northern end of what is presently referred to as 'The West Bank'. Its chief city, then called Samaria but now known as Nablus, was about thirty miles north of Jerusalem. It was near the ancient site of Shechem, where Abram had built his first altar in the Promised Land.[1]

Years later, when Jacob returned from living with Laban, he bought a patch of ground from Hamor, Shechem's founding father; and he too erected an altar there.[2] Perhaps remembering his father's conflicts with the Philistines over water, Jacob dug his own well. It exists even to this day, and must have been an astonishing feat: it's over a hundred feet deep. But it was reliable and prolific enough to supply water for his whole tribe, and their large herds of livestock. Thus it was a symbol of God's grace.

When one of Hamor's sons raped their sister Dinah, Jacob's sons slaughtered all the Shechemites. Out of fear of revenge from other Canaanites, Jacob abandoned the land and the well, and relocated further south.

Years later, after the whole family had moved to Egypt, Jacob knew he was about to die. Prophetically, he gifted this land in Shechem to Joseph, doubling Joseph's share of the Promised Land.[3] Joseph was later buried there, after his bones had been brought back to Israel during the Exodus.[4] His tomb still exists, only a few hundred yards from his well. The well lies below a neighbouring hill called Mount Ebal, whereas his tomb is nearer another hill called Mount Gerizim.

---

[1] (Gen 12:6–7)

[2] (Gen 33:18-20)

[3] (Gen 48:22)

[4] (Josh 24:32)

Shechem lay in a natural amphitheatre between these two hills. This formed the ideal setting for a national covenant-renewal ceremony after Israel's return from Egypt.[5] Having crossed the Jordan, Joshua re-circumcised the nation, celebrated Passover, then marched on Jericho and Ai. From there he led his army to Samaria where he built an altar on Mount Ebal. The fact that he was doing so in the same place both Abraham and Jacob had built their first altars, would have been lost on no-one.

The altar stones were inscribed with the words of the Ten Commandments, and burnt offerings and peace offerings were sacrificed. Then they renewed their covenant with Yahweh. The ceremony centred on the Ark of the Covenant, and involved half the nation speaking blessings from Mount Gerizim, then the other half pronouncing curses from Mount Ebal. The whole ceremony had been prophetically prescribed by Moses before his death, including all the blessings and curses.[6]

So Shechem's geography spoke of a life lived between blessing and curse, between life and death, between heaven and hell. But it also spoke of God's covenant faithfulness, and grace. Whether Israel stayed obedient to Yahweh's Law, was to determine whether they could stay in the land and under God's blessing longterm.

A recipe for rivalry between Judah & Ephraim

Once Joshua had apportioned the land, Shechem became Ephraim's leading city. During the time of the Judges, leaders emerged from different tribes at different times. Deborah was from Ephraim; and though Gideon was of the tribe of Manasseh, he had a concubine in Shechem. After Gideon's death her child Abimelech ruled briefly from Shechem. And later another Ephraimite named Pirathon judged Israel for eight years. By comparison there was only one judge from the tribe of Judah throughout that four-hundred-year period.

Once the twelve tribes changed from a confederacy and became a kingdom, old sibling rivalries re-emerged about the issue of birthright: who had the right to lead the tribes? Jacob's first three sons had disqualified themselves,

---

[5] (Josh 8:30-35)

[6] (Deut 11:29-30; Deut 27:1-28:68)

and technically Judah should have been next in line. However before he died, Jacob had adopted Joseph's sons (Manasseh and Ephraim) as his own. Then, perhaps remembering Joseph's prophetic dreams, he had given him a double portion of land, apparently giving Ephraim the birthright.[7] Nevertheless on his deathbed, he had named Judah as the tribe from whom Israel's rulers would come.[8] Confusing, huh?

Saul was a Benjaminite, but David was of the tribe of Judah. And Judah was the first tribe to appoint David as their king, after Saul's death. The other tribes held out for six years, but eventually all twelve united and David moved his capital from Hebron to Jerusalem, on the border between Judah and Benjamin. In Jewish eyes this indicated God was choosing Judah over Ephraim; and Mount Zion, not Mount Gerizim, as the place of His Presence.[9]

But when David was reinstalled as king after Absalom's rebellion, Ephraim initially objected. And after Solomon's death, it was at *Shechem* that the nation gathered to crown Rehoboam. When he refused to ease Solomon's harsh rule, the kingdom fell apart: he ruled Judah from Jerusalem, while Jeroboam became king of the ten tribes, with *Shechem* as his capital.

The racial purity issue

The northern kingdom, who had claimed the name Israel, underwent frequent changes of dynasty due to its kings' idolatry. The curses pronounced from Mount Ebal came into operation. Eventually it was invaded by Assyria and ethnically cleansed, its inhabitants replaced by immigrants from other parts of the Assyrian Empire. They worshipped their own gods; blending this with worship of Yahweh, whom they saw as a local god.

Later, the Southern Kingdom was also taken into captivity, this time by Babylon: but unlike the Northern Kingdom, the Judaean exiles were allowed to return seventy years later. Meantime Samaria remained racially mixed.

The Jews began rebuilding their temple in Jerusalem, under the leadership of Nehemiah and Ezra and with prophetic encouragement from Haggai and

---

[7] (1 Chron 5:1-2; Jer 31:9)

[8] (Gen 49:8-10

[9] (Ps 78:67-70)

Zechariah. Nehemiah was adamant about racial purity, and wouldn't allow the Samaritans' leader Sanballat, any part in the rebuilding.[10] Sanballat tried to get round this by marrying one of his daughters to a son of the High Priest; but Nehemiah discovered and drove the young couple away.[11]

Religious rivalry

Despite all this, the Samaritans saw themselves as children of Jacob. They held to the Torah, just as the Jews did; but only the Torah, not the historical books or the prophets. They believed Moses was the *only* true prophet, until another prophet like him should come.[12] They called this future prophet *'The Taleb'*, meaning the One who would return and restore all things. So their view of Messiah was significantly different than that of the Jews: more focused on His prophetic ministry than His nature as Redeemer King.

Their version of the Torah replaced the tenth commandment with one commanding that a Temple be built on Mount Gerizim, which they did in 400 BC or thereabouts. Excavations show it had a massive foundation, remarkably similar to the rebuilt Temple in Jerusalem. They celebrated Passover and the other feasts there, with a near-identical ritual to that of the Jews. So from a Judaean point of view, the Samaritans and Mount Gerizim represented a copycat religion right on their doorstep.

History moved on, and Babylon was overthrown by the Medes and Persians; then later the Greek Empire became the new occupying power. Antiochus tried to wipe out Jewish culture, deliberately defiling the Temple. The Jews fought back, reclaiming their own land and rededicating the Jerusalem Temple. In 128 BC the Jewish rebels' leader John Hyrcanus razed the Samaritans' temple to the ground. Worse still for the Samaritans, when Rome occupied the land they designated Samaria as part of Judaea!

The intense antipathy meant that Jews from Galilee going up to Jerusalem often faced hostility from Samaritans. Though their most direct route lay

---

[10] (Neh 2:19-20,4:1-3, 13:1-3)

[11] (Neh 13:23-28)

[12] (Deut 18:15; 34:10)

through Samaria, many preferred to go the long way round via Jordan in order to avoid the risk of attack in Samaria.

In Jesus's time, there were probably as many Samaritans as Judaeans. Today, there are probably only a thousand Samaritans still alive, but they still worship on Mount Gerizim. Having sought to prevent inter-racial marriages for centuries, they are now trying to boost their numbers by intermarriage with Jewish women!

The relevance of this context, to the woman at the well

History meant that the woman at the well lived under a counterfeit religion. Yet both faiths believed in the same God, and that He was One. The controversy about which religion had the truth, was ongoing.

The geography of Samaria, with Mounts Ebal and Gerizim, spoke of judgement based on one's life and deeds: things in which the Samaritan woman knew she had failed.

The well had sustained Jacob's family through very difficult times. Finding such a prolific water supply, at that depth, had been a major miracle for him. She too had a difficult life, ostracised by her fellow women. But now she was about to experience a greater miracle than Jacob: a permanent supply of living water, entirely by grace!

Living water, in a spiritual desert (4:3-42)

Jesus uses His exhaustion as an opportunity in disguise. He breaks all social norms, to bring the water of spiritual life to a Samaritan woman. Taking this 'God-opportunity' led to massive results, and teaches us about effective evangelism.

A cross-cultural opportunity

Eavesdropping on Jesus's conversation with the woman is fascinating! His weariness speaks of His humanity. Yet He was about to reveal His divinity to the Samaritan, more directly than He had yet done to any Jew.

This passage fits John's overall narrative purpose perfectly. He records the Samaritan woman's conversion, *"that you may believe that Jesus is the Christ, and that believing you may have life in His Name".*[1]

Jesus started by humbling Himself to ask for the most basic of needs - water. He did this, knowing it would provoke her curiosity. Jewish rabbis believed that talking to a woman, even your own wife, was a waste of good time - time that could have been better spent studying Torah! And a *Samaritan* woman was even worse. Yet He made no attempt to avoid her, but instead crossed all the cultural barriers to engage her.

There are numerous clues in the account, that suggest this woman was not respectable. The disciples were astonished that Jesus was talking with her, and thought she must have an ulterior motive.[2] She was alone at the well in the midday sun, when they hadn't expected anyone to be around. When she went back to the town, it was the men she spoke to, not the women. And it was the possibility of hearing more of her colourful backstory that drew them to see for themselves.

Some say that she was just someone who had been extremely unfortunate in life. She'd married five men, each of whom then died or divorced her.

---

[1] (20:31)
[2] (4:27)

Maybe some of her marriages were 'levirate' marriages: marriage to a brother of your deceased husband, so that you could have a child to inherit his land.[3] But in general the rabbis disapproved of more than three marriages under any circumstances. So this explanation seems unlikely.

When Jesus sent out the Twelve on mission, He told them not to go to the Gentiles or Samaritans[4]. To the Syro-Phoenician woman[5], He says He has only been sent to the tribe of Israel. But here He seems to apply a different logic: He accepted that this Samaritan woman was a child of Jacob, as she later claims.[6]

Jesus reveals His identity to her

Having provoked her curiosity, He invited her to think about who He really was. *"If you only knew who is speaking with you, and how generous God is, you would have asked Me, and I would have given you living water!"* Living water meant flowing water: in a stream, or fresh from a spring. Water that wasn't stagnant, not water from a well or cistern.

Like Nicodemus, she failed to see beyond the metaphor. Jacob's well was able to meet a whole tribe's needs. But it was very deep, and Jesus had no bucket. Did he perhaps know of a surface spring nearby? Did he know something Jacob didn't?

But Jesus was in fact offering her the gift of the Spirit.

Later, on the last great day of the Feast of Tabernacles, Jesus cried out, *'If anyone is thirsty, let him come to Me and drink. He who believes in Me, as the scripture has said, out of his heart will flow rivers of living water.' - He was speaking of the Spirit.*[7]

The Feast celebrated the Presence of God with Israel during the Exodus, when a miraculous rock which gushed water, followed the Israelites wherever they went. Paul says that that rock was in fact Christ.[8]

---

[3] (Matt 22:23-28)
[4] (Mt 10:5)
[5] (Mt 15:21-28)
[6] (4:12)
[7] (8:37-39)
[8] (1 Cor 10:4)

The Samaritans would have been well aware of this scripture. In their liturgy, it is said of the Taleb that *'water shall flow from His buckets'*[9]. So she would understand that Jesus was claiming to be the Taleb.

Jesus tells her that the water He gives, becomes a spring within the individual. They will never ever need to drink again - in fact, there will be an outflow of living water to others too.

One can sense the beginnings of faith, the woman's incredulity gradually being overtaken by hope. She will never need to come and fetch water again. She will never be thirsty again! Jesus had said that all she needed to do was to ask! This would have been, to her, the ultimate prosperity gospel. So she asked ...

But Jesus was about to pop the balloon.

Jesus reveals her identity, to her

'Go, bring your husband and come back.' Jesus's requirement for giving the Spirit, was that she fetch her husband. He required that she walk in the light. And He would not give her the living water unless she brought her man. Her heart must have sunk, as she glumly stated, *"I have no husband"*. She did indeed have a man, but not a husband. The price of this gift was confession and repentance. Jesus, as usual, went straight to the heart of the matter.

The woman's reply is true; but not the whole truth! Jesus graciously compliments her on her truthfulness, but then exposes her unconfessed sin. He will not countenance hypocrisy. He gives her a word of knowledge, revealing His omniscience. This was further evidence of His divinity.

(Seen in the light of omniscience, hypocrisy is sheer folly. Jesus can see every dark secret of our hearts, and what we whisper in private will one day be shouted from the housetops. If we don't walk in the light, or pretend we don't sin and never have, we deceive only ourselves, and maybe others[10]*; but not God. We cannot have fellowship with Him without walking in the light.*

What does it mean to you, to know that Jesus knows you inside out?)

---

[9] (Num 24:7)
[10] (1Jn 1:5-10)

If her past was as we suppose, she would have spent enormous mental energy hiding the truth about herself:-

- Hiding why her husbands divorced her
- Hiding her relationships with other men
- Hiding from stigma from other women
- Hiding even from herself, from facing her own sinfulness.

Knowing that she was fully known and yet accepted, and by a Jewish rabbi at that, would have conveyed massive grace in place of rejection & exclusion.

Tim Keller writes, *"To be loved but not known is comforting, but superficial. To be known and not loved is our greatest fear. But to be fully known and truly loved is a lot like being loved by God. It is what we need more than anything. It liberates us from pretence, humbles us out of our self-righteousness, and fortifies us for any difficulty life can throw at us"*.[11]

The Samaritan woman doesn't seem to have been fazed or frightened by Jesus's exposure of her past. She doesn't shrink from the Light of the World. Instead, she focusses on what Jesus's supernatural knowledge says about Him. The secrets of her heart having been disclosed, she is forced to acknowledge Him as a prophet.[12] But she is not yet ready to acknowledge Jesus as *The* Prophet, the Taleb of Samaritan hopes.

<u>He uses her sidetrack to teach about worship</u>

Her subsequent question about where one should worship, is telling. *'Our fathers'*[13] refers back a hundred and fifty years to when the Samaritans' temple on Mount Gerizim was destroyed by John Hyrcanus.

The whole debate between Jews & Samaritans about the Temple's location, turned on whether a single verse said God *had chosen*, or *would later choose*, somewhere as the Temple site.[14] From the Samaritans' point of view,

---

[11] (Timothy Keller, "The Meaning of Marriage: Facing the Complexities of Commitment with the Wisdom of God")

[12] (1Cor 14:24,25)

[13] (4:20)

[14] (Deut 12:5)

Abram's first altar was in Shechem[15]. Mt Gerizim was where blessings were shouted over Israel, on entering the Promised Land. Jacob's altar, his well, his tomb, and the birthright land were all in Shechem. So there were reasons to back the Samaritans' claim, that Gerizim was God's dwelling place.

A charitable view is that she was genuinely asking Jesus how she should worship God. But more likely, she was trying to divert the conversation away from her personal life, by engaging this rabbi in theological controversy.

Once again, Jesus will not be deflected. He challenges her about *true* worship. The word can also be translated as *genuine:* genuine worship. Worship that focusses on physical buildings, is idolatry: not true worship. The hour of His death is under three years away; and forty years later, the Jews' Temple will be destroyed just as the Samaritans' temple had been. Neither nation will then be able to claim their temple is uniquely God-ordained.

But once the temple of His body had been destroyed on the cross, He would rebuild it in three days. His resurrection would establish that He Himself had always been the true Temple, the way into the Presence of God. *'No-one comes to the Father, but through Me'*.[16]

Jesus refers to God as 'the Father', underlining the need for relationship with Him. The Samaritans put great emphasis on God being spirit: their alterations to the Torah seem to have been focussed on removing anthropomorphisms. And as Jesus has just taught Nicodemus, one cannot see the Spirit, only observe His effects. So the Samaritans' knowledge of God was limited to the numinous, *as it is for many today*. They worshipped what they did not know.

Although Samaritans held only to Moses' Torah, they also believed in the resurrection. And they seem to have been in eager expectation of the Taleb or Messiah, just as Israel was. But the revelation of God to the Jews was far greater, containing all the prophecies of Messiah, and all the prophetic writings. Nevertheless Jesus repeatedly tells the Jews that they do *not* know God[17] in the sense of intimate relationship (Gk: ginosko).

---

[15] (Gen 12:6-7)

[16] (14:6)

[17] (5:42, 8:19, 8:54-55)

Far from ducking the racial issue, Jesus asserts that *'salvation is of the Jews'*. This may not have been as 'in your face' as it sounds. The Samaritan Pentateuch, like the Jewish Torah, acknowledged that Messiah would come from the tribe of Judah.[18] The stream of revelation would flow through Judaea not Samaria; but was not exclusive to the Jews.

In sending His Son to be the sacrifice for our sins, and to be the antitype of the Temple, the Father is looking for a new kind of worshipper. Because He is Spirit, we can only truly know Him through our spirits.[19] Genuine worshippers must worship Him in spirit and truth, not just with our souls and bodies.

What does this mean for our worship today?

Hymns, ritual, vestments, posture - all can help us worship, if handled rightly. And our day-to-day actions are as much part of our worship, as anything we do in church. But ultimately we must not rely on anything we do or say or sing, as true worship. *"We are the (true) circumcision, who worship God in the Spirit, rejoice in Christ, Jesus, and have no confidence in the flesh".*[20]

What type of service is best for a particular congregation, should be decided by how effectively it turns their attention to God. Not whether it is happy-clappy or silent, liturgical or congregational, emotional or intellectual, etc.

C S Lewis wrote, *"As long as you notice, and have to count the steps, you are not yet dancing, but only learning to dance. A good shoe is a shoe you don't notice. Good reading becomes possible when you need not consciously think about eyes, or light, or print, or spelling. The perfect church service would be one we were almost unaware of; our attention would have been on God".*[21]

Spirit and truth go hand in hand: Jesus promised that the Holy Spirit would lead us into all truth. So worship in spirit will always be worship in truth. While we *understand* with our reason, we *know* through our spirit. For example, at first I could not understand what it meant, that God was Spirit. But once the Holy Spirit revealed it to me as truth, my intellectual struggling

---

[18] (Gen 49:10)
[19] (3:8, 1Cor 2:9-11)
[20] (Phil 3:3)
[21] (C S Lewis, 'Letters to Malcolm, Chiefly on Prayer')

ceased. The supernatural life within us from being born again, the anointing of the Spirit[22], enables us to recognize truth. This Spirit of adoption witnesses with our spirit that we are indeed children of God[23], enabling us to cry out 'Abba, Father!' True worship is when our spirit and the Holy Spirit are free to collaborate and bring us into the kind of adoration we read of in Revelation.[24]

In the Tabernacle, after offering a lamb on the altar, the priests had to wash in the laver before entering the Holy Place. There they would pray at the altar of incense, with the light of the menorah and beside the 'bread of the Presence', before stepping through the veil into the Holy of Holies. Every aspect speaks of how we should come into God's Presence to worship, and every aspect speaks of Christ. He is the Lamb, the Laver, the Bread, the Light, the Incense, the Veil, and the 'Mercy Seat', where the Law is covered over with His blood and *'hides all our transgressions from view'*. True worship will always be focussed on the Person of Jesus, who is The Truth.

True worship must also be honest, real. God is Light, and will not fellowship with darkness. Hypocrisy is when we practice make-believe: hiding unconfessed sin, whilst pretending to worship. We must come without pretence: with hearts open to God, knowing He already knows us inside out.

We must worship on the basis of biblical truth, not church traditions. Jesus said of the Pharisees' focus on their oral law rather than the written Torah, *"These people draw near to me with their mouths, and honour me with their lips, but their heart is far from Me. And in vain they worship Me, teaching as doctrines the commandments of men".*[25]

So the worshippers God seeks, will worship Him

- out of the fullness of the supernatural life they enjoy
- focussed on God's incarnate self-expression (Jesus) as their temple
- With honesty and reality about their own spiritual walk

---

22 (1Jn 2:27)
23 (Rom 8:15,16)
24 (Rev 4&5)
25 (Mt 15:8-9, Isa 29:13)

• Prioritising biblical truth over their church's traditions.

The significance of Jesus saying, 'I AM'

The woman tries to postpone commitment and end the conversation, by pleading ignorance. She says that when the Taleb comes, he would explain everything in a way she could understand. Jesus bazookas this fob-off with a stunning assertion: He *is* the Taleb, the Messiah! This tired, dusty, hungry, thirsty traveller standing before her, is her long-hoped-for Taleb.

Although most modern translations quote Jesus as saying, *'I am He',* or, *'I am the Messiah'*, in fact the Greek just says, *'I am'*.

'I AM' in Hebrew is the word 'Yahweh' (often pronounced as Jehovah). This was the name by which Almighty God revealed Himself to Moses at the burning bush; His personal Name for all eternity.[26] I AM expresses the self-existence and eternity of God. He is not named by anyone else, but names Himself. He is not dependent on time or space, or contained by them. He was in the beginning, is, and always will be. He is eternal, Alpha and Omega.

The Jews held this Name in such awe, that they would never say it for fear of trivialising or disrespecting it. For any human being to say 'I AM' was utter blasphemy, likely to lead to annihilation by God.[27] (That was why, in Gethsemane, the soldiers fell on their faces when Jesus said, 'I AM'.[28])

Instead they referred to God as 'HaShem', the Name; or 'Adonai', Lord or Master. Wherever the divine Name appeared in their scriptures, they would substitute one of these words. Most bible translations continue this: wherever you see LORD, the original Hebrew was YWHW, or Yahweh.

It is hard for us, in egalitarian Western cultures, to relate to this awe of a name. The nearest recent parallel I can think of is in the Harry Potter novels, where the evil Lord Voldemort is spoken of as 'he who must not be named'. And as Dumbledore explains to Harry, the fear of the name engenders fear of

---

[26] (Ex 3:13-15)
[27] (Ex 20:7)
[28] (18:5,6)

the person. Old Testament writers remind us regularly that *'the fear of Yahweh is the beginning of wisdom'*.[29]

Because ancient Hebrew had no vowels, people debate whether the name would be pronounced as Jehovah, or as Yahweh. The very fact that we still today don't know how to pronounce God's personal Name, is part of the mystery. In Hebrew thought, one's name expressed one's character, the essence of one's being that was knowable by others. Knowing a god's name gave a person power and authority to speak 'in their name'.

In Philippians, Paul tells us that Jesus has been given 'the name which is above every name', that at the name of Jesus every knee shall bow, and every tongue confess that He is Lord. Christ's Hebrew name, Yeshua, means 'Yahweh is salvation'. And it is the authority of that Name that we use, every time we pray in the Name of Jesus.

Jesus is recorded as saying 'I am', fourteen times in John's Gospel: Seven of them are purely 'I AM': direct claims to being Yahweh[30], as in this instance. But seven others combine God's name with an aspect of who He is, <u>to us:</u>

- the **Bread of Life**[31]
- the **Light of the world**[32]
- the **Door of the sheepfold**[33]
- the **Good Shepherd**[34]
- the **Resurrection and the Life**[35]
- the **Way**, the **Truth**, and the **Life**[36]
- the **True Vine**[37]

We will look at each of these names in more detail, when we get to them. But for now, let it sink in: Jesus is God Incarnate, God with us, God *for* us.

---

[29] (Prov 1:7, 9:10, Ps 19:9)
[30] (See 4:26; 6:20; 8:24,28,58; 13:19; 18:5,6)
[31] *(6:35)*
[32] *(8:12;9:5)*
[33] *(10:7,9)*
[34] *(10:11,14)*
[35] *(11:25)*
[36] *(14:6)*
[37] *(15:1,5)*

The joy of witnessing

Curiously the disciples, on arriving back, didn't ask any questions; though they were very surprised. Perhaps they saw the look on the woman's face, as she took in the implication of what she had just heard. She hurried off to tell her friends, so stunned that she forgot her water jar! Her testimony was that Jesus knew all about her colourful past, and yet offered her eternal life.

Jesus too was energised by what had just transpired. His disciples arrived back with lunch, and urged Him to eat. instead, He started to teach them about the joy He found in doing His Father's will. This is the first of many teachings John records, about Jesus's relationship to the Father.[38]

As a boy, his *earthly* father would hold one end of a double-handled saw, and he the other, as they together cut through beams. Or Joseph would show Him how to do something, then watch as his son finished it off. In a similar way, His *heavenly* Father showed Him what to do, and gave Him works to finish. Just as Jesus had watched his earthly father in his carpentry workshop, and learnt from him exactly how to form a mortice-and-tenon joint, so too He watched His heavenly Father, copying Him exactly in every detail.

Jesus says that His secret super-fuel is to do the will of His Father, and to complete His work. Jesus was nourished, not just by reading the word of God, but by obeying it completely.

'Man shall not live by bread alone, but by every word that proceeds out of the mouth of God'[39]. Moses's saying was more true in Jesus's life, than it ever had been before. In Gethsemane Christ prayed, *"I have glorified You on earth. I have finished the work which you gave Me to do"*[40]. And on the Cross, He could cry out, *"It is finished!"*

There is a challenge here for those of us who are flagging, to fulfil the ministries the Lord has given us.[41] We may make the excuse that the time isn't yet right to harvest, and certainly most Judaeans would have held that witnessing in Samaria was a waste of time. But no sooner had the woman

---

[38] (5:19-20; 5:36; 6:38; 9:4; 10:25)

[39] (Deut 8:3)

[40] (17:4)

[41] (Col 4:17)

gone back to town with her breathtaking question *"Could this be the Christ?"*, than the local men began flocking down the hill towards the well. The hillside was white with their robes. We need faith and spiritual vision, to see the harvest ready for reaping - however hard the place we live in.

Whilst we often do not see the harvest that comes from our sowing, but someone else later leads that individual to Christ, ultimately there will be joy in heaven which both sower and reaper will share. And whilst one may plant and another water, it is always God who gives the increase.[42]

When Jesus set His disciples baptising[43], John the Baptist had laboured beforehand to bring the message of repentance. He had done the hard work, and they had reaped what they had not sown.[44] Now Jesus has been at work before them: He has planted the seed through the woman's testimony, and they are about to reap.

Jesus trained His disciples to look for people in whom God was already at work. We may plant, water, or reap - but it's always God who brings our witness to fruition. High-pressure salesmanship by evangelists, usually just puts people off!

Lasting fruit in Samaria

Samaritans would often give Jewish travellers a hard time[45]. But now, through the woman's testimony, they pressed Jesus to stay. No doubt whoever hosted them would have experienced Jesus's *shalom* peace[46]. There would have been deep, meaningful conversations late into the night.

Many came to personal faith that Jesus was indeed the Anointed One, Messiah or Taleb; and that His teachings were not just for Jews and Galileans, but for Samaritans too. He was the Saviour of the whole world. His own

---

42 (1Cor 3:6-9)
43 (4:1,2)
44 (4:38)
45 (Lk 9:51-56)
46 (Mt 10:11-13)

people had *'received Him not'*[47], but now *anyone* who would receive Him, was given the right to become a child of God.[48]

Jesus's great commission to His disciples was for them to witness throughout Judaea but also Samaria, en route to worldwide evangelism.[49] His stay there laid the groundwork for revival to break out a few years later, when Philip preached there.[50] Jesus's Name and its power impressed a famous local sorcerer, such that even he believed.[51] Peter and John were sent to release the outpouring of the Spirit there, and on their way home, preached the gospel in many Samaritan villages[52].

---

47 (1:11)
48 (1:12)
49 (Acts 1:8)
50 (Acts 8:4-8)
51 (Acts 8:9-13)
52 (Acts 8:25)

Lessons in evangelism, from John so far

How do you respond, when someone asks you about Jesus?

Ultimately Jesus's biggest question to us, is, *"Who do you say that I am?"*

Some are more gifted evangelists than others, but all of us can explain why we love Jesus. We don't need to be ashamed of what we have been, or are still: the gospel is about grace, and self-righteousness is a major turn-off.

So what tips can we garner from John's Gospel thus far?

From **John the Baptist**, we can learn:-

- Always make it about Jesus, never about ourselves
- Find joy and fulfilment in bringing others to Jesus, then get out of His way!
- Assert Jesus's divinity, and His intimate knowledge of God
- Seek a specific commitment to believe

The way Jesus talks to **Nicodemus**, suggests we should:-

- Recognise the unvoiced question the enquirer is really asking
- Adapt our approach to their worldview, without flattering or seeking to please them
- Emphasise the need to be born again, a radical new beginning
- Not be put off by ridicule or scepticism
- Use our own 'eye-witness' testimony: it carries great weight
- Explain that faith is more than assent: it means believing *into* Jesus
- Focus on Jesus's uniqueness; not man become god, but God become Man
- Explain He is the only eye-witness we have, about heaven and the afterlife
- Explain that we shouldn't hide from God's holiness, or be hypocrites

In Jesus's encounter with **the woman at the well**, we see that:-

- He takes a seemingly-random opportunity, to engage her
- He is not blinded to her need, by the prejudices of the time
- He uses His own need, to provoke her curiosity
- He confronts her sinfulness, but with grace and gentleness

- He re-purposes her sidetracking, to teach her about true worship
- He won't be fobbed off, but pushes for a decision by saying 'I AM'

True faith, or prosperity gospel? (4:43-54)

Jesus meets Herod's courtier, desperate about his dying child.
The Jews want to see miracles before believing:
but Jesus asks the man to believe before seeing.

Why did Jesus return to Galilee? (4:43-46)

Jesus was born a Judaean, so His comment about a prophet not being honoured in his hometown may refer to the hostility He'd experienced in Jerusalem. By contrast, He was welcomed on His arrival in Galilee.

However, in Judaea many people actually thought that Jesus was a Galilean, or perhaps a Samaritan[1], which undermines this interpretation.

Prior to this, Jesus had been in Galilee at the wedding in Cana. Following that, He had toured Galilee announcing the Kingdom of God, and then had come home to Nazareth[2]. There He had claimed to fulfil Isaiah's description of Messiah's ministry. But His childhood neighbours couldn't accept that a local carpenter's son could possibly be the Messiah.

In Nazareth, Jesus had quoted the same proverb, about a prophet receiving no honour in his own country. He backed it up with stories from Elijah and Elisha's experience. Nevertheless his family's neighbours tried to kill Him, and He had to move His mother and siblings to Capernaum for their own safety.

So if Jesus knew that

- He would receive no honour in His childhood home, and that
- His message had put His whole family at risk not long before,

why, when He had just experienced such a welcome in Samaria, did He return to Galilee? Humanly, it made no sense.

Jesus knew from Isaiah that the light of the gospel was to come to *'Galilee of the Gentiles'* first.[3] And many Galileans had been amongst those who believed, when they saw the miracles He did in Jerusalem during Passover.[4]

---

[1] (7:27, 50-52; 8:48)
[2] (Lk 4:14-30)
[3] (Isa 9:1,2)
[4] (2:23, 4:45)

Rather than going back to Nazareth, Jesus goes to Nathanael's home in Cana, where the excellent wine of the wedding feast was still remembered!

The Courtier's son healed (4:46-54)

John now recounts the second of the seven signs[5], carefully selected to reveal something more about Jesus the Messiah.

There are various echoes of the first sign: it occurs in Cana, three days after leaving Judaea; it starts with an initial rebuke, is validated by servants, and leads to belief. But there is one major contrast: the first sign is at a joyful event, the second has to do with the grief of a child's impending death.

The word translated 'nobleman' implies this man was close to the King: he was a courtier. He may even have been Herod's steward, Chuza, whose wife later became one of Jesus's most devoted followers.[6]

So a courtier requests a carpenter to come from Cana to Capernaum (twenty-five miles) to cure his child! He must have been pretty desperate.

Jesus demurs; on the grounds that '*seeing is believing*' is the opposite of '*walking by faith*'. The Jews routinely demanded signs to validate a man's ministry, before they would believe: but the resulting kind of belief was not saving faith.[7] The courtier must believe *first*, before seeing. He must trust Jesus enough to allow Him to operate however He chooses.

Why was this sign significant?

It teaches about the development and nature of true faith

The Jerusalem Jews had faith in Jesus's name when they saw the signs that He did, but it wasn't the sort of faith that Jesus could put much weight on.[8] Nicodemus saw beyond the miracles, to God's endorsement of Jesus: but he too wasn't yet 'born again'. In this instance, the nobleman's faith shows a progressive development. He first asks for a miracle; then takes Jesus at His word; then believes, along with His whole household.

---

[5] (4:54)
[6] (Lk 8:3)
[7] ((2:23-25)
[8] (2:23-25)

Faith sees beyond the sign, to grasp the spiritual reality to which it points.

"Faith based on signs and miracles must not be mistaken for true faith, which is why Jesus does not encourage it. It fails to honour God, since by it, He serves us rather than the other way round. We are left with a mistaken notion that we are in a position to dictate terms to him. Miraculous signs and miraculous answers to prayer, may have a certain value as a starting point, making us aware of God's reality, but they remain sterile, unless they lead on to a concern for the Christ to whom they point, and whose glory they signify.

"Beyond the miracles, we seek the Lord who works them. It is in obeying his commands and trusting his promises that true faith is expressed. Now we have ceased to dictate the terms of our relationship: we exist for him, not he for us. Now, we 'believe'." (Milne)[9]

It teaches about *prayer*

The courtier's prayer is *p*assionate, *p*ersistent, *p*ractical and *p*owerful. He is not put off by Jesus's initial apparent rebuff. He moves from a position of entitlement (because of his social standing) to humility, calling Jesus 'Master' or 'Lord'[10]. He accepts Jesus's word by faith, only discovering the next day that the healing occurred the instant Jesus spoke.

It reveals Jesus's *authority.*

The gospels show that when Jesus healed, He usually touched people or used other methods. But when He cast out demons, it was always by verbal command alone. His words had incredible authority, quite different from other rabbis.[11]

Some while after this episode, a Roman Centurion (also from Capernaum) whose servant was ill, also approached Jesus seeking healing.[12] However, unlike this courtier he seems to have grasped from his military experience, how spiritual authority works. Or maybe he had the advantage of having heard about the courtier's case previously?

---

[9] (Bruce Milne, 'The Message of John'; IVP, 1993)

[10] (4:49)

[11] (Matt 7:29)

[12] (Matt 8:8-10)

The nature of authority

Authority is always *something vested in a person, by their superior.*

The Centurion knew that his authority to command came from the fact that he himself was under authority. Had he mutinied against Caesar, his soldiers would have been under no obligation to obey. Likewise Pilate would have had no authority over Jesus, unless God had allowed it.[13]

Jesus's authority came from His obedience to the Father: it was *given* to Him. His Father gave Him all authority in heaven and on earth, that at the Name of Jesus every knee would do obeisance.

Power and authority are two different things, with two different Greek terms (dunamis and exousia). In the boxing ring, a heavyweight champion will be far more *powerful* than the referee. But the referee's *authority* enables him to stop the fight at any point, and separate the sparring contestants. In fact, John never uses the word for power. And yet our translations tend to treat them as interchangeable. Both the King James and the New King James versions translate John's various references to authority, as power instead.[14]

Just as the Centurion's authority came from his obedience to Caesar, Jesus's authority came from His obedience to the Father. And *our* authority is directly proportional to our obedience to Christ. As the song says, *"Kingdom authority flows from His throne, unto His own"*.

Only those who are fully submitted to Jesus, can operate in His Kingdom authority. Those who try to use Jesus's Name with authority, but are not themselves under His authority, risk being badly mauled by the Devil - just as the High Priest's seven sons were, at Ephesus.[15]

Jesus gave His disciples authority to heal, to cleanse lepers, raise the dead, and cast out demons. He could do this because all authority was given unto Him in heaven and on earth.[16] We should expect to see this Kingdom

---

[13] (19:11)

[14] (1:12; 5:26,27; 10:18; 17:2; 19:10,11)

[15] (Acts 19:13-16)

[16] (Matt 28:20)

authority operating in our own lives: in our prayers 'in the Name of Jesus', our witnessing, our teaching. He has been given *all* authority!

Jesus's authority was often questioned by the Judaeans. When He threw the money changers out of the Temple, they demanded a sign to prove His authority.[17] And when He re-cleansed it just after His triumphal entry to Jerusalem, again they questioned.[18] To them, a rabbi's authority came from the rabbi he had trained under. Since Jesus had never had rabbinical training, they couldn't accept He had authority: but it was self-evident that He did.[19]

In the next chapter of John, we will see just how extensive Jesus's authority is. It's not just about being able to command healing, or to expel demons. He has authority to give eternal life to whomever He will, but also to judge all mankind at the Day of Judgement! And this authority has been attested by multiple sources: John the Baptist, the miracles, the Torah, & Moses himself.

---

[17] (2:18)
[18] (Matt 21:23-27)
[19] (Mt 7:20)

Resurrection power in Jesus's voice (5:1-30)

Jesus speaks, and a helpless paraplegic gets up from his sickbed. This sign speaks of His power to call the dead to life and pronounce their judgement: but some can't see past the fact that it happened on a Sabbath!

Jesus seems to have been on His own at this point: there's no mention of any of the disciples. It seems they returned to their homes and jobs, while Jesus was on His first Galilean crusade. We don't know for sure which Feast it was, that Jesus had gone to: but majority opinion favours the Feast of Trumpets, in mid-September. He would have seen and observed all the pageantry and prescribed liturgy of the Temple ceremonies.

The pool of Bethesda

In the north-east corner of the city wall, near the Temple, there was a gate through which sheep from Bethlehem were brought for sacrifice. By it was a pair of large pools, surrounded by sheltering porches: one on each side, and one in between the two pools. These were crowded with chronic invalids.

Legend had it that an angel stirred up the waters from time to time, transiently conferring healing powers. But only the first person into the pool would be healed. Of course, none of these people could actually get into the pool under their own steam. So there would have been relatives, friends and well-wishers, to help them in the scramble to be first in. The chances of success, and healing, were probably less than winning the Lottery! Many must have eventually been taken home despondent.

During the Greek empire, the site had been dedicated to their god of healing, Aesclepion. So it was a kind of 'New Age' or alternative medicine thing, as far as the Jews were concerned.

One man was known to have been there thirty-eight years. His family had long since given up and gone home. But he insisted on being left there, even though there was no chance of him getting into the pool unaided. His only virtue was persistence, hoping against hope: some might have called it denial!

An unexpected healing

Whichever feast it was, the city would have been crowded with tourists. The paralysed man didn't know Jesus, and didn't ask for healing. As far as we know, Jesus had no entourage to mark Him out: but in the melee, He chose this man to showcase another aspect of His glory.

He said to the man, "Do you want to be healed?" - a strange question, you might think. But being disabled, and near the Temple, the man may have received lots of alms from Jews seeking merit with God. And recovery after all this time, would have meant taking up his responsibilities in life all over again: he was getting on in years.

If the man felt annoyed by this question and its undertone, he didn't show it. He just pointed out the reality that his friends and family had long since given up, and gone on with their everyday lives. He could apparently shuffle on his bottom, but never fast enough to be first.

Without any fuss, and without raising His voice, Jesus simply said, *"Rise, pick up your sleeping mat, and walk"*. And the man did just that! But while his back was turned to roll up his mat, Jesus disappeared into the crowd. The healed man had no opportunity to thank Him or find out who He was. After looking around for a while, he set off home, carrying his mat.

Grace vs Religion

As he passed the Temple, some of the super-religious Jews pointed out that carrying anything was one of the thirty-nine activities they had banned on a Sabbath. He explained that he'd just been healed from a lifetime of paralysis, but they weren't interested in that. He said that he was just following his healer's instructions: but couldn't tell them who it was had healed him. But he picked up that they weren't happy; and made a mental note to tell them, if he ever did find out who the mystery man was. Otherwise he might be excommunicated, or so he had heard.[1]

For thirty-eight years he'd been excluded from the Temple precincts. Disabled people were classed as spiritually unclean and unfit to enter God's Presence.

---

[1] (9:22)

So after dropping off his mat he came back, presumably to give thanks to God for the miracle he'd experienced. There, to his surprise, he found Jesus - looking for him. Jesus told him that the root cause of his paralysis had been personal sin. He warned the man never to repeat the sin, lest something worse befall him. Something worse than permanent paralysis? Scary thought.

We know that Jesus didn't believe that all sickness was down to personal sin. Jews believed that it could equally be a result of something one's parents had done, or that had happened whilst the person was still in the womb. And occasionally, God would allow sickness purely for His own glory[2], such as Job.

There is no mention of the man realising that Jesus was the Messiah, or coming to faith in any way. Rather, he goes off straight away to cover his own back, by telling the authorities who had told him to break the sabbath. So why on earth did Jesus choose *him*, out of all the invalids, to be healed? It just landed Him in deep trouble with the authorities. In fact, they began trying to work out how to get rid of him completely: how to murder him!

The answer lies in the next section. The larger purpose of this display of amazing grace, was to signify that Jesus would one day raise everyone from the dead! In His heartfelt love for His people, Jesus was willing even to provoke them to thoughts of murder, if by any means He could help them grasp that accepting Him was vital to their salvation. This is agape love! (Later, the Apostle Paul would emulate Jesus in this respect.[3])

Keeping the sabbath had been a key battleground when Antiochus Epiphanies, the Greek emperor and proto-antichrist, was trying to eradicate Jewish culture. A few diehards had held to observing it, even when it cost them their lives. Their movement later morphed into the Pharisees as we know them. Heroic resistance had ossified into spiritual myopia, and keeping Shabbat had become the be-all-and-end-all of their religious observance.

The fourth commandment just forbade work of the weekday variety, without going into detail. But the Jews had created layer upon layer of legalism

---

[2] (9:1-3)

[3] (Rom 9:1-3)

around it. They delineated thirty-nine different ways one could break this commandment, each having multiple sub-categories.

There are several other occasions when Jesus is challenged on this issue, and He responds in a variety of ways. He declared Himself Lord of the sabbath, and said that if it is OK to circumcise on a sabbath, then it's certainly OK to heal[4]. It was actually lawful to heal on the sabbath, according to Him.[5]

<u>Jesus claims authority as our Creator</u> (5:16-20)

When they challenged Jesus about telling the man to carry his sleeping mat, His answer inflamed them ten times more.

Although the sabbath commemorated God resting from His work on the last day of Creation, everybody knew that God couldn't have completely stopped His activity. Without His power sustaining it, the Universe would have ceased to be. In saying, *"My Father has been working until now, and I have been working"*, Jesus was claiming to have been working with the Father from eternity past, up till now. As the Prologue says, *"All things were made by Him, and without Him nothing was made that was made"*.[6] And Hebrews says He still *"sustains the Universe by the word of His power"*.[7]

The Jews realised that this claim, that He and the Father had been working together in Creation since eternity past, meant Jesus was claiming equality with God.[8]

His Sonship did not mean He was anything less than fully God, fully equal with the Father. But far from blasphemously exalting Himself, He *'did not count equality with God a thing to be grasped, but made Himself of no reputation, taking the form of a bondservant and coming in the likeness of men'*.[9] And He goes on to try to explain that not only has He been working as long as God has, but He has always done only what He sees the Father doing. He always operates in perfect harmony and complete unity with His Father.

---

[4] (7:21-24)
[5] (Mt 12:9-12; Mk 2:23-28; Lk 13:10-17)
[6] (1:3)
[7] (Heb 1:2,3)
[8] (5:17)
[9] (Phil 2:6-7)

And the Father always involves Him in everything He is doing: He shows Him everything, and will involve Jesus in even more jaw-dropping miracles.

Creators have authority over their creations. For instance, this commentary has a little note at the beginning saying '© Andrew Wright'. As its creator, I have authority over how it is used. This is trivial compared to Christ's authority over us as our Creator. Because we reject His authority, we think we have autonomy to act as we wish. We think there is no absolute truth, that everything is relative and that each person is entitled to their own alternative truth. And we believe that we can be whatever we want to be, that we do not have to accept how He created us.[10]

When God wanted to show Jeremiah what He was about to do, He took him to watch a potter working on a lump of clay. The pot was shaping up nicely, when an imperfection in the clay caused it to deform. The potter squidged it all down and began again: but this time, shaping it into a different vessel, *'as he saw fit'*.[11] Paul says, *'Will the thing formed say to him who formed it, Why have you made me like this? Does not the potter have power over the clay, to make from the same lump one vessel for honour and one for dishonour?*[12].

And Isaiah says, *'You are our Father; we are the clay, and You our potter; and we are all the work of Your hand'*.[13]

In commanding life into the invalid's broken body, Jesus was declaring Himself to be our Creator. In doing so, He was declaring His immense authority over all mankind. The Jews hated the implication, and began plotting how they could kill Him. Breaking the sabbath was the tip of the iceberg: the real issue was, He was claiming equality with God. The first commandment had taught them, *'You shall have no other gods besides Me'*, yet here was Jesus claiming to be God's peer, and calling God His Father.

As if to underline the issue, Jesus now tells them much more about His authority (5:19-30). The conversation went something like this:
"OK, so you think I'm setting myself up as some kind of rival to Yahweh, right?

---

[10] https://www.paultripp.com/articles/posts/the-doctrine-of-creation-article
[11] (Jer 18:1-6)
[12] (Rom 9:21)
[13] (Isa 64:8)

You've got totally the wrong end of the stick. I can't do anything on my own: I only do what I see Him doing, and I copy Him exactly. So what you see Me do, is what He is doing. Because He loves Me, He shows Me everything - and you'll see even more marvellous things than these".

In this passage we have the fullest unpacking anywhere in scripture, of John's statement that Jesus is the only-begotten Son of the Father. You'll remember that being begotten does not refer to Jesus being made man, but to *'eternal filiation'* - eternal fathering and eternal sonship. No matter how long eternity is, there is never a point at which Jesus no longer copies His Father, and never a point when the Father stops showing His Son everything He is doing.

So what are the 'greater works than these' of which Jesus is speaking, which the Father is going to show the Son?

Authority to raise the dead (5:21-23)

Just as Jesus has collaborated with the Father throughout the creation's history, so He will collaborate in its winding up.

Though the Sadducees denied its possibility, the Pharisees knew that God could raise the dead. Abraham had realised that if the same utterly faithful God had said *'Take your son Isaac and sacrifice him'* after saying *'In Isaac shall your seed be named'*, then God must have been planning to raise him from the dead.[14] Elijah had raised the widow's son back to physical life[15], and Elisha had raised the Shunammite's son. And Daniel had prophesied the resurrection into *eternal* life, of all those whose names were written in the Book of Life.[16]

Jesus claims He has the same authority as the Father, to give not only physical life, but *zoe* life: eternal life. As He says to Lazarus's sister, "I AM the resurrection and the life". And that decision whether or not to give someone zoe life at the Resurrection, inevitably involves authority to judge.

---

[14] (Heb 11:17-19)

[15] (1 Kings 17:17-24

[16] (Dan 12:1-3)

The reason the Father had given Jesus this authority, was specifically so that all should honour the Son just as they honour the Father. Anyone who doesn't honour the Son, is refusing to honour the Father who sent Him.[17]

Jesus taught us to pray, *"Hallowed be Thy Name"*. The fear of the LORD - reverence for Yahweh's personal Name - is the beginning of wisdom. As the commandment says, those who take His Name in vain will be held guilty before God.[18] If that is true of God the Father, and we are to honour His Son equally, how should we handle the Name of Jesus? Is it just a spell to be tacked onto the end of our prayers, as the sons of Sceva did? Or should we hold it in highest honour and use it reverently?

This claim to equal honour is a fresh claim of Jesus's oneness with the Father. If we are to worship Him as we worship the Father, and the scripture says *"You shall have no other gods beside Me"*, then He and the Father are One! Though sent by the Father, They are still One: there is no diminution of His divinity, in the incarnation. Those such as Jehovah's Witnesses who say that He is in some way a lesser god, dishonour the God they claim to serve, by saying this.

<u>Authority to judge mankind</u> (5:24-30)

The chief priests and rulers considered themselves qualified to judge whether Jesus was Messiah. But Jesus here told them that instead, He would judge them. And the judgement would be based on whether they had honoured and worshipped Him as God! Whether they had accepted His word and believed that He was speaking for God.[19]

He goes on to say that very soon, the dead would hear His voice, and those who heard would live.[20] Once again, the phrase *'the hour is coming'* refers specifically to the hour of His death. When He died, many saints emerged from their tombs and appeared to the residents of Jerusalem.[21] How extraordinary that must have been! And yet, it was merely a foretaste of

---

17 (5:23)
18 (Ex 20:7)
19 (5:24)
20 (5:25)
21 (Matt 27:51-53)

what is to come: a sign that the One they had judged, will indeed return in glory to judge the living and the dead.

At Christ's second coming, *'the Lord Himself will descend from heaven with a shout, with the voice of an archangel, and with the trumpet of God. And the dead in Christ will rise first. Then we who are alive and remain will be caught up together with them in the clouds, to meet the Lord in the air. And then we shall always be with the Lord'.*[22] The Rapture will involve not only those believers alive at His return, but those who've died throughout the centuries.

Looking even further into the future, He says that eventually a day will arrive when every single soul that ever lived will hear His voice and be resurrected to be judged by Him. There will be many surprises, people who thought themselves worthy being turned away, and others who felt themselves utterly unworthy being welcomed into the Father's House.[23] Jesus's judgement will be absolutely righteous and completely free of self-interest, because His only criterion will be His Father's glory, not His own.[24]

Jesus says, this judgement has in effect already happened, for those who have accepted Him.[25] Those who have accepted their own sinfulness and need for Christ to take their place under God's judgement, and who obey His words day by day, have already passed from death to life. They already have this resurrection life, this *zoe* life which only Jesus can give.

I wonder what the Jewish authorities were feeling, when they heard this? They were judging Jesus, but He was claiming divine authority to judge them. How do *you* react, when you feel judged? For me, pride rises up and says, 'Who do you think you are?' Yet we are very ready to criticise & condemn!

All judgement belongs only to God, and to Him alone. By His standards, all have sinned and fallen short of the glory of God. And *'the wages of sin is death'*. Will we shout and wave our fists at Him when He judges us, telling Him that He doesn't understand what a hard life we had, and that it was all really His fault? It will all be to no avail.

---

[22] (1Thess 4:16-17)
[23] (Matt 25:31-46)
[24] (5:28-30)
[25] (5:24)

Far better to accept His judgement today, and accept the astonishing plea bargain He is offering: that if you will only confess and believe, He will accept His Son's death on the Cross as having paid your penalty in full.

Jesus says, *"Judge not, lest ye be judged. For with what judgement you judge, you will be judged: and with the measure you use, it will be measured back to you. Why do you look at the speck in your brother's eye, but do not consider the plank in your own eye? Or how can you say to your brother, 'Let me remove the speck from your eye, when there is a plank in your own eye? You hypocrite!"* [26]

We need God's help even to remove these major blockages in how we judge ourselves. Paul tells us that he doesn't trust his own assessment of himself, but asks the Lord to be his judge.[27] David prays, *'Search me, O God, and know my heart: try me, and know my anxieties; and see if there is any wicked way in me, and lead me in the way everlasting'.* [28]

Backing up His claims (5:31-47)

Jesus now backs up His incredible claims of authority, in various ways:-

1. If He was blowing His own trumpet, His testimony would be discounted unless there were external corroboration.[29] And yet, whilst He has come in His Father's Name and is being rejected, others who come in their own name will be believed.[30] *(Apparently within fifty years after Jesus's death, the Sanhedrin assessed sixty-five false claims of messiahship as valid!)*
2. John the Baptist was like a powerful searchlight, picking out Jesus.[31] For a time some of the Jewish leaders had accepted his authority as a prophet: but this meant accepting his testimony about Jesus. So eventually they had to deny John's authority, if they were to deny Jesus's. This was difficult, as the population largely revered him, long after his death.[32]

---

[26] (Matt 7:1-5)
[27] (1Cor 4:1-5)
[28] (Ps 139:23,24)
[29] (5:31)
[30] (5:43)
[31] (5:32-35)
[32] (Mt 21:23-27)

3. The miracles bore even weightier witness that God had sent Him[33]. Only God could do some of the things Jesus did, such as raising Lazarus from the dead. Either Jesus was God, or was collaborating with God, just as He had collaborated with His father Joseph in their carpentry workshop.
4. The Father Himself, the Invisible God, had testified of Him.[34] At Jesus's baptism, the Father had said, *"This is My beloved Son, in whom I am well pleased"*. And at the Transfiguration, God had repeated this and added, *"Listen to Him!"*
5. Though they had never heard or seen God, they had memorised the Torah and the prophets from beginning to end. Yet Jesus says, *"You do not have His word abiding in you, because you do not believe the One whom He has sent".* The whole purpose of the Torah & the Prophets, was to testify of Jesus: yet the leaders refused to come & receive eternal life from Him.
   If we are unwilling to receive Christ, the scriptures cannot make sense, no matter how much we study them. Instead the Jews had created a religion based on human merit in keeping the commandments.[35] That was why they were so focussed on the finer points of the Oral Law. They were focussed on receiving honour from one another, not from God.
6. Rather than Jesus's words being the standard by which they are judged, as will be for the rest of humanity, *their* accuser will be Moses. They trust in him, but don't believe his writings! Moses had prophesied of a future Prophet like himself, who would speak everything that God commanded Him. And he had warned that God would condemn anyone who refused to hear that Prophet's words, which He would be speaking in God's Name[36].

The whole purpose of scripture, is to bring us into living relationship with Christ, and God. The Holy Spirit, who authored the scriptures, will often use them to speak with us, and reveal more of Christ. But in the words of the hymn, "Beyond the written page, I seek Thee, Lord. My spirit longs for Thee, Thou living Word!"

---

[33] (5:36)
[34] (5:37)
[35] (5:39)
[36] (Deut 18:15-19)

From Megastar to Madman (6:1-71)

Overnight, Jesus's massive following from His Galilean crusade evaporates. His challenging teaching about being the Bread of Life, bursts the bubble of 'Jesus mania'.

Once again John skips over a lengthy period of Jesus's ministry in Galilee. Jesus returned there after attending the feast mentioned in 5:1. If that was the Feast of Trumpets, and we're now nearing Passover[1], then He's spent around six months on crusade in Galilee. If it was a different feast then it may have been longer. Meantime His cousin John-the-Baptist has been imprisoned by Herod in a dungeon of his castle at Machaerus, just northeast of the Dead Sea. Herod's wife, who hated John for criticising their marriage, takes the opportunity of a feast to manipulate Herod into beheading John.

The news of John's death reaches Jesus at about the same time as Herod realises that Jesus is becoming massively popular. Herod starts to fret that perhaps Jesus is John's reincarnation, and seeks to bring Him in for questioning. But Jesus retreats across Lake Galilee to a deserted area outside Herod's territory, hoping He and His disciples can get space to rest and mourn. However word gets out and large crowds follow Him on foot to the other side of the Lake. He welcomes, teaches and heals them all day. Meantime the crowd grows and grows, and feeding them becomes an issue.

The miracle of the feeding of the five thousand, is the only miracle that figures in all four gospels. Each author had a different agenda, focussing on different aspects & details. All four accounts dovetail into a single narrative, but only John recounts Jesus's subsequent teaching about the event. That teaching pricked the developing bubble of Jesus mania: most of His followers concluded He was crazy, and returned disillusioned to their everyday lives. His reputation went from megastar to madman, in the space of a few hours.

We'll first revisit the narrative, integrating the four accounts: then look at Jesus's teaching about the meaning of the sign.

---

[1] (6:4)

The feeding of the five thousand

Jesus's boat landed not far beyond the mouth of the Jordan; near Phillip's home town of Bethsaida. This is near the foothills of the Golan Heights, and more than two hours walk from Capernaum. But the boat's sail would have been visible from there, and so crowds followed Him both on foot and by boat. They did so *'because they had witnessed the signs He had performed on the diseased'*: some were seeking healing themselves, others just intrigued.

Despite having to give up His hopes of getting some space, He set aside His personal sorrow and grief. He welcomed them, healed many, and taught them about the Kingdom of God.[2] Acceptance, healing, revelation: no wonder they hung on His words, and forgot the time.

The disciples realised that sundown was nearing, and the crowds were still growing. They advised Jesus to send everyone off, to find food and lodging for the night in nearby towns. But He said, "No: *you* give them food to eat".

He asked Philip, who knew the area, where they could buy bread. Philip pointed out that even buying snacks would cost far more than they had in the team's kitty. Jesus told them to find out whether anyone had any food to share. The only offer was from a young man whose Mum had made him a packed lunch: two sardines and five cheap barley-bread buns. (Passover comes just as the barley harvest begins, after a long hiatus in food supplies.) Andrew told Jesus, but He wasn't fazed. He knew all along what He was going to do.

Passover being in March, before the scorching summer heat, the grass was lush and green. Jesus organised the crowd into groups of fifty or a hundred, and told them to sit down. Then He gave thanks to God and publicly shared out the lunchbox between the Twelve: half a bap and half an inch of sardine each! They then gave a portion to each group, to pass around. Even in the biggest groups, as the food was passed from one person to the next, it kept on multiplying and never ran out. Amazingly, five thousand men *and* their wives and children all had plenty to eat! Afterwards, as the disciples cleared

[2] (Lk 9:11)

up, each of them filled his daysack with left-overs. What they had thought totally impossible, was possible with Christ.

No doubt in Jesus's mind He was thinking of the following Passover, when He would give Himself as the bread of life. As the 'bread of the Presence' foreshadowed, He would be *broken for many, for the forgiveness of sins*. His sacrifice would be sufficient for the sins of all mankind, but each would need to pass on the miracle if all were to be fed. The grief of losing John, would have been dwarfed by His horror at becoming sin for us.

Nationalist expectations threaten to destroy Jesus's mission

The astonishing symbolism of this Passover meal was completely lost on the huge crowd. Instead, they focussed on Passover's meaning as a commemoration of Israel's liberation from Egyptian slavery. Nationalism was always fiercest over Passover; and Herod, the Romans' puppet King, wasn't even a Jew but an Edomite! Worse still, he had just executed John the Baptist, someone they all held to be a great prophet.

Little wonder then that there were whisperings that they should pressure Jesus to be the military Messiah they'd been hoping for.[3] Jesus, as always, knew what was in mens' hearts. In the wilderness, he had resisted Satan's offer to make Him a political Messiah: and He recognised the same temptation now. Before their plan could be hatched, he sent the crowds away. He also sent the disciples back to their boat despite their reluctance[4], telling them He'd join them back in Capernaum. Then He disappeared up the mountain to pray.

He would have sought the Father's heart, as to how to disabuse those who envisaged Him as their military leader. And I imagine He would have reconfirmed His willingness to be the sacrificial 'Lamb of God'. In response (I believe) the Father revealed to Him exactly what to say the following day; how to counter the Galilean crowds' nationalist assumptions, whilst also revealing the spiritual meaning of the sign. And how to steady the Twelve's resolve, in the face of mass disillusionment.

---

[3] (6:15)

[4] (Mk 6:45)

Jesus's authority over wind & waves

As the sun set, a storm blew up and the disciples' boat was buffeted. A strong headwind meant they had to row; very difficult in such rough water.

Seeing they were in trouble, Jesus set out walking across the lake. As He got near them, they saw what they thought was a ghost[5], and were terrified. But He told them "Don't be afraid: I AM"[6] - affirming once again His divine authority over creation. Peter tested whether it really was Jesus, by walking on water himself. But after fear threatened to drown him, he was rebuked for lack of faith! John decorously skips over that, as it's irrelevant to his point.

The others now knew it was Jesus, and happily took Him onboard. He calmed the storm, then warped space-time so that the boat immediately reached the shore. So many miracles in such a short space of time! The disciples were filled with awe, and worshipped Him saying, *"Truly, you are the Son of God"*[7].

They landed at a place called Gennesaret, slightly south of Capernaum. Again, word got around; and very soon all the local invalids were presented for healing. They all wanted to touch the fringe of His robe, because Malachi had prophesied that Messiah would bring healing in His tzittzit - the tassels on the fringe of His robe. Anyone who did so, was completely healed[8].

John's account includes Peter walking on water, but skips over these healings at Gennesaret; why?. Most commentators count Jesus's walking on the water as one of John's seven signs; but others feel it should be counted as part of the feeding of the five thousand. Certainly it's given only a few lines. So how does it show us more of Christ's glory?

Jesus would have known there was a storm brewing in the atmosphere, both physically and spiritually, when He sent His disciples off across the lake. He could just as well have gone with them and found somewhere to pray after landing. The experience of their own powerlessness against the elements, and of Jesus's authority over any storm the powers of darkness could whip up, strengthened their faith in Him. When everyone else abandoned ship,

---

[5] (Matt 14:22-33)
[6] (6:20)
[7] (Mt 14:33)
[8] (Mt 14:34-36)

Peter could say, *"Lord, to whom else shall we go? You have the words of eternal life. And we have come to believe and know that You are the Christ, the Son of the living God"*.[9] At least for the time being, he had learnt to look at Jesus rather than being afraid of the storm.

Jesus returned to Capernaum, only for the crowds to track Him down again. News of the previous day's astonishing events had spread like wildfire in Capernaum. They were puzzled because they knew He hadn't left in the disciples' boat. Local ferries from Tiberias had picked *them* up after the storm, and brought them home; but how had Jesus got back before them?[10]

John records four conversations Jesus has with different groups of people, each with a different agenda:-

- The ordinary local Galileans[11], interested in more free meals
- Judaeans[12], senior Pharisees sent there to assess His messiahship claim
- People who'd followed Him[13] but couldn't stomach this new teaching
- The Twelve[14]: committed so thoroughly there was no-one else to go to

The vast majority take offence, decide Jesus is crazy and go home. Only the Twelve stick with Him. He's gone from megastar to madman overnight.

We'll look at His response to each of these groups in turn:-

A Person, not prosperity (6:25-40)

The locals who find Jesus first, ask how He got back so quickly. Jesus's answer[15] seems like a non-sequitur, as is often the case! (Exploring such apparent mismatches often leads to fresh revelation. He always addresses the true issue *underlying* the questioner's query.)

He says they're seeking Him purely because He's fed them. This might sound judgemental, but it was based on reality. Unlike the Jerusalemites, they were

---

[9] (6:68-69)
[10] (6:22-24)
[11] (6:25-40)
[12] (6:41-59)
[13] (6:60-71)
[14] (6:67)
[15] (6:26)

poor peasant-farmers, focussed on the most basic of needs. From October to February there were no fresh crops, but by Passover the barley was just ripening. (Perhaps that's why the little boy had barley buns in his lunchbox!) The winter had been long and hard, and they'd just had their first square meal for a long time.

Jesus points them to the meaning of the miracle. There is a kind of bread that gives eternal life, and which should be higher priority than their earthly food. This food was only available from the Son of Man, just as had happened the day before, when Jesus blessed and broke the barley loaves.

It was natural for them then to ask, *"Well if that's the case, Jesus, what must we do to earn this food?"*[16] They assume that the food must be bought; that they'll have to earn it from Him. But Jesus's answer is, *"Just believe in the One God sent".* We cannot earn eternal life: it's by grace, through faith.

Israelites being hard-nosed pragmatists, they demanded a sign. *"If you are asking us to trust you more than Moses, show us a miracle as big as when he gave our ancestors bread in the Sinai desert!"* This is more than just a healthy dose of scepticism: it's the blindness of materialism. Jesus has just given them as much bread and fish as they could eat, in a desert place!

Moses had been clear that it was God, not him, who met their needs.[17] But now, God was doing something even greater, giving them the true bread from heaven - something much better than manna, let alone barley bread.

They responded like the woman at the well had done: *'Lord, give us this bread always'*. Jesus has nurtured their awareness of their spiritual hunger, and now they seem eager to receive.

The first I AM

"I AM the Bread of Life", says Jesus. This is the first of His great self-revelations, the seven 'I AM's which show us how His divine grace meets our spiritual needs. The Bread of God is a Person, not a material substance.

---

[16] (6:28)
[17] (Ex 16:8)

The Old Testament contains various compound names of God, expressing how He is the answer to our needs: for example, 'Yahweh-raphah'[18], the LORD is my Shepherd. Jesus declares Himself to be the God who meets all our spiritual needs, using a series of such God-names. But it is relational, not transactional: not *'I supply the Bread of Life'*, but *'I am the Bread of Life'*. Our need is met in our relationship with Jesus. We must continually look to Him; to nothing and no-one else.

Of the seven titles, the first five were for all to know, but the last two were only revealed to His most committed disciples, the Twelve. The seven are:

- *I AM the Bread of Life; the Bread of Heaven, the Living Bread*[19]
- *I AM the Light if the world*[20]
- *I AM the Door of the sheep*[21]
- *I AM the Good Shepherd*[22]
- *I AM the the Resurrection and the Life*[23]
- *I AM the Way, the Truth and the Life*[24]
- *I AM the True Vine*[25]

We will consider each of these names in due course. But notice what John is doing as he skilfully weaves his tapestry. He is introducing a set of different threads. He has focussed on the miracles, the signs. Now he is telling us more directly, who Jesus is *to us*.

Paraphrasing, Jesus continues *"You have seen Me, and as yet do not believe. Everyone whom the Father gives Me, will come to Me; and I will always welcome such. Whatever My personal preferences, I came down from heaven to do the Father's will not My own. His will is that I should shepherd His flock so carefully that not one is lost, until I raise them up at the Last Day.*

---

[18] (Ps 23:1)
[19] (6:35,41,48,51)
[20] (8:12;9:5)
[21] (10:7,9)
[22] (10:11,14)
[23] (11:25)
[24] (14:6)
[25] (15:1)

Furthermore, His will is that until then, anyone who sees Me and believes in Me should have wonderful fellowship with both Me and My Father - a new dimension of life, that will continue on into eternity".[26]

Jesus tells them they haven't yet come to true faith. But in the sovereignty of God, some will come. And they need not fear being turned away. Everyone who comes, will be accepted and welcomed.

This saying of Christ speaks of the power of the Father's electing grace: everyone the Father gives Me, *will definitely* come to Me. Because the Father's will is that Christ should lose none of the elect, He (Christ) will never reject them, but will definitely raise them up at the last day. This theme continues throughout John's gospel, but is particularly explicit in John 10 and John 17. (Judas's apparent exceptionalism receives specific explanation[27].) Those who believe we must choose between Calvinism and Arminianism, and favour the latter, find this passage very uncomfortable. And yet John also has many passages where Christ obviously holds people accountable for their choice as to whether they believe in Him or not.

Eternal life involves feeding on Christ (6:41-59)

A group of Judaeans now seize on Jesus's 'I AM' claim. Two themes from the previous chapter re-emerge: resurrection, and the Last Day. Then, Jesus was speaking in Jerusalem: now, He meets those same Judaeans in Galilee! Why were they present in Capernaum?

Matthew says they were still bent on discrediting Jesus.[28] Their charge was that Jesus falsely claimed to have come down from heaven, when everyone in Capernaum knew His earthly parents. They cannot conceive that His heavenly origins and His earthly roots are both true: that '*Jesus Christ is come in the flesh'*. They cannot believe in His incarnation.

We might paraphrase Jesus's response like this: *"Don't bad-mouth Me amongst yourselves, like the Israelites did to Moses. The fact that you don't grasp who I am, just shows that the Father hasn't revealed My glory to you.*

---

[26] (6:36-40)
[27] (6:70, 17:12)
[28] (Mt 15:1))

You're not amongst the people He has given Me, whom I will raise up at the Last Day. The scripture says that all true children of Jerusalem will be taught by God Himself, and will have great peace[29] *- through coming to Me.*

"This being 'taught by the Father' doesn't refer to anyone actually seeing Him. He can only be known through Me, who came from His bosom companionship. But anyone who believes that I have come in the flesh, that I am the Son of God, already has that new quality of life: life in communion with the Father and the Son. Because I AM the bread of life - the source of that kind of life."

He then repeats His claim, referring them back to the Exodus account[30]: Though their ancestors had eaten bread from heaven in the form of manna, every single one of that first generation died because of unbelief.

"That bread couldn't even prevent physical death. But this bread means your souls will never die, and your bodies will be raised to life for all eternity. I AM the living bread. In My very Person is this self-existent, divine life[31]*, which I communicate to people as they digest who I am. The food that I'll give is My humanity: that's what they'll need to digest. I'll freely lay down My body-and-soul life, to purchase eternal life for the world."*

This triggered a fierce debate between different Pharisees, about what Jesus could possibly mean.[32] How could He give them His flesh to eat? Eating the flesh of the Passover lamb was an element of the passover meal, so they perhaps should have grasped the metaphor. But like Nicodemus, they are stuck in literalism.

Jesus exacerbates their confusion by lobbing in another hand-grenade.[33] Not only must they eat His flesh, they must also drink His blood!

"It is essential for anyone wanting eternal life, to eat My flesh and drink My blood! Just as physical food and drink are necessary to sustain human life, my flesh and blood are what sustains spiritual life. You can't live eternally, unless

---

[29] (Isa 54:13))
[30] (6:49)
[31] (1:4)
[32] (6:52)
[33] (6:53-55)

you feed on Me by faith, abiding in Me and I in you. But if you are joined to Me like this, I will raise you up on Judgement Day.."

To my knowledge, there is no parallel whatsoever for this in the Old Testament. When Moses forbad eating blood of any kind, he said God would set His face against anyone who did such a thing. And to Noah[34], God had said He would demand a reckoning from anyone who ate flesh with blood in it. That was the origin of all the detailed regulations about kosher food. Eating or drinking blood would have been anathema to a Jew. (If you think of modern-day vampire movies, the very idea still causes revulsion.) Spoken in the Capernaum synagogue[35], these remarks caused such offence that most of Jesus's disciples abandoned Him.

Blood could only be used for sacrifices, because *'The life of the flesh is in the blood, and I have given it to you upon the altar to make atonement for your soul'.*[36] In this quote from Leviticus, the Hebrew word translated 'life' is 'nephesh': but this word is far more commonly translated as 'soul'. In fact it's the word used of Adam's creation, when God breathed into clay and it became a living *nephesh*. Blood was sacred because it contained God's gift of body-and-soul life, given to both men and animals. In that sense, *nephesh* corresponds to a combination of the Greek words *bios* and *psyche*.[37]

Why did Jesus choose to teach His Judaean inquisitors in particular, on this very difficult topic? Unlike the Galileans, there was no risk of them declaring Him Messiah! His tone is quite different; whereas His teaching of the locals invites them to believe, this teaching warns them about unbelief, reminding them about their fathers' deaths in the wilderness.

Perhaps, as with Nicodemus, He expected them to have greater depth of understanding of the Old Testament. God came and indwelt Israel in the shekinah at the mercy-seat; and the Feast of Tabernacles celebrates that the dwelling-place of God is with man. But both those refer to God's Presence in the community, rather than an interior, personal indwelling.

---

[34] Gen 9:3-5)

[35] (6:59)

[36] (Lev 17:10)

[37] {See Appendix 2)

The nearest Old Testament analogy is the way Moses' face changed after he'd been in the Tent of Meeting. The glory of God shone within him, albeit transiently. Paul sees this as a 'type' of indwelling, and talks about how as we gaze at Jesus, we are changed from one degree of glory to another[38].

But Jesus's reply is also, in a curious way, an answer to their objection that He couldn't be both Mary's son, and sent from heaven. He calls Himself the bread of heaven, and appropriates the holy Name of God in saying 'I AM the Bread of Life'. But He also says He is going to give real human flesh and blood as a sacrifice, implying a real death but with Himself also the High Priest.

Communion and indwelling

Commentators argue whether this passage refers to the Lord's Supper, though that wasn't instituted till much later in Jesus's ministry. Unlike the other gospels John barely mentions the passover meal, let alone the institution of the new covenant. Here the context is all about food that sustains life; about Jesus's identity, not substitutionary atonement.

If John's gospel was designed to complement the Synoptics[39], we could view this chapter as balancing their teaching on the sacrament. 'Receiving mass' or 'taking communion' does not of itself sustain spiritual life, unless to the participant it is an act of worshipping Jesus in spirit and in truth. We can take communion without discerning that we are eating the body of Christ; this brings sickness rather than healing.[40] It is belief in Him as the One who came from above, the incarnate Son of God full of grace and truth, that saves.

Whatever tradition we come from, Jesus's final remark takes another leap.

'He who eats My flesh and drinks My blood abides in Me, and I in him. As the living Father sent Me, and I live because of the Father, so he who feeds on Me will live because of Me'.[41]

Feeding on Jesus, He says, is similar to His *eternal filiation* by the Father. There is a communion, a shared mission and a shared life. As the Father

---

38 (2Cor 3:18;4:6)
39 (See appendix 1)
40 (1Cor 10:1-22;11:27-30)
41 (6:56-57)

continually shares His heart with the Son, and the Son continually listens and perfectly mimics Him, so is this lifelong process of feeding - or we might say, *abiding* in Him.

Like a skilful composer, John is quietly introducing a major new theme. Jesus will massively develop this theme, of eternal life being in Him and our life coming from union with Him, in His farewell discourse (John 14-16). For John it is the lifelong theme of his spirituality. His *"fellowship was with the Father and the Son, that which he had seen with his eyes, touched and handled with his hands, concerning the Word of Life"*.[42] His summary of his testimony was that *"God has given us eternal life, and this life is in His Son. He who has the Son has life. He who does not have the Son of God does not have life."*[43]

Evangelicals major on communion as a means of grace, in that it is a remembrance of Christ's sacrifice, and a reminder that He will come again. The Anglican liturgy puts it like this: *"Take and eat this in remembrance that Christ died for you, and feed on him in your heart by faith with thanksgiving. .... Drink this in remembrance that Christ's blood was shed for you, and be thankful."*[44] Requiring self-examination and confession of sin, it focusses on the grace created in us by His death, of devotion and obedience to Christ. Whereas the doctrine of trans-substantiation, whether taken materially or metaphorically, speaks about us receiving Christ: the *uncreated* grace of Christ condescending to indwell us.

Could it be that we have thrown out the baby with the bath water? That in rejecting the doctrine of the physical transformation of bread and wine into the flesh and blood of Christ, we have under-emphasised this amazing gift of Christ indwelling us, and its affirmation and strengthening through celebrating the Lord's Supper?

Spiritual truth can only be grasped by faith, through the Holy Spirit (6:60-66)

Jesus's many disciples also struggled with this teaching: despite having just witnessed many healings, and having all been fed from one child's lunchbox.

---

[42] (1 Jn 1:1-3)
[43] (1 Jn 4:11,12)
[44] Anglican liturgy for Holy Communion

In one sense, who can blame them?! Our Western worldview is built on understanding as much as we can. What we can't understand, we either ignore or reject as false.

Without them saying anything, Jesus knew. He knew they were on the verge of taking offence: that they were starting to question the truth of His words. He knew He was destined to be the *'stone of stumbling, the rock of offense'* that Isaiah had prophesied.[45] He knew He would be *'despised and rejected by men'*.[46] So there was no defensiveness in His response, though His heart must have grieved. Motivated solely by love not rejection, He challenged them to have ears that hear by faith.

The disciples' nascent faith that He had come from above - faith in His incarnation - had been undermined by the Judaeans' attack line: *"How can he be the Son of God, when his mum and dad live just down the street?!"*[47] But if they can't believe He came from God, what will they think when they see Him ascend to His Father, as the Son of Man whom Daniel predicted?

"The words that I have spoken to you are spirit and are life. But there are some of you who do not believe. That's why I said that no-one can come to Me unless it has been granted to Him by My Father".

In case they had misunderstood His earlier remarks, He tells them it is *not* His physical flesh that gives life. Physically eating means nothing, and cannot give *zoe* life. Human life is flesh and blood: *nephesh* in Hebrew, *bios* and *psyche* in Greek. But these are useless to gain *zoe* life.

But there is a deeper truth: man cannot receive spiritual truth by intellectual understanding. Nicodemus had studied for years, but couldn't grasp the new birth. Our *psyche* includes our mind, will, and emotions. But *'since in the wisdom of God, the world through (its) wisdom did not know God, it pleased God to save men through the apparently-foolish message of the cross.'*[48] We *understand* through our minds: but we *know* through our spirits.

---

[45] (Isa 8:14; Isa 28:16; Ps 118:22; 1 Pet 2:4-8)
[46] (Isa 53:3,4)
[47] (6:42)
[48] (1 Cor 1:18-21)

Though they could not understand Jesus's words with their minds, when received through the Holy Spirit He says His words *'are spirit and they are (zoe) life'.* There is a life-giving quality to them, which can only be received in our spirits, through the ministry of the Holy Spirit.

Because these words can only be received by faith through the ministry of the Spirit, those of His disciples without true faith would gain nothing. And Judas, who had spent three years under Jesus's teaching, would betray Him.

Assurance, through the Spirit's witness (6:67-71)

Have you know times when your heart has been thrilled by a bible verse, or by a good preacher? That is the witness of the Spirit, to which Jesus is referring here.[49] And it is one of the safeguards that carry us through times when we don't understand what God is saying.

The apostles already had that witness, though not yet indwelt by the Spirit. At this juncture when everyone else was abandoning Jesus, He asked whether they too wanted to be released from their discipleship. *(He never forces anyone to continue following!)* Peter's answer was strong and faith-filled. As ever their spokesman, he says that no-one else has words that communicate eternal *(zoe)* life.

During the stormy crossing of the lake the day before, Jesus's ability to walk on water, His command over nature and His ability to shrink space-time had convinced the Twelve that it was right to worship Him as God[50].

They have come to believe (by faith) and to know (by the Holy Spirit) that He is *"the Christ, the Son of the Living God"*. They have grasped the truth of the incarnation! This is a truth that can only be known by revelation from the Father, through the Holy Spirit.[51] And it's the foundation stone of the Church.

There is only one other way in which someone can know that Jesus is the Christ; and that is, through demonic insight.[52] Judas knew that Jesus was the Christ, but his knowledge was demonic. The fact that someone can live as a

---

49 (15:26; Acts 5:32; 1 Jn 2:27; 1 Jn 4:6)

50 (Matt 14:33)

51 (Matt 16:15-18)

52 (Matt 8:28-29; Lk 8:26-28; Acts 19:13-16; Jas 2:19)

disciple, apparently close to Jesus, and yet later betray Him or us, should not take us by surprise.

Why did Jesus deliberately offend so many, just as His popularity peaked?

This teaching, about Jesus being the manna that sustains our spiritual lives, was God's divinely-appointed sieve to sift out all those whose discipleship was not based on true faith. This was His Father's answer to Jesus's prayer on the mountain, how to stop the zealots making Him a military Messiah.

These disciples turned away from His word, because they wanted a Messiah who would set them free militarily. Later, He would say, *"If you continue in My word you are My disciples indeed. And you shall know the truth, and the truth shall set you free".* Only the *logos* of Jesus can set us truly free! And even then, only if we continue in it, no matter how difficult we may find it and how unpopular it is with others.

Some questions to ponder

- How do you react, when people try to pressure you into what they want you to be? Is your reaction to go along with it for a quiet life, or for popularity and prominence? Or do you withdraw and pray, then do what the Father tells you, however costly that may be?
- What is your experience of the words of Jesus? Are they 'words of eternal life' to you? Do you experience the witness of the Spirit - that bubbling of joy within you - when you hear preaching or teaching about Jesus? Do you find the word of God brings you into deep fellowship with the Father and the Son? Or is it all too difficult, too strange and seemingly mystical, when you just want some practical solutions in life?
- What is your experience of taking communion? Do you experience Jesus's risen Presence in the breaking of the bread, as the Emmaus disciples did? We can get bogged down in thinking we ought to be more penitent, more aware of our sins and of the agony of the Cross. But for the disciples going to Emmaus, it was a wonderful revelation, full of joy, and all about Jesus's

identity as the Risen Lord, 'the Son of God with power' [53].
How do *you* 'feed on Him by faith'?

- Have there been times in your life when you have taken offence at things Jesus has said? Or when He has seemingly not answered your prayers in the way that you wanted? Are there still issues about things that have happened to you, where you need to say, "Lord, I don't understand, but I trust You"?

53 (Rom 1:4)

Good man, con man, mad man, or God-man?

(7:1-52)

Jesus forces the Jews to face the issue of His identity, by hijacking the Feast of Tabernacles.

The first Passover John mentions, was when Jesus cleansed the Temple. Then, after Nicodemus, the Samaritan woman, and the man at Bethesda, we hear of another Passover at the feeding of the five thousand. Following that, there was the great controversy about His claim to be the bread from heaven, and the collapse of His Galilean fan club. It seems that despite this, He continued his ministry there for a further six months, but in a more low-key manner. He didn't want to return to Judea, where He was a marked man[1].

As summer turned to autumn, His siblings began planning the annual trip to the Feast of Tabernacles. This was the most popular feast of the year, perhaps because of the joyful floodlit dancing each night in the temple courts. Jews from all across the diaspora[2] would hurry to get there: not just those in Israel. They would set up makeshift shelters of branches from local trees, in every spare corner of the city and its suburbs; even on rooftops.

The feast celebrated God's presence with Israel in the wilderness, during the Exodus: and His provision of both water from the rock, and light at night from the cloud of Shekinah glory. During that period, God had literally dwelt among them, His Presence covering & filling the Tabernacle.

The ritual & symbolism of the Feast

Over the centuries, an elaborate ritual had built up around the Feast. It involved daily trips by a priest from the Temple down to the pool of Siloam, to fill a gold jug with water. He would return through the water gate into the altar court. Trumpets would sound as he arrived back, and the priests would process around the altar. Just as the morning sacrifice was offered, the jug was poured into a funnel at the top of the altar. The water ran down a channel inside the altar onto the Temple floor, eventually finding its way into

1 (5:18)
2 (Acts 20:16)

the Kidron brook that ran below the Temple Mount. Then as the sacrificial offering was made, the worshippers would sing the 'Great Hallel', culminating in Psalm 118 which spoke clearly about Messiah's coming. And they would shout hallelujah, 'God be praised!'

On the last "great day" of the feast, all the ritual was ramped up: instead of three trumpet blasts, there were seven: and instead of circling the altar once, the priests did so seven times.

The Feast of Tabernacles spoke of past, present, and future:-

- Moses's instructions meant that it fell on the anniversary of the giving of the law on Mount Sinai. The Jewish lectionary was timed so that they would read the last chapter of Deuteronomy, followed by the first chapter of Genesis, on the last day of Tabernacles. And every seventh year, the Torah was read through from beginning to end during Tabernacles, as had happened under Ezra[3]. Furthermore, Solomon's Temple had been dedicated and filled with God's glory, during the Feast of Tabernacles.[4]
- It fell at the end of the olive harvest, the last harvest before winter. Though Israel has the same annual rainfall as the UK, it occurs almost entirely during the winter months; so this festival also represented a prayer for God to send the rain needed to grow the following year's crops.
- It also looked forwards to the future arrival of the messianic kingdom, when Messiah-God would dwell amongst man once again, as He had during the Exodus. He would rule the world from Mount Zion, and nations who refused to send a delegation to worship during Tabernacles, would experience drought the following year.[5]

<u>God's timetable</u> (7:1-10)

Tabernacles being such a major crowd-puller, Jesus's siblings suggested it would be an opportunity to remind His followers of His miraculous powers. They couldn't understand why He was keeping such a low profile, despite the

---

[3] (Deut 31:10-13; Neh 8:13-9:3)

[4] (2Chr 5:3)

[5] (Zech 14:16-17)

pressure there had been for Him to become a military Messiah. And presumably they were unaware of the plot to kill him in Jerusalem.

Maybe they were hoping that some of His glory would be reflected onto them too. But there was an element of scepticism in their suggestion: John records that they did not truly believe in Him.

Jesus explains to them that His challenging of sin has made Him 'persona non grata', unlike them. Any true presentation of the gospel will bring opposition and hatred from some, as well as acceptance and repentance from others. The gospel causes division, as we see happening amongst Jesus's hearers.

His brothers are totally unaware of God's agenda and timetable. And they haven't yet recognised that their elder brother is the Word Incarnate! They know nothing of God's divine scheduling, and so for them any time will do. But all appointments that ignore God's *kairos* timing are equally meaningless in the eternal scheme of things.

Jesus turns down their proposal, on the grounds, that *"His time has not yet come"*. In John's gospel, this phrase always refers to His impending crucifixion. Jesus had a clear and strong sense of God's timing for every event in His life. They could do whatever they wanted, whenever they chose: but He was constrained to stick exactly to his Father's schedule. This was part of His perfect obedience, but also meant He was protected from untimely arrest[6]. We see this repeatedly throughout the gospel, particularly as He nears the Cross.[7]

Jerusalem abuzz: is Jesus the Real Thing? (7:11-13)

Jesus's brothers would have taken the traditional route: from Galilee across the Jordan and down through Trans-Jordan, back across the river and up to Jerusalem. This was to avoid going through Samaria, where one could expect an inhospitable response from the Samaritans.

Once they had left, Jesus too set off - but incognito. The Judaean authorities were expecting Him to come. They remembered His sabbath-breaking

---

[6] (7:30)

[7] (12:7,23,31,36; 13:27,33 etc)

instruction to the man at Bethesda, and were ready to arrest Him on sight. They put the word out amongst the crowds: if anyone spotted Him, they were to report it. Jesus's reputation had spread far and wide, but public opinion was divided as to whether He was a good man or a charlatan.[8] Maybe the Pharisees had been putting out 'fake news' to blacken His name; or maybe it was because He'd refused to become a military Messiah.

There was lots of talk about Him, but whispered; because the authorities had decreed that anyone confessing Him as Christ would be banned. Not only from the Temple ceremonies, but even from the synagogues in their home towns[9]. Interestingly, John makes a distinction between the pilgrims and the local Jerusalemites.[10] it seems that the pilgrims, unlike the locals, are unaware that the authorities have put a price on his head.[11]

<u>The source of Jesus's authority</u> (7:14-24)

Halfway through the Feast, Jesus went into the Temple and began teaching.

The Jewish elite were astonished, not just by His bold-faced courage, but by His knowledge of the scriptures. Maybe they had forgotten His astonishing teaching as a twelve-year-old prodigy.[12]

The rabbis categorised people into spiritual grades depending on whether they had learnt the Torah as a child, studied the Mishna (the'Oral Law') as a teenager, or gone on to be discipled by a learned rabbi.

They labelled the grades as follows:-

- Torah ✓, Mishna ✓, Student of the Learned **X** : *'people of the land'*
- Torah ✓, Mishna **X**, Student of the Learned **X** : *'uneducated man'*
- Torah **X**, Mishna **X**, Student of the Learned **X** : *'sub-human'*!

In their view, Jesus was *uneducated*, since He had joined His father in the carpentry trade just after His Bar-Mitzvah.

---

[8] (7:12)
[9] (9:22)
[10] (7:12,25)
[11] (7:20,25)
[12] (Lk 2:41-47)

Authority, they believed, was passed down from rabbi to rabbi through the generations; and a rabbi's standing depended on who he had studied under.[13] And yet here was Jesus, teaching with an authority everyone recognised as surpassing theirs,[14] and challenging their monopoly of power.

Though there's no mention of them actually asking Jesus about this, as always He knew what was in mens' hearts. His authority He said, came direct from the fountainhead of God Himself. So it could not be corroborated in the usual way. Only those truly desiring to do God's will - who had surrendered all personal pride - would know whether His teaching did come from God, or was made up. Those seeking their own glory, even by gaining a reputation as a great rabbi, were tainted by unrighteousness; whereas someone completely committed to God's glory would always speak spiritual reality.

This shows us how to test who we listen to, as Christians. Are they seeking to impress, and build their own empire? Or are they humbly glorifying Christ, as John the Baptist did?[15] Is their teaching based on human wisdom and intellect, or does it come from reverent fear of the Lord?[16]

Though Jesus had had no secondary education in Jewish eyes, His heart's desire was always to please the Father. And because of this, people recognised that His teaching was true. In the same way, if our teaching is focussed on Him and not on ourselves, people will recognise it as truth.

In return, Jesus challenges them about the controversy over the healing at the Pool of Bethesda eighteen months previously.[17] The logic of His argument is best conveyed by paraphrasing it:-

"You've been accusing me of breaking the law of Moses, by telling a man to pick up his mat on the sabbath. You felt this was enough to justify killing me without trial, even though this is murder. That doesn't speak well of your respect for the Law! All this fuss about one miracle I did, healing that man

---

[13] (Acts 22:3)
[14] (Mt 7:29)
[15] (3:30)
[16] (Prov 1:7; 9:10)
[17] (7:21-24)

who'd been paralysed for thirty-eight years. And yet you regularly circumcise children on the eighth day, even if that falls on a sabbath.

"The only reason Moses spoke about circumcision at all, when it had been in force ever since Abraham, was so that you would know it was OK to do good for someone on the sabbath. His regulations about the sabbath are not meant to prevent you obeying what God had already decreed. If it's OK to circumcise a small part of a man's anatomy, how much more is it OK for Me to heal someone's whole body on the sabbath?"

Moses in fact only spoke once, very briefly, about circumcision.[18] God had instituted circumcision as a sign of His covenant with Abraham[19], long before the sabbath was instituted by Moses. Jewish teachers recognised that an earlier commandment took precedence over a later one, and that this specifically applied in the case of circumcision. So their judgement of Him was inconsistent; based on appearances rather than righteousness.[20]

Controversy about Jesus's origins (7:25-36)

The crowd of pilgrims, unaware of the authorities' intention to kill Jesus, thought he had become paranoid as a result of being demonised.[21] But the locals, who knew what was really afoot, were puzzled by the fact that Jesus was able to preach in the Temple at all.[22]

They reasoned that perhaps the Sanhedrin had concluded that He really was the Messiah. Against this, they thought, was the fact that Jesus's origins were known - whereas Messiah would suddenly appear out of total obscurity. This belief may have been based on Malachi's prophecy, *"The Lord whom you seek, will suddenly come to His Temple"*.[23] Though they knew that Messiah would be born in Bethlehem[24], they thought He would suddenly burst onto the public stage later in his life.

---

[18] (Lev 12:1-3)
[19] (Gen 17)
[20] (7:24)
[21] (7:20)
[22] (7:25,26)
[23] (Mal 3:1)
[24] (8:42)

Jesus, fully aware of what was being rumoured, addresses the Jerusalemites directly in the Temple: and He uses their thinking to teach them about His incarnation! Again, it's easiest to convey the logic of his argument by paraphrasing:

"Yes, you know me, and you think you know where I'm from, namely Nazareth. But again, you are judging by superficial appearances. I was born to Mary and Joseph, but actually I was sent by the true and living God, the Ultimate Reality of the Universe. You don't know Him, but I do: because actually, I came from Him, and He sent me."

Jesus says that whilst He came of His own free will, He was also sent: by God. John records this saying many times. Christ's mission was at God's initiative.

"God so loved the world, that He sent His only-begotten Son", the Son who had been in His bosom for all eternity, His beloved Son in whom He was well pleased - to be rejected and crucified. He sent Him so that *"whoever believes in Him should not perish, but have everlasting life"*. Our God *is* love: and the incarnation and atonement prove it.

Jesus's claim to deity[25] was enough to tell the listeners they should turn Him in to the Temple authorities: but because He was working in lockstep with God's timing, no-one had the guts to actually lay hands on Him. Even the Temple guards, though specifically told to seize Him, did nothing. They knew that many of the crowd were in fact convinced that He was Messiah, because of all the miracles He had done.[26]

Jesus's words are gradually bringing each hearer to a crisis. Each person must make their own decision and come to their own belief: is He for real? Is He truly the Messiah, the Son of God?

Their eternal destiny hangs on this one choice.

---

[25] (7:29)

[26] (2:23)

The authorities realise they must shut the debate down, by taking Jesus into custody. But faced with a volatile crowd and Jesus's statement that He'll be leaving soon anyway, they decide discretion is the better part of valour.

Forcing the issue, Jesus claims to be Israel's wellspring (7:37-42)

The Feast is drawing to its conclusion; and after a final night of celebration, the Great Day has arrived. As dawn breaks, the priest draws water from Siloam, returns to the blaring of trumpets, and processes round the altar seven times. He climbs the altar ramp and empties the jug, just as the morning burnt offering is being lit. The worshippers reach a glorious climax in the Great Hallel: and then, there is a reverent silence.

Suddenly, a lone voice cries out amongst the congregation, *"If anyone is thirsty, let him come to Me; and let him drink, if he believes in Me. For as the scripture has said, 'Out of His belly shall flow rivers of living water'"*[27]

N.B. There is much debate about exactly how to read the Greek of verses 37 & 38. The traditional interpretation is that the 'he who believes in Me' connects with the 'out of his belly' clause. But more recent interpreters have read it as a couplet (as above) followed by a statement which may have been Jesus's words, or may be an interpretative comment by John.

If one reads it as I have shown above, then a second issue arises: is the scripture referring to living water flowing from Jesus, or from the believer? In one sense you could argue that it's moot. But there are no other scriptures referring to the Spirit flowing from a believer, whereas many refer to living water flowing from Messiah.

Can you imagine the impact Jesus's shout would have had?

He was forcing a decision about His identity. He was claiming to be the Rock from which Israel drank in the Exodus[28], the altar from which flows the river of life[29]. He longed for Jerusalem to recognise its Messiah, and be saved from destruction.[30]

---

[27] (7:37-38)
[28] (Ex 17:1-7)
[29] (Ex 17:6; 1Cor 10:4; Ez 47:1-12; Rev 22:1,2)
[30] (Mt 23:37-39; Lk 19:41-44)

In Israel at that time, there were no water mains or taps. Water is essential for life; three days is the longest one can survive without it. And the Feast of Tabernacles was seen as a prayer to God for the autumn rains.

There were huge *cisterns* carved out of the rock (in places like Masada), which could hold enough water to see you through a long siege. But they sometimes leaked, or got polluted. There were *wells*, sometimes very deep, but which could provide a reasonably reliable source for limited volumes. Best of all however, were the high-volume springs from underground rivers in the limestone: so-called *'living waters'*. They burst forth from rocks, just like the water supply during the Exodus.

Controversy about His identity heats up (7:43-52)

The whole crowd of worshippers began discussing, *Is* this man the Prophet whom Moses foretold, whom we should all obey?[31] *Is* He the Messiah?

There were some for whom logic said no. Micah had predicted that Messiah would be born of David's line, in Bethlehem.[32] They don't seem to have known that this was true of Jesus.

Some wanted to arrest Him; but again, no-one did.[33] The Temple police returned empty-handed and overawed. The Pharisees were particularly incensed by their failure to arrest Jesus. They ridiculed the guards for being fooled like the common people had. Again, they display their arrogance and pride, saying that the top people have unanimously decided He's a conman.

But one lone voice refused to agree: Nicodemus, 'the Teacher of the Jews', whose integrity had driven him to risk his reputation by visiting Jesus at night. He reminds them that it is illegal to convict a man without a fair trial.

Nicodemus's family were very prominent in Jerusalem, very well known and influential. But he must be a Galilean himself, they mock, to have overlooked the *fact* that no prophet has arisen from Galilee! (They were actually wrong. For Jonah had come from Gath-Hepher, a town on the border of Zebulun!)[34]

---

[31] (7:40)
[32] (Mic 5:2)
[33] (7:44)
[34] (2Ki 14:25; Josh 19:13)

Chapters 7-9 of John all deal with the Jews' reactions to Jesus's claims.

For Jew or Gentile, there are only the same four possible conclusions. Is He:-

- Good? But if He claims to be God but isn't, He cannot be a good man.
- Bad: a fraud?
- Deluded, or demonised?
- Or God?

The mystery of His incarnation, which John sees as pivotal, is the issue.
Is Jesus Immanuel, the Word who became flesh and 'tabernacled' among us?

Grace upon grace (7:53-8:30)

Jesus shows amazing grace, in dealing with a trick question: should a young woman caught in adultery be stoned? He offers her grace, whilst challenging her lifestyle. But He also confronts the hypocrisy of her accusers, warning them their window of grace will close soon.

> NB: John 8:1-12 is regarded by many scholars as unlikely to have been written by John himself, but rather, added at a later date. It is true that the very earliest manuscripts of this gospel either skip it completely, or leave a blank space where it should be. However :-
>
> - Of the early manuscripts, the majority do include it, and place it at this point.
> - It is certainly consistent with Christ's character
> - Its themes tie in with the sections before and after it

The setting

On the final day of Tabernacles, Jesus had hijacked the whole ceremony by shouting *"If anyone is thirsty, let him come to Me; and let him drink, if he believes in Me".* He turned the whole event into a pointer to His identity.

We don't know what He did for the rest of that day, but we do know there was intense debate amongst the pilgrims as to whether He was Messiah. We also know that the Temple authorities were wanting Him arrested, but the police refused to do so, because they knew He was claiming to be God. The authorities were furious, but couldn't do much about it.

Everyone went home, but Jesus went to the Mount of Olives. From the Temple you walk down into the Kidron valley to its east, then cross the stream and up the Mount of Olives. Here there was a garden called Gethsemane, which means 'olive press'.

The olive harvest finished just before the feast of Tabernacles, so the press may still have been in use. There was a three-stage process to the pressing:-

1. Baskets of olives would be stacked atop each other, so that the lower ones were crushed by the weight, & oil began to ooze. This was what we call *extra virgin* oil, used for holy purposes such as anointing.

2. Then a huge wooden beam would be lowered onto the baskets, to crush them more. This produced the virgin oil, used for food and cooking.
3. Lastly, the beam would be loaded with massive rocks, to extract the last drops of oil for other everyday uses such as lamp oil.

This was a place where Jesus often went to pray; He would have been talking with His Father, perhaps foreseeing when He would be crushed by our sin. Six months later, just before He was crucified, He would pray there three times: with such intensity, that drops of blood were squeezed from His pores.

Early in the morning, He returned to the Temple: to the Court of the Women, where people had been dancing during the Feast. At night, the court was floodlit by sixteen oil lamps, mounted on four tall lampposts. These were periodically refuelled by priests with pitchers of oil. And elders of the Sanhedrin would perform dances with flaming torches. Though it was the middle of the lunar month and the harvest moon was full, these lamps were so bright that the whole city had a canopy of light; wherever you lived in Jerusalem, you could see to walk around safely.

The woman trapped in adultery, the men trapped in hypocrisy (8:1-11)

Having stood up to shout His message the day before, Jesus now sits. This is how rabbis teach when they are training their disciples[1]. He is teaching those who have believed in Him during the Feast.

He is interrupted by a gaggle of men dragging a screaming, struggling woman towards Him. The men are scribes (teachers of the Law) and Pharisees. *(Most scribes were also Pharisees, but not all Pharisees were scribes.)* Their aim was to entrap Jesus with a 'gotcha' question, like modern-day reporters do to politicians.

Surrounded by these men, the woman is made to stand in front of Jesus and His audience of new disciples. She is probably dishevelled and tearful; likely a teenager; and certainly terrified. She has been caught in the act of adultery, for which the penalty is death by stoning. Somehow these men had emerged from the shadows just as she and her lover were at their most intimate.

---

[1] (Matt 5:1)

But her boyfriend had abandoned her and escaped. He too was liable to death by stoning, and should have been arrested. The whole scenario is so inherently unlikely that it must have been a 'set-up', arranged specifically for the purpose of entrapping Jesus. The woman was just a pawn.

Reminding Jesus that the Law of Moses stipulated stoning, these super-spiritual men ask Jesus whether He agrees with it.

> NB: *The only form of adultery for which the Torah specifically mentions stoning, is when a betrothed virgin is unfaithful: this suggests that she was likely in her teens.*

- If He agrees, she dies there and then: though the Roman authorities might take a dim view of the death penalty being administered without their say-so. More importantly, Jesus's reputation for grace and forgiveness would be blown apart. His new disciples would be appalled.
- But if He refused to condemn her, He would be instantly discredited for contradicting the Law of Moses.

Either way, they thought, they had Him cornered! How can God be both just, and forgiving? It seemed impossible to them, though of course we now know the answer![2]

Jesus leaned forwards from His seat, and began writing in the dust. Many ingenious theories have been put forwards as to what He was writing, but the truth is, scripture doesn't give us any clues. *(The theory I like best, is that He was writing out lists of the sins each of the men had committed.)* The men aren't impressed by His silence, and badger Him for an answer. He looks up briefly, and says, *'Let anyone who is sinless cast the first stone'*. Then He goes back to writing on the ground.

The Law required witnesses to be of good character; not complicit in any way in the sins of which they are accusing others. And their testimonies had to match exactly. They had to have actually seen the action they were accusing the person of. For example, it wasn't enough to have seen two people entering a hotel bedroom together! Convictions for adultery, and thus stonings, were very very rare.

---

[2] (Rom 3:23-26)

If the men had entrapped her, and then watched without intervening to prevent adultery, they were complicit. Indeed, they too were deemed guilty of adultery[3]. The penalty for false witness was that the witness suffered what the victim would have; so they risked being stoned themselves!

Whether it was this knowledge, or an awareness that they too had sinned sexually in their youth, we don't know. One or two of the older men, perhaps with longer life experience, began to slip away. That unnerved the younger ones, and they too quietly left, until only the young woman was left.

Why she didn't flee, we don't know. She must have already sensed something of the holiness and grace of Jesus. Jesus asked her if there was anyone else left who might condemn her. She says *'No'*, calling Him Lord, acknowledging that her judgement is now solely in His hands.

Jesus's verdict, *"I do not condemn you either"*, is technically correct; since she can only be found guilty if there are witnesses. But He is saying something much deeper. He is saying, "I forgive you and will pay the death penalty for your sin - at Calvary in six months' time. I will carry your cross. It is through Me that God can be both just, and your Justifier."

This is truly costly grace.

Grace upon grace

In his prologue, John wrote: *"Of His fullness have we all received, grace upon grace. For the Law was given through Moses, but grace and truth came by Jesus Christ. No-one has seen God at any time. The only-begotten Son, who is in the bosom of the Father, He has declared Him".*[4]

This episode epitomises the glory of Jesus's character: He is *'the only-begotten Son of the Father, full of grace and truth'*.

The way Jesus handles the apparent conflict between the demands of the Law, and His fullness of grace, is incredible. In His verdict on the woman, He combines grace with challenging truth: *"I do not condemn you; go and sin no more!"* But there is also grace for the Pharisees: time for them to reflect as

---

[3] (Mt 5:8)
[4] (1:16,17)

they wait for His response, privacy from His gaze as they weigh His answer, and opportunity to recognise their own hypocrisy before it is too late.

But it is not 'cheap grace' for the woman. 'Go, and leave your life of sin', He tells her. And then He says to His disciples, *"I AM the light of the world. He who follows Me shall not walk in darkness, but shall have the light of life".*

I AM the light of the world. (8:12)

This is the second of Jesus's statements of how His nature meets our needs. Just as the Temple lights had reminded them of the shekinah glory which hung over the Exodus campsite at night, Jesus the Light of the world will give them the light of *zoe* life. Just as the cloud had guided them through the unmapped wilderness, He will illuminate their journey through life.

In it, He takes His hearers back, yet again, to the Exodus. In chapter six, He referred to Himself as the ***manna***. In chapter seven, He says He is the ***rock*** that gushes out the water of life. Now in chapter eight, He says He is the ***light***, the cloud of glory that covered Israel, illuminating them at night and guiding them during the day.

Light has multiple effects, and powerful symbolism.[5] It dispels the darkness, exposes uncleanness, and purifies. It enables us to see where we are going. The word carries overtones of purity, truth, enlightenment and holiness. Jesus has all of these qualities and effects; He is utterly pure, true, and holy.

Light and life go together in Christ: *"In Him was life, and the life was the light of men"*[6]. When we are born again and receive *zoe* life from Him, His life in us gives us that light. We become *'sons of light'*, and manifest His qualities. Our lives continue His role as the light of the world, even though He has now returned to the Father.

Anyone who follows Jesus will not continue to walk in darkness. It is not possible to walk in darkness and have fellowship with the light. *"This is the message which we have heard from Him, and declare to you, that God is light, and in Him is no darkness at all. If we say that we have fellowship with Him, and walk in darkness, we lie, and do not practice the truth. But if we*

---

[5] (See appendix two)

[6] (1:4)

walk in the light as He is in the light, we have fellowship with one another, and the blood of Jesus Christ His Son cleanses us from all sin".[7]

Jesus will go on to elaborate this theme further: *"Are there not twelve hours in the day? If anyone walks in the day, he does not stumble, because he sees the light of this world. But if one walks in the night, he stumbles, because the light is not in him"*[8]. And again, *"A little while longer, the light is with you. Walk while you have the light, less darkness overtake you; he who walks in darkness, does not know where he is going. While you have the light, believe in the light, that you may become sons of light".*[9]

Walking in the light

This story is usually called 'The woman caught in adultery': and we have seen the astonishing grace Jesus extended to her - combined with a challenge to live in purity. It is grace that makes repentance and restoration possible. In its absence, only condemnation and stigma remain.

But there is another side to this episode, namely 'The men caught in hypocrisy'. These scribes and Pharisees saw themselves as *'a guide to the blind, a light to those who are in darkness'.*[10] They thought they could see, when in fact, they were blind.[11] Worse, they were blind *guides*! Blind guides who strain out a gnat whilst swallowing a camel. Their hypocrisy would condemn them to hell.

Jesus repeatedly warns His disciples, *'Beware the leaven of the scribes and Pharisees, which is hypocrisy'*. He knows the heightened risk for those who seek to walk with God: how easy it is for religious zeal to slowly morph into hypocrisy, within our hearts. How easy it is for Christian leaders..

- to condemn alternative lifestyles, on the bandwagon of popular opinion
- to hide the areas of failure in their own lives, 'to protect the church'
- to seek the approval of men, by comparing others unfavourably

---

[7] (1Jn 1:5-9)
[8] (11:9-11)
[9] (12:35-36)
[10] (Rom 2:17-24)
[11] (9:40,41)

But hypocrisy isn't confined to those in leadership positions. Maintaining our reputation and respectability is a powerful drive in our everyday lives. We use spiritual lipstick and moral face cream to hide the blemishes. It is so much easier to point the finger at someone else, than to acknowledge the truth about ourselves. To try and remove the specks of dust from others' eyes, whilst ignoring the cataracts in our own.

Judging ourselves is very difficult. *'The human heart is desperately wicked and deceitful'.*[12] John says, *'If we say we have no sin, we deceive ourselves, and the truth is not in us'.*[13] There is no such thing as sinless perfection, and the Christian who thinks he has reached such a state is deeply deceived. As the Holy Spirit leads us into holiness, we will become more and more aware of our sinfulness.

In my own experience as I grow older, I find that God's spotlight shines more and more on my heart attitudes, rather than on specific deeds. Paul says he doesn't trust his own judgement of himself but rather, submits himself to God's scrutiny.[14] We can but plead, *"Search me, O God, and know my heart. See if there be any wicked way in me, and lead me in the way everlasting."*[15]

He knows that we have a tendency to judge by appearances, without looking into the heart. Unlike Him, we cannot judge justly, because we do not know mens' hearts. That is why He says, *"Judge not, lest you be judged"*[16].

We see many examples in scripture of people being judged by their own words. For example Nathan uses David's own words to convict him about Bathsheba. And Jesus tells us that on the Day of Judgement, its will be our own words that come back to haunt us. The things we said, the emails we wrote, the trolling we indulged in, the vendettas we pursued.

For church discipline to bring cleansing and healing, rather than being destructive, it must not be exercised by individuals. There must be at least two or three believers gathered together, with Jesus present amongst them,

---

[12] (Jer 17:9)
[13] (1Jn 1:8)
[14] (1Cor 4:3,4)
[15] (Ps 139:23,24)
[16] (Mt 7:1)

and then our judgements will either bind or loose, in heaven as on earth[17]. But first of all we should have done everything in our power to bring the straying sheep back into the fold.[18] We must come with Jesus's grace and forgiveness; but we must also address real issues rather than ignore them.[19]

So in summary, 'walking in the Light' means:-

- Striving to live in holiness and listening for His guidance
- Seeking to help each other to do so
- But also facing our own hypocrisy and failings
- Repeatedly and continually opening ourselves to His scrutiny
- Letting His utter purity reset our moral plumb-line
- Confessing and repenting of what He shows us
- Relying on His grace, for forgiveness and empowerment to change

The Pharisees harden their hearts (8:13-30)

Rather than face their own hypocrisy, the Pharisees are incensed by Jesus's fresh claim to deity. There was an added edge to it, in that they counted themselves as *'a guide to the blind, a light to those who are in darkness'*[20]. Here was Jesus saying *'No, it's not you, but Me: I am the light of the world'*.

His light forces men to choose:

"This is the condemnation, that the light has come into the world, and men loved darkness, rather than light, because their deeds were evil. For everyone practising evil, hates the light, and does not come to the light, lest his deeds should be exposed. But he who does the truth comes to the light, that his deeds may be clearly seen, that they have been done in God"[21].

Having tried to silence Him by arrest, and to discredit Him by trickery, they now seek to undermine His testimony on a technicality. Quoting His own

[17] (Mt 18:18-20)
[18] (Mt 18:10-14)
[19] (Mt 18:15-17)
[20] (Rom 2:17-24)
[21] (3:19-21)

words[22], they charge that blowing His own trumpet, however subtly, implies lack of integrity.

Jesus answers them with their own legalistic logic, which is easiest to convey in a paraphrase:

"Whilst it's true that in earthly matters, there might need to be two or three human witnesses, this issue - whether I am God's divine light for the world - is a heavenly one. I know My heavenly origins and destiny, but you don't, and can't. Your judgement is fundamentally flawed in a case such as this, because your worldview is limited to the natural world.

Unlike you, I am not judgemental. But if I were to judge, I'd always be just: because I'd have My heavenly Father's all-knowing, all-wise perspective on it.

If you really want to argue legal niceties, remember that the Law says you only need two eye-witnesses who agree, to prove a case. Heavenly issues require heavenly eye-witnesses; I am one, and My Father (who by the way, sent Me as His ambassador) is the other. He backs up everything I teach, through the miracles He enables Me to do."[23]

At this point, the only weapons they have left are sarcasm and ridicule. *"Really? So tell us then - where is this mysterious Father you talk about?"*

"The very fact you can ask such a question, shows you've completely missed the point. When you look at Me, you are seeing the Father. But as it is, you don't recognise either Me or Him."[24]

Although the Twelve also struggled with this issue, the Pharisees' failure to recognise Jesus's one-ness with the Father was more culpable given their knowledge of the Law and the prophets. They could not comprehend His incarnation: that whilst remaining part of the Godhead, He was *'Jesus Christ come in the flesh'*.

They hated Him and wanted to kill Him; but even though He'd placed Himself right in the lions' den, no-one touched Him: God's *kairos* moment hadn't yet quite arrived. But Jesus was well aware it wasn't far ahead.

---

[22] (5:31)
[23] (8:13-18)
[24] (8:19)

"I'm warning you, your window of opportunity is fast closing: I'm leaving shortly for somewhere beyond your reach. You'll search for Me in vain, and die in your sin - the sin of not believing in Me."[25]

This puzzled them. The only way they could think of Him escaping, would be if He were to commit suicide! Heaven was a shoo-in for them, in their minds: only if he went to hell would they be unable to follow.

"No, no! You're fatally complacent! Your roots are earthly, mine are heavenly. You are at home in this sinful, rebellious world: I am from above, holy, unlike you. Far from being entitled to enter heaven, you will die still marked for judgement, unless you believe that I AM - that I am God."[26]

Now they were rattled. This was serious. For the first time they asked genuinely, *"Who are You?"*

"I've been telling you for so long, and you still don't believe. There are so many charges against you which I will pronounce judgement on in due course, but My Father's scheduled that for a later date. When you finally have Me killed, you'll suddenly realise you've crucified the Son of God; everything I ever did or taught was straight from Him. You detest and despise Me; but My Father is continually present with Me, delighting in My obedience."[27]

Many were convinced by Jesus's response, and began to believe.

But Jesus doesn't slacken His pace. He starts to teach them about the total depravity of their human hearts. Even though they have some kind of belief, they are still 'children of the devil', so used to lying and deception that they can't hear the truth Jesus is telling them. They're still enslaved by sin: and only ongoing longterm obedience to His word will set them free, so that they can be assured of their place in God's house.

---

[25] (8:21)
[26] (8:23-24)
[27] (8:25-28)

Sin's slaves, and sons of Satan (8:31-59)

Jesus disabuses the Jews about their 'favoured nation' status as Abraham's offspring. Rather, He says. they are children of the devil, and enslaved by sin. Predictably, they react with hostility, trying to stone Him.

Our last chapter ended with Jesus telling the Pharisees, that if they didn't believe in Him they would die in their sins. Their assumption was that as ultra-righteous children of Abraham, they would automatically go straight to heaven. Whereas if Jesus committed suicide, He would go to the lowest hell.

The Jewish view of sin

The Jewish view of sin was very different to Christ's teaching, as we shall see. To Jews, sin meant disobeying a specific commandment. They thought that ...

- Though born sinless, everyone had an inclination to do evil from their youth[1], and thus sinning was an inherent part of life. Sin which was purely against God was covered by the annual 'Day of Atonement'; whereas sin against man was only covered if one appeased one's victim.
- If one was completely righteous, one would enjoy both this life and that of the world to come. In practice, those who sinned often did suffer in this life, which made atonement for their sins. Failing that, one could buy atonement through sacrifices (korbanot); providing it was accompanied by repentance, and restitution where relevant.
- Upon death, any un-atoned-for sins involved a stay in one of the lower levels of Gehenna (hell), until atonement had been earned. But everyone would eventually reach Paradise, except the utterly evil. They would be sent to the lowest Gehenna, from where they would be annihilated.

I emphasise that this is the *Jewish* view of sin, not a Christian view. However you will probably recognise its similarity to doctrines taught by some 'Christian' denominations. Some teach that all will be saved eventually, or that sin can be atoned for by buying indulgences, or by spending time in Purgatory. Or that the worst that can happen is that you cease to exist

---

[1] (Gen 8:21)

(annihilation) rather than endlessly suffering in the Lake of Fire. Others hope that God will look favourably on their good works and overlook their sins: or that judgement is more like scraping through an exam on the day, rather than continuous assessment!

But Jesus says that eternal life is a gift of pure grace, given by Him to those who believe in Him and hold to His teaching. We can never earn a ticket into heaven; we must be born again and become children of God.

Having temporarily silenced His opponents, Jesus begins teaching those Judaeans who have apparently believed in Him.[2] There is no indication that these are other than genuine believers. But a few verses further on, we find Judaeans accusing Him of being demonised[3]: are these the same group?

Some argue that there were believing and unbelieving Judaeans mingled together. My own conclusion is that many of the 'believers' took offence as Jesus continued teaching, just as the Galileans had done in 6:60. Jesus knows that only a sustained holding to His teaching will bring about genuine discipleship.[4] *"Blessed is he who does not take offense because of Me."*[5]

So why was what Jesus said, so offensive to them?

<u>Slaves to sin</u> (8:32-36)

Jesus starts by telling them that if they continue to hold to His teaching (His *logos*) they will come to know the truth, and the truth will set them free.

In earlier times, we English used to sing, *"Rule, Britannia; Britannia rules the waves. Britains never never never shall be slaves"*. Jews, despite being under the Roman Empire's rule, had similar nationalistic pride. Overlooking their captivity in Babylon and successive occupations by the Persian, Greek and Roman empires, they say, *'We've never been in bondage to anyone, so how can you say we need to be set free?'*

Jesus's reply makes them more uncomfortable. Sin isn't something trivial that will be dealt with routinely next Day of Atonement. It actually enslaves you.

---

[2] (8:31)
[3] (8:48,52)
[4] (8:31)
[5] (Matt 11:6)

You become addicted to it; in bondage. Your appetite to sin more, grows and grows. The defilement it causes gets deeper and deeper. The Holy Spirit strives against this[6], but eventually God gives us up to unbridled passions[7].

Slaves have no security: they can be thrown out at a moment's notice, as Abraham did with Hagar.[8] Whereas a son will never be treated like that.[9]
In other words, if you are enslaved by sin, you can have no assurance that you will remain a member of God's household. But if the Son of God sets you free - looses you from your bondage to sin - you will be truly free!

Children of Satan, not of Abraham or of God (8:37-50)

They had claimed that their freedom came from being Abraham's physical descendants. (The Greek word is actually 'sperma'.) Because God had promised Abraham that after slavery in Egypt they would then live free in a land God had cleared of other nations[10], they believed God had guaranteed their freedom.

Jesus acknowledges that they are indeed Abraham's biological descendants; but their behaviour is so different to his that they must be someone else's children.[11] Abraham promptly accepted any uncomfortable truths God spoke to him, such as about his offsprings' future enslavement in Egypt, or the judgement coming on Sodom. Whereas Jesus's teaching* is like seed falling on rocky ground: it finds no soil to grow on in their hearts, despite coming directly from the Presence of God. Their actions (in seeking to kill Him) show that their role model is someone completely different from Abraham's God.

As yet, Jesus hasn't said who He thinks *is* their true father. Nevertheless they reply indignantly, *'Abraham is our father'*[12]. Jesus replies that they may be Abraham's biological descendants (*sperma* again) but they are not his children (*tekna*). Their plot to kill Him, despite Him telling them truth, proves that they have some other father.

---

6 (Jas 4:4-10)
7 (Rom 1:24-30)
8 (Gen 21:9-10)
9 (8:35)
10 (Gen 15:13-21)
11 (8:37,38)
12 (8:39)

Increasingly offended at the idea of being spiritually illegitimate, they shift the goalposts. Hadn't Yahweh God Himself acknowledged them as His sons, when He said to Pharaoh, *"Israel is my firstborn son"*?[13]

Jesus's reply to this changed paternity claim revolves around His identity. He *proceeded* (past tense) and *comes* (present tense) from the Father[14]. Whilst 'proceeded' can simply refer to where something came from, it carries undertones of coming out of the heart of God, or emanating from Him. Just as the Father is continually begetting Him, He is eternally proceeding from the Father. He is *eternally filiated*, to use theologians' language. He has come not on His own initiative, but because the Father sent Him. If they were genuinely sons of God, if they loved the Father, they would also love His only-begotten Son, the exact image of His Person.[15]

Not only do their specific sins create a bondage to further sin, their underlying tendency to sin comes from a sinful nature which is totally hostile to God. Their inability to comprehend what He is saying, or to accept and obey it, is because *their true father is Satan*![16]

Whereas God gives light and truth, the devil is a murderer and the root source of all lies.[17] Way back in the Garden of Eden, he lied to Eve that *'You will not surely die'*. That lie then led to Adam's sin; and death entered the world, infecting all future generations.[18]

When the Devil lies, he is speaking his mother-tongue, so to speak. He is so fluent in lying, so plausible, that he deceives the whole world.

And they have become so used to lies that they can no longer discern truth when they hear it. Worse, it sounds so weird to them that they do not believe it.[19] But, He says, though many accusations have been levelled, no-one has proved anything against Him. So there can be no grounds for their disbelief.[20]

---

[13] (Ex 4:22)
[14] (8:42)
[15] (Heb 1:3)
[16] (8:44)
[17] (8:45)
[18] (Rom 5:12)
[19] (8:45)
[20] (8:46)

Ultimately, if they were of God, they would be able to hear Him and understand. (He will later say, *'My sheep hear My voice'.*[21]) The fact that they can't, proves that despite what God said about Israel being His firstborn son, *they* are not of God.

To sum up Jesus's logic, they cannot be true children of Abraham because:-

- Their behaviour doesn't match Abraham's: they are seeking to kill Him
- They are rejecting what He's said to them, despite its truth

Nor can they be children of God, because

- In wanting to kill Him they show their likeness to the devil, a murderer
- They do not love the One who's from the Father & reveals His nature
- The very fact He's telling them the truth, puts them off
- They cannot grasp what He is saying, because they are not of God

Jesus's statement that their real father is actually the devil, so incenses them that they accuse Him of being a demonised Samaritan[22]. Unlike when the Pharisees said Jesus was possessed by Beelzebub, and He warned them that blasphemy against the Holy Spirit was unforgiveable, here He just calmly refutes them. But since His whole desire is to honour the Father and not Himself, their dishonouring of Him in this way pits them against God. God seeks those who will honour His Son, and judges those that won't.[23]

<u>The gospel of eternal life</u> (8:451-59)

Jesus returns to His gospel message: *"Amen amen, anyone who keeps My word (logos) will never taste death"*[24]. Whereas the devil is a murderer and loves death, Christ brings life. Jesus wants disciples to have complete assurance about death, providing they hold to His word.

Amen means 'True.' We use it to signify our agreement with something that has just been said. Jesus also uses it, but the difference is that He puts it *before* the statement, rather than afterwards; and He repeats it twice. God

---

[21] (10:27)
[22] (8:48)
[23] (5:22-23; 8:50)
[24] (8:51)

cannot lie, so He isn't saying this to distinguish truths from lies. Rather, He is wanting to impress on us the seriousness of this truth.

Jesus repeats this promise that we will not taste death, over and over again; culminating in His statement to Martha, *"I am the Resurrection and the Life, he who believes in Me, though he may die, he shall live. And whoever lives and believes in Me shall never die"*[25]. Death has lost its sting, and we can triumph over it in Him![26] We *'fall asleep in Jesus'*, and wake in His Presence. All because He, *'by the grace of God, has tasted death for everyone'*[27].

Jesus's apparent claim to bestow immortality on His followers provokes total incredulity.[28] They cannot understand His manner of speech and cannot conceive the spiritual truths He is teaching. But they rightly see this claim as making Jesus far more eminent than Abraham or any of the prophets. That naturally leads them to conclude that this is outrageous boasting: *"Who do you make yourself out to be?"*

If that were true, Jesus replies, if He were honouring Himself, it would count for nothing. But the truth is that the Father, Yahweh the God of Israel, is the One honouring Him.[29] The Jews are lying when they claim to know Him. Jesus knows Him, and if He were to deny that, it would be just as big a lie. Knowing Almighty God means keeping His word: and Jesus never does anything except what He sees the Father doing.

<u>A brief detour on the taste of death!</u>

What is the *taste* of death, of which Jesus speaks?

Death in Christ is sweet: death outside Christ is bitter. It is bitter for those suffering bereavement, but it is also bitter for those faced with terminal illness. Hezekiah mourned his impending death, for various reasons:[30] But he realised that facing death can also safeguard our walk with God.[31]

---

[25] (5:24; 6:47; 11:25,26)
[26] (1Cor 15:54-57)
[27] (Heb 2:9)
[28] (8:52,53)
[29] (8:54)
[30] (Isa 38:3, 9-19)
[31] (Isa 38:15, Ps 90:10-12)

Confronted with loss of independence and dignity, hopes that will never now be realised and relationships which will never now be reconciled, we are forced back to total reliance on God's grace. We enter the place of rest which still remains for the people of God, where we have 'ceased from our works': ceased struggling in our own strength.[32]

The contrast of Abraham's attitude to Christ

Unlike the disbelief and dishonour He is experiencing from His listeners, Jesus says, Abraham was overjoyed at the thought of seeing the Lamb of God. When by faith he said to his son Isaac, *'God will provide Himself the Lamb'*[33], he was seeing into the future prophetically.

Although he had been told, *'In Isaac shall your seed be named'*[34] and he knew that the promise of the Land of Israel was made not to himself but to his seed, he had realised that Isaac was not the Lamb of God. There was Another yet to come, who would offer Himself as the ransom-sacrifice for the sins of the world. And he knew that that sacrifice would take place on the very same mountain where he had tried to sacrifice his son: *'On the mountain of the Lord it will be provided'*.

As a result of his obedience in offering Isaac, God promised him, *'In your seed shall all nations be blessed'*. That is why you are now reading this: because *'now in Christ Jesus the blessing of Abraham has come upon you Gentiles'*[35].

Once again, the blindness of the Jews' fallen natures prevents them grasping the implication of what He is saying; and they query how He and Abraham could ever have met, since Jesus is under fifty.

Jesus claims to be the eternal God

Just as Jesus took His time before making it explicit that their true spiritual father is Satan, so here He has been biding His time to allow the implication of His earlier statements to sink in.

---

[32] (Heb 4:9,10)
[33] (Gen 22:8-18)
[34] (Gen 21:12)
[35] (Gal 3:14)

If He can confer eternal life, He must Himself have eternal life. If Abraham saw Him, then He must have existed two thousand years before this conversation took place. Now He reveals the whole extent of the truth: *"Before Abraham was born, I AM"*[36].

This was a crystal-clear claim to share the awesome Name of God. The same Jews who'd begun to believe, now took up stones to kill Him for blasphemy.[37]

Abraham's life had a beginning and an end: Jesus's life has neither. He has come *'in the likeness of Melchizedek'*, whose priestly ministry was not the result of some earthly decree, but *'through the power of an endless life'*[38]. He is the Alpha and Omega. *"In the beginning was the Word, and the Word was with God, and the Word was God."*

Jesus is the great 'I AM', the ever-present One, the eternally-Living God. He will never go deaf or blind with old age, or fail to see our needs or hear our cries. He will never lose His power to save. He has been, and will be, our dwelling place in all generations: from everlasting to everlasting, He is God![39] We are called to experience the living Presence of God in the fabric of our everyday lives.

If you want this truth to sink deeper into your heart, I suggest you read Isaiah chapters forty to fifty-five, highlighting every time you see the word 'LORD' in capital letters. The upper case formatting indicates the underlying Hebrew is 'Yahweh', 'I AM': Jesus! Now go through it again with a different colour pen, marking all the times you see the word 'I': each of these occurrences tells you something about His activity, past present and future. There are so many such statements that the highlighting will look like an Impressionist artwork!

---

[36] (8:58)
[37] (8:50)
[38] (8:50)
[39] (Ps 90:1,2)

Application:

We can read this passage superficially, and assume it only applies to the Jews of Jesus's day. But if so, what value has it to us? These same truths apply as much to us, as to them. Unless we realise what we have been saved from, and how radical that salvation is, we will never stay the course.

Jesus is not interested in having disciples who think that following Him is merely a lifestyle choice. Having pushed the issue of who they think *He* is[40], He now addresses who they think *they* themselves are. Remember that He is here speaking to those who have believed in Him!

- Firstly, *their response is one of entitlement*. We are special, we are God's chosen people, we are under His blessing like no-one else is. We are children of Abraham. We have a free pass to enter heaven without having to pass through Gehenna or purgatory. There is a spiritual elitism, an arrogance, a sense of entitlement. Does that ring any bells about attitudes amongst fellow Christians, or indeed your own heart? It is the opposite of believing in God's grace as your only hope.

- Secondly, *they are unaware of their own bondage to sin*. They see sin as something everyone does, which can't be too serious and anyway will be dealt with on the next Day of Atonement. They have no idea of its power to enslave: that in sinning, they are obeying Satan and thereby becoming his slaves[41]. Whether through gross sin, or 'respectable sins' such as refusal to forgive, we give the enemy a beach-head in our hearts, into which he can pour demonic spirits.[42] Even Christians can sometimes need deliverance.

Ultimately however, it is only abiding in His word which will undo the enemy's lies and reveal the sinfulness of sin to us. It is only this *'prolonged obedience in the same direction'* that will ultimately set us free. But that is Jesus's intent and desire: He came to preach liberty to the captives[43].

---

[40] (John 7)

[41] (Rom 6:15-19).

[42] (Eph 4:25-27)

[43] (Lk 4:18)

Are there any areas you are conscious of, in which you repeatedly experience failure and sin? Be encouraged : He came to set you free. And His promise is, *'If you continue in My word, you will come to know the truth, and the truth will set you free.'* Keep confessing, keep coming to the Cross, keep claiming and proclaiming the blood of Jesus, keep giving testimony.[44]

- Thirdly, *they have no idea how corrupted their inner nature is*. Individual episodes of sin are certainly not trivial; but our underlying heart's desires are those of Satan himself! His defining characteristics manifest themselves in our hearts, and drive our actions. His murderousness drives our anger and road rage, drives the niggling resentments in our marriages, keeps us from forgiving others and letting go of vendettas. His nature as the 'father of lies' expresses itself in our pretentious respectability, our hypocritical judging of others, our self-deception and 'white' lies.

As I get nearer my own trial before the judgement seat of Christ, I become more and more aware of these heart attitudes within myself. Unlike individual sins, I cannot reassure myself that I will try harder to avoid entering into temptation next time. This is who I *am*, without Christ. Only as I learn to die to myself and let Christ indwell me, let Him take the driving seat of my life, can I hope for change.

-Fourthly, *they do not realise they are deaf to the voice of God*. They have believed so many enemy lies, each one strengthening their mental strongholds against God's word[45], that they cannot grasp Jesus's words.

Later, He will say, *'My sheep hear My voice'.*[46] He is not referring to the dead but the living: us! It is your right as a child of God to hear the Good Shepherd's voice. The devil may tell you that that is only for prophets and mystics; but that is a lie. His voice is 'as the sound of many waters': He has many channels of speech, and huge bandwidth, sufficient for every believer to hear His specific word to them.

---

[44] (Rev 12:11)
[45] (2Cor 10:3-5)
[46] (10:27)

Messianic mudpacks (9:1-41)

Jesus heals a man's congenital blindness - a miracle marking Him as Messiah.
The man's testimony results in his being ostracised,
but he comes to see Jesus as the Son of God, and worships Him.
The Pharisees become more and more hardened in their blindness.

Context

The day after His shock intervention at the Feast of Tabernacles, the scribes and Pharisees sought first to discredit Jesus in front of His disciples, then to disqualify Him with legal arguments. The debate about His identity got more and more heated: but Jesus countered by declaring that *their* identity was that of sons of Satan. Eventually, when He claimed to have existed as God Almighty before Abraham's birth, they tried to stone Him. Jesus suddenly became invisible, and walked straight through them and out of the Temple.

Chapter nine starts with Jesus 'passing by', accompanied now by His disciples. How closely this linked to the previous section, John doesn't say. But Jesus's gaze fixes on a blind man, presumably a beggar. Temple entrances were prime sites for begging, as alms-giving was a way of making atonement. It may have been the same place where Peter later healed a paralysed man.[1]

The gospels record various occasions where Jesus gazed at someone before healing them. It seems as though a person's eyes were His window into their soul. Sometimes His gaze engendered faith: but being blind, this beggar would not have seen Jesus's look. However he probably registered that a group of people had stopped, and may have overheard the disciples' question, "Who sinned?". And blind people often develop increased sensory awareness in other ways, to compensate for their lack of sight.

Congenital blindness: who sinned?

With Jesus's teaching fresh in their minds on how we are all enslaved by sin and by nature children of the devil, it was natural that the disciples should ask Him this question. They knew God visits the sins of the fathers on the

---

[1] (Acts 3:2)

children to the third and fourth generation; but Jews also believed that it was possible for a baby itself to sin, while still in its mother's womb.

Underlying their question was the assumption that all suffering is the result of sin. We know that this is true in general, in that there was no suffering before the fall of man, and there will be none in the new creation. And the paralysis of the man at Bethesda seems to have been due to sin.[2] But we also know it is not always the case that specific suffering is due to a specific sin. In Jesus's own time, there had been a major disaster when a tower at Siloam had collapsed, killing many.[3] Jesus said that the disaster didn't mean its victims were more sinful than anyone else.

The book of Job describes the intense suffering of a man who was righteous. In his case, it was the result of a Satanic attack. But the attack was allowed by God, and used by him to bring Job to the wonderful realisation that *"I know that my Redeemer lives, and that one day, I will see him with my own eyes"*. At the end of the book, God reveals His awesome majesty to Job; humbling him, and bringing him to a new place of deeper surrender.

Nowadays, we tend to think of much suffering as being either random, or the result of natural disasters such as famines, floods, pandemics, wars and so on. But we still often ask ourselves privately, 'What did we (or they) do to deserve such suffering?' And it multiplies our suffering when others imply that we must have done something bad - like Job's friends did.

Jesus flatly denies that the sins of the man's parents, or his own actions in the womb, could have caused this man's congenital blindness. In one sense, he doesn't answer the disciples' question. Rather than looking backwards, He looks forward to the opportunity it presents for the man to experience, and for Him to demonstrate, the wonderful compassion of God.

Jesus is very aware that his time on earth is limited. It is in fact less than six months till his crucifixion, and He has just miraculously escaped being stoned. *"I must work the works of Him who sent Me, while it is still day; the night is*

---

[2] (5:14)

[3] (Lk 13:1-5)

coming, when no-one can work"[4]. In the Middle East, as in tropical Africa, sundown comes very swiftly and suddenly. And in the absence of electric lights, such as we have today, it is completely impossible to work.

He is very conscious of completing the work that His Father has given him to do, so that on the cross He will be able to shout, *"it is finished!"* And He wants to convey to the disciples, the urgency of their own witness and work after He is gone. There will be a period immediately after His death, *"when no man can work"*: but after that, *they* will be *"the light of the world"*[5]. But for now, while He is still in the world, He is the Light of the world.

A Messianic miracle

That light has been demonstrated in the grace and forgiveness Jesus offered the woman caught in adultery; but also, in exposing the hypocrisy of those who used her as a pawn. It has been shown too, in his teaching about our fallen nature and the effects of sin. Now it will be shown in the opening of the eyes of this poor man. This miracle will manifest Jesus's glory, just as each of the previous signs have. And by enabling this man to see for the first time in his life, it will illustrate that Jesus is indeed 'the light of the world'.

This miracle was one of three that Jewish authorities knew from their scripture, *only Messiah could perform*. Along with cleansing lepers and driving out deaf-mute spirits, this was ultimate proof that Jesus was Messiah.

No doubt, as he listened intently, the blind man would have sensed that something major was about to happen. If this Man was indeed the Light of the world, might He heal him?

Jesus spat on the ground, and used the dust to form a paste of mud. He then applied mudpacks over the man's closed eyelids, and told him to walk down through the city to the Pool of Siloam.

The Pool of Siloam to which Jesus sent this man, was only rediscovered in 2004. It was right at the southern end of the City of David, and was supplied via King Hezekiah's incredible water tunnel deep under the city. The water came from a spring five hundred yards away, outside the city wall: hence

---

[4] (9:4)
[5] (Matt 5:14)

why it was named 'Siloam' which means 'sent'. Designed to enable Jerusalem to withstand sieges, it was protected by a long, buttressed wall with towers at either end. Archaeology suggests these were built during the Greek Empire's occupation, but rebuilt sometime during the first century: backing up the historicity of Luke's account. The High Priest would have visited it every morning of the Feast, to fill the golden jug for the ceremony.

We are not told how the man managed to get to Siloam: presumably someone led him there. But everyone would have noticed the mud packs on his face, and wondered what was going on. He would have been well known in the city, recognisable to many from their trips to the Temple.

Once he had washed, he needed no helper to find his way back! For the first time in his life, he could see. Imagine how startlingly bright the colours would have seemed, how fascinating to see the life of the city which he had previously only been able to hear. And how intense it would be, to make eye-contact with your parents, friends and loved ones, for the very first time ever.

Why? Why did Jesus choose this incredibly odd method to bring healing to the man? We think of "mud in your eye" as meaning you are unable to see! We know that saliva was thought to have healing properties in those days, and some commentators think there is a link with the story of God creating Adam out of clay. Jesus's instructions made the man's healing dependent on his obedience, just as when Elisha told the Syrian Naaman to go to the Jordan and wash. It also guaranteed there would be many witnesses of the miracle, and that Jesus could quietly exit before pandemonium broke loose.

Legalism blinds one to God's grace

Importantly, all this happened on the sabbath: and there were at least three specific ways in which Jesus's action broke the detailed laws the rabbis had created. Firstly, one was not supposed to heal on the sabbath unless a man's life was at risk; secondly, mixing saliva and dust into a paste was forbidden; and thirdly, using such a paste as eye ointment was specifically forbidden too!

Jesus's healing of the man at the pool of Bethesda eighteen months previously, had led to accusations that he was a sabbath-breaker. Whilst His concern was to be getting on with His Father's agenda, the Pharisees' concern was to do with the details of their law. But behind that was their desire to discredit and eventually kill him.

The man's family & neighbours were astonished when they saw him, and couldn't quite believe their eyes! When he confirmed that he *was* the same man they'd known for years as a beggar, they asked him how his eyes had been opened. Of course, at this point he had not actually seen Jesus, but he must have heard someone use His name. By now, Jesus had withdrawn, and the man had no idea how to find him again.

Everyone knew that the authorities had been trying to arrest Jesus and have him killed. The Sanhedrin had issued an edict that anyone who publicly acknowledged Jesus as the Messiah would be excommunicated[6]: perhaps this was why they took the man to the Pharisees?[7]

The leaders quizzed him all over again, about *how* he had been healed. But they couldn't agree on whether the miracle meant that Jesus was a holy man, or alternatively, that he was breaking God's law. So they asked the man what he thought: and he said "He is a prophet". At this point he hasn't recognised Jesus as *the* Prophet, of whom Moses had spoken.

This was the beginning of this man's journey into faith. Later he will testify that Jesus is from God[8] and then believe that Jesus is the Son of God[9], eventually coming to worship Him. En route he gives feisty answers to those who want him to deny the reality of his experience. In this, he is very unlike the man at the Pool of Bethesda, who seems broken and passive[10], and rather than coming to faith, immediately betrays Christ to the Jews[11].

<u>Sanhedrin in denial</u>

Since the Sanhedrin couldn't agree what this sign meant, they decided to investigate further. If Jesus was a charlatan and this man's testimony was false, his parents would be the best people to corroborate or discredit his

---

[6] (9:22)
[7] (9:13)
[8] (9:33)
[9] (9:35-38)
[10] (5:7)
[11] (5:15)

testimony. So they called them in and asked them three questions: (a) Is this your son? (b) Was he born blind? (c) How was he healed?

The man's parents confirmed the first two questions; but could not be eye-witnesses as to how or by whom he was healed. Whilst they presumably were overjoyed at their son's healing, they weren't willing to face being ostracised from the synagogue on his behalf. Being banned from the synagogue was a serious matter. It was as shameful as being excluded from the community of Israel the Exodus, such as had happened to Miriam[12]. Since he was past the 'age of majority', they argued, let him answer for himself.

During the Babylonian exile, when they had nowhere to worship, Jews began gathering in small groups (called in Greek, synagogues) to read the Law of God. The Temple was the only place authorised for sacrifice, so they had no altar. But each synagogue had an 'ark', which contained the scrolls of the Torah and Prophets.

The service would start with the Shema (Hear, O Israel, the Lord our God, the Lord is One), then blessings and prayers, then a set reading from the Torah and an optional reading from the Prophets, perhaps accompanied by a sermon.

Reading and expounding the word of God was central to the life of the local community; but along with that the synagogue also functioned as a hub for education and civil governance of the local Jewish community. (The word 'synagogue' simply means 'coming together for a purpose': its Hebrew equivalent is Knesset.)

In Nehemiah's time he set up 'The Great Synagogue', a gathering of 120 elders of Israel which would later develop into the Sanhedrin. And in Jesus's time there was a synagogue within the Temple, presumably where the rulers met. But there were also around four hundred separate synagogues within the city: apparently any group of more than ten men would be

[12] (Num 12:14)

In Jesus's time, exclusion from the synagogue took three forms. The least serious involved a public rebuke, and lasted a week. The next, lasted a month. But the most serious was indefinite, and involved total ostracism. No-one would talk to you, help you, employ you or do business with you; and all your property would be confiscated.[13] If a local synagogue excommunicated you, you could go somewhere else. But if the Sanhedrin banned you, you were barred from all synagogues, everywhere. It seems that this is the type of ban which had been promulgated here. And it must have happened very recently, since just a few days earlier, there had been people confessing faith in Jesus within the Temple itself.[14]

The man now faced a third interrogation. He was invited to *'give God the glory'* - a phrase meaning to confess one's sin.[15] They certainly didn't want him giving *Jesus* any glory! They were convinced (they said) that He was a charlatan.

To disagree with their opinion meant going directly against the Sanhedrin: and if his parents knew the dreadful cost that would involve, presumably he did too. Nevertheless, whilst denying any opinion about Jesus's character, he would not deny the reality of what had happened: *"One thing I know: that though I was blind, now I see"*.

They pressed him to explain exactly how the miracle was performed,[16] perhaps hoping to elicit some inconsistencies that would discredit his account. But by now he understood that their real motives had little to do with getting to the truth. He referred them back to his previous answer, suggesting sarcastically that they too wanted to become disciples.

They began cursing him for stupidity: they are disciples of Moses, who everyone knew heard directly from God - whereas he is following this fellow from God-knows-where. In this they spoke truth; they thought they knew Jesus's earthly origins[17], but certainly didn't know the God who sent Him[18].

---

[13] (Ezra 10:8)
[14] (8:30)
[15] (Josh 7:19)
[16] (9:26)
[17] (7:27)
[18] (7:28,29)

The man would not be intimidated: quite astonishing for someone who has been vulnerable all his life long. He mocked them for not knowing Jesus's origins. The simple fact that He had done a miracle never seen before, attested that He had God's ear. As such, He cannot be a sinner, but must be from God. The man might have added that this miracle was known to be one that only Messiah could perform[19] - but they already knew that.

They responded with pure arrogance, as they had previously.[20] Since he had never been able to study either the scriptures or the Mishnah, let alone been 'a student of the learned', they saw him as no better than an animal. Ignoring what Jesus had told them about their own origins as children of the devil, they castigated him as 'completely evil by birth' - and excommunicated him.

<u>The blind man sees who Jesus is: the Pharisees don't</u> (9:35-41)

Now comes the meat of the chapter: the meaning of this sign. How does it help us see the glory of Christ, *'full of grace and truth'?* [21]

Jesus heard that the man had been thrown out of the synagogue, and thus knew that the authorities considered he had acknowledged Jesus as the Christ.[22] He tracks him down and asks, *"Do you believe in the Son of God?"*

The man, who hasn't yet come to a full realisation of who Jesus is, addresses Him as *'Lord' and* asks for clarification *'that I may believe in Him'*. He has such a different attitude to the Pharisees, who only ask so as to condemn Him.[23]

Jesus now opens the man's eyes a second time: this time, his spiritual eyes. *"You have both seen Him and it is He talking with you".* He who was born blind, spiritually as well as physically, can now see in both realms! The man falls to the ground and worships Jesus as God: he has seen *"the light of the knowledge of the glory of God in the face of Jesus Christ".*[24]

His physical blindness, whilst very real, is symbolic of his need for spiritual enlightenment. Like the rest of mankind, all of us, we are 'born blind' and

---

[19] (Isa 35:5, Matt 11:2-5)
[20] (7:45-52)
[21] (1:14)
[22] (9:22)
[23] (Mt 26:63)
[24] (2Cor 4:8)

need Jesus to give us spiritual vision. Jesus is indeed 'the Light of the world'! *'In Him was life, and the life was the light of men'*[25].

Jesus goes on to explain what the man has just experienced. The Pharisees were judging Jesus, not the man himself. Jesus's incarnation forces people to make a judgement about His identity. Their judgement of Him, is what will determine His judgement of them on the Last Day.

Whilst He did not come into the world to condemn people but to save them, those who won't believe in His Name - won't believe that He is the *I AM* - are condemned already. *"Light has come into the world, and men loved darkness rather than light, because their deeds were evil. They refuse to come to the light, lest their sins should be exposed"*.

Apparently the Pharisees were shadowing Jesus, for there were some present listening to His words.[26] They must have realised that His remarks were directed at them, for they ask, *"Are we blind too?"* Jesus tells them it is their hypocrisy that is tying them to their sins and preventing them seeing.

Just as the blind man showed a progressive growth in faith, they show a progressive hardening of their heart. They start from the view that Jesus is not from God[27], question the miracle[28], label Jesus a sinner[29], and finally are pronounced blind sinners themselves[30].

Those who ask *'Who is He, Lord, that I may believe'* receive their sight. But those who claim spiritual insight and refuse to acknowledge their sinfulness, thereby bind themselves to their sin and become blind to who Jesus really is.

The Jews' blindness is part of God's plan

Whilst there is definitely personal responsibility for the Jews' refusal to accept the Light, there is also a deeper dimension to their blindness.

---

[25] (1:4)
[26] (9:40)
[27] (9:16)
[28] (9:18)
[29] (9:29)
[30] (9:31)

When Isaiah saw the Lord in the Temple, he was told to *"Go and tell this people: keep on hearing, but do not understand; keep on seeing, but do not perceive. Make the hearts of this people dull, and their ears heavy, and shut their eyes; lest they see with their eyes, and hear with their ears, and understand with their heart, and return and be healed".*[31]

Paul says that the Jews' minds were blinded, and there is a veil over their hearts when they read the Old Testament, in that they cannot see that all Moses's writings are testifying of Jesus. But nevertheless when a Jew turns to Christ, that veil is taken away.

He declares that this is all part of God's mysterious plan which should keep us Gentiles humble: *"Blindness in part has happened to Israel until the fullness of the Gentiles has come in. Then all Israel shall be saved, when Christ returns as the Deliverer and turns away all ungodliness from Israel"*[32]

This chapter highlights a major theme of John's gospel: that

the Incarnation brings about both salvation and judgement, depending on a man's response to the Person of Jesus Christ.

Believing in Jesus is the 'work' that God looks for.[33] *Unbelief* brings condemnation here and now[34]; whereas *belief* means a man has already passed from death to life[35]. Those children of the devil who receive Him, are given authority to become children of God.[36] Whereas those who shy away from His purity, inherit all their ancestors' guilt: they are 'a brood of vipers', and won't escape the condemnation of hell[37] but will die in their sins.

God's very act of injecting His Son into human history separates men into two camps: the redeemed, who receive and love Him, and the condemned, who reject and hate Him.

---

[31] (Isa 6:9-10)
[32] (Rom 11:25-26)
[33] (6:29)
[34] (3:18)
[35] (5:24)
[36] (Eph 2:1-7)
[37] (Mt 23:33)

Our wonderful Shepherd (10:1-42)

In contrast to the Jewish leaders, Jesus's role is that of a good shepherd: genuine, protecting, committed, understanding, self-sacrificing and reliable. He makes His last appeal to the Judaeans, to grasp His true identity.

At this point in John's Gospel, the mood begins to change: from the conflict with the Jewish authorities, to sorrowful love. It makes perfect sense that after sustained attack from the Jewish leadership, and having just told them they are spiritually blind, Jesus now speaks about the nature of godly leadership and His role as the good shepherd.

Six hundred years earlier, the prophet Ezekiel had castigated Israel's leadership as being selfish, uncaring and cruel shepherds.[1] He had prophesied that God Himself would become Israel's true shepherd; re-gathering them, feeding them, protecting and blessing them. *"I will establish one shepherd over them - My servant David. He shall feed them and be their shepherd. And I, the LORD, will be their God, and my servant David, a prince among them."*

The Judaeans clearly recognised this Messianic reference, for it re-inflamed the debate about Jesus's identity.[2] Eventually one day they swarmed Him in the Temple cloisters, demanding He declare once-and-for-all whether He was Messiah. His reply led to fresh attempts to stone or arrest Him, and He went into internal exile on the far side of the Jordan.

An overview of the chapter

Israel had suffered from bad shepherds (leaders) down through the centuries. Ezekiel prophesied against them, saying God would require accountability for the ways in which they had abused His flock.[3] The priesthood had become so money-grabbing under Annas and Caiaphas, that the Temple had become 'a den of thieves'.[4] But the Pharisees were no better: Jesus repeatedly warned

---

[1] (Ezek 34)
[2] (!0:19-21)
[3] (Ezek 34:1-10)
[4] (Mk 11:17)

His disciples against their hypocrisy. Indeed it is on them that Jesus focusses a fearsome list of *woes*, or curses, just before His crucifixion.[5]

The Pharisees and Sanhedrim have just crystallised their cruel self-interested motivation in their handling of the man born blind: a 'lost sheep of the House of Israel'. They are the thieves and hired hands to whom Jesus will refer.

But the focus here is not so much about condemning their failures, but to bring out the wonderful character of the Good Shepherd:-

- the wonderful love & care of the Shepherd for His sheep
- the incredible bond between Him & them, similar to Him & His Father
- the utter security of the flock, in His care

Though most read this chapter as continuous, John inserts a time marker (the Feast of Hanukah) halfway through. This feast took place three months after the Feast of Tabernacles, in the depths of mid-winter.

The feast had been instituted in 164 BC, when Jewish guerrillas recaptured the Temple from Antiochus Epiphanes, ruler of the Greek Empire. A tiny amount of holy oil for the menorah lamps, lasted for seven days while the rededication of the Temple took place. So the feast's theme was about overcoming evil rulers through recommencing true worship.

Another key to comprehension, is that Jesus uses the shepherd illustration in several different ways. The Pharisees can't grasp it at first[6], so He repeatedly tries again[7]. He uses and re-uses the same simile of sheep and shepherd, to show out different aspects of His character as the Good Shepherd.

We might summarise these different aspects as:-

- Genuineness (vss 1-5)
- Protectiveness (vss 7-10)
- Courageous commitment (vss 11-13)
- Relationship with each sheep, not limited to one flock (vss 14-16)
- God-authorised self-sacrifice (vss 17-18)

---

[5] (Matt 23:1-36)

[6] (10:6)

[7] (10:7-18,26-31)

- Eternal care (vss 27-30)

Shepherding in Israel

Before we can properly understand what this passage would have conveyed to its original hearers, we also need to know something about shepherding in Israel, which was quite unlike modern-day sheep farming in UK!

Judaea had a long thin plateau running north-south with deep gorges radiating out from it to the Jordan (east) and the Mediterranean (west). This high ground was rocky, much more suited to sheep farming than cultivation. Vegetation was sparse, meaning the shepherd regularly had to find new pasture and move the flock.

There were no walls to enclose the sheep: it was more like the high moorland commons of northern England. But the sheep didn't get 'hefted' to a particular patch of land, and so were prone to wander. This meant that unlike here in UK, you would never see a flock unattended. A shepherd was with them constantly.

As well as a knapsack of food, the shepherd carried a 'rod' (crook) and a 'staff' (cudgel) as his two main tools. There were plenty of sheep-rustlers around; lions, bears and wolves were commonplace; and a wandering sheep might well get stuck on a ledge or in a gorge, and need rescuing. If a sheep *was* lost, the shepherd was held responsible - unless he could produce its hooves or horns to prove it had been eaten by a predator.

Another major difference was that sheep were kept primarily for their wool rather than for meat. This meant they lived much longer, and the bond between sheep and shepherd was much deeper. Each shepherd spoke to his sheep in a unique 'tongue' quite distinct from ordinary Hebrew. He would have specific names for each sheep, often based on their distinguishing features. Though not hefted to any particular place, the sheep *were* attuned to their shepherd's voice. So it was possible to have a common sheepfold for a village, where flocks would mingle overnight, but for them to gather to their own shepherd when called in the morning.

Since shepherds didn't have sheepdogs, their leading the flock had to rely on attraction from the front, rather than threatening from behind! The shepherd went ahead of the sheep, which meant he could look out for patches of good grass, and places for them to drink. He never required them to go somewhere he had not already been ahead of them.

There were two different sorts of sheepfold: the large communal one just mentioned, which had a sturdy, lockable door and a guard each night; and much smaller sheepfolds out on the hills. Those were suitable only for a single flock, and had a narrow entrance but no door. When the shepherd had gathered his flock, he would lie across the entrance such that he himself was the 'door of the sheep': nothing could go in or out unless he allowed it.

How shepherds called their flocks

In 1860, H.V.Morton observed how a Jewish shepherd talked to his sheep:

"Sometimes he talks to them in a loud sing-song voice, using a weird language unlike anything I have ever heard in my life. The first time I heard this sheep and goat language I was on the hills at the back of Jericho. A goat-herd had descended into a valley and was mounting the slope of an opposite hill, when turning round, he saw his goats had remained behind to devour a rich patch of scrub. Lifting his voice, he spoke to the goats in a language that Pan must have spoken on the mountains of Greece. It was uncanny because there was nothing human about it. The words were animal sounds arranged in a kind of order.

No sooner had he spoken than an answering bleat shivered over the herd, and one or two of the animals turned their heads in his direction. But they did not obey him. The goat-herd then called out one word, and gave a laughing kind of whinny. Immediately a goat with a bell round his neck stopped eating, and, leaving the herd, trotted down the hill, across the valley, and up the opposite slopes. The man, accompanied by this animal, walked on and disappeared round a ledge of rock.

Very soon a panic spread among the herd. They forgot to eat. They looked up for the shepherd. He was not to be seen. They became conscious that the leader with the bell at his neck was no longer with them. From the distance came the strange laughing call of the shepherd, and at the sound of it the entire herd stampeded into the hollow and leapt up the hill after him"

Having set the scene extensively, now we'll focus on what the passage itself tells us about Jesus, our wonderful Shepherd! He is ...

<u>Our genuine Shepherd</u> (10:1-5)

Jesus's arrival as the Shepherd of Israel has none of the skulduggery of a sheep-rustler. He's genuine; and both the doorkeeper (?John the Baptist) and His own sheep recognise Him. They are attracted by the sound of His voice, whereas they will flee from a stranger's voice.

We will hear much more about this deep bond between the Shepherd and His sheep as we go on. But inwardly, we recognise that *'We are His people, the sheep of His pasture'.*[8] Not hefted to a particular congregation or denomination so much as to the Shepherd Himself.

The context shows that the sheepfold is Israel; this sheepfold is large enough to have a door keeper, meaning it contains multiple flocks - the different sects & interest groups within Israel. The psalmist addresses God as the *Shepherd of Israel*[9], calling on Him to come and save the nation.

The thieves and robbers are the Pharisees and Sanhedrim whom Jesus has just been dealing with. Thieves come stealthily, whereas robbers use overt force. We see both in operation, in their stealthy attempts to have Jesus arrested or to discredit Him; and the use of authoritarian force in shutting His followers out of the synagogues.

Not all Israel will respond to the Shepherd's call: only His own sheep. And He will call them by name - individually. He will call out a remnant - a small handful - from amongst the nation as a whole, for *'Not all Israel, is Israel'*[10]. They will hear His voice, in the sense of believing His teaching: unlike the Pharisees[11]. And they will follow Him: follow His teachings; follow Him in bringing the gospel message to a hostile world; follow Him in feeding His sheep; follow Him in denying themselves and taking up their crosses.

---

[8] (Ps 100:3)
[9] (Ps 80:1)
[10] (Rom 9:6)
[11] (10:26)

Peter writes to Christian leaders: *"Shepherd the flock of God which is among you, serving as overseers, not by compulsion but willingly, not for dishonest gain but eagerly; nor as being lords over those entrusted to you, but being examples to the flock; and when the Chief Shepherd appears, you will receive the crown of glory that does not fade away".*[12]

<u>Our protecting Shepherd</u> (10:7-10)

Jesus recycles the simile for a different purpose. This time He is talking of a small sheep pen out in the fields, suitable for only one flock, one shepherd. The shepherd Himself is the door. *"No-one comes to the Father, but by Me."*[13]

There had been many false saviours and false Messiahs, prior to Jesus; and there would be many more after.[14] Each time, the Roman Empire stepped in to quash rebellion, and the followers were massacred. When a Jewish city was under siege, its gates would be shut up. So to be able to come and go unmolested was a Jewish aphorism for a life that is absolutely secure and safe. With Jesus, His followers come into the sheepfold (now meaning the Church) through Him: and they can go in and come out, not in the sense of intermittent church membership, but of security!

"The LORD *will preserve you from all evil; He shall preserve your soul. The* LORD *shall preserve your going out and your coming in, from this time forth and even forevermore."*[15].

Unlike the thief's motives, which are about death and destruction, Jesus's motive is that we might have ever-increasing spiritual life. Not just enough to stay alive, but an overflow, a surplus to give to others. As we'll see later, that life consists of knowing the only true God, and His Son Jesus.[16] He wants our relationship with Him to grow deeper and deeper!

"The Lord is my Shepherd; I shall not want. He makes me lie down in green pastures; He leads me beside the still waters. He restores my soul. He leads me in the path of righteousness for His name's sake. Yea, though I walk

---

[12] (1Pet 3:2-4)
[13] (14:6)
[14] (Acts 5:35-37)
[15] (Ps 121:8)
[16] (17:3)

through the valley of the shadow of death, I will fear no evil; for You are with me; your rod and your staff, they comfort me."[17]

Our courageous, committed Shepherd (10:11-13)

Wolves were a common threat for a flock. If wolves attacked, the hireling shepherd thought only of saving his own skin, and ran away. Jesus's point is that the man who works only for reward thinks chiefly of the money; the man who works for love thinks chiefly of the people he is trying to serve. Paul warned the elders of Ephesus that grievous wolves would come, not sparing the flock.[18]

The Greek word translated good is 'kalos'. There was a separate word for inner goodness; but *kalos* meant outward, observable goodness. It could also mean attractive & beautiful: so *noble* might be a nearer match in English.

But there is another more vital issue of translation hidden in the Greek: the words for 'life' in verses 10 and 11 are not the same!

The ultimate thief, the Devil, comes to kill and steal and destroy. But Jesus came so that we might have ***zoe*** life: eternal, spiritual life, coming from our fellowship with the Father and the Son.[19] The noble shepherd stands His ground between us and the enemy, taking all the ridicule and shame and humiliation they can heap on Him; and ultimately laying down His ***psyche*** (human life) for us sheep: totally focussed on our welfare not His own.

This is agape love in action:

"Greater love hath no man than this, that a man lay down His life for His friends."[20]

"God demonstrates His own love towards us, in that while we were still sinners, Christ died for us."[21]

The key to Christs's character is that unlike the hired hand, He is committed to caring for us[22]: *you matter, to Him*. Satan will often tempt us to believe

---

[17] (Ps 23:1-4)

[18] (Acts 20:29)

[19] (17:3)

[20] (15:13)

[21] (Rom 5:8)

[22] (10:13)

that He doesn't care; that He's angry with us, or so distant that He can't be bothered with our trivial problems. But the truth is, He cares; and this is a massive reason to pray: *"Cast all your cares upon Him, for He cares for you".*[23]

<u>Our deeply-aware Shepherd</u> (10:14-16)

Another aspect of the noble Shepherd is that He knows His sheep.

There is something deeply reassuring in knowing that you are known. I once experienced a nurse calling me back to consciousness after a long anaesthetic, and the fact that she knew my name felt like I was hearing the voice of God! Our parents are a great source of this comfort, and spouses too. But still for most people there is a hunger to know and to be known more deeply: a spiritual loneliness, if you will.

The noble Shepherd knows His sheep. He knows each of us is different, with our own unique strengths and struggles. He knows we are all wayward soul-wise, and spiritually helpless. He knows every detail of our life history, everything that has shaped and formed us. And He loves us unconditionally.

His knowledge of us is both supernatural (omniscience, such as He showed with Nathanael) but also natural. Since He has been tempted in every way that we are (though He never sinned), He sympathises with us in our weaknesses, and is the ideal Intercessor.[24]

His heart's desire is for us to know Him; and to know Him more and more deeply. And that through Him, that we might know the Father.[25] This is the essence of eternal life[26] - to know Him, and His Father.

John later writes, *"That which was from the beginning, which we have heard, which we have seen with our eyes, which we have looked upon, and our hands have handled, concerning the Word of life, ... This we declare to you, that you also may have fellowship with us; and truly our fellowship is with the Father and with His Son Jesus Christ".*[27]

---

[23] (1Pet 5:7)
[24] (Heb 4:15)
[25] (14:7-9)
[26] (17:3)
[27] (1John 1:1-3)

Our knowledge of Him, our fellowship with Him, comes in different ways.

We gradually grow in our grasp of the revelation He has given us in scripture. We grow in our assurance of His goodness and mercy.[28] We grow in our experience of His victory over the world, the flesh and the devil in our lives.

But John is referring to something beyond these. True, he had entered heaven and seen Jesus in His glory.[29] But a one-off vision is not what he is referring to. *Fellowship* is a daily reality of the awareness of God's Presence, as both Father and Son: daily communion with them, as real as when John's eyes had seen Jesus on earth, or heard Him, or touched Him.

Our knowing of Christ, is to be like His knowing of His Father.[30] He was continuously aware of His Father's heart, and His Father's intentions and actions. He is continually fathered through all eternity, His Father showing Him everything He is doing.[31]

Calvary lay only six months away at this point. It is because Jesus knows His Father's heart, that He is about to lay down His life for the sheep. But Jesus can see way beyond that: He can see that the Father has given Him multitudes of sheep that are 'not of this fold'; non-Jews. The gospel is to be preached 'to the Jew first, but also to the Gentiles'.[32] They too will hear the voice of the Son of God, calling them into life.[33]

<u>Our God-ordained sacrifice</u> (10:17-18)

The Shepherd is the Lamb of God!

The Shepherd, out of His voluntary submission to the Father, yearns with His Father's heart for the redemption of mankind. He will not die of natural causes, or of man's malice, or as a miscarriage of Roman justice; but voluntarily. He will lay down His *soul*-life willingly, which is why the Father says of Him, *'This is My beloved Son, in whom I am well pleased'*[34].

---

[28] (Ps 23:6)
[29] (Rev 1:9-17)
[30] (10:15)
[31] (5:19-20)
[32] (Matt 28:20; Rom 1:16)
[33] (5:25)
[34] (Mt 3:17)

Before the foundation of the world, He had committed to being 'the Lamb whom God would provide'; the real sacrifice to whom all other sacrifices pointed. When He came into the world, He said: *"Sacrifice and offering You did not desire, But a body You have prepared for Me. In burnt offerings and sacrifices for sin You had no pleasure. Then I said, 'Behold, I have come In the volume of the book it is written of Me - To do Your will, O God.' "* [35]

His sacrifice is for us wayward sheep. *"All we like sheep have gone astray; we have turned everyone to his own way; and the Lord has laid on Him the iniquity of us all."*[36]

The Father had not only authorised Him to lay down His own life, but also to take it again.[37] Christ died in order to rise, and by rising, to be glorified, and be seated at the Father's right hand - with the glory He had in eternity past[38]. From there, He would pour out the Spirit, so that all His flock might have eternal life[39].

<u>Our everlasting Shepherd</u> (10:27-30)

The flock have been given to Jesus by His Father. While He was in the world, He lost none of them except Judas, the 'son of perdition'. On leaving the world, He prays that His Father would keep them from the evil one, by sanctifying them with His word of truth. Father and Son are utterly One, just as much in keeping and sanctifying His people as in their original salvation.[40]

Because the Father is greater than all, and has given Jesus the highest of all names, no-one will be able to snatch any true saint out of Their hands. Occasionally we hear of children being snatched on the street; but we are as safe as if we were being held between our Father's hand on one side, and our big brother's hand on the other.

As sheep, we are inherently wayward, prone to wander and stray. But we are *'kept by the power of God, through faith, for a salvation ready to be revealed*

---

[35] (Heb 10:5–7)
[36] (Isa 53:3-6)
[37] (10:17,18)
[38] (17:5)
[39] (10:28)
[40] (10:30)

in the last time'.[41] Providing we follow the shepherd and stay with the flock, we are utterly secure in His care: not even Satan can snatch us away.

This security-which-endures marks out all true saints.

> *Blessed assurance, Jesus is mine!*
> *Oh what a foretaste of glory divine!*
> *Heir of salvation, purchase of God,*
> *Born of His Spirit, washed in His blood.*

Christ and the Church

What does this passage teach us about Christ's relationship with the Church?

- He calls people individually into the Church. For example, Peter James & John; Phillip[42]; Matthew[43]; Zacchaeus etc etc. Each one has been individually given to Him by the Father; entrusted to His care. We cannot become His by joining a particular church, going through a particular rite, or being born to Christian parents: we must be called personally, by Him.
- Though He calls from different sheepfolds - Jews first, Gentiles later - we are all one in Christ Jesus. Our unity is in the Shepherd. He is the Head of the Church. There is to be one flock: Jews and Gentiles together will form a new man, a new type of human society[44] without barriers of race or culture.
- His sheep recognise His voice. Mary Magdalene thought He was the gardener, until she heard Him speak.[45] It is a promise of Christ, that you too will be able to recognise His voice. If you don't feel you can, or envy others their apparent ease in hearing, claim Christ's promise from the Father.
- He leads us: He is the *Great* Shepherd; all others are under-shepherds. He nurtures and nourishes us[46], leading us to fresh pastures and still waters;

---

[41] (1Pet 1:5)
[42] (1:43)
[43] (Matt 9:9)
[44] (Eph 3:11-19)
[45] (20:15,16)
[46] (10:9-10)

restoring our souls day by day. He will never ask us to face something He has not faced, or go somewhere He has not gone before us.

- He knows us inside out. He knows each of us, just as He knew Nathanael.[47] His desire and intention is that our knowledge of Him goes deeper and deeper, that the life that comes through our fellowship with Him and His Father grow more and more abundant. The steamed-up mirror of our present sight will clear, till we know Him as fully as we are known.[48]
- We are utterly secure in His hands. Nothing and no-one in heaven or earth or under the earth, can abduct us from His care.[49]

The role of pastors

The word 'pastor' is just the Latin version of the word 'shepherd'. Jesus is referred to as 'the Great Shepherd of the sheep'; everyone with a pastoral ministry, whether ordained or informal, is an 'under-shepherd' who models themselves on Jesus's example. Every aspect of Jesus's character which is brought out in this chapter, is necessary in such a role. But most of all, we need His shepherd heart.

Shepherds must feed their flock with the word of God, and enable them to drink of the Spirit. They must beat off attacking predators with their cudgel, but also rescue sheep from their own stupidity using a crook. Sometimes a fierce attack will come which causes the sheep to scatter and become even more vulnerable: we see this when churches suddenly fall apart. These are the wolves. But other times, people within a congregation try to develop a following of their own and draw members away, forming sects within the church and eventually leading to schisms.[50] They are the thieves.

Whatever the form of attack, if we are pastors we need to step in between the flock and the threat; even if it means the attack then focusses on us. Very often the attack will come against us, as it did with Jesus: for the enemy knows that if he can strike the shepherd, the sheep will be scattered and be

---

[47] (1:47-50)

[48] (1Cor 13:12)

[49] (Rom 8:35-39)

[50] (Acts 20:26-35)

that much more vulnerable to predation. We need Jesus's *courage*, His *care* for each individual, His *commitment* to shepherd everyone God has entrusted to us, His *compassion* for their weaknesses and foolishnesses.

<u>Jesus's identity challenged again</u> (10:19-42)

Jesus's teaching about the good Shepherd who would lay down His life and take it up again, caused intense controversy amongst the Jews. Some were clear He was crazy, possessed by a spirit of megalomania.[51] Others realised the significance of healing a man with congenital blindness.[52] It seems that this theme of Him being the good Shepherd was dominant throughout this climactic period between Tabernacles and Hanukah. Passover, and Calvary, lay only three months ahead.

Three months after Tabernacles, came the Feast of Dedication, (now known as Hanukah). This feast had been instituted by Judas Maccabee following his guerrilla war to reclaim the Temple from the Greek emperor Antiochus, who had desecrated it. Its rededication climaxed in the re-lighting of the Menorah; the seven-branched candelabra in the Holy Place, signifying the Spirit's presence and the light of the Spirit-inspired word of God.

Jesus was walking in Solomon's Cloister. Being on the east side of the mount, it would have offered some shelter from the winter winds. Knowing everything about the Temple was symbolic, He was perhaps thinking of how His body would soon be defiled at Calvary, and then raised to life and glorified. He knew He would be rededicated to serving the Church, through His dual roles of being our High Priest and pouring out the Spirit. In fact He dedicated Himself to this new role, the night before He was crucified.[53]

His meditation was rudely interrupted by some Jews, who surrounded Him threateningly, blocking any avenue of escape. They were annoyed by Jesus's refusal to clarify whether He was the Messiah they were expecting, or not? Though He had declared Himself to the woman at the well[54] and the man

---

[51] (10:20)
[52] (10:21)
[53] (17:19)
[54] (4:25,26)

born blind[55], and had confirmed His disciples' understanding[56], He had studiously avoided declaring it publicly: because His role as suffering Servant was so different from the military Messiah-ship the people hoped for.

He knew the term carried all kinds of mistaken connotations, and would likely lead to Him being forced to become an earthly King[57]: and He knew that His Kingdom was not of this world. It would also have brought down the wrath of Rome prematurely. But these zealous Jews, whose Pharisee ancestors had formed the backbone of Judas Maccabee's forces, wanted a black-or-white, yes-or-no answer. The Feast, with its commemoration of national liberation, had perhaps stirred them to think it was now or never, to rebel against Rome.

Disconcertingly, Jesus says He has *already* told them: His miracles, especially the Messianic miracle of healing a man born blind, have clearly demonstrated who He is. All His signs were done in His Father's Name. Just as Peter would later use the authority of Jesus's Name to heal the lame man at the Temple gate[58], so Jesus was operating not in His own authority, but in His Father's power. The fact that God enabled these miracles, attested His identity.

They have had many proofs of Jesus's identity, and yet they still don't believe. Their unbelief shows that they cannot hear His voice: to them it is like the mysterious sing-song tones of a shepherd to his sheep. This in turn shows that they are not His sheep: they are not part of the flock which His Father has given Him. In fact, as He had told them[59], they belong to a different flock, whose 'father' is the devil!

They may pride themselves on their religious observance and patriotic fervour, but they will never know or be known by Him, or follow Him. When He sits on His throne of judgement, He will say to them, *"I never knew you; depart from Me, you who practice lawlessness!"*[60]

By contrast, those who can hear His voice, *are* known by Him and *do* follow Him, and have utterly secure spiritual life. No sheep-rustler, however

---

[55] (9:35-37)
[56] (Mt 16:13-16)
[57] (6:15)
[58] (Acts 3)
[59] (8:43,44)
[60] (Mt 7:23)

determined, will ever be able to abduct them from His Father's grip. Father and Son are both determined to keep them safe: *"I and the Father are one".*[61]

<u>Another attempt to kill Him</u> (10:31-42)

This was just too much for the Jews: to be excluded from Messiah's kingdom, whilst others much less worthy (in their eyes) were utterly secure inside. But Jesus had at last given them justification for stoning Him for blasphemy. His last statement, they recognised, was more than just a claim to be in complete agreement with God. It was a claim to be God!

Their lifetime mantra, the Shema, said: *"Hear O Israel, the LORD our God, the LORD is One"*. But here was a man (the Greek means a human being, rather than a god) making Himself out to be God. In calling God His Father, He was claiming to be the Son of God: the unique, one-of-a-kind, only-begotten Son of the Father. And their Law said, *"He who blasphemes the name of the Lord shall be put to death; all the congregation shall stone him".*[62]

They got ready, picking up loose stones from the Temple's ongoing construction work. But Jesus challenged them saying, *"Which of My miracles, done in My Father's Name, is any justification for you to stone Me?"*

Under the Law, even if a so-called prophet did great miracles, if he led them astray from worshipping only Yahweh, he was to be killed.[63] They explain that it is blasphemy, not miracles, they are stoning Him for.

In response, Jesus quotes briefly from Psalm 82:6. The complete verse says, *'I said, "You are gods, and all of you are children of the Most High"'.*

The psalmist was referring to the appointment of judges amongst the people, just before the revealing of the Law at Sinai.[64] Those judges had become corrupt and unjust, showing favour to the wicked and failing to defend the poor and fatherless. They did not know or understand God's ways.

God declares that though He has appointed them as 'gods', like Him in having the power of life and death, they will nevertheless die like other men.

---

[61] (10:30)
[62] (Lev 24:16)
[63] (Deut 13:1-5)
[64] (Ex 18:18-26)

Jesus's argument goes like this: "If the word of God which you so prize, calls fallible Jewish judges 'gods', then why do you count it blasphemy for the one appointed as judge of all and sent into the world by Almighty God, to call Himself Son of God?"

He continues, "If I am not doing works which only Almighty God can do, then don't believe My words. But if I am, then even though you don't believe my words, believe the evidence of your eyes. Then you will know, and come to understand My and My Father's mutual indwelling." His unity with the Father is more than functional: it is unity of substance within the Godhead.

In referring to His sanctification by His Father, Jesus is referring them to the meaning of the Feast. If they are celebrating the dedication of the physical Temple after a period of defilement, why would they not celebrate the Father's dedication of His only-begotten Son, the living Temple, so that *'whoever believes in Him should not perish, but have everlasting life'*?

This is Jesus's last plea to the Jewish leaders to believe. It's their last opportunity to avoid the terrible curses He will pronounce if they do not.[65]

His argument was enough to stop them stoning Him, but not enough to prevent them seeking to arrest Him. Maybe they felt the issue needed to be tried before the Sanhedrin? As on several previous occasions, Jesus escaped. His time had not yet come, and His Father was still protecting Him.

Jesus now realises that He needs to lower the temperature, till Passover. He and His disciples withdraw to the place where He had been baptised by John, on the far side of the Jordan river[66]. This was where He had identified with mankind through baptism, and where His identity had been so clearly announced by John the Baptist. It was where His Father had declared, *"This is My beloved Son, in whom I am well pleased"*.

The locals remembered those events well, and realised that everything John has said about Him had proved true - even though John himself had done no miracles to validate his ministry. Many believed in Jesus at this time: the contrast with the skeptical Judaean leaders could not have been more stark!

---

[65] (Mt 23)

[66] (10:40)

Death defeated! (11:1-57)

Jesus demonstrates His authority over death, by raising Lazarus to life just outside Jerusalem. This puts the last nail in His own coffin.

Background

Bear with me as we study the context, before we dig into this chapter.

Where *was* Jesus when Lazarus fell ill?

He was at the site where John first baptised[1]; but where was that? We know that John baptised in various places, depending on where there was water.[2] The Jordan can virtually dry up in summer.

Matthew says Jesus was baptised by John in the 'wilderness of Judaea'; near Jerusalem, from where people flocked[3] to hear the Baptist. John's gospel refers to the site as *Bethany or Bethabara,* depending which manuscript you read. In either case it is specified as *'beyond Jordan'*, distinguishing it from the Jerusalem suburb of Bethany where Lazarus's family lived.

By the time Jesus arrived back at their house, Lazarus had been dead four days.[4] Their message would have reached Him within a day, and He replied with an encouraging response[5]; but then He delayed two days before setting off. Given the return took another day and He arrived four days after Lazarus died, death must have occurred very soon after they'd sent the messenger.

Jesus's comment that *"This sickness is not unto death"*[6], would thus have been spoken *the day after Lazarus had actually died.* The disciples assumed He meant Lazarus would recover naturally, and so there was no rush to return. But actually, He was delaying so as to amplify the impact on the disciples' faith. He had previously raised a widow's son, and Jairus's daughter, just after they'd died. But this was in a different league.

---

[1] (10:40)
[2] (3:23)
[3] (Matt 3:1-6)
[4] (11:39)
[5] (11:40)
[6] (11:4)

Jewish beliefs and customs about death

In Jewish thinking, a person's soul lurked near their body for three days after death, hoping to be able to return. By day four, the face of the dead man was changing colour as decay progressed: so the soul gave up, and departed. While the soul was still present, mourners made a big show of weeping and wailing, so that the deceased would know they really cared.

On the day someone died, their nearest-and-dearest would tear their inner garment from the neck downwards a handsbreadth, to express that their heart had been torn apart by the loss. They would visit the grave repeatedly for three days. For the first week they would not wash, anoint themselves, or wear shoes. Studying, and business of any kind, were also forbidden. Mourning continued for a month and then they were supposed to sew up the rip, signifying that mourning was now over.

Bodies had to be buried outside the community, since tombs were considered unclean. Not every town had a communal graveyard and anyway, they were mainly for the poor. Many families would have a grave cut into the rock, where over the years a number of family members would be buried. It seems Jesus didn't know where Mary & Martha had buried Lazarus[7]: though they had a rock-cut tomb with the traditional large millstone to seal it[8].

Where graves were near roads or paths, they were whitewashed every spring to ensure that pilgrims coming up for Passover would not accidentally become defiled by walking over them.

The fact that Martha and Mary had many good friends in Jerusalem, meant that there were lots of mourners to witness Lazarus's resurrection. So no-one could claim this was fake, or that he'd merely fainted!

Bethany's identity as 'House of affliction'

Bethany's name is now thought to mean 'House of affliction': and overall, the picture that emerges is of a town given to caring for the sick, the destitute, and pilgrims.

---

[7] (11:34)

[8] (11:39)

Anyone leaving Jerusalem for Jericho would have first come down from the Temple to the Kidron Valley, then climbed up the Mount of Olives: past Gethsemane and then through a huge graveyard. An estimated 150,000 Jews have been buried there over the last three thousand years, including prominent rabbis, and even David's son Absalom. Many of the tombs are cut into the rock, with a stone disk rolled across the entrance. Coming over the brow of the hill, the traveller would then descend to Bethany, which was around one-and-a-half miles from Jerusalem, before proceeding to Jericho.

Galileans coming to the feasts, used this road in the other direction. Having crossed the Jordan and come down its eastern bank to avoid Samaria, they would cross back at Jericho and walk up from there to Jerusalem. So Bethany was their last resting place before entering the city.

Archaeologists have discovered many ossuaries there from Jesus's time, with inscriptions of Galilean names. This suggests that not all the pilgrims made it (!) or else that many Galileans had settled there. Interestingly, while Jesus's first recorded encounter with Mary and Martha is in Galilee, by this point they have moved to Bethany. And Jesus stayed with them regularly during his visits to Jerusalem. Specifically, we know that He stayed with them during the week before the crucifixion, and He set off from there the day He entered Jerusalem on a donkey. And when He ascended, it was also from Bethany![9]

Bethany held a hospice for the sick and dying, run by the Essene sect. This sect, known for their community at Qumran where the Dead Sea scrolls were found, believed that Jerusalem and the Temple had become defiled by illness and death. So they chose three places round Jerusalem where they could care for such people outside the city. One of these was Bethany.

This may explain why, soon after Lazarus's resurrection, a banquet in His honour was held at the house of 'Simon the Leper'.[10] Normally lepers were kept well away from others, and were considered very unclean.

Lazarus's tomb still exists to this day, though now with a mosque built over it. The town now has the Arabic name, 'El Azariyah', commemorating the

---

[9] (Lk 24:50-53)

[10] (Matt 26:6,7)

amazing event that happened there. There is even a two-thousand-year-old house which claims to be that of Martha and Mary.

<u>The family's character and social standing</u>

Jesus's first encounter with this Galilean family is recorded in Luke 10:38-42. It was a curious household, with three unmarried adult siblings sharing a home. They seem to be unusually close: and Mary at least, had enough wealth to own a jar of highly expensive perfume, worth a year's wages. We can only guess at why this was the case. Had their parents died? Were Martha and Mary with Lazarus for safety, as single women? We are not told.

And why had they moved to Bethany? It was a town that cared for the sick, the destitute, and pilgrims. If Mary, Martha and Lazarus moved there from Galilee to be involved in such work, that would explain why they were apparently held in high esteem by many Jerusalemites.

Judas's objection to Mary's wasting the ointment, is the only time we hear the poor being mentioned in the gospels. Jesus's response that *'The poor are always with you'* fits well with the town's role as an almshouse.[11]

Everything we are about to read, fits with their characters. On that first occasion Mary sat at Jesus's feet hanging on His every word, whilst her elder sister Martha got more and more frustrated at her lack of support. Here, Martha's the practical one who sets out to meet Jesus before He is surrounded by weeping and wailing. Mary collapses at His feet in grief.

As we read on into John 12, we find Mary - as usual - at Jesus's feet, anointing Him for burial. She alone has realised that Lazarus's resurrection is going to cost Jesus's life. It represented the last straw for the Sanhedrin, and led to their formal decision to kill Him.

The following day He would ride down through the graves on the Mount of Olives, coming as the Lord of Life and Death to the city where He was to be crucified.

With all this context in mind, let's now dive into the chapter itself.

---

[11] (Mk 14:5-7; Mt 26:8–11; Jn 12:4–6)

Jesus summoned: Lazarus at death's door (11:1-16)

John starts by pointing out the depth of Mary's love for Jesus: she would subsequently bathe Jesus's feet with ultra-costly perfumed oil, then let down her hair to wipe the dirt off his feet. John-the-Baptist had counted himself unworthy to undo Jesus's sandal buckle: but Mary's love made her unashamed to express her devotion.

Mary knew Jesus loved her brother. She counted on that drawing Him back to Bethany, though she knew how dangerous that would be. The sisters must have been desperate, to ask Jesus to take this risk. It seems they had faith that Jesus could heal their brother, but only if He came soon, and in person.

If Jesus was in Bethabara, it took the messenger a day to reach Him. Jesus responded with a message that seemed reassuring: Lazarus's illness wouldn't end in death, but would bring glory to God. But by the time the messenger arrived back, Lazarus had already died: in fact, he'd died later the same day the message was sent. Had Jesus got it wrong, and given a false prophecy? The sisters' trust must have been shaken.

Worse, Jesus delayed coming for two days: was His mission more important to Him than their brother's life? But John knew that Jesus loved the whole family deeply.[12] In fact, it was *because of* His love that He delayed coming.[13]

Having made the decision to return, He invited His team to come with Him. They thought He was crazy to take the risk[14], but Jesus said they'd be safer with Him than staying back[15]. Just as there were (in Jewish timing) always twelve hours of daylight, when sunlight showed up any trip hazards, so until God brought the day to an end, He was absolutely safe doing the Father's will. This is *kairos* timing.

He then told them that Lazarus was asleep. The word He used means lying down or resting, but can also be used of death. Since He had said that Lazarus's illness wasn't terminal, they presumed Jesus meant he was now recovering. But Jesus clarifies that actually, Lazarus is *dead*! Strangely, He's

---

[12] (11:36)
[13] (11:5,6)
[14] (11:8)
[15] (11:9,10)

glad for *them* that He hadn't returned earlier. The extra delay will make the miracle all the greater, and develop their faith further.

Now they understand why Jesus is going, and that it's important they go too. In this instance, Thomas, known since the resurrection as 'Doubting Thomas', shows most courageous faith. Even if it costs him his life, he wants to follow Jesus. In the end ten of the Twelve *were* actually killed for Jesus's sake: Thomas subsequently took the gospel to India, and after twenty years was martyred there in AD 72 in Mylapore.

Jesus stretches Martha's faith (11:17-27)

Martha hears Jesus is coming. Ever the practical one, she leaves Mary and the mourners, to be able to greet Jesus in relative privacy. The encounter shocks her to the core. This man who she has cooked for, who has stayed in her house, who's her brother's best friend and her sister's hero, tells her that He is also the awesome Source of resurrection life! She comes face-to-face with the truth of the incarnation: He is fully God, though also fully Man.

As the account develops, watch Jesus stretching Martha's faith step by step:-

Her starting point:

"If you had been here my brother would not have died. But even now, I know that whatever You ask of God, God will give You."[16] She has faith in Jesus's ability to heal disease, but not death; and not from a distance. But she also has great faith that God grants Jesus's prayers. In this, she is right!

The first challenge to her faith:

Jesus challenges her by saying, *"Your brother will rise again'*. Lazarus may have died, but that isn't the end of the story.

She replies, *"I know Lazarus will rise again in the last day".*[17] She has faith in the eventual resurrection of the dead, but not in a here-and-now resurrection. We might imagine her thinking, 'Miracles have happened for other people in the past, and may happen for Lazarus after death, but not for me, and not today".

---

[16] (11:22)
[17] (11:24)

The revelation:

Jesus challenges her limited grasp of who He really is: *"I AM the resurrection and the life. He who believes in Me, though he may die, he shall live. And he who lives and believes in Me will never die. Do you believe this?"*

Jesus reveals that He is God, using the 'I AM' formula of Yahweh's divine name. Resurrection life is not some remote event in eternity future: it is already present in His Person, right in front of her, talking with her.

Jesus is, in His very Person, both *the* Resurrection and *the* Life. This is the same truth He had spoken in the Temple a year earlier.[18] His voice has power to call the dead to life, both physically and spiritually. The Father, who is the source of all eternal life, has given Jesus the same life *'in Himself'* - that is, in His own right[19]: and has also given Him the power to communicate it to whomever He wills[20].

When someone believes in Jesus, God judges them as righteous in Christ, and they never have to experience the judgement of God: they have passed from death to life. This life becomes ours, through our union with Christ.[21]

The Greek word for life used here is '*zoe*', meaning spiritual life - as opposed to '*psyche*' which means soul life, or '*bios*' which means bodily life. Though *zoe* is often translated as eternal life, the difference from ordinary life is not primarily about *duration* but *dimension*. There is a new, deeper, spiritual dimension to our lives which can never die. It starts now, not after death. Our bodies, which remain mortal, will eventually put on immortality. But our souls are already immortal!

The word Jesus uses here for death ('thanatos'), He also uses when referring to passing from death to life.[22] It refers not only to physical death, but also spiritual: it is the opposite of zoe life. If zoe life means union and communion with God in Christ, then death means separation from the life of God.

---

[18] (5:25-29)
[19] (5:26)
[20] (5:21)
[21] (1Jn 5:11,12)
[22] (5:24)

Two implications:

- *"He who believes in Me, though he may die, he shall live".* This sentence is easy enough: if a believer dies, as Lazarus just has, their physical death does not end their spiritual life (zoe), which goes on beyond the grave. And they will in due course experience bodily resurrection.

We have previously discussed that there are two distinct Greek words for 'in'; one refers to position, the other to movement. The sort of belief He is talking about, is 'belief *into* Me': not just belief that He is a wonderful man who once lived, but a belief that joins and embeds us in Him.

- *"And he who lives and believes in Me will never die".* This sentence is harder to interpret, for Christians who have eternal life and believe in Jesus, *do* go on to suffer physical death. The translation is unhelpful: Jesus actually said, 'shall not die unto the Age'. Jews believed that this present age would be followed by the Messianic Age. So Jesus was saying, everyone who believes in Me will be alive in My messianic Kingdom.

"The dead in Christ will rise first, then we who are alive shall be caught up together with them in the clouds to meet the Lord in the air. And thus we shall always be with the Lord"[23]

The second challenge:

Jesus challenges Martha again: *"Do you believe this?"*

Martha responds, *"Yes Lord, I believe that You are the Christ, the Son of God, who is to come into the world".*[24] This is a remarkable theological statement which acknowledges both Jesus's anointed manhood, and His full divinity. But there is more, when she says *"..who is to come into the world".* She has realised that Jesus will come again.

Theologians have two different Latin words for faith. 'Assensus' means theological assent to a doctrinal statement, whereas 'fiducia' means practical trust and reliance on a person. Martha has now accepted the truth that Jesus is both God and Man. But she has one more step to make. She must practically rely on this truth!

---

[23] (1Thess 5:17)

[24] (11:27)

Jesus sends her to fetch her sister. Once Mary has arrived, the stage will be set. It seems Mary did not need the conscious challenges Jesus gave Martha. Her faith was heart-rooted, not head faith.

The third challenge:

When Jesus goes to open the tomb, Martha is horrified: *"Lord, his corpse will be so rotten that he'll stink - it's four days now, You know!"*

As next of kin, Jesus needed her consent for the stone to be removed.

In this, His final challenge to stretch Martha's faith, Jesus encourages her to hold on to the specific promise He'd sent back with the messenger: *"Did I not say to you that if you would believe you would see the glory of God?"*

More than any of the other six 'signs', this miracle reveals the glory of God. And Martha still needs that revelation. But it will only be granted, if she relies on Jesus as the resurrection - and consents to the exhumation.

> As we watch Martha's faith being stretched, where are we on that continuum?
>
> - Generic belief in Jesus's power, that 'anything is possible' to Him?
> - Belief that Jesus Himself is the Source of eternal life?
> - Belief that He is both really man, and Son of God?

Jesus is moved to tears (11:28-37)

Jesus now sent Martha to fetch Mary. She tries to do so covertly, so that Mary too could meet Him in privacy. But despite the three days official mourning having passed, her friends have stayed out of concern for Mary. So when they realise she is leaving, they follow her.[25]

As with Martha, there's a note of regret, perhaps even anger, in Mary's comment: *"Lord if you had been here my brother would not have died"*. Unlike Martha, Mary doesn't soften this remark by a statement of trust. How

---

[25] (vss 28-31)

easily we blame God for apparently not answering our prayers in the way we want, when He has something better in mind!

Instead she falls at His feet weeping, which sets the mourners off wailing. Though fully aware He is about to raise Lazarus, Jesus nevertheless is distressed by this. He has deep compassion for her, being Himself *'a Man of sorrows and acquainted with grief'*.

But He is also deeply angry at the effects of Adam's sin on the whole human race, whereby death came into Eden. And perhaps He is angry too, that no-one has faith that He can raise Lazarus from the dead.

Some of the bystanders see His grief and are touched by His empathy. Others mock the fact that though He healed the man born blind, He hasn't been able to prevent Lazarus's death.

Jesus asks where they've buried Lazarus, and they invite Him to come and see. The tomb would definitely have been outside the village: but given that Bethany was on the eastern flank of the Mount of Olives, it may have been within the huge graveyard on the Mount's western flank.

As He approaches the tomb, the full horror of death comes home, and He too starts to weep. We can easily slip into thinking of God as distant and detached from human suffering; our own, and others'. Indeed in Greek thought, it was a given that God was impassive, untouched by human emotion. Jesus, who declares the Father's heart to us[26], shows us otherwise.

<u>Jesus calls Lazarus back to life</u> (11:38-44)

Jesus's anger remained, as He was shown to the grave. Lazarus's tomb was just the same as the one He Himself would be buried in, a few weeks later: it had a large millstone across the entrance. The reality, as Martha knew, was that inside there would be a stench. Lazarus had been dead four days, and in that climate decomposition would be well underway. His soul would have departed. What could Jesus be thinking of, asking to enter and see the body?

As next of kin, Jesus would need her consent for the stone to be removed. He reminds her of His message: *"Have faith, and you will see the glory of God"*;

---

[26] (1:18)

and she tremblingly agrees. Some of the mourners step forwards and put their shoulders to the stone, exposing the interior darkness to the bright daylight. They step away, covering their faces as the stench floods out.

Jesus paused and looks up to heaven, thanking His Father for hearing Him. This tells us He had previously prayed privately for Lazarus to be raised to life. He had known God would raise Lazarus, when He said, *"This illness is not unto death"* three days earlier. In fact, He also knew that it would end in glory for Himself, which would bring glory to God.[27]

Presumably He had prayed to His Father as soon as He heard the news that Lazarus was seriously ill. In doing so, He was demonstrating eternal life: continual fellowship with Father, utter dependence, doing only what He was shown to do.[28]

He thanked His Father not because this answer to prayer was special, for God *always* heard His prayers. He wanted the bystanders to know that the authority He was about to manifest, came not from Himself but from His Father! What was about to happen, was solely because He had been sent from the Father. Then He shouts, *"Lazarus, come out!"*

As the song goes, *'Kingdom authority flows from His throne, unto His own; His Kingdom reigns'*. Kingdom authority always comes from above, through prayer, to surrendered hearts. From His prayer, came assurance; from assurance, came authority; and from authority, came the command: *"Lazarus, come out!"*

During Jewish burials, the body was anointed with aromatic oils then laid with the feet at one end of a long sheet of linen. The rest of the sheet was then folded back over the face and body, back down to the feet. Then the arms and legs were bound together with thin strips of linen. Bound like this, it would have been very difficult to move. Some think that Lazarus miraculously levitated out of the tomb; others, that he was able to shuffle. Either way, he needed to be untied, before he could be re-clothed and free to move again.

---

[27] (11:4)
[28] (5:19-20; 17:3; 1John 1:3)

This miracle was witnessed by many Jews from Jerusalem[29], and had a dramatic effect in setting the stage for the Triumphal Entry a few days later. News of Lazarus's resurrection meant there were thousands of people wanting to see Jesus. He rode down the Mount of Olives through the massive graveyard, proclaiming His kingship over life and death.

But whilst many ordinary people believed, as far as the Sadducees and Chief Priests were concerned it sealed His fate. In their eyes, He *had* to be killed.

But why were they so opposed?

The Sadducees' hatred of resurrection (11:45-57)

At one level, the reason for their opposition was obvious. They were concerned that if Jesus's influence continued growing, the Romans would step in to crush possible rebellion. And in doing so, the Temple would be destroyed; and their lives of priestly privilege would end. It was in their interest that this one man should die, rather than the whole nation.[30] They began to actively plan how to achieve this.

Strangely enough, their decision had exactly the opposite effect. Eventually in 70 AD Jerusalem was destroyed by a Roman army; the Temple was razed to the ground; and the Sadducees vanish from human history completely. Even their writings completely disappeared. As Jesus said, *"He who seeks to save his own life, will lose it: whereas he who loses his life for My sake and the gospel, will keep it unto eternal life".*

In the short term however, their decision meant that Lazarus's newly-restored life was at the expense of Jesus's imminent death.

Jesus again withdrew, but this time only twelve miles or so, to a village called Ephraim. The Passover was near, and He knew that His crucifixion was fast approaching.

However there is a deeper reason why the Sadducees hated Him. Whereas the Pharisees hated Jesus's teaching about *grace*, the Sadducees hated the idea of *resurrection* and eternal life.

---

29 (11:18,19; 12:9-11; 12:17-19)

30 (11:49-50)

Like the Pharisees, the Sadducees were a sect of Judaism that had arisen during the war of liberation from the Greeks, one hundred and fifty years earlier. Antiochus Epiphanes had deliberately defiled the Temple in order to destroy Jewish national identity and assimilate them into Greek culture. But Judas Maccabeus led a revolt and eventually managed to drive them out. He re-dedicated the Temple in 136 BC.

During that conflict, the *Pharisees* had sought to preserve the nation's identity by holding to traditions such as circumcision, Torah, and Shabbat. Many of them had paid with their lives for doing so. The *Sadducees* however emphasised Temple worship as the heart of Jewish identity, thus elevating their own status as custodians of the Temple and all its sacrificial rituals.

After the Roman conquest of Jerusalem by Pompey the Great in 63 BC, the Sadducees collaborated with Roman magistrates of the Roman government and the Herodian puppet-kings. What concerned them most was to avoid Rome shutting down the Temple, as Antiochus had done.

In terms of their civic responsibilities, the Sadducees represented the state in international negotiations; collected taxes; equipped and led armies; and served as judges in domestic law courts. They held the majority of seats in the Sanhedrin, though the Pharisees were also well represented.

This led to criticism from other interest groups that the Sadducees were collaborators with the enemy. They were also unpopular because they used the need for perfect sacrifices to create a gravy train for themselves. They were the elite: wealthy, powerful, and driven by self-interest.

Doctrinally, the Sadducees were miles apart from the Pharisees. *'The Sadducees say that there is no resurrection, and that there are neither angels nor spirits, but the Pharisees believe all these things'.*[31] Focussed on maintaining material wealth and power, the thought of the last being first and the first being last, was not what they wanted. they found the concepts of resurrection and eternal life anathema.

They later ridiculed Jesus's teaching about the resurrection using the hypothetical example of a woman who had been married to seven different

---

31 (Acts 23:6-9)

men. In the resurrection, whose wife would she be?[32] Jesus replied using a text from the Torah stating that God remained the God of Abraham, Isaac and Jacob, long after their deaths. Since God is not God of the dead, they must have risen from the dead. The patriarchs proved that resurrection was real!

Caiaphas was the fake High Priest appointed by Rome for that period; but Jesus, we know, is our true High Priest. Caiaphas was concerned to preserve his own life of privilege and wealth, whereas Jesus was about to lay down His life for us. Caiaphas was completely unaware that his words about Jesus actually represented unconscious prophecy: whereas Jesus lived in permanent intimate communion with the Father. And He was about to be restored to His previous glory, sitting at the Father's right hand.

Summing up

Lazarus's resurrection was the climax of the series of miracles John selected, and it caused a furore during a season of heightened nationalist fervour, setting the stage for the Triumphal Entry.

As a miracle, it was astonishing; but eventually of course, Lazarus died of old age as we all do. As a sign, it pointed to Jesus's total authority over death and the resulting bodily corruption. He has the keys of death and hell! He Himself *is* the resurrection and the life.

Jesus's prayer before calling Lazarus back to life, is a powerful example of eternal life working out in reality. It demonstrated a life lived by faith in God and continuous communion with Him, from which came assurance and authority.

Believing in our bodily resurrection is one of the great anchors of faith, helping us ride out the storms of life. But as for Martha, it is often major personal loss that helps stretch our faith and lay hold of Jesus's promise - that we too will one day experience that glorious resurrection.

[32] (Matt 22:23-32)

Jesus's last appeal to the Jews (12:1-50)

After a banquet in His honour, and Mary's extravagant worship, Jesus rides into Jerusalem - to acclaim from its citizens, but the chagrin of the rulers. As the Passover countdown progresses, Jesus explains what His death will mean, and makes His last appeal to the nation.

This chapter marks the end of the section of John's gospel written *'that you may believe that Jesus is the Christ, the Son of God'*; and a shift to focussing on what it means to *'have life in Him through believing'*[1].

The Jews' decision to kill Jesus, is counterbalanced by three affirmations: Mary with her anointing oil[2]; the triumphal entry[3]; and acclamation by Greeks[4]. Jesus teaches about the purpose and significance of His imminent death, and how it is a role model for discipleship. John then inserts an explanatory note about why the Jews ultimately rejected Jesus, before recording Jesus's last appeal to them.

Mary worships Jesus extravagantly, as her Lord (12:1-11)

Jesus returns to Bethany once again, shortly before Passover. Jerusalem was already full of Passover pilgrims, because ritual cleansing prior to the Feast took seven days. Jesus, of course, had no need of cleansing.

He is welcomed like a visiting ruler, with something akin to a state banquet! Lazarus, living proof of Jesus being the Lord of Life and Death, sat right next to Him. The sisters are true to character, Martha waitressing while Mary worships: but there is no grousing this time! Martha too is full of love for the Lord, now deeply aware that Jesus is the resurrection and the life.

Everyone present must have known how incredibly dangerous it was for Jesus to return to Jerusalem[5]. But whether any of them realised His death was only six days away, is debatable. Though Jesus had repeatedly told them that the

---

[1] (20:31)
[2] (12:1-8)
[3] (12:9-19)
[4] (12:20-36)
[5] (11:16,57)

Priesthood would arrest Him and turn Him over to be flogged and crucified[6], Luke says they had no idea what He was talking about.

It seems however that Mary *had* understood: for her actions were purposeful, according to Jesus. Perhaps she had grasped that *'I am the resurrection and the life'* implied He himself would die and rise again?

Assuming the banquet seating took the usual form of long couches, with guests reclining on their left elbow, Jesus's feet would have been easily accessible to Mary. Martha was already serving the food, and Jesus and the guests were already seated. Presumably his feet had already been washed on arrival, as this (along with a kiss and some plain anointing oil) was considered the bare minimum for hospitality.[7]

Bustling to and fro, Martha notices that Mary has momentarily disappeared. When she comes back, she has a beautiful alabaster jar of ultra-precious perfume, which she starts to pour over Jesus's feet. The aroma instantly overrides the smell of the food, and the room goes dead silent. Every head turns. She removes her hair clips and kneels down, using her beautiful tresses to wipe his feet dry. Then she empties the rest of the jar - far more than was needed - over His head.[8] Presumably it flowed down over His robe, like when a new High Priest was anointed.

Jesus knew her heart, and realised she'd kept the oil laid by, ready to anoint Him for burial after His crucifixion.[9] In the event, only Joseph (of Arimathea) and Nicodemus had access to His body before He was buried. How Mary knew this would be her only chance to use it, we aren't told.

What she did, was a showstopper that evening. But as He prophesied, it is still being talked about two thousand years later, wherever the gospel is preached. It's such a clear example of what it means, to truly believe in and love Jesus.

---

[6] (Mk 10:32-34; Matt 20:17-19; Lk 18:31-34)

[7] (Lk 7:44-47)

[8] (Matt 26:6-13; Mk 14:3-9)

[9] (12:7)

How to adequately convey Mary's worship?

In those days, a woman's long hair was her glory, and a symbol of being under authority.[10] The usual pattern was that under God, Christ was the head of every husband, and the husband was the head of his wife.[11] David heard God tell Messiah to sit at His right hand, till all his enemies had been put under his feet.[12] Mary wanted to be the first! She wanted Jesus as her spiritual husband, her covering.

Washing a guest's feet was a job for the lowest of the low. The task was assigned to foreign slaves, not Jewish ones, for that reason. John the Baptist counted himself unworthy even to unfasten Jesus's sandals. Even Jesus, when washing the disciples' feet, had a bowl and a towel to use. But like David, Mary was willing to be *'even more undignified than this!'*[13] She really let her hair down (!), and was totally uninhibited in her worship of Jesus.

Judas's reaction

It was this action of Mary's that triggered Judas to go to the High Priest and offer to betray Jesus.[14] He belittled her sacrifice, saying it would have been better spent on the poor of Bethany. But John tells us that Judas used to embezzle money from the team purse, normally used to buy provisions or to give to the poor.[15] His remark was totally hypocritical.

He had begun to worship Mammon, long before this; and Mary's willingness to count everything loss for Christ, must have deeply challenged him. But rather than learning from her example, he took his sinning to its natural conclusion, and sold Jesus out for thirty pieces of silver.

The Servant King enters Jerusalem. (12:12-19)

The city would have been crowded with Passover pilgrims: Josephus estimates 2,700,000, not counting the defiled and the foreigners! Probably

---

[10] (1 Cor 11:15)
[11] (1 Cor 11:3)
[12] (Ps 110:1)
[13] (2 Sam 6:22)
[14] (Mk 14:10)
[15] (13:29)

Bethany itself would be crowded with guests. Those who'd seen the banquet would have told their friends in Jerusalem, who then came out in hordes to see Jesus *and* Lazarus. He was now living proof of resurrection, a doctrine so hated by the priesthood that they decided he too must be killed.

The morning after the banquet, Jesus sets off to walk into Jerusalem: an hour's walk at a usual pace, up from Bethany over the brow of the Mount of Olives, passing Bethphage en route. En route He commandeers a young donkey, then rides down through the huge graveyard, past the garden of Gethsemane, across the Kidron brook and up onto the Temple Mount. The Lord of life, the Raiser of the dead - the One who'd said *'The dead shall hear the voice of the Son of God, and those who hear shall live'* - rode in humble majesty through death's domain!

Passover was a volatile time in Jerusalem, when revolts and rebellions could break out. So a show of force by the occupiers was necessary to 'keep the peace'. As Jesus approached from the east, Pontius Pilate was approaching from the west; on a warhorse, with a large contingent of Roman soldiers.

Someone ran ahead of Jesus to bring the news of His approach, and pilgrims surged out of the city. Soon He was surrounded, His followers from Bethany behind and the Jerusalemites and pilgrims in front. They pulled down palm branches, symbols of national identity, to create a carpet for Jesus; spreading their own cloaks over it as symbols of allegiance to His rule.

And as at Tabernacles, they shouted the 'Great Hallel': *"Save <u>now</u>, I pray, O LORD; O LORD, I pray, send <u>now</u> prosperity. Blessed is He who comes in the Name of the LORD. God is the LORD, and He has given us light; bind the sacrifice with cords to the horns of the altar. You are my God, and I will praise You. You are my God, I will exalt You".*[16]

They are blessing the One who comes in the Name of the LORD - that unspeakably holy Name, which they refer to as HaShem. The Pharisees thought this worship was sacrilege, and tried to get Jesus to rebuke them, but

16 (Ps 118:25-28)

He refused.[17] It was pointless to try, He said, for if they were silenced, the very stones would cry out in worship of Him!

Nationalist fervour was rising, as it had done the previous Passover when Jesus fed the five thousand.[18] Perhaps in order to damp it down, Jesus sends two disciples to commandeer a donkey and its colt.[19] The colt had never been ridden before. Then He mounts it and continues His procession. The contrast with Pilate's warhorse could not have spoken more clearly.

His Kingdom is 'not of this world'; not to be achieved militarily or by force. Nevertheless, even the disciples didn't grasp the significance of Jesus's mode of transport. John brings out its meaning, by quoting Zechariah. As is often the case, the context of the quote matters:

"Rejoice greatly, O daughter of Zion! Shout, O daughter of Jerusalem! Behold, your King is coming to you; He is just and having salvation, lowly and riding on a donkey, a colt, the foal of a donkey."[20]

The Pharisees recognise that it is game over! The whole city, even some Greek proselytes[21], are flocking to see Him.

<u>The Greeks</u> (12:20-26)

Usually Greeks would have been unwelcome to the Jews; they remembered how Antiochus had tried to wipe out their national identity and defile the Temple. And yet, some had come to Passover to worship. Why?

- They may just have been Greek proselytes to Judaism

- Jesus had taught, healed, and fed the *four* thousand, in the Decapolis, the Greek cities in Jordan. Philip's home was Bethsaida, near there. And Philip and Andrew are both *Greek* names.

- Jesus re-cleansed the Temple day after the Triumphal Entry[22], according to the synoptic gospels. He had re-opened the Court of the Gentiles as 'a house

---

17 (Lk 19:39)
18 (6:14,15)
19 (Mt 21:1-3, Mk 11:1-7)
20 (Zech 9:9-10)
21 (12:20)
22 (Matt 21:12-13; Lk 19:45-46)

of prayer for all nations'. The Greeks may have sought Him out to ask what this meant for them.

It seems so ironic that just as the Jewish leaders are turning irrevocably against Jesus, the Gentiles are recognising Him! But Jesus is not seduced by the adulation of the multitude; or by the approach of the Greeks with its seductive hint of worldwide fame. He has already been offered, and refused, the kingdoms of this world, if only He would worship Satan.[23]

The Greeks' request seems to have been a spiritual time signal for Jesus. He knew that His crucifixion must be witnessed by Gentiles as well as Jews. He had told Nicodemus, *"And I, if I be lifted up, will draw all peoples to Myself."*[24] And Isaiah had said, *"My servant will be raised and lifted up and highly exalted ... So shall He sprinkle many nations"*[25]

Suffering servant, not military Messiah

"The hour has come that the Son of Man should be glorified".[26] This would have been music to the nationalistic crowd's ears. They had prayed, 'Save *now, LORD*': surely Jesus their Messiah was about to do so!

But His next words painted a sobering picture.

"A seed remains just a single seed, unless it falls into the ground and dies. If so it sprouts and grows, producing lots of grain." Jesus's Messiahship is not about leading His followers into battle against Rome. His victory will be won by Him alone, and by apparent defeat and death. Nevertheless His sowing of Himself will bring life to millions. *'He will see the fruit of the travail of His soul, and be satisfied.'*[27]

But the principle applies not just to *His* death. *"He who loves his life in this world, will lose it; and anyone who hates his life in this world, will keep it for eternal life. If anyone serves Me, let him follow Me; and where I am, there My servant will be also."*

---

[23] (Mt 4:8,9)
[24] (12:32)
[25] (Ps 52:13)
[26] (13:1,17:1)
[27] (Isa 53:11)

Seen through the lens of Messiah-mania, this could have sounded a bit like Jim Jones's gospel: mass suicide in order to gain the afterlife. But once again, our translations are badly misleading. There are two different words for life in play. And 'eternal' refers not to eternity, but to the age of Messiah's coming Kingdom. A more accurate rendering would be something like this ...

*"He who prioritises his soul-life (**psyche**) in this world, will lose it (destroy it, ruin it, render it pointless); and anyone who hates his soul-life in this world, will safeguard it for spirit-life (**zoe**) in Messiah's age. If anyone serves Me, let him follow Me; and where I am, there My servant will be also."*

As Jim Elliott famously wrote, *"He is no fool, to give what he cannot keep, to gain what he cannot lose"*.

Serving Jesus involves walking the path He walked. This is John's equivalent for Paul's phrases, *'taking up one's cross'*, *'crucifying the flesh'*, *'dying to self'*, or *'walking by the Spirit and not according to the flesh'*. True service means sticking close to Jesus[28]: and it leads to honour from the Father.

Jesus is well aware of His own inner struggle.[29] His human nature, *'tempted in every respect like we are'*[30], is horror-stricken at facing death on the Cross. *"I have a baptism to be baptised with; and how am I straitened till it be accomplished!"*.[31] His humanity revolts at the thought of crucifixion, and would dearly love to pray to avoid it. But His spirit knows that the cross is the ultimate purpose of His incarnation, and always has been since before the foundation of the world. His two natures are wrestling together, but He chooses to pray, *"Father, glorify Your name!"*

Inner conflict between our flesh and our spirit

Let's detour to explore this inner conflict a bit further.

Each of us has three dimensions of life:

- bodily life (Greek='bios'), through which we experience the world;
- soul life (Gk='psyche') , through which we experience human society; and

---

[28] (12:26)
[29] (12:27,28)
[30] (Heb 4:15)
[31] (Lk 12:50)

• spirit life (Gk='zoe'), through which we can know and experience God.

Our soul consists of our mind, will and emotions. Our soul and body together constitute what scripture calls our 'flesh': fallen human nature. When the Bible talks about 'the lusts of the flesh' it is talking about sinful thoughts, feelings and desires.

Because Satan is the 'prince of this world', he has perverted the way we look at the world, and the way the world appears to us. He wants to draw us away from God, just as he did with Eve and Adam. Things that God has forbidden, now seem attractive 'must-haves'. If we love the world and indulge our flesh nature, eventually our soul will face judgement and perish in the Lake of Fire.

Loving the world is diametrically opposed to loving the Father[32] and His Son. If we love God, we will find ourselves in a continual struggle to overcome our flesh and instead, walk by the Spirit. But the fruit, the outcome, will be resurrection of our body and soul into eternal life.

Jesus speaks repeatedly about this issue in the Synoptic gospels, under the metaphor of taking up our cross and following Him. In fact all the New Testament authors speak of this struggle, and give lots of explanation about how it applies in different aspects of our lives. For example,

- Paul says, *"Walk by the Spirit, and do not fulfil the lusts of the flesh. For the flesh lusts against the Spirit, and the Spirit against the flesh"*[33]. He goes on to list seventeen specific examples of 'the works of the flesh', contrasting them with 'the fruit of the Spirit'.
- James says, *"Friendship with the world is enmity with God ...Or do you think the scripture says in vain, "The Spirit who dwells in us yearns jealously?'"*[34].
- Peter says, *"Since Christ suffered for us in the flesh, arm yourselves with the same mind, for he who has suffered in the flesh has ceased from sin, that he should no longer live the rest of his time in the flesh for the lusts of men, but for the will of God".*[35]

---

32 (1Jn 2:15-17)
33 (Gal 5:16,17)
34 (Jas 4:4,5)
35 (1Pet 4:1,2)

- John says, *"Do not love the world or the things in the world. If anyone loves the world, the love of the Father is not in him. For all that is in the world - the lust of the flesh, the lust of the eyes, and the pride of life - is not of the Father but is of the world".*[36]

Identifying our own carnality

Identifying where our own soul-life is blocking the fruit of the Spirit, is an ongoing issue for believers. Christ's aim is that we become like Him in every respect: but our human hearts are desperately wicked and self-deceiving.

Paul says that the 'natural man' (non-believer) cannot receive the things of God at all, while the 'spiritual man' can. But he identifies an intermediate category he calls 'carnal': believers whose relationships within the church are characterised by jealousy, quarrels, and divisions. Such folk are like unweaned babies, not yet able to take solid spiritual food[37]. This is the flesh nature obstructing our spiritual growth.

Some ways in which I observe my own flesh-nature in operation, include:-

- Seeking affirmation and honour from others rather than from God
- Indulging and excusing my own passions - greed, lust, anger etc
- Self-righteousness; defensiveness, reluctance to admit I was wrong
- Placing my own intellect in judgement over the word of God
- Shying away from witnessing, for fear of ostracism
- Blaming God, rather than embracing 'trials' as His way of strengthening me

What about you? How do *you* presently experience this struggle?

Jesus's determination to do God's will (12:27-28)

"Father, glorify Your Name!" This is the Gethsemane prayer, *"If it be possible, let this cup pass from Me. Yet not my will, but Thy will, be done O Lord".*

The depth of devotion to His Father's glory shown here, is just what He'd taught the disciples to pray: *'Hallowed be Thy Name, Thy Kingdom come, Thy will be done'*. This is what that prayer implies. We pray daily for our needs,

---

[36] (1Jn 2:15,16)
[37] (1Cor 2:14-3:4)

forgiveness, and protection: forgetting that all these should be secondary to a burning desire for His Kingdom, His power, His glory: whatever it costs us.

When He chose to accept His Father's commission, He said: *'Sacrifice and offering You did not desire; My ears You have opened.'* God did not want mandated sacrifice or required offerings, but freewill obedience born out of love. *'Burnt offering and sin offering You did not require. Then I said, "Behold, I come; In the scroll of the book it is written of me. I delight to do Your will, O my God, and Your law is within my heart."'*[38]

But lest we think that it was easy for Jesus to stick to His initial resolution, Hebrews tells us: *"Though He was Son, yet He learned obedience by the things which He suffered"*.[39]

This is the 'Calvary Road' of which Roy Hession wrote: taking up our cross, and following Jesus in crucifying our flesh. *"A servant is not greater than his master. If they persecuted Me, they will persecute you also"*.[40] Or as Paul expressed it, *"I count all things loss ... that I may know Him and the power of His resurrection, and the fellowship of His suffering, being conformed to His death."*[41]

"I have glorified it, and will glorify it again": The Father had already glorified His Name in sending His only-begotten Son to redeem us. Now He promises His Son that the sacrifice will not be in vain. While men may see the Cross as ultimate shame and defeat, it will in fact be the ultimate instrument of glorifying God's Name.

The bystanders heard this Voice as thunder, or else thought that an angel had spoken - though the words imply that it is Jesus's Father responding to Him. The voice is not for Jesus's reassurance, but so that the hearers will realise that a turning point in redemption history has arrived.

---

[38] (Ps 40:6-8)
[39] (Heb 5:8)
[40] (15:20)
[41] (Phil 3:8-10)

<u>Powerful effects of His coming crucifixion</u> (12:28-33)

Unlike the crowd, Jesus already knows *how* God's Name will be glorified through His crucifixion. He has seen joy beyond the cross: He knows that when He sees the fruit of His suffering, it will all have been worth it.

<u>Judgement of this world</u> (12:31)

The world's sin will be exposed by its unbelief.[42] In crucifying Jesus, the awfulness of sin is fully exposed. But the cross also judges those who believe as righteous: rather than exposing, it covers (atones for) believers' sin.

"He who believes in him, is not condemned; but he who does not believe, is condemned already; because he has not believed in the name of the only begotten Son of God. And this is the condemnation, that light has come into the world, and men loved darkness rather than light, because their deeds were evil."[43]

<u>Expulsion of its evil ruler</u> (12:31)

Satan, the Prince of this world, its supreme ruler, will be expelled.[44]

"He has taken our sins out of the way, having nailed them to the Cross. Having disarmed principalities and powers, He made a public spectacle of them, triumphing over them in it"[45].

Satan's authority to reign over us, and to pressure us into disobeying God, has been broken.[46]

<u>Drawing multitudes to Himself</u> (12:32)

Being lifted up is the same phrase Jesus used with Nicodemus.[47] It implies honour and fame; but it actually referred to the cross. The manner of His death convinced many of His true identity. For example, think of the Roman

---

[42] (16:9)
[43] (3:18,19)
[44] (16:11)
[45] (Col 2:14b,15)
[46] (Eph 2:1-3)
[47] (3:14,15)

soldier's comment at the Cross, *"Truly, this was the Son of God"*. But many other onlookers also repented at His death.[48]

This was the supreme joy set before Him. With the foresight of eternity, He saw His future bride the Church, pure and ready for her wedding: cleansed through His blood, and longing deeply for the day when full union with Him would be consummated. Maranatha!

These three aspects of the Cross, help us understand different emphases in the worldwide church. *Evangelicals* focus on its efficacy in substitutionary atonement. *Orthodox* churches focus on Jesus's victory over the powers of darkness. And *liberal* Christians focus on the drawing power of the cross, as an example of God's love. All three are true, but only when held together!

<u>Why the Jews didn't believe</u> (12:34-43)

The hearers rightly connected Jesus's reference to the Son of Man as Messianic, and His use of 'lifted up' as referring to a departure or death. But the Judaism of that time expected Messiah to be victorious and to reign eternally[49]: they hadn't registered that Messiah would be cut off[50].`

They asked what kind of 'Son of Man' He was. They still could not grasp how to marry up what He was saying, with the partial insights they had gleaned from the Jewish scriptures. They had read that Messiah would remain forever, and couldn't reconcile this with Jesus dying or departing.

The issue of Judaism's rejection of Christ, would have been very relevant to any Jews reading John's Gospel in AD 95. 'The Way', as the early Christians were known, had grown far beyond being seen as a sect within Judaism. Gentile believers had become stand-offish from their Jewish brethren, despite Paul's teaching about the One New Man and Israel's temporary stumbling. Meantime Roman persecution of Judaism had gone on growing after Peter and Paul's martyrdom, eventually leading to Titus's sacking of

---

[48] (Lk 23:47,48)
[49] (Lk 23:47,48)
[50] (Dan 9:26)

Jerusalem and the Temple. Jesus's prophecy of judgement on Jerusalem for rejecting Him, had been fulfilled.

How could it have come about, that *'Messiah came unto His own, and His own received Him not'*?

There is a terrible tragedy in that verse, but also a majestic mystery of grace - for Jews as well as the Gentiles.

Six hundred years beforehand, Isaiah had seen 'the light of the gospel of the glory of God in the face of Jesus Christ'.[51] Despite the wonderful revelations of Messiah in his prophecies, especially the 'Songs of the Suffering Servant'[52] and Messiah's manifesto[53], the Jews would not believe and would be unable to recognise *'the arm of the Lord'* (His intervention in history) when Jesus was born. Paradoxically his prophetic ministry would have the effect of blinding Israel's eyes, blocking their hearing and hardening their hearts.[54]

Paul says of the Jews,

'I do not desire, brethren, that you should be ignorant of this mystery, lest you should be wise in your own opinion, that blindness in part has happened to Israel until the fullness of the Gentiles has come in. And so all Israel will be saved, as it is written: "The Deliverer will come out of Zion, and He will turn away ungodliness from Jacob; for this is My covenant with them, when I take away their sins".

Concerning the gospel they are enemies for your sake, but concerning the election they are beloved for the sake of the fathers. For the gifts and the calling of God are irrevocable. For as you were once disobedient to God, yet have now obtained mercy through their disobedience, even so these also have now been disobedient, that through the mercy shown you they also may obtain mercy. For God has committed them all to disobedience, that He might have mercy on all.

Oh, the depth of the riches both of the wisdom and knowledge of God! How unsearchable are His judgments and His ways past finding out! "For who has

---

[51] (12:41; 2Cor 4:4)

[52] (Isa 42:1–4; Isa 49:1–6; Isa 50:4–11; Isa 52:13–53:12)

[53] (Isa 61:1-4)

[54] (12:40; Isa 6:10)

known the mind of the Lord? Or who has become His counsellor? Or who has first given to Him and it shall be repaid to him? For of Him and through Him and to Him are all things, to whom be glory forever. Amen."[55]

The Jewish leaders *were* deeply culpable for rejecting Christ despite His many Messianic miracles, and for fabricating charges which led to His crucifixion. But it is also true that God's sovereignty was at work, preparing the way for the gospel to come to the Gentiles.

Eventually before Christ's return, the gospel will be brought back to the Jews and God will *'pour on the house of David and on the inhabitants of Jerusalem the Spirit of grace and supplication; then they will look on Me whom they pierced. Yes, they will mourn for Him as one mourns for his only son, and grieve for Him as one grieves for a firstborn. In that day a fountain shall be opened for the house of David and for the inhabitants of Jerusalem, for sin and for uncleanness'.*

At the personal level, however, salvation is available now to any Jew who turns to Christ. *"But even to this day, when Moses is read, a veil lies on their heart. Nevertheless when one turns to the Lord, the veil is taken away."*[56]

Judaism's failure to accept Christ as 'come in the flesh', had multiple causes:

- misunderstanding Moses and the scriptures
- refuting the evidence of miracles
- ignoring John the Baptist
- self-righteousness (Pharisees)
- self-interest (Sadducees)
- the overarching eternal purposes of God

But John mentions one last reason that many Jewish leaders, though they were convinced by Jesus's teaching, did not publicly acknowledge Him. That was the fear of being ostracised by the Pharisees, and put out of the

---

[55] (Rom 11:25-33)
[56] (2 Cor 3:15)

synagogue.[57] Social standing was ultimately more important to them than God's approval.

Jesus's last appeal to the Jews (12:35-36,44-50)

We know that Jesus was deeply grieved at the fate that was to befall Jerusalem and the Jews, because of their rejection of Him. He wept as He made His triumphal entry. Even as He was led out to be crucified, He told those weeping for Him, to weep instead for the city.[58]

There is a strong sense of urgency as He warns the Jews that time has almost run out.[59] His life, which was the light of men, was about to be snuffed out. Believing in the light, even if only for the few hours remaining, offered them the possibility of becoming 'sons of light': starting to reflect His character.

Exposing ourselves to the light of Christ's life inculcates goodness, righteousness and truth. It means separating ourselves from the works of darkness, perhaps even exposing and challenging sin: and making the most of the time allotted to us[60]. It also means being continually ready for Christ's return[61].

There is an urgency in this last appeal, that we need to take note of.

From this point on, John's account of Jesus's public ministry is finished. He turns instead to Jesus's role teaching His disciples about life in the Spirit[62]; interceding for them and us[63];and offering Himself as the Lamb of God, crucified and raised again for the sins of the world [64].

---

[57] (12:42,43)
[58] (Lk 23:27-31)
[59] (12:35)
[60] (Eph 5:8-16)
[61] (1 Thess 5:5).
[62] (1 Thess 5:5).
[63] (John 18)
[64] (John 19-21)

Self-sacrifice v. Self-protection (13:1-30)

The night before the Cross, Jesus celebrates Passover, washing His disciples' feet to teach them Kingdom humility and love. Prophesying imminent betrayal causes consternation amongst the Twelve.

There is debate about whether this meal was the same Passover meal described by the Synoptics. John doesn't mention anything about the institution of the Lord's Supper: but then, he also leaves out the majority of stuff described in the other gospels. His overall purpose in writing was to complement the other gospels, whilst selecting episodes from Jesus's life that fit his twin purposes *'that you may believe that Jesus is the Christ'* and 'that believing, you may have life in His name'.

John's account of Jesus's last evening with His disciples flows smoothly from the foot-washing into the meal; and then after Judas leaves, His teaching about going to the Father. But there is an apparent break at the end of chapter fourteen, when Jesus says, *"Arise, let us go from here"* - only to continue His teaching for another two chapters.

We have all experienced occasions when a visitor goes to leave, but then the conversation restarts and their departure is delayed! But some see this as the point where Jesus and team leave the Upper Room on their way to Gethsemane. If so, the 'true Vine' metaphor may have been prompted by passing the Temple, which had a huge vine carved in stone over its entrance.

Jesus's focus, during the Last Supper

The next five chapters are known as the 'farewell discourse'. The crucifixion is only hours away (though the disciples perhaps don't realise this) and they are celebrating Passover with Jesus. Even on the verge of awful suffering, humiliation and death, He is more concerned for them than for Himself.

Jesus knows that the climax of His work has arrived: the 'kairos' moment in history, when the Lamb of God must be sacrificed for the Father's glory. It was to demonstrate God's righteousness, so that He might be both just *and* the justifier of anyone who has faith in Jesus[1].

What is central in Jesus's mind however, is not the sacrifice but the returning home to His Father.[2] The whole of the next five chapters revolve around this theme: His return to His Father, why the disciples should rejoice rather than fear this, and how their relationship with Him will morph into a relationship with all three members of the Trinity, as His life flows into them and enables them to continue His mission.

He uses the time to prepare for the massive shift they will experience, from

- knowing Him 'in the flesh', to knowing Father & Son 'in the Holy Spirit';
- asking Jesus anything and everything, to asking the Father in Jesus's name;
- observing Jesus's character, to bearing the fruit of the Spirit themselves;
- assisting Jesus in His mission, to incarnating that mission themselves.

<u>Agape love defined for all time</u>

Also central is His agape love for His disciples.

In the Old Testament there is a special word for God's love, which is *'hesed'*. *Hesed* is the Hebrew word used for covenant relationships such as between man and wife, David and Jonathan, God and Israel. It is difficult to translate, as it encapsulates many shades of meaning in English: love, goodness, kindness, faithfulness, mercy, devotion, and favour. Some translations use compound words such as 'loyal love', 'steadfast unfailing love', 'faithful love', and perhaps best of all, 'loving kindness'.

God describes Himself to Moses as *"compassionate and gracious, slow to anger, and abounding in hesed and truth; who keeps hesed for thousands, who forgives iniquity, transgression and sin".*[3]

When the Old Testament was first translated from Hebrew into Greek, the Greek word 'agape' was often used to translate 'hesed'. For example it is used in translating the greatest commandment, *"You shall hesed/agape the Lord*

---

1 (Rom 3:26)

2 (13:1)

3 (13:1)

your God with all your mind and with all your soul and with all your strength"[4]. This command shows us that hesed/agape love is not just intellectual assent, nor just an emotion, nor just practical loyalty: it is all of these, rolled into one.

Jesus had loved the disciples *'as His own'*. He regarded them as His family.[5] He was very aware that each of them had been given to Him by His Father[6], and that He was responsible for keeping them from the enemy - the 'Prince of this world'. He now demonstrates His agape - His loyal, steadfast, unfailing, gracious, merciful love - in devoting their last meal together to teaching them about living in His resurrection life, after the Cross.

Though He had come into the world, His Kingdom was *'not of this world'*[7]. Now He is about to leave the world, and His concern is to prepare the Twelve to make the transition from knowing Jesus *'after the flesh'* to knowing Him *'in the Spirit'* and as one member of the Trinity.

Washing the disciples' feet (13:1-17)

Van Gogh's famous painting of the disciples seated upright at 'The Last Supper' gives us quite the wrong impression. For ceremonial meals such as this, the Jews had adopted the Greek custom of using long, broad benches around three sides of a table. Guests would lie on the benches using their left arm to prop themselves up, whilst their right hand was free to take the food. This symbolised freedom and relaxation, unlike the first Passover when the people were told to eat standing up, ready for a speedy departure.

Each disciple's lower body and legs would be on the outer edge of the bench, behind their right-hand neighbour. Their head and upper body would be in front of the person to their left. Given there were thirteen people at the start of the meal, Jesus as celebrant would have been in the middle of the middle table, with two disciples on each side. This means that John must have been to Jesus's right, given that he was able to lean back and whisper his question to Jesus. And Peter must have been to John's right.

---

[4] (Deut 6:5)
[5] (Mt 12:48-50)
[6] (17:6-12)
[7] (18:36)

It seems Judas was next to Jesus but on His left, as Jesus was able to pass him the sop. This was a place of honour, sometimes left vacant for Elijah.

Everyone had taken their place, ready to start; but though the home-owner had apparently provided basin and towel, there was no servant to wash their feet. This task was considered beneath the dignity even of a Jewish slave. But it was also an expected courtesy whose omission conveyed lack of respect, let alone love, for a guest.[8]

Luke tells us that this very evening, the Twelve had been arguing amongst themselves about who should be considered the greatest. Presumably they were angling for the leadership role, once Jesus had gone![9] Jostling for position had been a recurrent issue, sometimes even involving pushy parents lobbying Jesus.

I imagine that as the meal was prepared and served, the Twelve would have quietly debated who should deal with their dirty, smelly feet before they took their places! *"I'm not doing it - You do it!" "No, I'm not doing it: someone else should."* All twelve took their places, tacitly refusing to humble themselves: and Jesus as Master of Ceremonies was due to bless the food, when He did the unthinkable.

He, the Lord of Glory, the Son of God, the Messiah, got up from the feast, stripped off down to His loincloth and put a towel around His waist. Then He knelt at their feet one by one, tenderly washing them in the basin then drying their feet and toes. The One of whom John the Baptist had said, *"I am not worthy to undo the buckle of his sandals"*, shamed their pride and competitiveness by taking on Himself the form of a servant.

His mindset was one of utter humility, although He knew He was equal with God.[10] He laid aside His flesh-life, with its *'pride of life'*, as a statement that He was willing to lay down His life for them at the Cross. Truly, He loved them to the end; to the uttermost. They must have wept at the memory of this event, once they understood after Calvary.

---

[8] (Lk 7:36-50)
[9] (Lk 22:24-27)
[10] (Phil 2:5-11)

Peter seems to have felt the shamefulness most keenly. Assuming Jesus was working clockwise around the table, he was the fifth to be washed. He crystallised the inappropriateness of letting Jesus wash his feet. But Jesus was about to teach them (and us) a much deeper, multi-part lesson - relevant to every day of our lives:-

- We must allow Jesus to wash our feet, otherwise we can have no fellowship with Him. The metaphor is about letting Jesus cleanse us from our sin. *"If we say that we have no sin, we deceive ourselves, and the truth is not in us. If we confess our sins, he is faithful, and just to forgive us, our sins, and to cleanse us from all unrighteousness".*[11] Refusing to acknowledge our own sinfulness is just another form of 'the pride of life', and means we cannot receive our portion, our inheritance in Christ.
- When Peter then asks Jesus to wash his hands and head as well (!), Jesus extends the metaphor. *"He who has had a bath needs only to wash his feet to be completely clean; and you are clean"*. Later He says, *"You are already clean, because of the word (logos, torah, teaching) I have spoken to you".*[12] One who has believed in Christ has been cleansed in such a fundamental way, that whilst daily life may bring need of fresh cleansing from sins and defilements, he is still regarded by Christ as a 'saint': someone sanctified and set apart by God, to be holy and blameless in His sight[13].
- *'A servant is not greater than His master'*. If you rightly accept Me as your Teacher and Lord, you must follow My example and wash each others' feet. But what does this mean? It can't be just a ritual. Yet equally obviously we cannot cleanse each other from sin or defilement, though we should be praying for each other in this respect[14].

  Paul explains the implications in his letter to the Philippians: it means having Jesus's mindset[15], His servant-heartedness. Not competing for honour and status within the church, but putting others' interests first as

[11] (1 Jn 1:8-9)
[12] (15:3)
[13] (Eph 1:1-7)
[14] (Jas 5:16)
[15] (Phil 2:5)

Timothy did[16]; if necessary risking our lives to serve them, as Epaphroditus did[17]; and seeking reconciliation where we have been arguing with others[18].

Taking Jesus's command literally, the early Church did practice ritual foot-washing for some decades, but eventually it was abandoned. Maybe the example of Judas had something to do with this. He too had let his feet be washed, even though at that very moment he was looking for the right opportunity to betray Jesus! Outward observance of any ritual, even allowing Jesus to wash our feet in person, does not guarantee inward change.

Jesus prophecies Judas's betrayal. (13:18-30)

As yet, Jesus hasn't explicitly said He is about to leave, though He knows that His crucifixion is only twelve hours away. He has spoken about 'being lifted up'[19] and warned them He'll only be present a little longer[20]. The disciples knew the rulers were plotting to kill Jesus, but also that they were trying to avoid doing so during Passover, for fear it would lead to riots[21]. The word was out, looking for informants who could betray Him quietly.[22]

Having just told them they must love and serve one another, it must have been a huge shock when He told them there was a traitor in their midst![23] The Passover meal was a deeply sacred evening, celebrated as a family. But no sooner had it started, than He announced one of them would betray Him. It would come out of the blue, like a ju-jitsu kick.

A couple of days earlier, Judas had agreed to betray Jesus to the Chief Priests for the sale-price of a slave; thirty pieces of silver[24]. So whilst the foot-washing may have finally shown Judas that Jesus would never be a military Messiah, that wasn't the immediate cause. Judas had long since made the

---

[16] (Phil 2:19-21)
[17] (Phil 2:25-30)
[18] (Phil 4:2)
[19] (12:32-33)
[20] (12:35)
[21] (Mk 14:2)
[22] (11:57)
[23] (13:18)
[24] (Mt 26:14-16)

choice to serve Mammon rather than God. For years he'd been embezzling funds from the team moneybag. Greed and fraud had become so habitual that he only realised too late that he had doomed himself.

Why does Jesus choose this moment for such a deeply unsettling prophecy? We see resulting consternation in the series of troubled questions it provokes from the disciples.[25]

All twelve had been personally chosen by Jesus: even Judas, who was a devil.[26] Had Jesus not forewarned them, they might have been tempted to doubt His omniscience. The primary function of prophecy is not just to foretell the future or to accredit the prophet, but so that we may know with hindsight that the LORD is in control of history.[27] Jesus wants them to know, that He knew in advance this would happen: He is "I AM". Though none of them had seen it coming, He was fully aware, and apart from warning Judas, did nothing. He knew it was His Father's will, and would bring about salvation and the ingathering of His Bride.

Bolstering their faith that He is the Son of God, is vital for their future mission. If He is not God, then *'we are of all men most to be pitied'.*[28] But if He *is* the Son of God, then anyone who receives those He sends, receives Him: and those who receive Him, receive the Father who sent Him.

The knowledge that Judas will betray Him, deeply disturbs Jesus.[29] He has known it all along from scripture; so it is not the surprise factor that causes this. Rather, it is His compassion, even for Judas.

"The Son of Man goes just as it is written of Him, but woe to that man by whom the Son of Man is betrayed! It would have been good for that man, if he had not been born". Then Judas, who was betraying him, answered, and said, "Rabbi, is it I?" He said to him, "you have said it".[30]

---

[25] (13:36,37; 14:5,8,22)

[26] (6:70)

[27] (For example, Ezek 11:10, 12:20, 36:11,23,36,38 etc etc)

[28] (1Cor 15:19)

[29] (13:21)

[30] (Matt 26:24,25)

His evident distress heightens the disciples' consternation and sorrow. How can they trust one another once Jesus is gone, if they don't even know who did it? Their concern has changed from "Who is the greater?", to "Who is the traitor?" If they knew, maybe they could protect Jesus? Even worse, what if their own hearts are deceiving them?

In their newfound introspection, each asks Jesus, *"Is it I?"* Presumably Jesus makes no reply. So Peter asks the one person he's sure it *can't* be, 'the disciple whom Jesus loved', for help. Being on Jesus's right, all John needs to do is to lean back against Jesus's breast, and whisper, *"Who is it, Lord?"*

Judas's fate is sealed

In fact, the answer to the question lay in the original prophecy. *'The one who eats My bread'*, the one who personally accepts an extra portion directly from Jesus, the one whom He seemingly honours, will be the betrayer. Jesus quietly explains the hidden meaning to John, then dips the bread in sauce and hands it to Judas.

The bread was unleavened bread, meant to symbolise sincerity and truth. Usually, Jews ate sourdough bread, where each new batch contained a small lump from the previous batch to provide the necessary yeast. Leaven symbolised sin, and before Passover every family would ceremoniously hunt out fallen breadcrumbs to purify the whole house ready for the feast.

The sauce would have been horseradish sauce, the 'bitter herbs' symbolising both the bitterness of their lives as Egyptian slaves, and the bitter cost of their redemption: the death of all the firstborn sons in Egypt. Accepting the sop was the height of hypocrisy for a man who was about to be utterly insincere and betray his master and friend to an especially bitter death.

The disciples (apart from John, and perhaps Peter) still can't work out who is the one. It was important for them *not* to know: otherwise they might have turned on Judas and prevented him from the dire deed. To forestall this, Jesus sends Judas out with a coded command. The others thought it meant some element of the feast had been missed out in the preparations, or else that he should give alms to the poor: a Jewish way of earning righteousness before worshipping God.

Something quite horrific now happens in the spiritual realm: *Satan himself* enters into Judas. In all the other gospel accounts of demonised people, they still have freewill to approach Christ, even if being near His holiness causes the spirit to throw a fit. But in Judas's case, he has so opened the door by his habitual filching, and now by agreeing to betray Christ, that Satan personally enters him. Far from throwing himself on Jesus's mercy as all the other demonised people did, Judas goes out into the night to the High Priest, to seal the deal. He is *'the son of perdition'* [31].

Now free to speak at liberty, Jesus starts an extended discourse. He teaches them about the wonderful effects His death and resurrection will bring, along with the terrible cost of being identified with Him and carrying on His work.

---

[31] (17:12)

The Upper Room: gateway to a new dimension

Just before He is crucified, Jesus describes to the disciples what they will experience when joined to Him in resurrection life.
This is a huge challenge to our low expectations of spiritual experience.

An overview of the 'Upper Room discourse' (13:31-17:26)

These chapters are Jesus's last testament, His last opportunity to teach His team and prepare them for the massive storm that is about to hit. As always, His concern was not for Himself: *"Having loved His own who were in the world, He loved them to the end".*

The disciples were in consternation. Though He had told them repeatedly, that he would be betrayed and crucified[1]; and though they knew that returning to Jerusalem might mean death, His revelation that He was about to be betrayed nevertheless came as a bombshell. A meal celebrating their fellowship as a team, and prefaced by the deep intimacy of Jesus washing their feet, was completely upended by Jesus's announcement. The traitor was actually one of them!

Once Judas had left, Jesus was free to reveal to them all the wonderful benefits of the Cross, which now lies only hours ahead. It will bring about :

- His glorification and ascension to the right hand of the Father
- Intimate fellowship with Father, Son and Holy Spirit - not just Him
- His resurrection life flowing through them, bearing wonderful fruit
- Their bond with each other enabling them to withstand the world's hostility
- His mission - to bring men back to the Father - continuing through them

This teaching is like a portal through spiritual space-time. What He teaches them is so far beyond anything He's said before, that He has to introduce its themes little-by-little; reiterating and expanding them gradually throughout the discourse. There is a kind of corkscrew flow, coming back to the same themes repeatedly, each time developing or underlining them further.

---

[1] (Mt 16:21f;17:12;20:17f)

His method is partly determined by the need to reassure and calm them. They are afraid of losing Him because He is going to the Father. Fear is the opposite of faith; and His words will bear no fruit unless heard with faith. Despite all His teaching about His identity, culminating in saying *"I and the Father are One"*, the disciples hadn't yet really grasped that *'He who has seen Me has seen the Father'*.

There is also a broader unifying theme that seems to me to underlie the whole discourse. He is ***preparing them for transition into zoe life: knowing God as Father, Son and Holy Spirit***.

He first addresses the disciples' fears of losing Him when He returns to His Father[2]; using their questions to deepen their grasp of His divine nature. Then He explains that they will move from physical discipleship to spiritual communion with all three members of the Trinity; Father and Spirit as well as Himself. Far from having to find their way without Him, both He and the Father will come to them! His resurrection life will bring them a peace deeper than anything the world can give.

Next He teaches them how to maintain the fruit-bearing flow of His life into their lives.[3] This would mean love for His teachings; prayer; and keeping His commandments - especially in loving one another as He had loved them. All these were evident in the early Church after Pentecost.[4]

Their union with Him will mean experiencing the same hatred and persecution He'd suffered. But the Holy Spirit, their new Encourager, will glorify Jesus through them. He will convict people that disbelief is sin, declaring Jesus's innocence, and pronouncing judgement on Satan. He will also guide the disciples into *all* truth, teaching them more about Jesus.

Though He has helped them see that the cross is essential, and their fear has been assuaged, they are deeply saddened. But though they *will* weep and lament, their sadness will suddenly be replaced by utter joy. Just as a woman

---

[2] (John 13 &14)

[3] (John 15)

[4] (Acts 2:42)

forgets her horrendous labour pains as soon as she has her baby in her arms, their trauma will be wiped away by the joy of seeing Him again.

Their relationship with Father God will blossom as they experience Him answering their prayers, and Jesus will also reveal more about Him to them. They can take heart meantime, that He has already overcome the world.

Finally[5] He takes them into the inner sanctuary of His own prayer life, as He prays first for Himself, then for them, then for all future generations of believers - including you and I. He prays that we may behold His glory and the eternal love between Father and Son, becoming one in Christ and manifesting His name to the world.

The challenge of these chapters

When Jesus talks about us knowing Him[6], knowing the Holy Spirit[7], or knowing the Father[8], he is obviously talking about something more than mere knowledge *about* Him or *about* Them. Thomas and Philip had spent three years following Jesus, listening to His teaching, observing His life. And yet, Jesus says, they have not 'known' Him - and thus have not known the Father. Knowing Him is something deeper than having heard Him preach the Sermon on the Mount, or having observed His miracles.

Some will think the kind of 'knowing God' of which Jesus speaks, is unattainable mysticism. Or that it's unwise to open oneself up to experiences, such as the 'Toronto blessing'. But He's definitely talking about something real and genuine, which He sees as a present-day fruit of eternal life[9]. Paul talks about it frequently[10]. And John later claims to be living in this joyful 'fellowship with the Father and with His Son'[11], and wanting to link others into it too.

---

[5] (John 17)
[6] (14:7,9)
[7] (14:17)
[8] (17:3)
[9] (17:3)
[10] (Phil 3:10)
[11] (1Jn 1:3,4)

Others may see the essence of knowing God as being obedient to Him. Certainly that is part of it. But the commandment is to love God with all of our heart and soul as well as our minds and strength. That has to include feelings. The woman who anointed Jesus's feet wept with gratitude, and her tears were part of her worship. And though the Ephesian church had excelled in labouring patiently, in holiness and doctrinal discernment, Jesus said *'I have this against you, that you have left your first love'*.

> *N.B. In everyday English, we make a distinction being knowing about someone, and knowing the person themselves. The Greek idea of knowledge was an awareness of facts about a static reality; but Hebrew thought focussed on life as a dynamic process, and knowing meant entering into ongoing relationship with something or someone. This required not only understanding, but choice. So for instance, Adam having intercourse with Eve is described as 'knowing' her. And God's knowledge of us, is linked with His choice - His election - of us, to salvation.*

These chapters represent the same challenge (if not more) to us as to the disciples. They are deeply experiential, yet they speak of realities few have experienced: resurrection life within us enabling us to know and fellowship with the Father as well as His Son; the Spirit teaching us, not externally but internally; the love and joy and peace of Christ flooding our hearts and changing us into His likeness. Which of us would claim to have fully plumbed in our own experience, the depths Jesus is describing here?

Let us approach these chapters with a faith that says,

"Lord, take me deeper. Let me recognise the wind of the Spirit more sensitively. Introduce me to Your Father personally. Let my dried-up heart flood with fresh love for You. Sustain me and prune my life to bear more fruit. Let the sap of your vine bring all the beautiful character traits of the Spirit into fruition in me. Lead me into that abiding fellowship with You and Your Father, that You desire. Show me how to live out Your love for my brothers and sisters. Teach me to pray in the power of Your authority. Re-ignite within me Your love for the world, a passion to bring men back to the Father."

Separation anxiety about losing Jesus (13:31-14:14)

Hours before the crucifixion, Jesus breaks the news: His departure is now imminent. The disciples are panic-stricken.
Jesus uses their questions to teach them about knowing the Father.

Once Judas had left, Jesus was free to speak about the true meaning of the cross. None of the rulers of that age - neither the Sanhedrin nor the Romans, and especially not Satan - understood its hidden wisdom, for *'if they had, they would not have crucified the Lord of Glory'*[1]. What they thought would be His humiliation, was in fact to be His triumph over them.[2] In it, 'the ruler of this world' would be judged.

How does the cross display God's glory? (13:31,32)

We usually see the cross as a mark of shame, as did the Jews and Romans. The Romans used crucifixion as a means of humiliating and cowing their enemies. The Jews saw it as meaning that the victim was especially cursed by God. So it must have puzzled the disciples, when Jesus spoke of it as *'being glorified'*.[3]

In English we use the noun 'glory' to mean honour or distinction. (For more about its etymology, see appendix two.) Of course to a Jew it also meant the radiance of God's Presence. His shekinah glory had hovered over the Israelites as they journeyed through the desert at night, and later it filled the Holy of Holies in the Tabernacle. This glory of God was hidden when Jesus came to earth: he *'veiled it in flesh'*, He *'laid aside His majesty'*, and humbled Himself to become man. It was only once the Father had revealed to Peter that Jesus was Messiah, the Son of God, that Jesus revealed this glory to three of the disciples, in the Transfiguration.[4] But it remains hidden from the world to this day: so what did Jesus mean?

What does *God* define as His glory?

---

1 (1Cor 2:7,8)
2 (Col 2:15)
3 (14:31)
4 (Matt 17:1-9)

Astonishingly, despite experiencing the shekinah for months, and the terror of God's Presence on Mount Sinai, Moses nevertheless asked to see God's glory. His reply was, *"I will show you all My goodness".*[5]

The next day He elaborates: *"The LORD, the* LORD *God, merciful and gracious, long-suffering, and abounding in goodness and truth, keeping mercy for thousands, forgiving iniquity and transgression and sin, by no means clearing the guilty, visiting the sins of the fathers on the children and the childrens' children to the third and fourth generation".*

God's own definition of His glory, is that it lies in attributes of His heart.

Read those Exodus verses again. Don't they read exactly like a description of the cross? In it God's mercy and grace, His patience and goodness and truth are demonstrated. He does not ignore sin by simply clearing the guilty. Jesus's sacrifice of Himself was the *only* way God could be both *'just, and the justifier of the one who has faith in Jesus'*[6]. It demonstrates the holiness and justice of God. In it, He kept covenant mercy for thousands of Old Testament saints whose sins had meantime been covered over by sacrifices and offering.

The One who would make all that ritual obsolete would arrive and pay the full penalty for all mankind's sins. On the Cross, God visited the sins of Jesus's ancestors right back to Adam, on Jesus - who called Himself '*the Son of Adam*'. (*Adam* is the Hebrew word for *man*.)

It therefore makes perfect sense that Jesus saw the cross as His glorification. For in it, all these heart attributes of God - the things which God declares are the core of His glory - are shone out. He endured the Cross, despising its shame[7], for the joy that He foresaw, of being restored to heaven's glory. He is our supreme role-model of what it means to live by faith.

Perhaps our view of the Cross needs to change. We need to see its glory; to boast about what Christ achieved there.[8] We are about to discover many wonderful truths about the effects of Jesus 'going to His Father'. Not only is

---

[5] (Ex 33:18-34:7)
[6] (Rom 3:23-26)
[7] (Heb 12:2)
[8] (Gal 6:14)

it our redemption and Satan's defeat, it also brings us into union with Christ and wonderful communion with all three members of the Trinity.

Jesus's obedience glorified His Father God; and in return, God glorified Him immediately thereafter, declaring Him *'to be the Son of God with power, by the resurrection from the dead'*[9]. He was given *'the Name which is above every name'*, that at the name of Jesus every tongue on earth or in heaven would kneel in obeisance. Forty days later, Christ ascended to the Father in a victory parade, to receive the gift of the Spirit and pour it out at Pentecost[10].

A new commandment: loving one another as Christ loves us (13:33-35)

Jesus had previously told His detractors that He would soon be beyond their reach[11], and that they would die in their sins if they didn't believe in Him. Now He tells His disciples that they too cannot yet go where He is going.

He addresses them as *'little children'*; a term John re-uses in his first letter, referring to those whose sins are forgiven and who have put a simple faith in God. But it also expresses tender concern for them; even as He Himself is just about to face being scourged, mocked, spat on and nailed to the cross.

He has taught them to *'love your neighbour as yourself'*, as second in importance only to loving God with every fibre of one's being. But now He institutes a *new* commandment - for His disciples to love one another.

So how is this new?

Theologians go down rabbit holes about it being new because it is part of a *new* covenant. But the answer is actually very simple. Those of us who are not narcissists, regularly beat ourselves up about our failings. Those who seem harsh towards others, are usually secretly equally harsh on themselves. In other words, they are loving their neighbour as themselves - but not loving them as Jesus does.

Look through the gospel accounts of how Jesus dealt with His disciples' failings, and you will find grace upon grace. When James and John want to call down fire on a Samaritan village. When their mother lobbies for them to

---

[9] (Rom 1:4)
[10] (Ps 68:18, Eph 4:8)
[11] (8:21,24)

have positions of honour in Jesus's kingdom. When just before the Passover meal, they are still arguing over who is the greatest. He always responds with grace, never puts the person down, but challenges them by His example.

Alternatively look back to your own experience of how Jesus has dealt with you over the years. Has He loved you in the same way you love yourself? Or has His love been infinitely more gracious and patient?

When I first met Him, I was overwhelmed by the fact that He knew me far more deeply than anyone else; and yet He accepted and loved me deeply. And my experience over the years is of His incredible patience and gentleness in dealing with my waywardness and unfaithful heart.

Loving one another as He loves us, is different from loving others as we love ourselves. Paul explains to the Colossians, *"As the elect of God, holy and beloved, put on tender mercies, kindness, humility, meekness, long-suffering; bearing with one another, and forgiving one another, if anyone has a complaint against another; even as Christ forgave you, so you also must do. But above all these things put on love, which is the bond of perfection".*[12]

This bond of love will draw them back together when they are scattered after His crucifixion. We hear of no recriminations or blaming one another, though this would be common after such a tragedy. It is a hallmark of *'walking in the light'.*[13] It is the ground of our assurance.[14] It is a manifestation of God's indwelling[15], and gives us confidence to face the Day of Judgement[16]. But just as God's love within us witnesses to us, so it also witnesses to others.

Tertullian, a Roman theologian in about AD 200, meditated on the effect Christian martyrs had: *"'Look', they say, 'how they [Christians] love one another' (for they themselves hate one another); 'and how they are ready to die for each other' (for they themselves are readier to kill each other)". "See how these Christians love one another".*

---

[12] (Col 3:12-14)
[13] (1Jn 2:8-11)
[14] (1Jn 3:10-19)
[15] (1Jn 4:7-12)
[16] (1Jn 4:17-21)

Anxious questions amongst the team (13:36-14:9)

The disciples are so shocked by the news of a betrayer and of Jesus's imminent departure, that they seem to have difficulty thinking outside the box. Jesus uses their questions to lead them on, following each answer with a provocative statement that will draw out their real fears.

Peter's question

As usual, Peter is first to engage his vocal cords! Passionate in his protestations of willingness to die for Jesus, he is the one who will shortly slice off the servant's ear in Gethsemane. He will shadow the arrest party back to Annas's courtyard, only to desert when a servant girl claims to have recognised him.

Behind his question, *'Where are you going?'* is another, '*Why can't I come?*' Peter couldn't imagine that his bravado actually hid a willingness to deny Christ for his own safety.

Jesus's answer is infinitely tender, knowing that one day Peter *will* be crucified in Rome for his loyalty to Jesus[17]. *"You can't come just now; but later, you will."* When Peter reiterates his willingness to die, Jesus pricks the bubble, with a prophecy that he will disown Christ that same night.

Jesus now speaks to the group as a whole, about how to handle the fear they're experiencing. He asks them to extrapolate from God's provision for their day-to-day needs on mission, and trust *Him* in the same way.

Jesus's whole purpose in going away (He says) is not to abandon them, but to prepare a place for them to be with Him. Just as a Jewish bridegroom would spend months building an extra room onto his father's house before collecting his bride, so He needs to go and prepare likewise. We know there will be a glorious day when He comes to call His bride, His Church, home. The dead will be raised first and then we who are alive will join Him in clouds of glory, for 'the marriage feast of the Lamb'!

In many situations in life, our fears are like Peter's. In a situation we don't understand, we forget to trust what our past experience of God's faithfulness

[17] (21:18,19)

has taught us. Our Father notices when even a hair of our head falls to the ground: and Jesus is just the same.

Jesus now deliberately provokes the next question. Peter had asked, '*Where are You going?*' Jesus says they already know the answer: not only His destination, but also the way to get there.[18]

Thomas's question

Thomas, who was always honest about what he was thinking, challenges Jesus.[19] *'We don't know where you're going, so how could we possibly know the way?'* Peter asked 'Why?': Thomas asks, 'Where? How?'

This elicits another of Jesus's seven 'I AM' statements: *"I AM the Way, the Truth and the Life - no-one comes to the Father except through Me".*

There is only one way to the Father, says Jesus; and it's through Me. This precludes all syncretism, all worship of anyone other than the Trinity. But if you reject this saying of Christ's as untrue, you cannot reasonably trust anything else He taught. He is *the* gate, the only gate, of the sheepfold.

As we journey to the Father, we must move in three dimensions:-

- *The way* refers to the way we live, the observable change from a worldly lifestyle to a Christ-centred one. This change was so clear in the early Church, that Jesus's followers were originally known as 'The Way'.
- *The truth*. To journey in the Way, our corrupted values and beliefs need reformation by truth. Lifestyle stems from one's beliefs, which in turn depend on who you believe. Paul urges the Philippians, *"Have this mind in you, which you saw in Christ Jesus"*. Jesus taught and lived out the truth about God; and His Spirit and the scriptures written under His influence, lead us into more and more truth throughout our lifetime.
- *The (zoe) life*. Correct beliefs are fine, but we know that even devils believe in Jesus, and tremble at His name. It is only by the power of Jesus's resurrection life flowing into us, that we can bear the fruit of His character -

[18] (14:4)
[19] (14:5)

love, joy, peace, patience, kindness, goodness, gentleness, faithfulness and self-control.

Jesus Himself is the answer to all of our needs. We are called to love God with all of our heart, our mind and our strength: but we can only do so as we focus on Christ's life, Christ's teachings, and His Spirit. Many nowadays believe that all ways to God are equal, but Jesus is unequivocal: the *only* way is through Him. Before we can know the Father, we must follow the Son.

Again, He follows His answer with a provocative statement.[20] *"My destination is the Father. If you had really recognised who I am"* (the only-begotten Son of the Father[21], and the exact image of His Person[22]) *"you would have known My Father too. From now on you do know Him and have seen Him."*

<u>Philip's question</u>

Philip now chimes in, frustrated by all this figurative language.[23] He's a pragmatist who believes in experience, not mysticism.[24] *"Just <u>show</u> us the Father - that's all we need."*

Philip wants to know the Father, without having to follow the Way: to worship, without having to trek across Arabia following the star. But at the same time, he discounts much of what Jesus has said, as mystical mumbo-jumbo. How like him we evangelicals are!

Knowing the Father is the complete antidote to all fears and anxieties. Philip has crystallised his deepest inner need, but hasn't realised it is met in Christ. He hasn't clocked that every time Jesus teaches, He is simply speaking God's words. And that every time He works a miracle, He is enacting God's activity.

Thus he completes a trinity of unbelief amongst the disciples: they do not yet know the Father! But man's built-in hunger to know God, has already been provided for in Christ: *'We beheld His glory, glory as of the only-begotten of the Father'*.

---

[20] (14:7)
[21] (1:14)
[22] (Heb 1:1-3)
[23] (16:25)
[24] (1:45,46)

A different kind of knowing (14:9-14)

This 'knowing of the Father' is a central theme in the rest of the discourse.

When they meet the resurrected Christ[25], they will know that Christ is in God[26] and that they are in Him and He in them: through the Holy Spirit's indwelling, they will experience communion with their Lord and their God. Father and Son will come and dwell in them[27].

This is obviously not referring to factual knowledge. Philip has walked on Christ's heels for three years, has known His habits, His character, His teachings - and yet doesn't 'know' Him in the sense Jesus is meaning.[28]

The Greek word Jesus uses is 'ginosko', from where we get English words such as 'diagnosis' and 'prognosis'. They imply a knowing which goes beyond the facts of an illness to understand its cause, and beyond knowing the cause to foreseeing its likely future course.

'Ginosko' is also the word used in the Greek translation of the Old Testament *(the Septuagint)* for Adam 'knowing' his wife Eve, which led to the conception of her first child. No mere factual knowledge, that!

Greek & Hebrew ideas of knowledge differed. To the Greek mind, knowledge was static & factual; whereas to Jews, it was relational & dynamic. Just as in marriages, it involved loyalty, commitment, & mutual respect to maintain one's knowledge of another.

Philip had not *diagnosed* the reality of Jesus's divine essence - His 'only-begottenness', His being of one substance with the Father. He had not realised that anyone who grasped who Jesus was, was actually seeing God Incarnate, the exact image of God's Person. He had not internalised what Jesus had said, *"I and the Father are One"*.

Union and indwelling amongst the Trinity

[25] (14:19)
[26] (14:20)
[27] (14:23)
[28] (14:9)

Jesus starts to explain the nature of the Godhead.[29] God the Father manifests Himself through His Son. Every time one of the seven signs occurred, Philip (without realising it) was observing God manifest in the flesh[30]. In the physical realm, God was in Christ. And in the spiritual realm, Christ was and is in God: the Lamb of God, in the midst of the Throne of God.[31] He is the eternal Logos of God, who indwells the bosom of the Father.

This is the first time Jesus has taught them about indwelling; and He goes on to teach astonishing truth about Father, Son and Holy Spirit all indwelling *us*. There is communion between the Holy Spirit and our human spirit. And we become one spirit with Christ.[32]

Indwelling is something that can only occur Spirit-to-*spirit*. It does not happen in our intellect or feelings or will, which are all aspects of our *soul;* though we may experience the Spirit within us through feelings, thoughts or urges. Some believe that our spirit and soul are one and the same, but whilst the two can be hard to distinguish, the Word of God can divide between them.[33] (For more on the difference between them, see the section on 'life' in appendix two.) The distinction is important, as without that, it's hard to grasp the reality of indwelling.

Believing into Jesus

In English we use 'in' to indicate both location (I am *in* my house) and movement (I'm going *into* my house). So though Greek has two quite distinct prepositions - 'en' for location and 'eis' for movement - both are often just translated as 'in', when referring to belief in Christ. So we miss the distinction between *three* kinds of belief, which are apparent in the Greek. These are:-

- believing a person, when they tell you something: accepting it as true
- believing in *(en)* a person: trusting them, believing they can do things, etc

[29] (14:10)
[30] (1Tim 3:16)
[31] (Rev 5:6,7)
[32] (1Cor 6:17)
[33] (Heb 4:12)

• believing into *(eis)* Jesus: believing in a way that joins you with Him

Jesus tells Philip that anyone who believes *into* Him, will similarly manifest the works of the Father.[34] *(This is such deep truth, my heart is singing!)*

The story is often told, of Houdini walking a tightrope across Niagara Falls.

- He first asked the crowd, *"Do you believe that someone could walk across the Falls on that rope?"* Those who said Yes, were believing it was possible. They believed him.
- Then he asked, *"Do you believe I can walk across that rope?"* That was asking, did they believe in him? He walked across the rope without falling to his death. *"Do you believe I can do it again, this time pushing a wheelbarrow?"* A few thought he could: they believed in him.
- Finally he asked those few, *"Then which of you is willing to sit in the wheelbarrow?"* That required the third kind of faith - for your fate and his to be joined: believing into him!

Why is this distinction about a two-letter word so important? Because it's the foundation of all New Testament teaching about our union with Christ.

<u>Union with Christ means union with the Father too</u>

This union is often seen purely in a judicial sense: we are baptised into Christ, and in the Court of Heaven His death is counted as our death and we are justified by faith.

But Paul teaches extensively about this union being much more than just legal. If we are united with Him in His death, we are also united with Him in HIs resurrection life. And we also share in the fellowship of His sufferings. We are welded into Him; and this union is the essence of truly knowing Him.

- *"For me to live is Christ, to die is gain."*
- *"I live; nevertheless not I, but Christ lives in me."*
- *"I count all things worthless, for the sake of knowing Him and being found in Him."*

---

[34] (14:12)

Our union with Christ is also a pre-requisite for abiding in Him: a branch cannot possibly bear fruit if it has never been joined to the Vine! Most of the rest of the discourse will make no sense at all, unless we have believed into Jesus and are joined with Him by faith.

But if we have and are, then the Father will manifest Himself through us, just as He did through Jesus. In fact He will do even greater works through us than He did through Christ. Because Jesus has ascended to the Father and is seated at His right hand, pouring out the Spirit and appointing various ministries!

In short, in being joined to Christ, we are also joined to the Father. We do not need to ask Jesus to ask the Father for us[35]; we can approach the Father directly, in the name of Jesus, knowing that Jesus will do *anything* to glorify the Father[36].

Up to this point, Jesus has used the disciples' own questions as a springboard for teaching them about the new dimension of life they are about to enter - life in union and communion with His Father as well as Himself. But He now begins to teach them about a third member of the Trinity: the Holy Spirit.

Read on for the next thrilling episode!

---

35 (16:26,27)

36 (14:13,14)

Communion with Father, Son and Holy Spirit

(14:15-31)

Jesus starts to reveal a new dimension to the disciples:
knowing the Holy Spirit's advocacy, the Father's love, and Christ's peace

How do you reassure your young child, if you have to go away for a while - say into hospital, or on a business trip?

You might use various approaches: promising them you will be back after three sleeps; placing them with people they trust; explaining why it's necessary; answering any fears they have; promising to bring them something back when you return - and so on. The reassurance works, because your child knows they can trust what you say.

All of these elements are present in the way Jesus deals with the disciples' separation anxiety. He gives them (and us) many wonderful promises:-

- I am going to prepare a place for you, and will come and collect you[1]
- You can still talk to me while I'm away: I'll respond to your prayers[2]
- The Holy Spirit will look after you, encourage & reassure you[3]
- I won't abandon you, I will return; & life will have a new dimension[4]
- You'll be joined with Me deeper than ever before, loved even more[5]
- My Father's going to come and live with us too! He loves you too[6]

In the previous chapter we saw how Jesus used the disciples' own fears & questions, to make His Oneness with Father God even more explicit.[7] In Christ's earthly life, God the Father has been present with Him, speaking through Him and performing the miracles they've witnessed. Everything they've observed of Jesus's character, grace and truth, is an exact image of

---

[1] (14:2,3)
[2] (14:13)
[3] (14:16,17)
[4] (14:19)
[5] (14:20)
[6] (14:23)
[7] (14:1-14)

the Father's heart. Coming to the Father is simply a case of living like Jesus, believing the truth He taught, and receiving the new kind of life He offers.

But now He goes on to open a broad new vista of life after His death and resurrection. Not only will He personally show Himself to them again, they will know God the Holy Spirit as an ever-present inner advocate; and they will experience direct, unmediated access to the Father's Presence and love.

The Holy Spirit: an inner Presence, and Advocate (14:15-18)

The disciples had known the Holy Spirit's presence with them, in Jesus. As Jesus said to Nicodemus, you can hear the sound of a gale even though you can't see the wind directly. They had watched as Jesus spoke to the storm on the Sea of Galilee. They had seen the ways demons fled at His command.

But now, says Jesus, you will know Him *in* you, in a way that non-believers can't. You'll receive Him, I will breathe Him into you:[8] just as I breathed the breath of life into Adam at Creation. Just as the air in your lungs sustains your bodily life, the Spirit will sustain your spiritual life, your 'zoe'.

Jesus describes the Spirit as '*another* Helper'. Greek has two distinct words for 'another'; the one used here means 'another *of the same kind*'. Jesus says the Spirit is another Person just like Himself. The same Greek word (paraclete) is used later[9] to describe Jesus's role in interceding for us with the Father when we sin. He is our 'Counsel for the defence' in Heaven's courtroom. And the Holy Spirit is our Counsellor here on earth.

Just as Jesus has been teaching, reassuring and strengthening their faith, the Holy Spirit will too. Just as Jesus is the exact image of the Father, the Holy Spirit is just like Jesus. But while Jesus has to leave to go to the Father, the Spirit will be present with them - *in* them - continuously and permanently,

The root meaning of 'paraclete' in Greek refers to someone called alongside to help, and means an advocate. When I was a family doctor, sometimes patients came in with a 'mental health advocate': someone who'd help them tell me their symptoms, and who could later explain to them what I'd said

---

[8] (20:22)

[9] (1Jn 2:1)

about the diagnosis and treatment. Likewise, the Holy Spirit prays for us and through us, when we don't know how to pray.[10]

John the Baptist had prophesied that Jesus would baptise His people *'with the Holy Spirit and fire'*[11]. The radical effect of being filled with the Holy Spirit is shown in the transformation of Peter from someone inwardly cowardly, to the bold, powerful preacher of the Day of Pentecost.

Jesus says the Spirit will remain with us permanently. The constancy of the Spirit's Presence is something we fail to appreciate. It's true, we may grieve Him by anger, or unforgiveness; and we can quench His gifts by distrusting Him. But He is constantly present within us. We can ask Him to intervene as our advocate whenever we are struggling with things, like that patient's advocate in my consulting room. Perhaps this is why Paul often refers to the *fellowship* of the Holy Spirit: He is our constant companion.

It is notable that Jesus refers to the Holy Spirit as 'He'. Greek has three genders - he, she, and it - and usually a spirit is referred to as 'it'. But the Holy Spirit is just as much a person as Jesus is. We should not think of Him as an impersonal force or vague influence. He speaks, has feelings, thinks & acts.

One thing many people struggle with, is the idea that a spirit can live within us. Yet we see this reality illustrated repeatedly in the gospel accounts of demonised people: the demon manifests itself by speaking through the person's voice or by acting through their body. *(Our Western worldview largely prevents us recognising this, though it happens in first-world countries not just in 'darkest Africa'.)* It seems that under certain conditions spirits can indwell a human body, and commandeer control of our emotions, thoughts, speech, health, and actions.

St Paul refers to our physical bodies as tents - temporary dwelling places for our spirits in this life - and there can be more than one spirit in the tent! Evil spirits each have a character or role - for example, lying spirits, or spirits of

[10] (Rom 8:26)

[11] (1:33, Matt 3:11)

anger, or infirmity. They all hate the Presence of the Holy Spirit. But God intends us to be temples, dwelling places for His Holy Spirit.[12]

The Holy Spirit indwells our human spirit, teaching us wonderful truths about God in our innermost being.[13] In fact, the Holy Spirit is the Spirit of Truth. He is the Spirit who inspired all the authors of the Bible to write what they did.[14] We may struggle to explain to someone else, why or how we know the spiritual truths we know; and we may even struggle to understand the truths themselves. But we know that we know that we know, because He has taught us Spirit-to-spirit.

He also gives us the gift of discernment between truth and lies[15], leading us into more and more truth over our lifetime. Sometimes as I read scripture or I hear a preacher, I will sense the Holy Spirit bubbling up within me and witnessing to the truth of what I am hearing. Likewise there are times when we hear an eloquent, passionate speaker but it leaves us cold. Or worse, we know what we are hearing *isn't* truth.

When we are tempted to doubt whether we are children of God after all, (perhaps when we've fallen into a recurring temptation or sin), He will come and witness within our hearts to the truth of our adoption, enabling us to cry out '*Abba, Father'*[16].

<u>How can we receive the Holy Spirit?</u>

Ultimately, it is not by anything we do, but by believing the promise Jesus gives us here.[17] The gift of the Spirit was promised by the Father way back in the times of Ezekiel and Jeremiah, as part of the New Covenant. And that New Covenant has been brought into force by the blood of Christ.

As Jesus speaks at the Last Supper, the fullness of the Spirit is present in Him. But once He returns to the Father, He will ask Him to pour out the long-awaited gift. The Spirit will 'proceed' from the Father and the Son, as the

---

[12] (2 Cor 6:14-18)
[13] (1 Cor 2:9-12)
[14] (2 Pet 1:20,21)
[15] (1 John 2:27)
[16] (Rom 8:15,16)
[17] (Gal 3:2)

creeds say: though sent by Them, He also comes of His own volition, to be our Advocate.

The only requirement on our part, is to love Jesus and keep His commandments. The disciples needed to obey Jesus's instruction to '*wait in the city*'.[18] In fact, when the Spirit does finally come, we find them in the exact same room where Jesus had made this promise[19], waiting expectantly in united prayer. In the same way when we seek the Holy Spirit nowadays, there will often be periods of prayer and devotional waiting before He comes. Part of the challenge is to trust that God will give you a good gift, not something harmful or crazy.[20] But the primary requirement is just to believe.

Union with Christ in His resurrection life (14:19-21)

Three days after the crucifixion, the disciples will see Jesus again, in that same room.[21] The doors were locked to keep intruders at bay, and yet Jesus appeared and stood in their midst. From now on, until His second coming in glory, He will appear only to those who love Him. The world will see Him no more: but those who love and serve Him will.

- We will know ourselves joined to Him in a new level of existence: resurrection life. Because He lives on that plane, we also will. He is the vine, we are the branches. His sap will flow into us, producing heavenly fruit - the same character traits which are the glory of God.
- We will know the unity of Son with Father; the eternal fathering of the Son by the Father, and the eternal obedience of the Son to the Father.
- We will know the truth of the incarnation, that '*Jesus Christ is come in the flesh*'.[22]
- We will know that He has now returned to the Father and is seated at His right hand, amid God's throne.
- And we will know that here on this earth, He is in us; but even more, that in the spiritual realms, we are in Him.

---

[18] (Lk 24:49, Acts 1:4,5)
[19] (Acts 1:13,14)
[20] (Lk 11:9-13)
[21] (20:19)
[22] (1Jn 4:2)

God sees us as saints because we are 'in Christ', justified by His blood, His obedience to the cross. We are complete in Him[23], lacking nothing necessary for life and godliness[24]. He is our wisdom. We are to 'seek the things which are above', where He is, rather than go after earthly pleasures.

Jesus promises to manifest Himself to us

Beyond the promise of a resurrection reunion with the Eleven, Jesus promises to *manifest* Himself; to anyone who shows their love for Him in obedience to His commandments[25], and treasures His teaching as the Logos of God[26]. What does this mean?

To manifest means to uncover, to make visible, to put something beyond doubt, to cause to shine out: its meaning is very similar to the word 'revelation'. Not everyone has Damascus Road experiences, mountain-top transfigurations or personal theophanies: but any believer may claim this promise of Jesus to manifest Himself.

Judas has one last question![27] Not Judas Iscariot, but his team-mate when they were sent out in pairs[28], who was also known as Simon the Canaanite[29]. His question is this: *"How will You manifest Yourself just to us, and not the world?"* He was presumably expecting Messiah's return to be one of great glory, visible to all nations. Why would Messiah skulk behind closed doors?

Jesus's answer is that such manifestations, whether resurrection appearances or subsequent epiphanies, are only for those who love Him and hold to His teaching (or 'logos'). The Son of God will never again subject Himself to the world's disbelief and taunts. Those who ignore or despise His word, ignore the fact that He is The Logos, sent by the Father. Their hearts are hardened against receiving revelation, and once Jesus has been given the name above all names, God will not expose Him to rejection and humiliation any longer.

---

[23] (Col 2:9,10)
[24] (2 Pet 1:3).
[25] (14:21)
[26] (14:23)
[27] (14:22)
[28] (Lk 6:16)
[29] (Matt 10:4)

We know that the Lord manifested Himself to Stephen as he was being stoned[30], and to Peter[31], and repeatedly to Paul[32]. And the whole Book of Revelation is 'the Revelation of Jesus Christ'[33] given through John by multiple visions of the Son of Man[34].

Are these experiences only for the original apostles, or is Jesus's promise true for anyone who knows and keeps His commandments out of love? Personally, I believe His promise still stands true.

Philip Wiebe, who was chair of the Philosophy Department at Trinity Western University and a serious scholar, investigated twenty-eight modern-day visions of Jesus, which he examined from psychological, neuropsychological, mentalist, and other perspectives. He was convinced that in at least some of them, something transcendent had happened. Hugh Montefiore, a well-known New Testament scholar at Cambridge University and later bishop of the Church of England, converted to Christianity from Judaism at age sixteen because he had a vision in which Jesus appeared to him. The Lord told him to "follow me" – words that, at the time, the young Montefiore did not know were drawn from the New Testament.

Jesus also promises that He will make His dwelling-place with each individual believer.[35]. His very last word to them before He ascended, was, 'Behold, I am with you always, even unto the end of the age'.

To sum up then, Christ promises us spiritual *union* with Him, and *indwelling*; *manifestation* when there is a special need for revelation; and *presence* with us. This is His all-encompassing answer to our separation anxiety!

---

30 (Acts 7:56)

31 (Acts 10:13-15)

32 (Acts 9:3-6; 18:9-10; 22:17-21; 23:11; 2Cor 12:1-5; 2Tim 4:16-17)

33 (Rev 1:1)

34 (Rev 1:9-19; 5:6-6:12; 14:1,14; 19:11-16; 21:5,6; 22:12-16)

35 (14:23)

Knowing the Father (14:7,9,21,23)

Jesus gently rebuked both Thomas and Philip for not realising they already knew the Father, present in Christ Himself.[36] He had previously said that the only way to the Father was through Him. So are we to understand that we can only know the Father - 'know' meaning deep, intimate relationship - indirectly via the Son?

Posing the question is enough to point to the answer!

Philip knew that a direct revelation of the Father would fully satisfy his heart's desire.[37] Then as now, every human being has an inbuilt longing to know they are 'fathered'; not in the biological sense, but relationally. Yet in the West, we have lost sight of this.

Since the Industrial Revolution, fathers have disappeared off to work each day. And marriage breakdowns and social mobility have added to the problem. Relatively few children experience the identity-forming input of their father, especially during their teens. We celebrate Mothering Sunday, but don't recognise the significance of fathering to anything like the same extent. Our culture believes that it is good for children to separate from their parents much younger than previous cultures ever did. Even with a stay-at-home Dad, how many of us would say that their earthly father gave them a really good image of what their Heavenly Father is like?!

The gospel clearly teaches that through making atonement, Jesus's purpose was *to bring men back to the Father*. He died, to create a *'new and living way'* directly into the Father's Presence.[38] He wants His disciples to be *'sons of your Father in heaven'*[39] and to find such deep rest in knowing they are fathered, that they no longer need to anxiously *'lay up treasures on earth'*[40], or worry about food or fashion[41]. He wants to turn the hearts of God's children back to their Father[42] so that they return to Him like the prodigal son

---

[36] (14:7,9)
[37] (14:8)
[38] (Heb 10:19-22)
[39] (Mt 5:43-48)
[40] (Mt 6:19-20)
[41] (Mt 6:25-32)
[42] (Mal 4:6)

did[43]. He wants us to know our status as beloved sons and daughters[44], so securely that in times of distress we reflexly cry out *"Abba, Father!"*[45]

Jesus has showcased the perfect son-to-father, father-to-son relationship throughout His ministry. He will reveal His intimacy with the Father much more deeply as He prays for them after finishing His discourse.[46] He will encourage them to use their own direct access to the Father in prayer[47], no longer needing Him as their intermediary.

Indeed, the *essence* of eternal life is to *know* both the Father and the Son.[48] John is still experiencing this reality years later, when he invites his readers to join him in *'fellowship with the Father and His Son Jesus Christ'.*[49]

Note how Jesus refers repeatedly to Himself and the Father as two distinct Persons. He is about to return to the Father. He will ask the Father for the Spirit. Anyone who loves Him will experience the love of the Father[50], and will know both Father and Son dwelling with him. The ultimate fulfilment of this will be in the New Jerusalem, when *'the dwelling-place of God will be with men'*[51]. But John wants us to know this in our present-day experience.

Paul obviously knew God deeply in this three-fold way. He expresses beautifully the distinct quality of each relationship, when he prays for the Corinthians "May the *grace* of our Lord Jesus Christ, the *love* of God, and the *fellowship* of the Holy Spirit be with you all" [52].

In my opinion, most Christians know God as one, or maybe two, members of the Trinity - not all Three. They may be very aware of the gifts and leading of the Spirit; or they may know Christ indwelling them. Few truly know God as their Father.

---

43 (Lk 15:11-23)
44 (1Jn 3:1,2)
45 (Rom 8:14-17)
46 (John 17)
47 (16:23)
48 (17:3)
49 (1Jn 1:3)
50 (14:21,23)
51 (Rev 21:3)
52 (2Cor 13:14)

Perhaps a testimony from someone I know, may help make this real:

"I met Jesus fifty years ago, in an overwhelming experience of His grace which came about as a result of seeking the gift of the Holy Spirit. But for decades thereafter, I had no idea I could also know the Father just as really.

"Then I met people who obviously did know Him as their true Father. I began to realise how my image of Father God had been distorted by childhood experience. My father was too busy with other more important things to notice his sons very much. One had to be either rebellious and a problem, or impressively good, to get attention. That inculcated a belief that Father God was the same: He had much bigger fish to fry, than my trivial prayers.

"Then one day Jesus personally introduced me to His Father! That experience radically changed me. All my striving to obtain others' affirmation, my anger at not receiving this, and my anxieties about having to rely on my own self-sufficiency - they all shrivelled. Not to say I am perfect, far from it! But I know I am Fathered, and that's made a huge difference emotionally and spiritually."

Take Jesus's description of what His life in us is like, and put it in the faith room of your heart. Then ask God specifically to know Him more deeply in all three Persons. Jesus died for this, and it's your birthright as a child of God.

The Cross as triumph, not defeat (14:25-31)

Having given them a glimpse of all that His returning to the Father will mean in terms of their new life & relationship with God, Jesus returns to the here-and-now, and the terrible reality they are about to go through.

They need not fret about remembering everything, because the Spirit will go over everything He's said, and unpack it all.[53] He's told them in advance so that when it happens, their faith in Him will be buttressed by the realisation that He knew all along.[54]

[53] (14:26)

[54] (14:29)

The crucifixion won't appear as some terrible miscarriage of justice (though it might at first), but rather as the supreme proof of Jesus's loving obedience to the Father.[55] His triumphant return to heavenly glory with the Father, having overcome the world and defeated its ruler, will be cause for joy. They will realise that He has been given *'the name above all names, that at the name of Jesus, every knee will bow'*.

This is a challenge to the way *we* think of the cross, not just them. Western orthodoxy focusses on the cross as atonement, sacrifice for our sin through enduring horrific torture and degradation. Eastern orthodoxy however focusses on the victory that Christ accomplished at Calvary.

When Jesus met Moses and Elijah on the Mount of Transfiguration, what did their conversation focus on? The *Exodus* that He would *accomplish* at Jerusalem.[56] Just as the Passover lambs had been used to bring about their deliverance from slavery to be able to worship, so Jesus will set them free to worship God without fear.

Christ's gift of peace (14:27)

The idea of someone giving us their peace seems strange nowadays, but was something the disciples would have been used to.

The Hebrew concept of peace *(shalom)* was far wider than the absence of conflict: it evolved the well-being of one's spirit as well as one's body and soul.[57] And it came from God looking favourably on that person.[58] It is a fruit of the Spirit, which develops in an individual's human spirit.[59]

Jesus had taught them to bestow their peace on any household that offered hospitality during their missions; if it turned out to be inhospitable, they should reclaim their peace[60], shaking the dust off their feet. Just as it is possible for someone to curse another, and that curse to really affect the

---

[55] (14:31)
[56] (Lk 9:28-31)
[57] (1 Thess 5:23)
[58] (Num 6:26)
[59] (Gal 5:22)
[60] (Mt 10:12-13)

person's life, so it is possible to speak blessing into another's life, from the inner storeroom of our heart.

The Roman Empire had established the 'Pax Romana' - Roman peace. Their dominance as sole superpower meant a stable world order. Many thought Messiah would come with greater military might, to overthrow Rome and establish world peace. But as Jesus told Pilate, *'My kingdom is not of this world'*. My peace I give unto you, but not in the way this world gives peace.

Peace is one of the qualities of God's Presence. He is the God of peace, as well as the God of love. The New Covenant prophesied by Ezekiel is a covenant of peace.[61] Jesus is our Prince of Peace[62], who was scourged for our peace[63]; and we have peace with God through Him[64]. His words are the foundation for our peace.[65] If we bring all our worries and cares to God, His supernatural peace will guard our hearts and minds, keeping them in Christ.[66]

When we consider Christ's supernatural peace displayed in this chapter, it is astounding. Facing flogging, mocking, utter humiliation and a horrific death, His heart is still at peace. Even after one of them has left to betray Him, and in the full knowledge the others will soon desert Him, He is able to give Himself to teaching them heavenly truth. There is no trace of anxiety or fear in His words.

There will be sorrow and distress in Gethsemane. And there will be anguish on the cross, as He experiences being forsaken by His Father. But at no point do we hear Him express fear, perhaps because He is so utterly secure in His Father's love. *'Perfect love casts out fear'*.

Even facing the approach of His sworn enemy, the Prince of this world, He is at peace. He knows the Enemy 'has nothing in Him'. Satan has not the slightest hold on Him, nothing whatsoever that he can use to accuse Jesus to the Father.[67] He has so thoroughly overcome the world and all the

---

[61] (Ezek 34:25, 37:26)
[62] (Isa 9:6,7)
[63] (Isa 53:5)
[64] (Rom 5:1)
[65] (16:33)
[66] (Phil 4:6,7)
[67] (14:30)

temptations Satan tried to lure Him with, He is so armed with the breastplate of righteousness, that the world will have to acknowledge He is going to the cross out of love for the Father.[68]

This should give us a cheerful resilience when we experience tribulation and accusation from the enemy: we are wearing the armour of Christ[69], we are hidden behind His riot shield so to speak.

It could have been very tempting to enjoy the warmth and security of the Upper Room for as long as possible; but perhaps to show Satan that He is resolute in purpose, Jesus stands up and sets off on the walk to Gethsemane.

En route, as they walk past the Temple with its entrance covered by a huge vine, He will begin to teach them how to guard their union with Him - how to 'abide in Him'. They are to be temples of the Holy Spirit, bearing fruit - much fruit - for His glory.

---

68 (14:31)

69 (16:33; Eph 6:13,14)

Abiding in Christ (15:1-17)

Once the disciples are in Christ, joined to Him through the cross and resurrection, they will need to maintain their relationship with Him.

Jesus has just taught His disciples that *"Because I live, you will live also. In that day, you will know that....you are in Me, and I am in you"*[1].

This union with Christ is portrayed in scripture in various corporate metaphors: for example He is the head of the church, we are the body; He is the husband, the church is the bride. But first there must be the individual connection, which comes from believing *into* Him.

I am the Vine, you are the branches (15:1-3)

This is the last of the seven great 'I AM' statements in John.

The vine was a common metaphor for Israel in the Old Testament; imagery perhaps rooted in the clusters of huge grapes which the spies brought back to Joshua.

But strangely, the vast majority of such OT references express God's disappointment at Israel's failure to bring forth good fruit.[2] Instead of justice and righteousness there were oppression and cries for help. The noble vine He had planted, had become degenerate[3], committing spiritual prostitution.

Asaph, a psalmist, saw Israel as a once-flourishing vineyard that spread over a vast area, but was then abandoned and re-wilded, the vine branches burned. He prays for a God-empowered 'Son of man' who will bring restoration - a *true vine* who will fulfil Israel's original calling.[4]

As they followed Jesus across Jerusalem to Gethsemane, the disciples would have passed the entrance to the Temple, which had huge clusters of golden grapes on the stonework on each side. Jesus had previously declared His body to be the true Temple.[5] Now He declares Himself to be the true vine!

---

1 (14:19,20)
2 (Isa 5:1-7)
3 (Jer 2:20,21)
4 (Ps 80:7-19)
5 (2:18-21)

Barclay[6] paraphrases Jesus's words like this: *"You think that because you belong to the nation of Israel you are a branch of the true vine of God. But the nation is a degenerate vine, as all your prophets saw. It is I who am the true vine. The fact that you are a Jew will not save you. The only thing that can save you is to have an intimate living fellowship with me, for I am the vine of God; and you must be branches joined to me".*

Jesus's concern is not about Israel as a nation, but us as individual disciples.

He focusses first on the Father's role as the vine-dresser. God is planting a new vineyard with a truly noble vine, and He wants to ensure there is fruit[7], abundant fruit[8], fruit that will glorify Him[9], lasting fruitfulness[10]. Vines need constant care for this to be so.

Over winter the vinedresser cuts away any branches that didn't bear fruit that year. Branches that can't find any support to climb on, do not develop foliage - so He lifts them up[11] and attaches them to a support. Then he prunes the fruit-bearing branches of all unnecessary foliage - so that *all* the sap will go into developing fruit.

N.B: In verse two, the word translated as 'He takes away',
can also be translated as 'He lifts up'

It is easy to skip over this aspect of Jesus's analogy, since none of us like being pruned. But if truth be told, we have all experienced times when our roles suddenly ended, illness or disability limited our activity, or it just seemed we were fruitless for a while. In fact young vines are routinely pruned so heavily for the first three years that they *cannot* bear fruit. So we can't judge one another by fruitfulness at a given point in time. It may be that this is a season of pruning in your life, but our Father's aim is always positive: to bring forth more fruit.

---

[6] (William Barclay, Daily Study Bible)
[7] (15:2)
[8] (15:5)
[9] (15:8)
[10] (15:16)
[11] (Vine's Expository Dictionary of Old & New Testament words, άιρεω, p1117)

N.B. Those who believe 'Once saved, always saved' have a problem with verses two and five: if the branch was once joined to Christ, and if we cannot lose our salvation, how can the branch be taken away, or cast out?

- *Some try to get round the problem by taking 'branch' to mean one's works, rather than the person themselves.*
- *But its straightforward interpretation aligns with the parable of the wheat and the tares, where Jesus says some who looked like wheat, actually end up being burnt because they are tares.*
- *Or with Jesus's account of His judging the peoples, where some who had prophesied and cast out demons in His name, are told to depart into the everlasting fire prepared for the devil and his angels.*
- *Or with those who, Hebrews says, 'have become partakers of the Holy Spirit'*

What is the fruit that Jesus has in mind?

Some commentators see the fruit as being those we bring to Christ, but most see it as the fruit of the Spirit.[12] We think of grapes as a source of delicious juice, but in nature their function is to carry seed; in other words, to reproduce. So maybe both meanings are in mind.

Jesus refers to the fruit bringing glory to God, and we have previously seen that God's glory is His goodness, His character.[13] In so far as our character reflects His holiness, His grace, His faithfulness, His love, we will bring Him glory: and we will attract others to Him. *'They will know you are My disciples, if you have love one for another'*.

The Greek word for pruning is the same as for cleaning. Jesus tells the eleven, that they are already clean because of His 'logos', His teaching. It has cut away their wrong ideas of Messiah, undermined their worldly competition for status, changed their ideas of holiness from external rituals to internal purity, and so on. Any remaining self-righteousness is about to be cut away at Calvary. But they will still need a lifetime's regular attention from the Father's pruning hook!

---

[12] (Gal 5:25ff)

[13] (Ex 33:18-34:7)

Active abiding (15:4-9)

Having put the primary emphasis on God's role, Jesus now shifts to their responsibility.[14] Abiding, or remaining, usually simply means staying where you are. But here Jesus is obviously envisaging active commitment.

Just as He has committed to indwelling us, we must commit to indwelling Him. We must abide in Him in the spiritual realm, and He must abide in us in the way we live. Otherwise, we will not develop any of the character-fruits that glorify Him: and instead, will start to wither.[15]

We cannot produce fruit if disconnected; but worse still, we are utterly useless. The wood of the vine is useful for nothing except to be burnt; and even then, it's no use as a fuel, for it burns too quickly.

There are various references to abiding, in both Old and New Testaments.

- David frequently refers to deliberately seeking God's Presence, and the joy and delight of worshipping Him.[16]
- Isaiah prophesies to a nation seeking protection through dubious political alliances, *"In returning and rest you shall be saved; in quietness and confidence shall be your strength".*[17] And again, *"Thou wilt keep Him in perfect peace, whose mind is stayed on Thee".*[18]
- Jesus tells His disciples, *"Take My yoke upon you, and learn of Me, and you shall find rest for your souls; for My yoke is easy, and My burden is light".*[19]
- In Acts we find the church at Antioch *'ministering to the Lord and fasting'* before receiving the Holy Spirit's instruction to ordain Paul and Barnabas.[20]
- Hebrews talks about a promise open to us, of *entering into rest*; a rest which comes from allowing the word of God to distinguish soulish activity from spiritual.[21] This entering into rest can only be by faith.

---

[14] (15:4)
[15] (15:6)
[16] (Ps 63:1-8)
[17] (Isa 30:15)
[18] (Isa 26:3)
[19] (Matt 11:29)
[20] (Acts 13:1-3)
[21] (Heb 4:1-12)

Some may object to this seemingly passive pursuit of God's Presence, pointing to all the scriptures about diligence in our Christian walk, and personal responsibility. But without time spent in devotion - in abiding and resting in God's Presence - we may tragically discover that our whole life's work has been wasted. We have built with materials which can't withstand the testing fire of the Christ's judgement seat.[22] Time spent 'abiding' is what fuels our passion to 'press on'.

<u>What does abiding mean in practice?</u> (15:9-17)

Jesus now puts flesh on the concept of abiding. Three themes stand out in His unpacking of its practical implications:

1. Love for Him, expressed in obedience to His commandments. Walking in His footsteps is not burdensome, but a cause of joy, fullness of joy[23]; especially following His command to love each other self-sacrificially[24]. Not competing for honour and status as they had done, but honouring each other and considering each other's interests before their own.

   John elaborates on this theme extensively in his first Letter. Love means actions not just words[25]; it is as we love one another that we experience God abiding in us[26]; and the old dictum, 'Love me, love my child' applies[27] not only to our relationship with Christ as God's Son, but also to all who have been born again.

2. Spending time with God, as His friends. Many Bible characters are described as servants of God, but only Abraham is described as 'the friend of God'[28]. What's the difference? Well, a servant simply obeys orders to do this, or do that: they are not told why, or what their master is trying to achieve by these actions. They don't know his heart's desires, or his future

---

[22] (1Cor 3:11-15)
[23] (15:11)
[24] (15:12,13)
[25] (1Jn 3:16-18)
[26] (1Jn 4:12)
[27] (1Jn 4:20-5:1)
[28] (Isa 41:8; Jas 2:23)

plans. Whereas a friend is in on his friend's inner thoughts and motivations.

Christ has told us everything the Father has revealed to Him! We know that Jesus will come again in glory, to judge the living and the dead. We know that His plan is to bring all things together under Christ's headship, and to make known His manifold wisdom to the heavenly powers, through the church. We know He is arranging every circumstance in our lives to mould us more into the likeness of Christ.

3. Prayer. As this moulding goes on, and we bear the fruits of God's character (which is no kudos to us, but all to Him who called us and ordained us for this destiny), our freedom and power in prayer grows and grows (v16). In fact prayer becomes itself a primary means of bearing fruit. Instead of seeking to change things (or people) by ourselves and our own actions, we 'work' through prayer. So that eventually, when we are called to give account, it becomes manifest that *'all our deeds are wrought in God'.*[29]

Closing off this exposition of abiding, Jesus underscores the pre-eminence of love. These things which He has just commanded - obedience, waiting on God, and prayer - are all subsumed in His supreme command, that we love one another. This will be vitally important as we face the implacable hostility of the world and its Prince, which is His next major concern.

---

[29] (3:21)

Hated, hunted - but heartened (15:17-16:16)

Jesus warns the disciples about the persecution they will suffer from now on. But He also reveals the Holy Spirit will be working with them to glorify Him.

Having told his disciples He is leaving to return to the Father, and having dealt with their anxious questions, Jesus has taught them about their future new relationship with the three members of the Trinity. He has given them His peace, and then taught them how to abide in Him; particularly emphasising the importance of loving one another.

The reason for that now becomes apparent: they will need that loving community to sustain each other against the hatred and persecution of the world. And they will need the very best Advocate!

The world's hatred of Christ's servants. (15:17-27)

The *world*, in this instance, does not just mean the total of human humanity, or worldly temptations. It refers to a real but spiritual kingdom, in implacable opposition to the Kingdom of heaven. There is no demilitarised zone between these two kingdoms, no coexistence or compromise. While it might seem that people hated Jesus *"without a cause"*, in fact their hatred was implanted by this kingdom of darkness.

This kingdom, 'the world', has a ruler: the prince of this world, also known as *'the prince of the power of the air'*[1]. His spirits operate through *'the sons of disobedience*' - human beings who are sold out to him. He has a hierarchy of spiritual forces beneath him: *'we do not wrestle against flesh and blood, but against principalities, against powers, against the rulers of the darkness of this age, against spiritual hosts of wickedness in the heavenly places'*[2].

This kingdom of darkness recognises those who have genuinely been chosen by Christ[3], and sees us as servants of another Master: to be persecuted just as He was, to be believed (or disbelieved) just as He was[4]. They think they are

[1] (Eph 2:2)
[2] (Eph 6:12)
[3] (Acts 19:15)
[4] (15:20)

safe, and indeed justified, in doing so; because they do not recognise that Jesus was sent by Almighty God[5].

Recognising that we are in a spiritual battlefield every day of our lives, is really important to understanding difficult things that happen along our way. When we experience seemingly unexplained hatred and opposition, especially in spiritual things, we are simply experiencing the same as Jesus. We are *"sharing in the fellowship of his sufferings"*. As the Body of Christ, in the absence of Jesus, Satan pours out his wrath on us instead.[6] We see this in the worldwide persecution of Christians, especially in places such as Iran and North Korea. Because we live in relative ease in the UK, we tend to forget that our nation's Christian heritage, which is so under threat at the moment, was originally won at the cost of great sacrifice.

Having told the disciples about their coming experience of the wonderful communion within the Godhead, and the love this will engender between them, Jesus does not hide from them (or from us) the tremendous personal cost in our daily lives. When He called Saul of Tarsus, He told Ananias, *"He is a chosen vessel of Mine to bear My name before Gentiles, kings, and the children of Israel. For I will show him how many things he must suffer for My name's sake".*[7]

Paul was hounded from place to place by posses of Jews, and nearly killed on several occasions: no wonder he referred to the Judaisers as '*hounds*'[8]. He suffered the thirty-nine lashes (one less than could kill a man) five times, from his Jewish detractors.[9] These would have been administered in the synagogue wherever he was at the time, in front of all the local Jews. Each time, he would have remembered that Jesus's back was torn to ribbons by the Romans' weighted scourge, for our sakes: '*by His stripes we are healed'*[10]. Truly, he knew what it meant to share the fellowship of Christ's sufferings: in those terrible experiences, he knew Christ's Presence deeply.

---

[5] (15:21)
[6] (Rev 12:17)
[7] (Acts 9:15)
[8] (Phil 3:2)
[9] (2 Cor 11:24)
[10] (Isa 53:5)

If Jesus hadn't come and preached to them, the Jews would at least have been innocent of guilt for rejecting Him. They would not have prayed that terrible, self-imprecatory prayer, *"His blood be upon us, and upon our children".*[11] But now, says Jesus, they are utterly without excuse. There are no mitigating factors whatsoever. Not only have they heard His words, they have observed the Father doing mighty miracles through Him, things which they knew only Messiah could do. So that in rejecting Him, they were directly rejecting God Himself. Jesus had not given them the slightest reason to hate Him. He had in fact fulfilled the Old Covenant so completely, that they had been unable to make a single charge stick against Him.[12]

<u>The issue of stumbling</u> (16:1-4)

Jesus's purpose in forewarning them was to protect them from 'stumbling'.[13] The Greek word is 'scandalise' - so we might read it as, to protect them from being scandalised. When a scandal occurs, we lose faith in the individual concerned: this is the essence of the word's meaning.

Someone whose faith was strong and upright, is tripped up by a life event that makes them question what they have believed. Spiritually, they are left lying on the ground badly bruised or injured.

It is a word that comes up many times in Jesus's teaching, but often with a different English translation: 'taking offence'. All the following footnotes use this same word, either as a verb or a noun: we can be stumbled by our own sinful desires[14], temptation by others[15], discouragement[16], persecution[17], bad example from our parents[18], the cross[19], the preaching of the cross[20], and betrayal by other believers[21].

---

11 (Matt 27:25)
12 (8:46)
13 (16:1)
14 (Matt 5:29,30)
15 (Num 23-25; Rev 2:14)
16 (Matt 11:21)
17 (Matt 13:21)
18 (Matt 18:6)
19 (Matt 26:31)
20 (1Cor 1:23)
21 (Matt 24:9,10)

Stumbling others, and stumbling or being stumbled ourselves, is a major risk for Christian disciples. We will need deep roots, pure hearts, loving care for others, and strong faith to withstand everything the world will throw at us. But knowing that Jesus told us this would happen, will be an anchor for our souls.[22]

<u>The Spirit will glorify Jesus, and unpack His teachings</u> (15:26-16:15)

Having told them the worst, Jesus now tells them what the help of the Holy Spirit will mean in practice.

Three of Christ's five references in this discourse to the Spirit's work, are in these verses. They seem to apply specifically to the apostles, whereas the earlier ones are of more general application.

Jesus says they must bear witness, *because they had been with Him from the beginning.*[23] This implies He is speaking solely to the remaining eleven apostles. Their eye-witness accounts would be essential for the gospel records, to establish the truth of His resurrection. When appointing Judas's replacement, this was their primary criterion: someone who could be an eye-witness of everything Jesus had said and done.[24]

When He speaks about the Spirit testifying[25], and them witnessing[26], in both cases the word is 'marturion' - the word from which we get our words 'martyr' and 'martyrdom'. All the apostles apart from John eventually died a martyr's death, Peter and Paul both being crucified in Rome. This was their ultimate witness - that they were willing to follow their Lord even in this.

As well as being their indwelling Advocate[27] and their Teacher[28], sent by the Father at Jesus's request, the Spirit's primary concern will be to glorify Jesus[29]. One means of His doing so will be to produce the God-glorifying

---

[22] (16:4)
[23] (15:27)
[24] (Acts 1:15-22)
[25] (15:26)
[26] (15:27)
[27] (14:16)
[28] (14:26)
[29] (16:14)

fruits of the Spirit. Another will be to empower the apostles' witness, both by bringing conviction of sin, righteousness and judgement to their hearers[30], and also by unpacking the truths Jesus was only able to pre-figure[31].

The Spirit is the *genuine* Spirit, the Spirit of truth. That is so precious in these days when everyone supposedly has their own truth, and alternative facts and conspiracy theories are rampant. He never lies to us[32] but continually teaches us truth in our inmost being. He writes the Law of Christ on our hearts and minds, as was promised in the New Covenant.[33]

<u>The Person of the Spirit</u>

Jesus tells them more about the Person of the Spirit, and His relationship to the Father and the Son.

The Spirit *proceeds* from the Father[34]. He is 'of one substance' with the Father, having the same character glories of love, joy, peace, patience, kindness, goodness, gentleness and self control. He is the outflowing of the essence, wisdom and power of God. He proceeds, in order to act, to do things. He is the carrier of the ongoing mission of God. He flows in royal procession from the Father to you and me. Truly, as the creed says, He is to be worshipped along with the Father and the Son.

N.B: The issue of whether the Spirit proceeds only from the Father, or from both the Father and the Son, became a major bone of contention between the Eastern and Western halves of the Church. Eventually this became the main cause of the schism between the Eastern Orthodox and Roman Catholic Churches in AD 1054.

Both the original Nicene Creed (AD 325) and the revised Constantinople version (AD 381) make no mention of Him proceeding from the Son. It was only in the sixth century that Roman churches began adding in the Latin word 'filioque' (and the Son) to their creed.

For those with wanting to explore further, Anselm's tract 'On the procession of the Holy Spirit' is available online in an English translation.

[30] (16:8-11)
[31] (16:12-13)
[32] (1Jn 2:27)
[33] (Ezek 36:26,27)
[34] (15:26)

As we saw in the Prologue, the Son is 'eternally begotten from the Father'. He is God, but He is also with God - continuously, even during His incarnation. He is completely One with the Father, being His exact image, sharing all His attributes, equal in power and glory, holiness, eternity and love.

The thing that distinguishes the Father from the Son is not any difference in roles, for all three Persons of the Trinity work together in all the acts of God. Rather, it is their relationship. The Father always has and always will be the Father, showing the Son everything that He is doing. The Son always has been and always will be the Son, saying and doing only what He hears and sees the Father saying and doing. This eternal relationship of begotten-ness is then expressed in history in the Incarnation.

But the Spirit's relationship to the Father is different. He *proceeds* from the Father. In general usage this means 'to go out from'; but the Spirit is never disconnected from the Father, never leaves Him. Nevertheless, He eternally proceeds from Him, just as a man's breath is visible on a frosty morning.

The Greek word for spirit, can also mean wind or breath; and in English we use 'inspiration' to mean breathing in, and 'aspiration' to mean sucking out. Theologians use the word *'spiration'* to describe what it means for the Spirit to proceed from God. He is sometimes referred to as 'the Breath of God'. Just as Jesus breathed on the disciples and said, *'Receive the Holy Spirit'*, 'spirating' the Spirit into them[35], giving them a spiritual 'kiss of life', so God breathes spiritual life into us by His Spirit proceeding into us.

During the BBC coverage of Queen Elizabeth's funeral, the camera panned back along the procession further and further into the distance, until it was lost from view. So it is with the procession of the Spirit: however far back or far forward you look, the Spirit is still proceeding from the Father. But just as Jesus's eternal begotten-ness was supremely manifested in time at the Incarnation, the Holy Spirit's eternal spiration was supremely manifest in history, on a day we call Pentecost.

---

[35] (20:21)

<u>The Spirit's role in ministering to the Church</u>. (16:12-15)

The Holy Spirit, being One with the Father, knows God's heart. We cannot imagine what God has prepared for those who love Him, but the Holy Spirit searches the mind of God then reveals them to us, Spirit to spirit.[36]

Like the Son, the Spirit never seeks His own glory. Rather, He always glorifies Christ. *'The Spirit of prophecy is the testimony of Jesus'*.[37] He loves to glorify Jesus and is delighted when that happens; just as the Father is delighted when His Son is honoured. Within the Godhead there is this glorifying and honouring of one another, which is to be the pattern for all our earthly relationships: husbands and wives, children and parents, bosses and workers. Mutual love, honouring and collaboration, all go together in the unity of the Spirit with the Father and the Son.

Like the Son, the Spirit never acts on His own authority. He takes what He has heard from Christ, who in turn has heard from the Father.[38] The Father reveals all things to the Son, who passes them on to the Spirit to teach us. There is nothing the Spirit teaches us, that Christ didn't know: all the treasures of wisdom and knowledge are and always have been hidden in Him, the Logos[39]. The Holy Spirit picks out these treasures of Christ, and reveals them to us.[40]

The extent of the Spirit's role in revelation runs from eternity past to eternity future, and covers everything that the Father has shown Jesus[41]. *'All scripture is God-breathed'*[42], because *'Holy men of God spoke as they were moved by the Holy Spirit'*[43]. There is nothing in the Bible that is solely the product of human thought or cultural insights of their time. Just as the spoken word cannot be vocalised without breath, the written word of God could not be expressed without the Breath of God.

---

36 (1Cor 2:10-12)
37 (Rev 19:10)
38 (16:13-15)
39 (Col 2:3)
40 (16:14)
41 (16:15)
42 (2 Tim 3:16)
43 (2 Pet 1:21)

As the Spirit had testified to Christ all the way through the Old Testament[44], so now He will testify with the apostles about Jesus's earthly ministry - the *history* recorded in the Gospels and Acts. He will also take Christ's *doctrine* - everything the Father had given Him - and expand and apply them in the doctrinal teaching of the Epistles and Pastoral letters. And finally He will *prophesy* things to come, which we see in Paul's teaching on the Resurrection and the Second Coming, Peter's teaching about Judgement Day, and John's massive Revelation.

Jesus says that there is much He would like to say, but they cannot yet bear[45]. Is He saying there will be stuff of which the disciples hadn't yet had even the slightest hint? Is He implying that the Spirit will reveal completely new truths to them - so-called 'progressive revelation'? Many would have us believe so: for instance the Muslims, Mormons, or Moonies. Or the modern counterfeit revivalists who claim to have had visions of angels and the like.

The New Testament certainly contains much that Jesus never taught explicitly. Paul calls these truths 'mysteries', not meaning esoteric secrets of the Illuminati or anything like that, but pre-existing truths that had not yet been revealed.

There are seven such mysteries mentioned in the New Testament:

- the mystery of the rapture[46]
- the plan of God to bring everything together under Christ[47]
- the mystery of the Gentiles' incorporation into the Church[48]
- the mystery of the Jews' temporary blindness[49]
- the mystery of the Gospel itself[50]
- the mystery of the Body of Christ[51]

---

[44] (5:46)
[45] (16:12)
[46] ((1Cor 15:51)
[47] (Eph 1:9)
[48] (Eph 3:5,6)
[49] (Rom 9:25)
[50] (Rom 16:25, Eph 6:19)
[51] (Eph 5:30-32)

• the mystery of the lawless one[52]

Paul counts himself, along with the other apostles, as 'stewards of the mysteries of God'.[53] These are the crown jewels of God's revelation. We have been charged with keeping them safe, whilst also putting them on display to the world. We are not some secret society, keeping truths to ourselves; nevertheless, knowledge of these mysteries does create a bond of fellowship.[54]

But if we are correct that these verses were addressed to the Eleven, and Jesus says the Spirit will guide them into *all* truth, then with the close of the apostolic era (and specifically with the Book of Revelation) all truth has been revealed. The church is built on the foundation of the apostles and prophets, and a foundation defines the boundaries of a building. Individuals may well receive gifts of prophecy, or words of wisdom or knowledge; but the overall boundary of Christian revelation has been set.[55]

The Spirit's three-fold ministry to the world

The Spirit is the primary driver of all Christian mission. *"He will testify of Me"*, says Jesus, *"and you also will bear witness"*. Just as the Son was sent by the Father to bring men back to God, so the Spirit is sent for the same loving purpose of God. He proceeds from the Father, because the Father's heart is longing for His sons to return from the far-off country.

As well as empowering the apostles to witness to the authorities[56] and enduing them with boldness and clarity, the Holy Spirit also works in their hearers[57]. We see this very clearly, in the accounts of the first sermons after Pentecost: when Peter preached, the massive crowd *'were cut to the heart, and said, What must we do?'*

They were *convicted* by the Holy Spirit. The word can mean reprove, rebuke, or convince. It doesn't refer to obtaining a conviction in a court of law, and it

[52] (1Thess 2:7)
[53] (1Cor 4:1)
[54] (Eph 3:9)
[55] (Rev 22:18,19)
[56] (Acts 4:1-10)
[57] (16:8-11)

is more than just proving the world wrong or intellectually convincing it. It is always associated with a sense of shame i.e. a degree of repentance. Perhaps a better translation would be, *'bringing the world to the conviction that'* they have sinned, Jesus is righteous, and this world is under judgement.

1. Despite their unbelief, the Spirit graciously brings them to the conviction that they have *sinned* by not believing in Christ. Many people will accept that things like lying, murder or adultery are sins; but few think of disbelieving Christ as a sin: and yet it is *this* sin that brings judgement. *'This is the condemnation, that the light has come into the world, and men loved darkness rather than light, because their deeds were evil'.*[58]

   It is by grace we have been saved, through faith: but even that faith is not of ourselves, but through the prior work of the Holy Spirit.

2. Since Jesus is no longer present, the Spirit will now be the one to bring conviction that our *righteousness* is like dirty rags[59] by comparison with Jesus - who alone was utterly righteous[60]. The whole Jewish system of washings, Temple worship, and alms was discredited. But so too is everything else *we* rely on, to justify ourselves in God's sight.

   No-one had been able to convict Jesus of sin during His lifetime.[61] And now God has declared Him righteous, by raising Him from the dead.[62] Peter proves this to the Pentecost crowd, by pointing out that unlike King David, the tomb could not hold Him[63]: there were no 'wages of sin' in His case.

3. Lastly, the Spirit convicts men of *judgement*, because the Prince of this world is judged. Behind every earthly ruler there is a spirit-prince, a 'world ruler of this present darkness'. And over them all, is the Prince of this world. He has been sinning from the beginning[64], when he introduced death into the human race by lying to Adam and Eve[65]. In believing him

[58] (3:17-19)
[59] (Isa 64:5)
[60] (1John 2:1)
[61] (8:46)
[62] (Rom 1:4)
[63] (Acts 2:29-36)
[64] (1 Jn 3:8)
[65] (8:44)

rather than God, they sinned and thus gave him authority over themselves and the whole of mankind.[66] So when Satan offered Jesus all the kingdoms of the world if He would just worship him[67], the world was truly his to give.

God had forewarned Satan of his doom to come through the 'seed of the woman' way back in Eden.[68] And even though his minions recognised Jesus as the Son of God who would eventually sentence them to eternal torment[69], the earthly authorities under his control failed to recognise what the cross would mean. "If they had, they would not have crucified the Lord of glory".[70] Satan was cast out of his authority over the earth[71] and Jesus's salvation, power and kingdom were established in its place[72].

Paul tells us that Christ triumphed over these spiritual rulers and authorities through the cross, disarming them and stripping them publicly[73] as a Roman conqueror would do to his foes. Satan has been disarmed through the blood of the cross; and he has been exposed as a con-man through the truth incarnated in Christ. Death has been defeated[74], and Satan has no more right to accuse us to God[75]. There is no more condemnation to those who are in Christ Jesus![76]

This is really bad news for unbelievers. For it says that God has appointed a date and time when the Man Christ Jesus will judge the world[77]. Satan's downfall means that everything he set up in opposition to God, will also be judged in due time.

These are the three core truths of the gospel message that the Spirit wants us to bring, so that He can work through our spoken message. We see this

---

66 (Rom 6:16)
67 (Matt 4:8-10)
68 (Gen 3:15)
69 (Matt 8:28-29)
70 (1 Cor 2:8)
71 (12:31,32)
72 (Rev 11:15; Rev 12:10)
73 (Col 2:15)
74 (1Cor 15:55; Heb 2:14)
75 (Rev 12:10)
76 (Rom 8:33,34)
77 (Acts 17:31)

clearly in Peter's two recorded sermons, first at Pentecost[78] for the Jews and later at Cornelius's house[79] for the Gentiles. And we see it too in Paul's preaching in Athens.[80] Preaching the love and grace of God without first preaching sin and righteousness and judgement, will only be of value if the hearers are *already* under the conviction of the Holy Spirit. But many in our day and age have no concept of sin or of coming judgement, so salvation is a meaningless word to them.

[78] (Acts 2:22-36)

[79] Acts 10:38-43)

[80] Acts 17:29-31)

Birthing salvation (16:16-33)

As Jesus faces a lonely struggle on the Cross,
He prepares the disciples for the agony and joy they will experience.
He warns them they will let Him down, but He will overcome,
giving them the victory.

Jesus finishes teaching about the disciples' new relationship with all three members of the Trinity; about how to maintain their indwelling; and about the persecution they will face as Christ's ambassadors once He's gone.

He brings them back to face the reality of His departure, His 'going to the Father': but this time, with an assurance that they will physically see Him again. Although He had answered their anxieties about His departure by teaching them about knowing and abiding in Him, nevertheless they get anxious again, questioning amongst themselves what He might mean.

When we don't understand

The disciples are thoroughly perplexed. They had been anxious about losing Jesus, because He'd said He was going to the Father. Now He says, that shortly after losing sight of Him *'because I go to the Father'*, they will see Him again, also *'because I go to the Father'*[1]. In their confusion they had questioned each other as to what He meant[2], but the problem was that they hadn't asked Jesus!

He knows their confusion and anxiety. He doesn't leave them struggling, but goes on to tell them that the next few days will be an emotional rollercoaster. Their agony at the crucifixion will be like that of a woman in labour just before delivery - overwhelmed by pain.

He Himself is only an hour away from terrible distress in the Garden of Gethsemane. He knows that strong emotion can block our ability to hear God. But He does not tell them they should keep a stiff upper lip, or pretend their emotions are unreal.

---

[1] (16:16)
[2] (16:17,18)

They *will* have sorrow: because of losing a dear friend in a horrific way; because of the world's gloating over His crucifixion; because of their dashed hopes. But just as the moment of birth changes the cries of labour into wonder, joy, and instant love, so His resurrection will change their sorrow into joy.

(We see this illustrated in the story of the disciples on the Emmaus Road. From discussing their dashed Messianic hopes and the strange report from the womenfolk, all of a sudden they found their hearts burning with joy).[3]

Paul says to the Philippians, *"Be anxious for nothing, but in everything by prayer and supplication, with thanksgiving, let your requests be made known to God; and the peace of God, which surpasses all understanding, will guard your hearts and minds through Christ Jesus"*. The world gives peace by distractions & pleasures, psychological self-management techniques and the like: Jesus gives us His peace when we entrust all our cares fully into His hands. We need to get into the psalmist's habit of bringing our doubts and fears to Him and letting the truth soak into our spirits again.

He later acknowledges that though He has been speaking figuratively,[4] the day will come when He will teach them plainly about the Father. Everything about His death, resurrection and ascension would become clear; through His teaching in the forty days after His resurrection, and the subsequent ministry of the Spirit.

The apostles later realised that it was the *Father* who had pre-planned His arrest, trial & crucifixion[5], having foretold Messiah's suffering through the prophets[6]. It was the *Father* who had raised Him from death [7]and exalted Him to His right hand[8], giving Him the Spirit to pour out on mankind. It was

---

[3] (Lk 24:13-33)
[4] (16:25)
[5] (Acts 1:23)
[6] (Acts 3:18)
[7] (Acts 1:24)
[8] (Acts 1:33)

the *Father* who had declared Jesus to be both Lord and Christ[9], giving Jesus the Name above every name[10].

Resurrection Joy (16:22)

When Jesus says they'll see Him again, what kind of seeing does He mean?

Greek has several nuanced words for seeing. Jesus here uses 'opsomai' - which means physical sight, but also perception and understanding. The disciples use a different word 'theoreo', which means to view attentively, or to 'see' as in visit someone.

It is clear that Jesus is talking about them seeing Him physically, not just spiritually. But what He is saying, is not only that they will physically see Him, but that they will 'get' who He is. And when they do, their sorrow will be turned into joy.[11]

This joy is the joy of the Emmaus disciples, whose hearts 'burned within them'. It's the joy of John Wesley, when his heart 'was strangely warmed' within him. It is the bubbling up of the life of the Spirit within us.

This joy is impregnable: no-one can take it from us. Like the peace of God, it passes understanding. It comes from knowing that Jesus is risen from the dead, and *He* is Lord!

It is the joy of the Lord's Presence:

- *"These things I have spoken to you, that my joy may be in you, and that your joy may be full"*[12]
- *"In your presence there is fullness of joy; at your right hand are pleasures forevermore"*[13]
- *"This day is holy to our Lord. Do not be grieved for the joy of the Lord is your strength"*[14]

---

[9] (Acts 2:36)
[10] (Phil 2:9-11)
[11] (16:20)
[12] (15:11)
[13] (Ps 16:11)
[14] (Neh 8:10)

New intimacy with Father

They have been asking Him lots of questions; but from now on, they will ask Him nothing. Two different words for asking are used here. In the Resurrection era, they won't need to ask Jesus *about* anything - but they will be able to ask the Father *for* anything, in Jesus's name[15]. The Father will no longer be distant or unapproachable.

Anyone who recognises Jesus, recognises the character of the Father perfectly imaged in Him. But now they will know the Father Himself, much more intimately. This is being 'in the bosom of the Father', if you will.

There will be no need for Jesus to ask on their behalf, because the Father Himself loves them. *"See what manner of love the Father has bestowed on us, that we should be called the children of God!"*.[16] Children have special rights - they can ask things of their father, that no-one else's child could. Jesus encourages the disciples to ask for all their needs, in specific prayer. Such requests are not beneath God's dignity.

Not asking, often comes from subconscious distrust: maybe from childhood experiences of being the unfavourite, or of deep disappointment that a parental promise wasn't kept. But now, any fear of disillusionment will have gone.[17] The Father's generosity is limitless: *"Ask, and it shall be given unto you: 'good measure, pressed down, heaped up and running over"*!

Answered prayer brings fullness of joy. Abiding leads to constant prayer for everything[18]; and the answers to prayer are fruit[19] which glorifies the Father. In fact when we stand before Christ's judgement seat, it is only the things wrought in God which will count.[20] We are to live as He did, in complete dependence on God.

(Note that this does *not* preclude us from praying to Jesus. Paul prays directly to Christ, pleading for the thorn in His flesh to be removed[21].)

---

[15] (14:13, 15:7, 15:16, 16:26-27)
[16] (1 Jn 3:1)
[17] (Mt 7:9-11, Lk 11:9-11)
[18] (15:7)
[19] (15:8)
[20] (3:21)
[21] (2 Cor 12:8)

Praying in Jesus's name

What does 'In My Name' really mean?[22]

None of the great prayers recorded in the New Testament end with the words, 'in the Name of Jesus'. We just don't hear Paul or Peter or John using that phrase in prayer: whereas it is used when claiming authority in healing and deliverance[23]. We don't need to remind Father of His Son's rank; but we may need to remind the enemy.

The name of someone, in the sense that the Bible authors used it, was what the person stood for, the substance of their character, or their authority. When we pray in the name of Jesus or baptise in the name of the Father, Son and Holy Spirit, what we are doing is acting in their authority, in their stead, according to their command, and consistent with their desires.

Sometimes however, we can unconsciously begin to use it a bit like a magic incantation. Jesus was actually a very common name in first-century Israel. Where there is no faith, no relationship, no submission to His lordship, the name Jesus is nothing but a word: as the Sons of Sceva found out[24]. The authority is not in the name itself, but in the relationship we have with the Named One.

There are three main strands of meaning in the words, "in My Name":-

Representing His wishes, on His behalf.

Ambassadors speak in their King's name, representing his views. Their words carry weight, because they are representing someone of power. They will have consulted with their King before ever speaking on His behalf.

In our passports it says, *'His Britannic Majesty's Secretary of State requests and requires in the Name of His Majesty all those whom it may concern to allow the bearer to pass freely without let or hindrance, and to afford the bearer such assistance and protection as may be necessary".*

---

[22] (16:23,24,26)

[23] (Acts 3:6; Acts 16:18)

[24] (Acts 19:13-17)

Just as our passports reveal the set will of our Monarch, we can confidently pray anything that Jesus prayed for us, or anything in Paul's recorded prayers. But we can also pray anything that we know is in line with Jesus's heart.

With His authority

When a policeman says, "Stop, in the name of the law", he can do so because he is standing in the place of the law and speaking on its behalf. To the degree that he speaks for the law, he can enforce the law and he has authority. When he steps outside of the law, he has lost his authority - even if he still says, "Stop in the name of the law".

All authority comes from above[25]: it is given by God. Even Jesus said, authority had been *given* to Him. This happened supremely at His ascension: it was in a sense His coronation. But He had authority over demons before that, and He gave His disciples that same authority.[26] Those who heard Him teach, recognised that His teaching was different from the scribes & Pharisees because He spoke with authority.

Just as when the Clerk of the Court says 'Court, rise!', everyone stands in honour of the Judge, so at the Name of Jesus every knee will bow. Name indicates rank and therefore authority. Jesus's Name is *"the Name above all names"*, and He was given that rank by Father God because He had humbled Himself so completely.

Standing in His righteousness

Rather than tagging 'in Jesus's name' onto the end of our prayers, it would be better to start with something like this:- *"Father, I come before you, not in my own power, not in my own righteousness, not in my own capability. I come before you in the authority of Jesus, your Son, who gave me access in this faith in which I stand, because of His blood. I come on the merits of Jesus, not on my own merits".* That's what praying in the name of Jesus is. When you come on the basis of Jesus's merits, then you are heard for Jesus's sake.

[25] (Rom 13:1; Matt 8:8-10)
[26] (Lk 10:19)

Prayer in Jesus's Name is yet another fruit of the Cross. Jesus could not have taught this earlier, which is perhaps why He doesn't mention it when teaching them the Lord's Prayer.

The Incarnation & Ascension are connected (16:28-30)

Jesus now simplifies His whole life story down to a return journey: *'I came from the Father into the world: now I'm leaving the world and returning to the Father'.*[27] The incarnation and ascension are matching bookends of His earthly ministry!

Right up to this point the disciples had struggled to grasp the truth that Jesus had come from the Father. But now they've finally understood.[28] And their love for Christ *and belief in His divinity* is deeply pleasing to God.[29]

Somehow, Jesus's statement caused the penny to finally drop, that He had come from God, and was God Omniscient[30]. But they only 'got' the first part: that He came from above. They don't yet seem to grasp, even though it's about to happen, that the crucifixion is the start of Jesus's return journey.

'Returning to the Father' refers to the whole time period from Gethsemane through the Cross, Christ's descent into Hades, the Resurrection, and His Ascension and Coronation. Though it has been a motif throughout the discourse, there's much the disciples haven't conceived of yet. Jesus will teach them more, after the resurrection.[31]

Why it matters, that Jesus returned to the Father

It is important for us to grasp the reality that Jesus is now seated at the Father's right hand, for a whole range of reasons:

Victory

Jesus is seated, because His work is done: the victory has been won, all that remains now is for all His enemies to be brought under His feet. When we are

---

[27] (16:28)
[28] (16:30)
[29] (16:27)
[30] (16:30)
[31] (20:17)

struggling in the battle, we need to look up to His banner of victory, signifying that He has overcome and in Him, we will too.

Heavenly Advocate

Our Advocate on earth is the Spirit, who lives in us and enables us to cry out *'Abba, Father'* when we doubt our sonship. But Jesus is our heavenly Advocate, at Father's right hand so that He can intercede when we sin[32], immediately reminding the Father that we are in Him and He is righteous.

Authority

He is at the Father's right hand, endued with all His authority. He has been given the Name above every name, the highest rank, with authority over everything life can throw at us - over Satan and his minions too[33]. Because He is at the Father's right hand, we can pray using His authority.

Infilling

He is at His right hand so that He can receive from the Father the promise of the Spirit, pouring it out in dreams and visions to young and old alike[34], revealing what He is doing to His friends[35], and His servants the prophets[36].

Commissioning

From His throne, He appoints some to be apostles, some prophets, some pastors, some evangelists and teachers. He oversees the development of His Body and equips the saints for the work of ministry[37], maturing our faith and shaping us into His image.

Fixing our minds on these heavenly realities, and the fact that our true life is hidden with Christ in God, enables us to view our earthly lives from above[38]. We can see our bodily passions for what they really are, and shed them as an eagle sheds its old feathers. Anger, malice, bad language, lust and envy drop

[32] (1Jn 2:1)
[33] (Phil 2:9-11)
[34] (Acts 2:17,18)
[35] (15:15)
[36] (Amos 3:7)
[37] (Eph 4:7-16)
[38] (Col 3:1-17)

away, and our new plumage of grace, humility, patience, kindness and love emerges.

When we let Jesus down (16:31,32)

The disciples thought they'd finally grasped what Jesus was saying, but He swiftly pricks the balloon of their self-deception. Within the hour, they would all desert Him. Everything He had taught them about selfless love would be ignored as they each put their own interests first, each fleeing 'to his own'. Their team unity would be shattered, as they scattered.

Jesus contrasts their faithlessness with the faithfulness of His Father[39]: *'He will always remain faithful, for He cannot deny Himself'*[40]. Faithfulness is written all the way through His character. They are about to have a salutary lesson in the deceitfulness of their own hearts. But ultimately, they can have peace, knowing that they are kept by the power of God, not by their own courage or resoluteness.

Peter would have been the one who experienced this most powerfully. Having sworn he would never deny Christ, he then denied Him three times, just as Jesus had prophesied. But Jesus had already interceded, *"that your faith might not fail"*.

After the resurrection, He would face Peter with the shallowness of his love.[41] Peter would have to cling onto the truth that though Jesus knew his heart, & its self-deception, He also saw a seed of genuine love. This would eventually germinate into a willingness to be crucified for Christ.

In the world, we will have tribulation: Jesus is quite clear about this. The word comes from a Roman word for a tool used to crush grain and separate it from the husks. Tribulation means trouble or affliction of any kind, not just persecution. Lot is an Old Testament example: he was a *"righteous man who was distressed by the filthy lives of lawless men"*[42]. His neighbours *"kept bringing pressure on him and moved forward to break down the door"* of his

---

[39] (16:32)
[40] (2Tim 2:13)
[41] (21:15-19)
[42] (2Pet 2:7)

house, wanting to rape his guests[43]. **Paul** lists the many forms of suffering he has endured: floggings, imprisonment, shipwrecks, betrayals, sleepless nights, exhaustion, hunger, thirst and cold. But he also includes the suffering of his pastor heart, dealing with Christians who've stumbled.[44]

But in addition to physical, mental and spiritual suffering caused by others, there is our own internal suffering when we know *we* have let Jesus down. Maybe the things the *world* loves, the not-of-the-Father loves - the lust of the flesh, the lust of the eyes, and the pride of life - have held sway in our hearts.[45] And like Peter, we realise that our loyalty and commitment to Christ are still very shallow.

In such situations, Jesus says, *"Be of good cheer"*.

Never let the enemy get double value for money, by causing you to beat yourself up, or doubt your own salvation. *"Be of good cheer!"* Why? *"For I have overcome the world"*: This is Jesus's very last word of teaching to his disciples.

Overcoming the world

Overcoming the world emerges as a major theme in John's Letters:-

- *'For this purpose the Son of God was manifested, that He might destroy the works of the devil. Whoever has been born of God does not sin, for His seed remains in him; and he cannot sin, because he has been born of God'.*[46]
- *You are of God, little children, and have overcome them, because He who is in you is greater than he who is in the world'.*[47]
- *'For whatever is born of God overcomes the world. And this is the victory that has overcome the world—our faith. Who is he who overcomes the world, but he who believes that Jesus is the Son of God?'*[48]

---

[43] (Gen 19:9)
[44] (2Cor 11:22-29)
[45] (1 Jn 2:15-17)
[46] (1John 3:8-9)
[47] (1Jn 4:4)
[48] (1Jn 5:4)

In Revelation, each of the letters to the Seven Churches ends with Jesus making a promise to those who overcome. For example,

- *'To those who overcome, He grants them to sit with Him on His throne, just as He also overcame and sat down with His Father of His throne'.*[49]

'Overcoming' implies a real struggle, not a walkover. And our experience, if we are honest, is that that is the case. I have just watched Liverpool - the predicted underdog - overcome Chelsea in a cup final. The struggle swayed back and forth, up and down the pitch, till the last three minutes of extra time; but then Liverpool's youngsters scored, and overcame. The whole team celebrated, with joyful hugs and high-fives all round, whilst the Chelsea players sat on the pitch, numb with defeat.

Ultimately, our victory doesn't depend on us:

- *'The sting of death is sin, and the strength of sin is the law. But thanks be to God, who gives us the victory through our Lord Jesus Christ'.* [50]
- *'But God forbid that I should boast except in the cross of our Lord Jesus Christ, by whom the world has been crucified to me, and I to the world'*[51]
- *'Who shall separate us from the love of Christ? Shall tribulation, or distress, or persecution, or famine, or nakedness, or peril, or sword? ... Yet in all these things we are more than conquerors through Him who loved us. For I am persuaded that neither death nor life, nor angels nor principalities nor powers, nor things present nor things to come, nor height nor depth, nor any other created thing, shall be able to separate us from the love of God which is in Christ Jesus our Lord'.*[52]

Jesus overcame worldly desires, at the Temptation in the wilderness; and He overcame worldly fears in Gethsemane. On the Cross, He triumphed over sin and death, and He *gives* us the victory over all the powers of darkness[53].

Hallelujah! The Lion of Judah, the Root of David, has prevailed![54]

---

[49] (Rev 3:21)
[50] (1Cor 15:57)
[51] (Gal 6:14)
[52] (Rom 8:35-39)
[53] (Col 2:15)
[54] (Rev 5:5)

<u>Jesus prays for His team of disciples</u> (17:1-20)

Filled with joy as He looks beyond the Cross and sees the fruit of His suffering, Jesus prays for the Eleven who will be the foundation of the Church

Apart from a few glimpses in the Psalms, there are very few records of Jesus directly addressing His Father. Mostly His conversations with His Father were in solitary prayer. This chapter is by far the longest account we have, of Their communication. It is right to approach with holy awe: we are being allowed to eavesdrop on the communication between the Eternal Father and His Son.

Within the Godhead, all three members are in perfect harmony at all times: there is no need for them to debate or discuss what they're going to do. Jesus is *"in the bosom of the Father"*, so close that He could hear His Father's heartbeat. But as a Man, He prayed just as He wants us to pray – like a little child sitting on its father's lap, asking, trusting, knowing it is loved.

Though God is sometimes addressed as Father of the nation in the Old Testament, there is nothing remotely like this *personal* intimacy - in which Jesus addresses God Almighty as *'Abba'*, Daddy.

Most commentaries approach this chapter from an analytic stance, comparing it with the Lord's prayer, or Jesus's prayer in Gethsemane; and breaking it down into three sections – Jesus praying for himself[1], praying for the apostles[2], and praying for the church down through the ages thereafter[3]. They view the Cross as the point at which Jesus was glorified; and they see Jesus's prayers for the unity of the church, and its vision of Christ's glory, as being fulfilled only when Jesus comes again in glory.

Such approaches sterilise Jesus's prayer of all relevance to our present-day lives: both our spiritual experience and our struggles to love each other within our local churches. They miss the mood of His prayer, which is one of joy; not the agony He will experience in Gethsemane. They divorce His prayer from its context - Jesus's teachings about the disciples' ingrafting into Christ

---

[1] (17:1-5)
[2] (17:6-19)
[3] (17:20-26)

and union with the Godhead; and the sharing in His sufferings and mission, which that will bring. And they overlook the fact that nowhere else do we *ever* hear Jesus praying for anything for Himself; even on the Cross.

In what follows, I've tried to explain how I understand what Jesus was praying - followed by paraphrasing each section to try and convey His heart:-

————————————-

The key to understanding (17:1)

The emotional tenor of Jesus's prayer is key to its understanding. He knew He had completed His mission of glorifying the Father through the miraculous signs and through His teaching[4]. He was praying not in desperation or sadness, but with a sense of joy[5] and purpose. Why and how could that be, when His crucifixion is only hours away?

Hebrews gives us the answer: *"Jesus endured the Cross, despising its shame, for the joy that was set before Him"*[6].

Isaiah says, *"When he sees all that is accomplished by his anguish, he will be satisfied. And because of his experience, my righteous servant will make it possible for many to be counted righteous, for he will bear all their sins".*[7]

Jesus was praying for the Church. By faith, He was looking beyond the Cross, and was filled with joy at what He saw. He was looking at His Bride-to-be, and how she would need to be prepared for their wedding.

'Christ also loved the church and gave Himself for her, that He might sanctify and cleanse her with the washing of water by the word, that He might present her to Himself a glorious church, not having spot or wrinkle or any such thing, but that she should be holy and without blemish.'[8]

I believe His whole prayer, is in fact a prayer for the Church: even the first part, when He seems to be praying for Himself.

---

4 (17:4)
5 (17:13)
6 (Heb 12:2)
7 (Isa 53:11, NLT)
8 (Eph 5:25-27)

The theme of Jesus's prayer throughout, is the Church He is about to die for. It is His beloved Bride, and the means of the Father's being glorified on earth throughout the future. This then makes perfect sense of Jesus going on to pray for the men who will be the foundation stones of the Church, and all those who will later be added to it as living stones.

This also explains why there are so many echoes of the Book of Ephesians, whose theme is the revelation of the mystery of the Church. The Church is the vehicle for *'displaying the manifold wisdom of God to the principalities and powers in the heavenly realms'.*[9] The Church is how the Son will glorify the Father, after Pentecost.

When was Jesus glorified?

Most commentators see Jesus's prayer to be glorified as referring to the cross; but this is counter-intuitive, and doesn't fit with what Jesus is saying. He's asking specifically to be restored to the glory He had with the Father *before the world began.*[10] The seven signs had already manifested the glory of His *character*[11]: that was not what He was asking. Rather, He was asking for the shekinah glory, the magnificent outshining that John later records seeing[12]. This was the glory He had veiled when He became Man.[13]

Given this, when was this prayer of Jesus answered by the Father?

Not at the cross, for sure. Not at the resurrection either, for although it *'declared Him to be the Son of God with power'*[14], that was only recognised after Pentecost. The only event that fits as being the answer to this prayer, is His *ascension*.

- Hebrews says of Jesus, *"who being the brightness of His glory and the express image of His person, and upholding all things by the word of His*

[9] (Eph 3:10)
[10] (17:5)
[11] (2:11)
[12] (Rev 1:13-17)
[13] (Phil 2:5-7)
[14] (Rom 1:4)

power, when He had by Himself purged our sins, sat down at the right hand of the Majesty on high".[15]

- And again, *"But now we do not yet see all things put under him. But we see Jesus, who was made a little lower than the angels, for the suffering of death crowned with glory and honour, that He, by the grace of God, might taste death for everyone".*[16]
- And again, *"When He ascended on high, He led captivity captive, and gave gifts to men. (Now this, "He ascended"—what does it mean but that He also first descended into the lower parts of the earth? He who descended is also the One who ascended far above all the heavens, that He might fill all things. And He Himself gave some to be apostles, some prophets, some evangelists, and some pastors and teachers, for the equipping of the saints for the work of ministry, for the edifying of the body of Christ".*[17]

The ***ascension*** was when Jesus's pre-incarnate glory was restored: it was His coronation. When a new monarch is crowned in Britain, they become head of the Church of England, and appoint bishops and archbishops. Similarly, the immediate result of Jesus's coronation was that He appointed apostles, prophets, pastors, evangelists and teachers; to build the Church.

So we might paraphrase the meaning of this verse, as follows:-

"Father, we both know that we've reached the pivot point of Your plan of salvation. I've completed all the miracles & signs, all the witnessing and teaching You gave Me to do. I've taught these dear men the kernel of everything We're about to achieve; and they're about to go through hell, just as I am. But the thing that keeps Me steady is that beyond all this apparently pointless suffering, I see something wonderful. Just like Isaiah prophesied, I can see that My death as a sin offering will bring life to multitudes. They will become My Body, and I'll be their Head, and through them I'll work out Your heart's desires. The Church will display Your incredible wisdom to the powers of darkness. All the shame and the agony will have been worth it, for the joy of seeing My Betrothed - My Bride-to-be.

---

[15] (Heb 1:3)
[16] (Heb 2:9)
[17] (Eph 4:8)

"For that to happen, I need You to restore the glory I shared with You, before the world began. Ever since I took this human body I've displayed the glory of Your character - Your grace and truth, Your holiness and love - in all My words and deeds. But I consciously laid aside the unapproachable magnificence of Our Throne, so that men could see what God looks like in the flesh. Now I need You to restore that glory; not just raising Me from the dead, but seating Me at Your right hand again and authorising Me to pour out the Holy Spirit. Only He can fill these men so full of power and authority, that Your plans will prosper in My hands. I'm not asking for My own sake, but so that I can glorify You further. It's the formation of the Church that will really really grind the devil's gears, and declare Your deep wisdom: that You've turned what he thought was ultimate victory, into his ultimate defeat.

The Church is the Father's gift to the Son (17:2-8)

Jesus recalls the history of the Church so far. He says repeatedly that He is praying for *'those whom You (Father) have given Me'*[18]. Though He has been given authority over all flesh[19], only a select few have been given to Him in this special sense. They have been given to Him *'out of the world'*.[20] To as many as have been given Him, to each and every one of these, He will give eternal life. To the rest, He will eventually pronounce judgement.[21]

The essence of true *zoe* life isn't that it's eternal and carries on beyond death, but rather an experiential relationship with the one true God, and His first missionary, Jesus Christ[22]. Union with the Father and the Son, by the Holy Spirit - as He has been teaching throughout the discourse.

The Church is the Father's gift to the Son. These men (and women) *'were Yours, then You gave them to Me'*.[23]

---

[18] (17:2,6,9,10,11,12,24)
[19] (17:2)
[20] (17:6)
[21] (5:21-30)
[22] (17:3)
[23] (17:6)

He chose us in eternity past

The Father chose us to be Christ's, in eternity past:

"Blessed be the God and Father of our Lord Jesus Christ, who has blessed us with every spiritual blessing in the heavenly places in Christ, just as He chose us in Him before the foundation of the world, that we should be holy and without blame before Him in love, having predestined us to adoption as sons by Jesus Christ to Himself, according to the good pleasure of His will, to the praise of the glory of His grace, by which He made us accepted in the Beloved."[24]

Jesus repeatedly taught that salvation was by God's sovereign choice. *'No-one can come to Me unless it has been granted to Him by My Father'.*[25] This teaching was what so angered the Jews, who thought that they were guaranteed a place in heaven by being sons of Abraham. But as Paul proves in Romans 9:6-13, Abraham's family tree showed covenant blessings were passed down only to the child of promise (Isaac vs Ishmael) and by God's election (Jacob vs Esau).

He drew us to the Son

The Father has given Him an exact number, everyone of whom will come to Him - because the Father causes them to be attracted by Him:-

"No one can come to Me unless the Father who sent Me draws him; and I will raise him up at the last day. It is written in the prophets, 'And they shall all be taught by God.' Therefore everyone who has heard and learned from the Father comes to Me"[26].

That is why Jesus now says, *'They have obeyed Your word'.*[27]

In accepting, protecting and raising us up, Christ is doing the Father's will

Christ will never reject anyone whom the Father gives Him; and He will never fail in keeping those truly given to Him. Nevertheless some who seem to be disciples, like Judas, will choose the path of apostasy.

---

[24] (Eph 1:3-6)

[25] (6:65)

[26] (6:44-45)

[27] (17:6)

"All that the Father gives Me will come to Me, and the one who comes to Me I will by no means cast out. ... This is the will of the Father who sent Me, that of all He has given Me I should lose nothing, but should raise it up at the last day. And this is the will of Him who sent Me, that everyone who sees the Son and believes in Him may have everlasting life; and I will raise him up at the last day."[28]

Having chosen to leave their careers and families, and by faith follow Jesus through thick and thin, these eleven disciples had gradually come to know what God was like.[29] They'd realised that everything Jesus did and said, came directly from God.[30] They had accepted His teaching even when they couldn't understand it, such as when He had spoken about being the Bread of Life. Unlike others who'd taken offence, they'd stuck with Him. And now, minutes earlier, they had finally grasped that He shared God's nature[31], and had been sent by His Father on a mission to save those who believed[32].

So we might paraphrase the gist of these verses like this:

"Father, I know You've given Me full authority over all mankind - authority to raise the dead and give eternal life to some, and authority to judge all those who reject Me. You've told Me to give eternal life to every single one of those you've chosen for Me. To bring them into Our union as a Trinity, so that by the Spirit they will know both You and Me experientially, not just intellectually. Now is the time, Father! Glorify Me, so that I can do just that.

"I've demonstrated Your nature fully to these men, whom You selected to be redeemed from this present darkness. You had chosen them and pre-destined them way back, to be moulded into My likeness through fellowship with Me. You somehow spoke to them, and attracted them to Me just as the prophet foretold when he said 'They shall all be taught of God'. They opened their hearts to Your voice, and followed Me. They've recognised that everything I said and did came first-hand from You.

---

28 (6:37-40)
29 (17:6)
30 (17:7)
31 (16:30)
32 (17:8)

I stuck exactly to what You told Me to say, and they accepted all My teaching - they didn't stumble or fall away like so many others. Little by little, they've grasped that I came from You: that You and I are actually one and the same in being, though We are separate Persons. Boy was that a struggle! But they finally got it, just a few moments ago. And they've also believed that I am Your personal Envoy, expressing Your mission of love to the world."

Jesus's three prayers for the Church's founders (17:11-19)

Jesus prays three things for His apostles, in view of His impending departure:-

To be kept in God's Name (17:11-12)

Modern paraphrases have, *'in the power of Your Name'* instead of *'in Your Name'*. But Jesus says that hitherto, He has kept them in the Father's Name; that being kept in the Father's Name is essential if they are to be one; and that only Judas, who was destined for perdition, has been lost. So it seems 'being kept in God's Name' means being kept loyal to Jesus and to each other.

Given how the enemy tries to turn Christians against each other, and how persecutors often seek to get believers to betray each other, this kind of protection will be badly needed.

Earlier, Jesus said that He had manifested God's Name to the disciples.[33] As we've seen, this means He manifested God's character; His grace and truth, His patience and love. So this petition may also mean, keeping them from falling back into worldly character traits.

To be kept from the Evil One, despite being in the world (17:14-16)

We have previously seen that 'the world' is the system of opposition to God in human society; driven and shaped by the Devil, but also empowered by our own fallenness.

John later expands on this theme: *"Love not the world or the things in the world. If anyone loves the world, the love of the Father is not in him. For all that is in the world - the lust of the flesh, the lust of the eye, and the pride of life - is not of the Father but is of the world".*[34]

---

[33] (17:8)

[34] (1Jn 2:15-16)

They no longer *"walk according to its course or according to the prince of the power of the air, the spirit now at work in the sons of disobedience, among whom we all once conducted ourselves in the lusts of our flesh, fulfilling the desires of the flesh and of the mind"*.[35]

Though they are *'not of this world'* any longer, it is vital to Jesus's mission that they *'go into all the world to make disciples'*, and He sends them just as the Father sent Him[36]. He knows that since they no longer conform, the world will hate them as it hated Him.

<u>To be sanctified by God's word of truth</u> (17:17)

Sanctification means both being set apart for holy purposes, *and* the practical holiness that such a calling requires. It is a gradual process, from the moment we are born again until we die.

Peter writes, *"His divine power has given to us all things that pertain to life and godliness, through the knowledge of Him who called us by glory and virtue, by which have been given to us exceedingly great and precious promises, that through these you may be partakers of the divine nature, having escaped the corruption that is in the world through lust"*[37]. And he goes on to outline a step-by-step sanctification programme: starting from faith and adding virtue, knowledge, self-discipline, perseverance, godliness, kindness, and love.

Jesus has previously spoken about how the Father lifts and prunes each branch of the vine[38] to bear more fruit. And earlier, He spoke about continuing in His word, in order to know the truth and be set free.[39]

This process of being sanctified by God's word is painful: the word of God actively separates between our soul and spirit, discerning the thoughts and intents of our hearts. Much that we thought was spiritual, is shown up as being fleshly. We find our inner selves naked before God's Presence, and needing to confess and repent.

---

[35] (Eph 2:2)
[36] (17:18)
[37] (2 Pet 1:3-4)
[38] (15:2)
[39] (8:31.32)

The good news is, we can *'approach Him boldly for grace to help in time of need'*, because we have a wonderfully sympathetic High Priest.[40]

In fact the whole process of sanctification is only possible because *'there is forgiveness with You, That You may be feared'.*[41] Without this, the utter purity of God's Presence would condemn us to despair. That is why Jesus vows to sanctify Himself for God's use as our ransom-sacrifice, so that we may be sanctified by the truth.[42]

Paraphrasing once again, the unabridged version of Jesus's prayer might have sounded like this:-

"I'm praying just for them: not for the whole mass of humanity. Though You've given them to Me, they are still Yours as well. And they are the evidence of my character, just like Yours. So it's in Your interest as well as Mine, I know, to hear My prayer for them.

"Coming back to glory means I'll no longer be here to protect them Father, and the hatred I faced from the world will be redirected towards them. Your holiness, Your antipathy towards sin of every sort, is why the world has such a problem with them. But You are their Father as well as mine. Keep them sheltered under Your Name, Almighty God. They're going to be scattered in the next few hours, and will badly need Your protection if they are to regroup afterwards.

While I was on earth, I safeguarded every single one You gave Me: not one of them was lost except Judas, and as the scriptures foretold, he was always going to desert. Keep the others loyal and true, both to Me and each other, just as You and I are One.

"I'm praying like this while still in their hearing, so that they'll catch the full measure of My joy Father. I'm so deeply elated at what I see they will become, and they are so precious to Me, that I will willingly endure all the shame and humiliation of crucifixion for their sakes.

---

[40] (Heb 4:11-16)

[41] (Ps 130:4)

[42] (17:19)

"The world hates them because Your word which I gave them, has changed them to be like Me. So it hates them just like it hates Me. I'm not asking You to take them out of that hostile environment, to become monks or hermits or anything like that: otherwise how would the world continue to hear the Good News? No, I'm asking however that You keep them from the evil one, the spirit who operates behind the scenes of this world's culture and values.

Take Peter, for example: You know the Devil tried to argue that Peter was so self-deluded that his 'faith' should be utterly destroyed. Father, keep him, and these other vulnerable disciples of Mine, safe when he attacks them in future.

"Lastly Father, let Your truth go on working within them so that they are refined more and more: so that they become more and more set apart for Your work. Just as You sent Me into this dark world, I've sent them; and the world is going to throw every possible form of temptation at them, to divert or disqualify them. Fleshly lusts, greed and covetousness, and subtle forms of pride - all the tricks of the Devil's trade.

They'll get sidetracked and then he'll tell them they're hopeless and that You've given up on them: he'll tempt them to despair. He'll try and use Your very words to condemn them. But here and now, Father, I consecrate Myself as their Ransom, the full satisfaction for their guilt: to provide the forgiveness they will need, so that they can live in awe of Your goodness rather than terror of Your judgement. I consecrate Myself as their Advocate in Your Presence."

Jesus prays for the future Church, His bride-to-be (17:20-26)

Having prayed about the immediate future of the apostles, Jesus's eagle eye foresees the needs of the Church down through the centuries. He prays for our unity, and our grasp of His glory.

Jesus now looks ahead down through the centuries and millennia, and the endless *'increase of His Kingdom'*. He prays for all future generations of believers, including you and me.

This is astonishing, in the context. His three years' ministry has produced only eleven solid disciples, and rejection by the vast majority of those to whom He was sent. *'His own received Him not'*. Even those eleven were about to abandon Him. Only the Father would stay with Him.[1]

Everything Jesus has prayed for the apostles, also applies to all subsequent believers[2]. But there are two specific things which particularly apply to these future generations. They are:-

Supernatural unity in real life (17:21-23)

Having been given eternal life - fellowship with all three members of the Trinity - Jesus prays that through their union with God, they may have the same unity as exists between Father and Son.

This unity:-

- Comes about through believers' communion with the Godhead[3]
- Will witness to the world at large that Christ was sent by God[4]
- Is cemented by God's character, which Jesus has taught the Church[5]
- Will demonstrate that God loves the Church, just as He loves Christ[6]

---

[1] (16:33)
[2] (17:20)
[3] (17:21)
[4] (17:21)
[5] (17:22)
[6] (17: 23)

This unity is created by the Spirit, not by human effort. It comes about when we are born anew into the family of God.[7] The Spirit of life in Christ Jesus indwells us, so that we become one spirit with Him[8], and thus with all other true believers.

This doesn't however mean uniformity, for the Spirit gives each believer diverse gifts, to be used for the common good.

It is not simply a unity of love, but is based on the teachings of the apostles[9]. It cannot therefore be created by doctrinal compromises between denominations over key doctrine. There can be no unity, for example, with those who deny that Jesus Christ is come in the flesh.[10]

Paul says Christian unity is maintained by our humility, gentleness and patience: but it also has a clear doctrinal foundation. "There is *one body and one Spirit, just as you were called in one hope of your calling; one Lord, one faith, one baptism; one God and Father of all, who is above all, and through all, and in all."*[11].

This doctrinal and experiential unity is something that each local church has to grow into. A church is immature if it is continually riven by passing doctrinal fashions, or by teachings which imply some believers are superior to others.

Ministry gifts are there *'for the edifying of the body of Christ, till we all come to the unity of the faith and of the knowledge of the Son of God, to a perfect man, to the measure of the stature of the fullness of Christ; that we should no longer be children, tossed to and fro and carried about with every wind of doctrine, by the trickery of men, in the cunning craftiness of deceitful plotting, but, speaking the truth in love, may grow up in all things into Him who is the head—Christ— from whom the whole body, joined and knit together by what every joint supplies, according to the effective working by which every part does its share, causes growth of the body for the edifying of itself in love'.*[12]

---

[7] (1:12)
[8] (1Cor 6:17)
[9] (17:20)
[10] (1Jn 4:2)
[11] (Eph 4:1-6)
[12] (Eph 4:11-16)

Whilst it is supernatural, our unity should be tangible to the world. Our love for one another should be so apparent to our neighbours, that it persuades them Jesus's message was truly of God; and that we are truly His disciples.

Many focus on the apparent disunity of contemporary Christianity, and conclude that Jesus's prayer will only be answered when He returns. But in doing so, they overlook the reality of the early church:

'Now all who believed were together, and had all things in common, and sold their possessions and goods, and divided them among all, as anyone had need. So continuing daily with one accord in the temple, and breaking bread from house to house, they ate their food with gladness and simplicity of heart, praising God and having favour with all the people. And the Lord added to the church daily those who were being saved.'[13]

'Now the multitude of those who believed were of one heart and one soul; neither did anyone say that any of the things he possessed was his own, but they had all things in common. And with great power the apostles gave witness to the resurrection of the Lord Jesus. And great grace was upon them all. Nor was there anyone among them who lacked; for all who were possessors of lands or houses sold them, and brought the proceeds of the things that were sold, and laid them at the apostles' feet; and they distributed to each as anyone had need'.[14]

Though Paul needed to teach the Ephesian church about the 'one new man', there *was* tangible unity between Jew and Gentile. For example, the churches in Achaia and Macedonia gave 'above and beyond' despite their own poverty, to support the Judaean believers in a period of famine.[15]

The reality is that Jesus's prayer is continually being answered by Father God in the here-and-now. It is answered in every sympathetic response within the Body of Christ, such that *'when one member suffers, all suffer; when one member rejoices, all rejoice'.* It is answered in every Christian ministry to the suffering church. It is answered in the welcome a Christian receives, wherever he goes, when he meets fellow-believers - of whatever ilk.

---

[13] (Acts 2:44-47)

[14] (Acts 4:32-35)

[15] (1Cor 8,9)

Our vision of Christ's glory (17:24)

What does Jesus mean, when He prays that the disciples '*may be with Him where He is, so that they can contemplate His glory*'?

Most commentators take this as referring either to the rapture, or to our experience when we die. But Jesus had already promised His disciples that having prepared rooms in His Father's house, He would come again and take them to be with Him[16]. Why would He have promised them something which the Father hadn't yet agreed to?

Could Jesus's prayer be referring to our everyday earthly life? And if so, how has His prayer been answered?

- We know that Peter, James and John had already seen Christ's divine glory,, on the Mount of Transfiguration. And they witnessed to it as a central truth in their letters.
- Stephen saw Jesus's glory as He was being stoned, and
- Paul was blinded by the glory of Christ on the Damascus Road. He also experienced being caught up to heaven, and seeing inexpressible glory. And
- John Himself, imprisoned on Patmos, had a wonderful revelation when He saw Christ's glory, first as the One amongst the candlestands and then as the Lamb in the midst of the throne of God.

But what about us? Are we simply to rely on others' experiences, or is Jesus praying for *us* to be able to contemplate His glory? And if so, why is this important?

Contemplating Christ's glory: a spiritual discipline

Paul teaches that in the New Covenant, unlike the Old, all believers can and should spend time gazing at Christ's glory:

But if the ministry of death, written and engraved on stones, was glorious, so that the children of Israel could not look steadily at the face of Moses because of the glory of his countenance, which glory was passing away, how will the ministry of the Spirit not be more glorious? For if the ministry of

[16] (14:3)

condemnation had glory, the ministry of righteousness exceeds much more in glory ... We all, with unveiled face beholding as in a mirror the glory of the Lord, are being transformed into the same image from glory to glory, just as by the Spirit of the Lord.[17]

Somehow, seeing Jesus's glory changes us into His likeness: which is what the Father has wanted all along:

For whom He foreknew, He also predestined to be conformed to the image of His Son, that He might be the firstborn among many brethren.[18]

The source of our hope and motivation

Though the process of becoming like Christ will not be completed till we meet Jesus face-to-face, the vision of Jesus's glory is what drives our sanctification in the here-and-now:

Beloved, now we are children of God; and it has not yet been revealed what we shall be, but we know that when He is revealed, we shall be like Him, for we shall see Him as He is. And everyone who has this hope in Him purifies himself, just as He is pure.[19]

Our vision of the Heavenly Man, described by John in Revelation, gives substance to our hope of our own bodily resurrection:-

"So also is the resurrection of the dead. The body is sown in corruption, it is raised in incorruption. It is sown in dishonor, it is raised in glory. It is sown in weakness, it is raised in power. It is sown a natural body, it is raised a spiritual body. There is a natural body, and there is a spiritual body. And so it is written, 'The first man Adam became a living being'. The last Adam became a life-giving spirit. The first man was of the earth, made of dust; the second Man is the Lord from heaven. As was the man of dust, so also are those who are made of dust; and as is the heavenly Man, so also are those who are heavenly. And as we have borne the image of the man of dust, we shall also bear the image of the heavenly Man."[20]

---

17 (2Cor 3:7-9,18)
18 (Rom 8:29-30)
19 (1 John 3:2-3)
20 (1Cor 15:35-49)

Our gospel is *"the gospel of the glory of Christ, who is the image of God …for it is the God who commanded light to shine out of darkness, who has shone in our hearts to give the light of the knowledge of the glory of God in the face of Jesus Christ".*[21] We cannot convincingly convey His glory, if we haven't spent time contemplating it ourselves.

Other than through Christ, the world has never known a god of *agape* love. Gods of might, of war, of fertility, of destruction, yes - all these, and many more, exist in the world's religions. But Jesus has declared the Father's Name; *God is love*. And He will go on declaring it, so that the Father's love for Him may flow through Him and into us, the Church, His Body, more and more.[22]

Summing up in paraphrase form, …

"Actually Father, I'm not just praying for these dear ones. By faith I can see the multitudes who will come to believe in Me as they spread the gospel, round the world and down through the ages. I can see My Betrothed, My Bride forming down through history, getting ready for our wedding feast to happen. I want Her to be utterly pure and spotless, made holy in every way through Your word. So there are two more things, and then I'm done.

Firstly Father, I'm asking that You will bind them together in unity like Ours. Just as We do everything in unison, and never seek Our own glory but glorify each other, that they would be one through their union with Us.

They'll have one Spirit, being one spirit with Me. And there'll be foundational truths which they all hold to, about who I am, who You are, what baptism means and the like. But there will also be doctrinal fashions which come and go, leading to factionalism and disunity. As well as the apostles' leadership they'll need prophets, pastors, evangelists and teachers. And every member will need to lay aside their pride to build up, and be built up by, the others.

Let them love one another as I have loved them, washing each others' feet in humility. Let them be so changed that it becomes undeniable for the world, that I was really sent by You. I've displayed the glory of Your grace and truth, and Our oneness, to them: now let that glory be manifest in their unity. Let

---

[21] (2Cor 4:5-7)
[22] (17:24)

them be connected to Me, as I am to You; so that it's obvious to all that not only did You send Me, but You love them as deeply as You loved Me.

"Finally Father, I want everyone You give Me to be allowed into My Presence, so that they can contemplate My glory. So far only Peter, James and John have seen it. I know You will open heaven and show them more in years to come. And of course they'll see My glory when I eventually return to reign on earth. But I'm praying for their day-to-day spiritual experience.

When You gave Moses the Old Covenant, he'd come into Your Presence day by day, and come out shining with Your glory. If that covenant was glorious, surely Your New Covenant is much more glorious? He was the only one in all Israel who had such encounters: but I want every one of My people to gaze on My glory until they too shine. Not with a fading glory like Moses, but a glory that gets brighter and brighter. It's the sight of My glory that will change them, and will motivate them to purify themselves more and more, ready for the day when they see Me face to face.

"The world doesn't recognise You Father, despite Your righteousness. They've made themselves lots of other gods - gods of war, gods of lust, gods of fertility and of destruction - but they've never known You as the God who is Love. These eleven men have realised that You sent Me, and I have declared Your nature to them and will go on doing so. In that way, the love that flows between Us as Father Son and Holy Spirit, will flow through Me into them - that the world may come to know You as You really are."

Jesus's arrest shatters Peter's self-confidence

(18:1-27)

Jesus calmly gives Himself up to His captors, protecting the disciples from arrest. Peter tries to defend Him, but is rebuked. His courage evaporates, and he denies Christ in order to save himself.

John's account of Jesus's arrest and trial is interesting for what it omits. It makes no mention of Jesus's desperate praying in the Garden, and almost nothing of His trial before Caiaphas. Its emphasis is on the sovereign power and majesty of Jesus: His control of all the circumstances and timing, and therefore the willing self-sacrifice involved. There is a striking contrast between Jesus's courage in pointing out the procedural injustices of His trial, and Peter's cowardly denial of any relationship with Christ.

The context

These events were happening at night, which in Jewish thought counted as part of the following day, the 'Day of preparation' when the Passover lambs were slaughtered.[1] It was only a few hours since Jesus had started to teach the disciples in the upper room. Five whole chapters of John are thus devoted to covering a time period of maybe three or four hours.

The garden of Gethsemane was just across the Kidron brook; this was actually a dry wadi, except after rain. Kidron's name means darkness, and it drains the valley of Gehenna, where Jerusalem's waste was burned. This valley was a symbol of judgement; there was so much rubbish that a permanently smouldering fire was necessary to consume everything the worms didn't eat.

There is a theory that Judas and his arrest party came to John Mark's home, (where the Upper Room was), before proceeding on to Gethsemane. That would explain why John Mark ran out in only his nightgown, to try and warn the disciples, But he arrived too late to do anything except watch.[2]

---

[1] (19:14)
[2] (Mk 14:51.52)

The High Priest was obviously expecting trouble. A *detachment* of troops suggests a significant number of Roman soldiers, as well as the Temple guards, Chief Priests and Pharisees. It would have been full moon; but the valley was deep and dark, and they may have anticipated Jesus trying to hide. Hence the need for lanterns and torches.

Though the fact it was night-time and outside the city was advantageous, the timing was unfortunate from the authorities' point of view. Their rules (see below) meant that Jesus had to be arrested & tried, presented to Pilate for the verdict to be rubber-stamped, then crucified and buried, all before the start of the official Passover the following afternoon.

It also presented numerous legal problems: trials were not supposed to be held at night, verdicts were supposed to be at least 24 hours after the trial, and sentencing was usually three days later. The Sanhedrin were supposed to assess charges made by others, not to formulate the charges themselves (which may be why Jesus was first taken to Annas, not Caiaphas). And once charged, they had to find two witnesses whose testimony agreed in every detail. Furthermore, Pilate was only available from 6:00-9:00 a.m.!

In Gethsemane (18:1-9)

The fact that Jesus "went forward"[3] (or in Greek, went out), suggests that the garden was walled. If so, He came out of the gate when He heard the troop arriving. Jesus deliberately placed himself between the disciples and the attackers, so that not one of them would be hurt.

John makes no mention of Jesus's prior struggles in prayer in the garden. The disciples were utterly exhausted and kept falling asleep, whilst Jesus was praying *"Father, if it be possible, let this cup pass from me; nevertheless not my will, but I will be done".*

Jesus's use of the divine name, "I AM", produces sheer terror amongst the arrest party. They pull back, and fall to the ground, whether out of awe for Him, or because they anticipate that God will strike Him dead with a lightning

---

[3] (18:4)

bolt. When that doesn't happen, they gather themselves up again; and the second time He says it, they don't seem to be intimidated at all.

Jesus, as usual, is focused on shielding His disciples rather than in any way protecting Himself. He is still concerned to fulfil His Fathers instruction to protect the men the Father has given him. His standing in the Garden's entrance, between His disciples and the threatening mob, and negotiating for their safety, is symbolic of what He will do on the Cross for us.

How often He has stood between us and the enemy, without us ever realising it! He made a once-for-all sacrifice, but also *'ever lives to make intercession for us'* so that *'if we sin, we have an advocate with the Father, Jesus Christ the Righteous'*.[4]

Peter's impetuous folly (18:10-11)

In the upper room, Jesus had told them they would need to be responsible for their own safety from now on. They'd need a money bag, a rucksack, and a sword, even if it meant pawning their coats; because He was going to be *"numbered with the transgressors"*.[5] Apparently they already had two swords, which He reckoned would be adequate.

So Peter had a sword (or maybe a dagger) on his person. Kudos to him for attempting single-handedly to fight off the Roman troops. He had previously said, *'I am willing to die for You'*[6], and now he proves he meant it.

Jesus has so thoroughly won His inner battle, that He rebukes Peter for trying to stop what the Father has ordained. This could seem ungracious! But we are so like Peter. We had rather display our zeal for Christ, than truly accept that we need Him to carry all the filth and corruption of our thought lives, our words, and our actions. Christ may need to block what we think is holy zeal, to bring us face-to-face with the cross, and His suffering in our place.

It seems strange that Peter cut off Malchus's ear: maybe the High Priest's servant dodged as the blow fell, or maybe he was wearing a helmet. Either

---

[4] (1Jn 2:1

[5] (Lk 22:35-38)

[6] (13:37)

way, the very last thing Jesus does with His hands before being shackled, is to heal the servant's ear.

"Shall I not drink the cup which My Father has given me?" The Cross was not just a terrible miscarriage of justice, although it was that. Rather, it was the Father himself who gave Jesus that awful cup to drink. There is such contrast between what the Father was asking His Son to do, and the tenderness of a father-son relationship.

Some say that to believe God Almighty would condemn His Son to crucifixion, is to believe in cosmic child abuse. However we believe it is the amazing grace of God, that He would ask His only begotten Son to bear the punishment which *we* were due.

The cup of God's wrath (18:11)

It seems that Jewish culture regarded drunkenness as humiliating, rather than glorifying it as we tend to. There are several references in scripture to wine being used to humiliate a beaten enemy. The subject would be forced to drink the cup right down to the dregs, so that they were utterly inebriated, trembling, perhaps incontinent or even unable to stand.

Ezekiel records God's coming judgement on Jerusalem as being like the earlier judgement and destruction of Samaria: *'Thou hast walked in the way of thy sister; therefore will I give her cup into thine hand. Thus saith the Lord GOD, Thou shalt drink of thy sister's cup deep and large: thou shalt be laughed to scorn: it containeth much. Thou shalt be filled with drunkenness and sorrow, with the cup of astonishment and desolation, with the cup of thy sister Samaria".*[7]

Isaiah records God telling Israel that they have drunk from the cup of His wrath, but now they will never have to drink of it again. *"Awake, awake, stand up, O Jerusalem, which hast drunk at the hand of the LORD the cup of His fury; thou hast drunken the dregs of the cup of trembling, and wrung them out... Thus saith the Lord thy LORD, and thy God that pleadeth the cause*

---

[7] (Ezek 23:31-33)

of His people, Behold, I have taken out of thine hand the cup of trembling, even the dregs of the cup of My fury; thou shalt no more drink it again."[8]

Jeremiah is told to take the cup of God's wrath around all the nations of the Earth, starting with Jerusalem, progressing out to every nation on earth, and then finally returning to Babylon. *"Thus saith the LORD God of Israel unto me; Take the wine cup of this fury at my hand, and cause all the nations to whom I send thee, to drink it".*[9] No nation can refuse: and the results are desolation, total inebriation, calamity, and warfare. This is not due to some earthly breakdown of world order, but because *"the LORD has roared from on high, shouting like men do when treading out the grapes".*[10]

In ***Revelation***, we hear of Babylon being forced to drink the cup of God's wrath, she having drunk the blood of the saints. The mystery woman[11] is adorned with gold and jewels. She proudly flaunts her blasphemies, and proffers a golden cup full of abomination and fornication - as if they were the most desirable of wines. She herself, however, is drunk with the blood of the martyrs. The nations and the kings are seduced by her temptations. But eventually her sins reach to heaven, and she is repaid twice over - out of the same cup she used to seduce others.[12] *"Great Babylon was remembered before God, to give her the cup of the fierceness of His wrath".*[13] Those who had received the mark of the beast are forced to drink from it, in the very presence of Christ!

The cup is thus not about a psychological struggle, however we understand Jesus's struggle in Gethsemane. Nor is it about the bodily agony: slow suffocation eased only by pushing against the nails. The cup Jesus refers to, is ultimately a cup of spiritual judgement, full of the wrath of God.

Judgement on nations, which we see playing out in front of our eyes every time we watch the news, is merely a large-scale outworking of the same

---

[8] (Isa 51:17,22)

[9] (Jer 25:15)

[10] (Jer 25:30-33)

[11] (Rev 17:1-6)

[12] (Rev 18:3-8)

[13] (Rev 16:19

wrath of God that *'is revealed from heaven against every individual'.*[14] We have so suppressed the truth within ourselves, that only the Holy Spirit can convict us of our sinfulness. The very things Babylon offered us, which seemed so attractive and good to us at the time, bring down the wrath of God on us.

'All have sinned, and all fall short of the glory of God. There is none righteous, no, not one.' And if we do not accept Christ by faith, if we do not acknowledge that He has drunk the cup of our judgement down to its dregs, we shall be forced to drink it ourselves, in His very Presence. We shall be stripped of all self-righteousness and exposed before His burning gaze.

Peter and John trail Jesus to Annas's palace (18:12-18)

During the time of the Maccabees, before the Romans took control, the ruling family had amalgamated the Kingship with the Priesthood. Jews regarded the High Priest as being appointed for life. But the Romans regarded it as a puppet role, to be regularly re-auctioned to the highest bidder.

Annas had been high priest years earlier, until deposed by the Romans. Nepotism allowed each of his sons to follow him in turn, keeping him in power behind the high-priesthood for many years. Eventually, he arranged for Caiaphas, his son-in-law, to become High Priest. That was the situation at the time when Jesus was crucified. in Jewish eyes, Annas was still the high priest; but in Roman eyes, Caiaphas was the present incumbent. Nevertheless, Jesus was first taken to Annas, not Caiaphas.

Caiaphas was the one who had argued to his fellow Sanhedrin members, that it was better for Jesus to be destroyed than for the whole nation to come under Roman wrath. John reminds us of this, in order to underline that this was a show trial. The priesthood had already decided that Jesus must die.[15]

Despite the knock-back of Jesus's rebuke, Peter recovers composure quickly. With another disciple, he shadows the arrest party back across the Kidron and up to the High Priest's palace. The other disciple, thought to be John, openly identifies with Christ by accompanying Him into the courtyard. It is

---

[14] (Rom 1:18)
[15] (11:47-53)

early spring, Jerusalem is two thousand feet above sea level, and the nights are cold: a brazier is the only source of warmth.

Apparently John was known to the High Priest, and so was allowed in without question. Why this was, is speculation. John's father Zebedee is thought to have owned a house in the city, and pickled sardines from Lake Galilee were a prized delicacy. So John may have been his father's sales rep to Annas.

Meanwhile Peter hadn't dared try and gain admission. John took his courage in both hands and negotiated Peter's admission, despite the risk that Peter would be recognised as Malchus's attacker. In all probability, most of the members of the arrest party would have been in the courtyard!

It nearly ended in catastrophe. The young woman peering through the spy-hole, thought she possibly recognised Peter as one of the shadowy figures with Jesus in the Garden. She knew John to be a disciple of Jesus, but was wary of letting any more in. Peter decided to duck the truth, and lie. Thus he began his descent into denying Christ, and having to face his own weakness.

Jesus's interrogation by Annas (18:19-24)

The narrative now returns to Jesus's interrogation within the Palace. John brings out the contrast between Peter's reflex dishonesty and Jesus's poised truthfulness.

Apparently there were at least twenty-two known Jewish laws relating to such legal procedures, which were broken during Jesus's trials before Annas and Caiaphas;-

1. *There was to be no arrest that was effected by a bribe.*[16]
2. *No steps of criminal proceedings were to occur after sunset.*
3. *Members of the Sanhedrin were not allowed to participate in the arrest.*
4. *There were to be no trials before the morning sacrifice.*
5. *There were to be no secret trials, only public.*
6. *Sanhedrin trials only to be conducted in the Hall of Judgment of the Temple*
7. *During the trial, the defence had the first word, before the prosecutors.*

---

[16] (Ex 23:8)

8. *The accused had to have at least one defender.*
9. *Must be two or three witnesses, whose testimonies agreed exactly*
10. *There was to be no allowance for the accused to testify against himself.*
11. *The high priest was forbidden to rend his garments.*
12. *Judges could not initiate the charges; they could only investigate them.*
13. *Accusation of blasphemy only valid if God's name was actually spoken.*
14. *A person could not be condemned solely on the basis of his own words.*
15. *The verdict could not be announced at night.*
16. *For death penalty, the trial and the verdict must be at least 24 hours apart.*
17. *Voting began with youngest, to avoid them being influenced by elders.*
18. *Unanimous vote of guilty suggested collusion & thus proved innocence!*
19. *The sentence could only be pronounced three days after the guilty verdict.*
20. *Judges were to be humane and kind.*
21. *Anyone condemned to death was not to be scourged or beaten beforehand.*
22. *No trials were allowed on the eve of the Sabbath or a feast day.*

These rules were not written down till much later, after the Temple and priesthood had been destroyed in *AD* 70. But the written code merely recorded longstanding oral law, current in Jesus's time. Each of the rules was there for a good reason: to avoid injustice and 'show trials' such as this, where the verdict had been decided long before the event.

Annas could perhaps claim he was free of legal restraints since he was now only the *honorary* High Priest. He seems to have been fishing[17] to try and identify a charge which would most clearly establish Jesus's guilt, making it easier for Caiaphas then to condemn Him. But Jesus challenged his question. An accused man's testimony could not be used against him, so why hadn't Annas asked any of the Jerusalemites who'd heard Him teach in the Temple?

Interrogation techniques haven't changed much over the millennia, and one of Annas's bodyguards decided to soften Jesus up by slapping the defenceless

[17] (18:19)

prisoner. Jesus again responded with supreme poise: quite unlike the parallel event when Paul was later treated in similar fashion.[18]

Peter later comments, *"When Christ was reviled, He did not revile in return; when He suffered, He did not threaten; but committed Himself to Him who judges righteously".*[19] Jesus is our role model for how to handle unjust suffering with patient endurance.

Jesus's poise under interrogation seems to have led Annas to conclude he was wasting his time: so he sends Jesus on to his son-in-law and the Sanhedrin, hoping they will have more success.

Peter is utterly broken-hearted (18:25-27)

As Peter is trying to stay warm near the brazier, its light makes his face more discernible. One of the arrest party realises he is unfamiliar, and questions him again about his possible allegiance. Peter denies Christ a second time.

An hour passes, as Jesus's interrogation is proceeding.[20] As it finishes, and the squad forms up again to escort Jesus to Caiaphas, a friend of Malthus notices Peter's accent and realises he is Galilean. He comments to his friends, then challenges Peter directly. Now facing the whole courtyard, Peter denies Christ vehemently; even calling down curses on himself as he does so.[21]

Just at that moment, a nearby cock crows - twice. This is commonplace in third-world urban settings, even today. The cockerel is in effect saying, "Wake up! Wake up!" But for Peter, it recalls Jesus's prophecy, and breaks his heart. His self-confidence was self-deception, and his vaunted courage had given way to cowardly lying.

Again, we are so like Peter. We put our confidence in our own strength, not in Christ. So when we find ourselves wanting, and the bubble of self-deception bursts, we '*go out and weep bitterly*', like Peter. We contain ourselves till no-one else is around, then we sink into despair: we have failed - again! But all along, our faith has been misplaced: faith in ourselves, not in Christ.

---

[18] (Acts 23:1-5)
[19] (1Pet 2:23)
[20] (Lk 22:59)
[21] (Mt 26:73-75)

Jesus turns from His interrogators, and looks across at Peter, catching his eye. But His look is not one of outrage or condemnation, but rather one of pity and grace. *'Peter, I told you this would happen, and you didn't believe Me. Now it's happened, and you are so ashamed of yourself you want to hide. But I also told you that I have prayed for you that your faith would not fail completely. The day will come when you reclaim your allegiance to Me. And when that happens I will use you to strengthen your brothers.'*

We so need to meet Jesus's gaze, not turn away from it, when we stumble or fall into sin. We so need His reminder that He has known our wicked, self-deceptive hearts all along. That He has prayed for us, and will re-establish us: indeed, will use our example, to strengthen others.

Take heart, brothers and sisters! *'When we are faithless, He remains faithful - for He cannot deny Himself'*. He is the Faithful One, so unchanging, *'full of grace and truth. And of His grace have we all received, grace upon grace'.*[22]

---

[22] (1:14-17)

The unprotesting sheep is shorn (18:28-19:16)

Caiaphas demands Pilate crucify Jesus, despite His innocence. Jesus is shorn of His dignity and de-humanised by the Roman soldiers - all for our sake.

John's account of Jesus's trial before Pilate, omits His interrogation by Caiaphas[1] and subsequent trial by the Sanhedrin[2], and also omits that Pilate asked Herod's opinion about Jesus[3]. All of these judicial hearings focus on the same theme however: whether Jesus is the King of the Jews.

The case against Jesus was presented to Pilate as a threat to Rome's authority. Jesus, they said, was forbidding others to pay taxes to Caesar, on the grounds that He was the King of Israel.[4] Actually, they knew this was entirely untrue. The Pharisees had tried to trick Jesus into saying this; but He had seen the trap and skilfully avoided it.[5]

Some say that the High Priests framed the charge in this way so as to secure Pilate's 'guilty' verdict, when their real concern was that Jesus was claiming to be the Messiah, the Son of God. But actually, to a Jewish mindset these are just two different sides of the same coin.[6]

Pilate queries the charge (18:28-32)

Pilate's day started very early, probably at daybreak. The Pharisees believed that entering the house of a Gentile caused ritual defilement. Especially so, when that Gentile represented an Emperor who claimed to be God! Their focus on religious observance blinded them completely to the reality that they were about to crucify God's Son.

They seem to have been surprised by Pilate's questioning them about the accusation. Maybe the fact that he had seconded Roman troops to go with the High Priest's arrest team, had led them to assume that he would simply rubber-stamp their verdict.

---

[1] (Mt 26:57-68)
[2] (Mt 27:1-2; Mk 14:53-65)
[3] (Lk 23:6-12)
[4] (Lk 23:2)
[5] (Lk 20:20-26)
[6] (Ps 2:7; 89:26-27)

When Pilate probed what the charge actually was, their reply was surly to the point of rudeness. So he responded in kind, telling them to go away and try Jesus themselves – which of course they had already done!

There were plenty of occasions when the Jews lynched someone by stoning them to death: for example, Stephen's martyrdom. But technically they were not allowed to execute a death sentence, without Rome's approval. And Pilate was not willing to give this without a proper trial. So he rubbed their noses in their own powerlessness, repaying their insolence.

That the Jews were intent on Jesus being *crucified* (a Roman execution), when they could easily have stoned him, was perhaps for three reasons:-

1. Crucifixion, under the law of Moses, indicated that a man was specially cursed by God.[7] That would discredit Jesus's claim to righteousness.
2. They could avoid popular unrest by presenting Jesus's execution as having been "out of their hands", should any of His followers kick up a fuss. Jerusalem at Passover was a volatile environment.
3. It fulfilled Jesus's own prophecy, given only a week before.[8] He must be "hung on a tree" if he was to become accursed for us[9], so that in turn in Him we might become the righteousness of God.

King of the Jews (18:33-39)

Determined to work out what on earth was going on, Pilate went back into his palace and called for Jesus to be brought before him. There is a note of surprise in his first question: *"Are you the king of the Jews?"* Pilate had dealt with Barabbas recently, and knew what a rebel looked like. Jesus didn't fit the stereotype! Instinct told him that it was out of jealousy that the Jews had arrested Jesus[10]; and his wife had also warned him not to condemn Jesus.[11]

N.B: *We know from history that Pilate was later demoted and sent to Gaul, where he committed suicide. His wife's nightmare came true.*

[7] (Deut 21:23)
[8] (12: 23–26; Mt 20:17–19)
[9] (Gal 3:13)
[10] (Mk 15:10)
[11] (Matt 27:19)

The phrase, 'King of the Jews', was very significant.

When Israel asked Samuel, the last of the Judges, to give them a king, he said they had rejected God from being their King. When the three wise men came to Jerusalem, they had asked, *"Where is the One born to be King of the Jews?"* And now when Jesus is crucified, Pilate affixes a sign over His head which says, *'Jesus of Nazareth, King of the Jews'*.

Given that this is the central accusation the Jewish leaders make, and that they end by saying *'We have no King but Caesar'*, Pilate's placard is a prophetic rebuke from the Holy Spirit: Jesus is indeed 'King of the Jews'. God is reaffirming His governance of the nation, through Jesus His incarnate Son.

Serene in His surrender to the Father's will, Jesus probed Pilate's question[12]: *"Are you asking off your own bat, or because others have said I'm claiming to be King of the Jews?""* The frame of reference - a Jewish religious viewpoint, or the Roman Emperor's view - would determine Christ's answer.

Pilate replies that he neither knows nor cares about Jewish law, but wonders what Jesus had actually done to provoke His own people to turn against Him.

In the synoptic gospels, Jesus simply answers Pilate's question by saying 'Yes'; but John now gives us more detail. Jesus acknowledges that He *is* a king, but His kingdom has nothing to do with this world. If it had, He would have instructed His followers to fight against the Jews, whereas in fact in Gethsemane He had told Peter to lay down his sword.

Being a Roman politician, this answer would have flummoxed Pilate. Otherworldly kingdoms weren't a category in his mindset! He can't grasp what Jesus is saying, and asks for clarification: *"Are you a king then, or not?"*

Jesus explained that His birth into this world was not as Pretender to the Throne of Israel. His incarnation was to bear witness to the truth, as the Logos of God. Everyone who loves truth, recognises Him and accepts Him.

Truth was another non-category in Pilate's thinking! Political expediency and keeping the peace were his core values, just as they are for politicians today. Despite perhaps thinking Him naive, Pilate is convinced of Jesus's innocence.

---

[12] (18:34)

Pilate re-emerges and announced this verdict to the crowd. In fact if one counts up all the different occasions Jesus was ruled 'not guilty', there were seven: in front of Annas[13], Caiaphas[14], and Pilate[15]. Even Herod could not formulate a charge against Him.[16]

A silent shearing

From this point on[17], Jesus says nothing more by way of self-defence. Even in front of Herod, he will not say a word.[18]

When a lamb is in distress, it bleats; but strangely enough, a sheep about to be shorn doesn't make a sound. Jesus was about to be unjustly shorn of all His dignity, His honour, His very clothes - and yet He was silent.

"He was oppressed and He was afflicted, yet He opened not His mouth; He was led as a lamb to the slaughter, and as a sheep before its shearers is silent, so He opened not His mouth".[19]

Peter quotes Jesus's refusal to defend Himself, as an example for us to follow when treated unjustly. *'What credit is it if, when you are beaten for your faults, you take it patiently? But when you do good and suffer, if you take it patiently, this is commendable before God. For to this you were called, because Christ also suffered for us, leaving us an example, that you should follow His steps: "Who committed no sin, nor was deceit found in His mouth"; who, when He was reviled, did not revile in return; when He suffered, He did not threaten, but committed Himself to Him who judges righteously; who Himself bore our sins in His own body on the tree, that we, having died to sins, might live for righteousness—by whose stripes you were healed'*[20].

How often we complain (outwardly or inwardly) at the injustice of our treatment, or of others' opinion of us? God notices, and commends, when we cease defending ourselves and instead entrust ourselves completely to

---

[13] (18:23)
[14] (Mt 26:59-60)
[15] (18::38; 19:4; 19:6; 19:12; Matt 27:24)
[16] (Lk 23:15)
[17] (18:38)
[18] (Lk 23:8,9)
[19] (Isa 53:7)
[20] (1 Pet 2:20-24)

the Righteous Judge. Jesus is our example of trustful humility, not threatening revenge or repaying insult with insult; but instead committing His spirit into His Father's care.

The whole of Psalm 37 is a wonderful commentary on this; in particular *"Commit your way to the Lord, trust also in Him, and He shall bring it to pass. He shall bring forth your righteousness as the light, and your justice as the noonday"*[21]. Have you been falsely accused? God will be your vindicator!

False Messiah freed; real Messiah flogged (18:39-40)

Though Pilate was convinced that Jesus was utterly innocent[22], the Chief Priests and elders continued pressing that He was claiming to be the King of the Jews[23].

Apparently Pilate had the habit of releasing one popular prisoner each Passover. (Given that the feast celebrated the Exodus, this was highly ironic. One man was freed, whilst the rest of the nation remained in bondage!)

So he tried the populist approach, seeking to bypass the leaders by appealing to Messianic sentiment in the crowd. This was a fatal mistake: in effect he was surrendering his own authority, the authority of the Roman Empire, to be governed by the mob's wishes. Once he had done so, he was left impotently arguing with them, until he finally capitulated.

He could not conceive that the crowd - the nation - would want him to crucify their Messiah. He was unaware that the Priesthood had foreseen this, and had already planted people in the crowd to chant for Barabbas rather than Jesus[24].

Barabbas was a rebel who had fomented an uprising against the Romans in Jerusalem. This had involved murder, presumably of someone he regarded as a Jewish collaborator.[25] He and his band of men had all been sentenced and were chained together, ready for execution.[26]

---

21 (Ps 37:5,6)
22 (18:38)
23 (Mt 27:12)
24 (18:40; Matt 27:20)
25 (Mt 27:16; Lk 23:19)
26 (Mk 15:7)

Barabbas's name means 'Son of the Father'. How ironic, that he was released whilst the real 'Son of the Father' took his place on the cross!

In some manuscripts, his name is given as '*Jesus* Barabbas', Jesus meaning Saviour as we know. He was in every sense a *false Messiah*, but fitted Jewish expectations of the role better than Jesus did. So perhaps the priests didn't have too much trouble persuading the crowd.

"Behold, the Man!" (19:1-5)

Having tried to appeal to their nationalism, Pilate now tries to appeal to their sense of pity, by flogging Jesus but then releasing Him.[27] This was probably the least severe form of flogging the Romans used, known as 'fustigatio'.[28]

The Praetorian Guard added their own brutal finishing touches to this punishment. They stripped Jesus naked then dressed Him in a regal robe, putting a crown of thorns on His head and a reed in His hand as a fake sceptre. Then, in mock homage, they took turns kneeling before Him and saying *'Hail, King of the Jews'*.[29] As they each did so, they spat in His face, slapped Him and beat Him over the head with the reed.

The crown would have been made out of long thorns from the date palm, forced onto His scalp and forehead. Date palm thorns are very toxic: even if pulled out straight away, they cause intense inflammatory swelling and large deep bruises. Perhaps this is what Isaiah foresaw when he prophesied, *'His appearance was disfigured more than any man'.*[30]

Pilate reiterates that as far as he is concerned, Jesus is completely innocent[31]; then exhibits Jesus in His purple robe and crown of thorns, saying *'Behold the Man!'*[32].

On that day two thousand years ago, the Jews' hearts were so hard, their ears so deaf, their eyes so blind, they didn't realise what they were doing.

---

27 (Lk 23:16)
28 (19:1)
29 (Mt 27:29)
30 (Isa 52:14)
31 (19:4)
32 (19:5)

Peter says *"The God of Abraham, Isaac, and Jacob, the God of our fathers, glorified His Servant Jesus, whom you delivered up and denied in the presence of Pilate, when he was determined to let Him go. But you denied the Holy One and the Just, and asked for a murderer to be granted to you, and killed the Prince of life, whom God raised from the dead, of which we are witnesses....Yet now, brethren, I know that you did it in ignorance, as did also your rulers. But those things which God foretold by the mouth of all His prophets, that the Christ would suffer, He has thus fulfilled".*[33]

The day will come, when the Jews will truly 'behold the Man' and will repent. *"I will pour on the house of David and on the inhabitants of Jerusalem the Spirit of grace and supplication; then they will look on Me whom they pierced. Yes, they will mourn for Him as one mourns for his only son, and grieve for Him as one grieves for a firstborn. In that day there shall be a great mourning in Jerusalem ... In that day a fountain shall be opened for the house of David and for the inhabitants of Jerusalem, for sin and for uncleanness".*[34]

The Second Adam

'Behold, the Man!': Pilate's invitation to the Jews, is also a powerful invitation for us today. He was *'the Man of sorrows, acquainted with grief. We hid, as it were, our faces from Him; He was despised, and we did not esteem Him'.*[35]

How hard it is to gaze at Jesus, our Saviour, battered and bruised, bespittled and mocked even before He was crucified - for us. *'Surely He has borne our sorrows ... He was wounded for our transgressions, bruised for our iniquities; the chastisement for our peace was laid upon Him, and by His stripes we are healed'*[36].

In that guardroom, the 'divine exchange' was already beginning. Jesus was despised and rejected by man, that we might be accepted by God. He experienced our sorrows, that we might have His joy. His flesh was torn to ribbons, that we might be made whole. He was disfigured, that we might become beautiful in God's sight.

---

[33] (Acts 3:13-21)
[34] (Zech 12:10-13:1)
[35] (Isa 53:3)
[36] (Isa 53:3-5)

The title Jesus used as His own by far the most often, was 'the Son of Man'. It appears many times in the Old Testament, mainly in Ezekiel; and there, it is indefinite and simply a generic term for a human being. But Daniel prophesied a divine being he referred to as 'One like unto a son of man', who would ascend the throne of God.[37] One who was both God and man.

In the New Testament, the term is used exclusively by Jesus alone, and applied to Himself. The Greek phrase He uses is actually 'the son of *the* man'.

What man was he referring to? Well, in Hebrew, since the original word for man was 'adam', 'son of man' is actually 'son of Adam'. He is the Second Adam, the One on whom the sin of the first Adam would be visited.

Truly, He is 'THE MAN'; the son of Adam, the Second Adam.

'Just as through one man sin entered the world, and death through sin, and thus death spread to all men, because all sinned … Therefore, as through one man's offence judgment came to all men, resulting in condemnation, even so through one Man's righteous act the free gift came to all men, resulting in justification of life. For as by one man's disobedience many were made sinners, so also by one Man's obedience many will be made righteous… through Jesus Christ our Lord'.[38]

Pilate's appeal backfires (19:6-16)

Seeing Jesus dressed in royal purple only incensed the High Priests further. The chanting grew ever louder, "Crucify Him! Crucify Him!". And the Chief Priests echoed this to Pilate. Once again, Pilate tries to duck responsibility. He suggests that the Jews crucify Him themselves, as he was not prepared to take responsibility for such an injustice. But in fact both he and they knew that that was illegal under Roman law.

Faced by the fact that there were no grounds for execution under *Roman* law, the priests finally declare the real reason they want Him dead. Under *Jewish* law, they explain, He should die because *He claimed He was the Son of God*.

---

[37] (Dan 7:13)

[38] (Rom 5:12-20)

Coupled with Jesus's statement that He was from another realm, plus his own assessment that Jesus was innocent, and his wife's warning, the Chief Priests' new statement really spooked Pilate. His fear that a riot was building, was overshadowed by the fear that he might be dealing with a supernatural being. Since Romans believed their Emperor was a god-man, this wasn't difficult for him to conceive.

He went back into the Praetorium and demanded Jesus tell him where He was *really* from. But Jesus said nothing. Astonished, Pilate goads Jesus with the reality that His destiny - life or death - is entirely in the governor's hands. Jesus still doesn't answer Pilate's question about His origins, but He does answer the underlying issue which is troubling Pilate. Who is really in control of, and therefore responsible for, what is about to happen?

Pilate's authority came from Caesar, in earthly terms. But Caesar's authority, like all civil authority, ultimately came from God.[39] If Jesus was the Son of God, Pilate was afraid of bringing judgement on his own head by condemning not just an innocent *man*, but the Son of God. On the other hand, Pilate was Caesar's puppet, charged with protecting Caesar's interests; and could expect to be charged with disloyalty if he did not do so.

Jesus, quite unfazed by Pilate's threat, said that the one who handed him over was guilty of a greater sin. Whether this referred to Judas or Caiaphas, is debatable; and it didn't exonerate Pilate, but said he *would* be culpable before God if he crucified Jesus. But others would be even more culpable.

Pilate's response was to redouble his efforts to find a way of releasing Jesus.

But the Jews piled on the pressure by saying that *'to free Jesus would not be consistent with being Caesar's friend'*.[40] The term 'Caesar's friend' was what we would call an Order of Merit within the Roman Empire. It was granted as a sign of the Emperor's special favour. In Pilate's case, he had been awarded the title after his patron in the Roman Senate, Sejanus, had recommended him to Caesar. But not long before Jesus's trial, Sejanus had fallen out of

---

[39] (Rom 13:1)
[40] (19:12)

favour and been arrested and executed. So Pilate's governorship was already vulnerable. Any hint of disloyalty to Caesar might well lead to his own death.

In Pilate's heart, the fear of man ultimately trumped the fear of God. His aides set the stage for sentencing, by bringing the Judgement Seat (in Greek, 'bema') outdoors, onto the Palace forecourt.

Determined that the Jews take as much of the responsibility as possible, he faced them with the fact that they were asking him to crucify their Messiah: *"Behold your King!"* But the calls for Christ's crucifixion just grow louder and louder. So he asks, *"Do you really want me to crucify your King?"* The chief priests reply, *"We have no king except Caesar!"*

Even coming from Jews whose personal interests aligned with Rome, this was an astonishing repudiation of Israel's Messianic hope. Those who believe that the Church has permanently replaced Israel at the centre of God's purposes in history, see this moment as the point where that happened.

We know however that God is not finished with Israel.[41] He has not cast away His people, but has reserved for Himself a 'remnant', chosen by God's grace.[42] For now, He has consigned the Jews to disobedience, so that they too may ultimately be saved by grace.[43] His faithfulness to His promises, and His astonishing grace, mean that whilst the Jewish nation may have been broken off from the olive tree of grace, it is only so that we Gentiles can be grafted in. Eventually, under great tribulation, Israel as a nation will acknowledge Christ as their Messiah, and He will return to reign on earth.

Hallelujah!

[41] (Rom 9-11)

[42] (Rom 11:5)

[43] (Rom 11:32)

It is finished! (19:17-42)

Christ's death completes the 'divine exchange'.
He is made sin for us, and experiences separation from God,
so that we can be forgiven and reconciled to God.

John, as far as we know, was the only one of the apostles who was present throughout the crucifixion. The accounts in the other gospels were therefore second-hand, either from the women who were present, or perhaps from others such as the soldiers[1]. Each gospel recounts different elements of the event, particularly Jesus's words while He was on the cross. But the fact that John was an eye-witness gives his account special weight.

Once Pilate had sentenced Jesus, He was flogged again[2], this time a more brutal flogging the Romans called 'verberatio'. It literally tore the flesh from the victim's back, leaving their bones and even their organs exposed.

The Crucifixion

Then Christ was led out to the crucifixion site, alongside one of the main roads out of the city, where His fate would be visible to everyone. It was customary to take the prisoners the long way round, carrying on their shoulders the crossbar to which they would later be nailed. Each victim would be accompanied by four soldiers, and a centurion would oversee the whole procession. In front of each prisoner a placard would be carried, giving their name and the crime for which they were being punished. Besides Jesus there were two others, probably Barabbas's henchmen.

Along the way many women watched, and bewailed what was happening.

Jesus was so weakened by the flogging that He could barely stay upright. A bystander, Simon from Cyrene (in North Africa), was commandeered to carry the cross-bar. Simon was probably in Jerusalem for Passover.

The exact location of Golgotha is uncertain, Jerusalem having been destroyed and rebuilt many times over the centuries. It is presently attributed to a site

---

1 (Mt 27:54)
2 (Mt 27:26)

which has a vague resemblance to the shape of a skull. But it only looks like that because up till two hundred year ago it was a quarry face!

Jesus was stripped naked and His hands nailed to the crossbar, which was then fixed to the upright post. His ankles were crossed and a single massive nail driven through them both, into the post. This nail's purpose was to prolong a victim's agony by slowing their suffocation. By pushing up on it, they could briefly alleviate their ribcage being stretched by their body weight.

As the soldiers were nailing Him, there would have been cries and groans from the other two men undergoing the same brutality. But Jesus prayed, *"Father, forgive them, for they know not what they do".*[3]

At first, the two others cursed at Jesus; but after a while one of them realised that whilst they were being justly punished, Jesus was innocent. He asked Jesus to remember Him, when He came into His kingdom: in other words, he believed that Jesus would return to reign! Jesus reassured him that he wouldn't have to wait that long, nor just be remembered. *"Today, you will be with Me in Paradise".*[4]

Jesus spent six hours suffering on the cross, drinking the cup the Father had given Him, the judgement for our sin.

David accurately prophesied many details of the crucifixion, in Psalm 22:

- Jesus's cry of dereliction[5]
- His being despised and ridiculed[6]
- His hands and feet being pierced[7]
- His garments being allotted amongst the soldiers[8]
- His cry, 'It is finished!'[9]

[3] (Lk 23:34)
[4] (Lk 23:43)
[5] (Ps 22:1)
[6] (Ps 22:6-8)
[7] (Ps 22:16)
[8] (Ps 22:18)
[9] (Ps 22:31)

Many believe that Jesus was meditating on this psalm throughout His crucifixion, for whilst it accurately describes His suffering, its second half also prophesies the wonderful outcome of redemption.

The first three hours were marked by intense humiliation as all the passers-by, the Chief Priests, and the Roman soldiers poured scorn on Jesus's claims to be Messiah, the Son of God.

But from midday till three o'clock a supernatural darkness came over the land. (It could not have been a solar eclipse, for Passover always took place at full moon.) Amongst its specific prophecies psalm twenty-two says, *"Many bulls have surrounded Me; strong bulls of Bashan have encircled Me. They gape at Me with their mouths, like a raging and roaring lion".* I believe this describes Jesus being tormented by Satan's most powerful demons, during these three hours of darkness.

Rejecting Christ's Kingship (19:19-22)

Pilate's inscription, *"King of the Jews"*, on the placard nailed above Jesus's head, caused intense irritation to the Chief Priests. Their charge had been that Jesus *claimed* to be King of the Jews, not that He actually *was!* Jesus had said that His Kingdom was not of this world: if it had been, He would have instructed His servants (such as Peter) to fight against the Jewish arrest party![10] But the wording was not accidental: Pilate had hand-written it[11] and refused to change it[12].

As we've previously seen, the Greek word translated 'Jews' didn't mean all those we would now refer to as Jews. Rather, it referred to the Judaeans, as opposed to the Samaritans and Galileans. Of course the Galileans were also descended from Abraham, and practiced Judaism: so in John's thinking, 'Jew' is not a racial or religious category. To further complicate things, John often seems to use 'Jew' to refer to the ruling classes in Judaea, rather than the Judaean population en masse.

---

[10] (18:36)
[11] (19:19)
[12] (19:22)

'King of the Jews' was thus a more specific term than 'King of Israel'. When Solomon's kingdom split, the northern tribes were known as Israel (perhaps because Israel had given the rights of the firstborn to Joseph) whereas the House of David (tribes of Judah and Simeon) were known as 'Jehudim' or Jews. Technically therefore Rehoboam was the first 'King of the Jews'.

So to the Judaean ruling class, Chief Priests and Sanhedrin and others, Pilate's wording implied that they had rebelled against their true King.

Jesus foretold this hatred by the Jewish leaders, in many of His parables.

- Evil vinedressers kill the King's son, in order to seize His inheritance[13]
- The King's Son's wedding feast, is spurned by the original invited guests[14]
- Citizens rebel against an externally-appointed King[15]

Of course, Jesus *is* the King of the Jews. He will return in glory, to reign in Jerusalem and sit on David's throne. The day will come, when Israel as a nation will recognise Jesus as their true Messiah.

But what does their hatred of His rule (as expressed at Calvary) teach us?

Firstly, it shows our *human rebelliousness*. Just as Satan rebelled against God, fallen man by nature rebels. Our flesh refuses Jesus to be our Lord. We may even accept Him as our Saviour, and yet in practice deny His Lordship. We water down His commands, ignore His teaching, despise His ministers, and reject His calling for our lives.

Secondly the placard tells us, *Christ reigns, by virtue of His cross*. Jesus of Nazareth is King of the Jews, and King of our lives also. In it, He triumphed over all the rival principalities and powers that would seek to have control of our lives.[16] He has been given the Name above all names, just because He humbled Himself and became obedient unto death, even death on a cross.[17]

Written in Hebrew, Roman and Greek, the plaque's message confronts us all.

---

[13] (Mt 21:33:41

[14] (Mt 22:1-14)

[15] (Lk 19:12-14)

[16] (Col 2:15)

[17] (Phil 2:5-11)

The division of His clothing (19:23-24)

If you were a Roman soldier, the only perk of crucifixion duty was the right to a share of the prisoner's clothing. We see here four men so brutalised by their work, that they are concerned only with who gets what from their victim's possessions. Their eyes are not on Jesus, or even on the crowd, but only on how the lots will fall. The contrast with the grief and compassion of Jesus's women followers, is striking.

Jews commonly wore five items of clothing: a turban, sandals, a belt, an outer robe and a tunic. The tunic was not an undergarment as we would think of it, but the primary item of clothing. In Jesus's case, it was made of a single piece of cloth, similar perhaps to our modern tabards. The other four items may have been apportioned according to the soldiers' seniority, but the tunic was too valuable to divide up: so they gambled for it.

This is the first of four ways[18] in which, John says, the crucifixion exactly fulfils Old Testament prophecy. Psalm 22, written by King David a thousand years earlier, predicts each of these details. Remember that John's gospel may well have been written primarily for a Jewish readership. So this tying together of the Old Testament and the New, this proving that Jesus was the fulfilment of the Jewish scriptures, was essential. *'These are written, that you may believe that Jesus is the Messiah, the Son of God'.*[19]

Over the centuries, commentators have seen other meanings in the seamless tunic. For example, the Jewish High Priest's robe was to be 'woven skilfully'[20], and Josephus describes it as being woven from a single length of thread. Some have interpreted Jesus's tunic as symbolic of His hidden High Priesthood, or of the unity of the Church.

Jesus's care for His mother (19:25-27)

As the eldest of Mary's sons, Jesus would have been responsible for her care. His brothers at this point were not believers, as far as we know. And there is no mention of any of them being there to support Mary, as she watched

[18] (19:24,28,36,37)
[19] (20:31)
[20] (Ex 28:39)

Jesus die. Though family ties usually took precedence in Jewish culture, for Jesus His disciples were His family.[21] But even in the midst of His own suffering, He was concerned that His mother be looked after.

John is believed to have been Jesus's cousin: in the absence of Jesus's own family members, he was the obvious choice. He was also 'the disciple whom Jesus loved'. Tradition has it that John looked after Mary for the rest of her life, and that she moved with him when he later became Bishop of Ephesus.

There is something significant in Jesus's words to Mary, and John: *"Woman, behold your son!"*; *"Behold your mother!"*. By these words He created a mother-son bond between them, much deeper than just dutiful care. Jesus can do that: He 'sets the solitary in families'.[22]

Whilst as believers we may find ourselves estranged from other family members, our duty of care to our parents remains. Jesus roundly condemned Pharisees who used the *corban* loophole to wriggle out of caring for parents.

The fact that John was present at the cross when a Roman soldier speared Jesus's side, suggests that he took Mary home immediately and then returned to his vigil. This might explain why he doesn't record some of Jesus's sayings mentioned in the other gospels.

It is finished! (19:28-30)

After John had taken Mary home, a three hour period of supernatural darkness ensued.[23] Towards the end of this, Jesus cried out, *"My God, My God, why hast Thou forsaken Me?"*[24] This was the ultimate trial of faith, for One who had never known what it meant to be Fatherless. He had never known being utterly alone, even when the disciples had abandoned Him, because the Father was always with Him.[25] But now, being made sin for us, as a man He sensed that the Father had turned away.

---

[21] (Mt 12:48-50)
[22] (Ps 68:6)
[23] (Mt 27:45-46)
[24] (Mt 27:46)
[25] (16:32)

How could this be? It is a mystery, that He who was both Son of Man and Son of God, could be cut off from God. Yet this is the essence of spiritual death. Jesus refers to it as being 'in the Outer Darkness, where there is wailing and gnashing of teeth'. This is the essence of Hell.

This is how Jesus knew that His work was finished. He had experienced what every one of us deserves, on our behalf. He had tasted death, the despairing death of one rightly cut off from God. He had de-fanged death.[26]

By now He was so dehydrated that His tongue stuck to the roof of His mouth.[27] He knew He would need liquid, to be able to fulfil scripture by shouting the last line of the psalm. So He said, *"I thirst"*. One of the soldiers fetched a sponge, soaked it with sour wine, then proffered it to Jesus on a reed.[28] The others believed He was calling for Elijah, and wanted to see whether the prophet would come. (Perhaps though they were Romans, they knew the Jewish tradition that Elijah would come at Passover to announce Messiah's reign; or that at the end of the Passover meal, a cup was filled with wine for Elijah?)

Jesus's final words came in quick succession. He shouted, *"It is finished!"* Not the last whimper of a dying man, but rather, a victory cry! Then He bowed His head and said, *"Father, into Your hands I commend My spirit"*[29]

Jesus had earlier said, *"My Father loves Me, because I lay down My life that I may take it again. No one takes it from Me, but I lay it down of Myself. I have authority to lay it down, and authority to take it again".*[30]

Jesus is here laying down His soul life as well as His bodily life; but committing His spirit into His Father's loving care. Was this Jesus giving up the struggle for life? No! Christ's death was entirely voluntary. He *chose* its manner and exact timing. In fact, Pilate was astonished when he heard that Jesus had already died.

---

[26] (1Cor 15:55)
[27] (Ps 22:15)
[28] (Mt 27:48-49)
[29] (Mt 27:50; Mk 15:37; Lk 23:46)
[30] (10:17-18)

<u>All-sufficient merit</u>

What was Jesus referring to, when He said, *"It is finished"*?

The most obvious answers are that His suffering was nearly over, His life's work was done, and the New Covenant had been brought into force.

He had

- taken our sentence of death (substitution),
- paid the full penalty (propitiation), and
- opened the door for us to enter the Father's Presence (reconciliation).

He had responded obediently to the Father's will, revealed the Father's heart of love, and made atonement for the sins of the world.

The Book of Hebrews offers us a wonderful exposition of what "It is finished!" means in practice for us. His sacrifice ...

- Means we no longer need to strive to establish our own righteousness. We can enter into a 'sabbath-day rest', relying totally on what He has achieved, not on our own works[31]
- Will never need repeating: it is once-for-all[32]
- Erases God's record of our lawless deeds: their *penalty* is gone[33]
- Cleanses not just our bodies but our consciences too, removing our *guilt* and enabling us to serve the living God[34]
- Removes the *power* of sin forever[35]
- Sanctifies and perfects us[36]

It is by faith that we receive all this. Faith *'is the substance of things hoped for, the evidence of unseen realities'*[37]. But there is no further sacrifice if we turn away.[38]

---

[31] (Heb 4:10)
[32] (Heb 9:12,14)
[33] (Heb 10:17)
[34] (Heb 9:14;10:1-4)
[35] (Heb 9:26)
[36] (Heb 10:14)
[37] (Heb 11:1,2)
[38] (2:3, 6:4-6, 10:26-29)

Not all Christians believe that it *is* finished. For instance, some believe that Christ's sacrifice is repeated time after time in the Mass: that the bread and the wine actually become the body and blood of Christ through transubstantiation, and that attendance at Mass is essential for the forgiveness of sins. Further, they believe that whilst Christ's sacrifice pays the *eternal* penalty of sin, there is also a *temporal* penalty. If we do not pay the latter during our earthly lives, either by our sufferings or by indulgences, we must spend time in Purgatory before we will be let in to heaven.

Even we who *say* we believe Christ has fully paid for our sins, often still condemn ourselves when we fall into sin. But scripture says, *"There is now no condemnation for them that are in Christ Jesus"*.[39] Christ is not taken by surprise when we do sin: He taught us to pray, *"Forgive us our sins"*. He intervenes as our Advocate with the Father, interceding for us.[40]

"If we confess our sins, He is faithful and just to forgive us our sins and to cleanse us from all unrighteousness"[41]

Let's make sure we have truly entered into the rest of knowing that *'It is finished"*! Our salvation stems completely from grace: grace upon grace.

<u>The blood and the water</u> (19:31-37)

Men could take days to die from crucifixion, and Passover was due to start at sundown. Because it's the same calendar date each year, it falls on different days of the week. If it is not on an ordinary sabbath, whichever day it falls on is classed as a special sabbath.[42] So the Jewish leaders wanted Jesus not only dead but buried, before sundown. They requested that Pilate expedite matters so the bodies could be removed.

When death by crucifixion needed accelerating, the easiest way was to break the victim's legs. Then they could no longer prevent suffocating under their own weight. Once death ensued, the soldiers could take the bodies to a communal grave for criminals.

---

39 (Rom 8:1)
40 (1Jn 2:1)
41 (1Jn 1:9)
42 (19:31)

After Pilate had agreed to the High Priest's request, the soldiers proceeded to break the legs of the other two men. But when they came to Jesus, He was already dead; so they didn't break His bones. Just to be on the safe side, one of them stabbed Jesus's heart from under His ribcage with a spear. John watched with astonishment as both blood and water flowed out.

Given that Jesus died at three p.m. and sundown was at six, He can only have been dead an hour or two at most. This is not long enough for blood to separate out into red cells and serum, and anyway blood usually clots when someone dies. The likely explanation is that the flogging had caused Jesus to lose so much blood that He was acutely anaemic. This would fit with His stumbling under the weight of the crosspiece, and feeling thirsty - since the body realises it needs fluid replacement. If He was so anaemic, His heart would have been working overtime and that can cause a collection of fluid to build up within the membrane around it (the pericardial sac). So a spear passing up through the diaphragm, through the pericardial sac and into the heart would produce a flow of blood and water.[43]

All well and good, but why does John make such a big thing of the blood and water? Theologians have puzzled over this for years.

John underlines that he is giving eye-witness evidence, *'so that you may believe'*. He then quotes two Messianic prophecies, predicting that
(a) Messiah's bones would be unbroken, like the Passover lamb[44], and
(b) that He would be pierced[45].
He regards these two facts as establishing Jesus's identity as Messiah.
But the prophecies make no mention of blood and water!

John subsequently returns to this issue in his first letter, saying that Jesus *'came by water and blood'*[46]*;* and that along with the Spirit's witness on earth, it is these two different fluids (blood and water) that prove Jesus's identity.[47] That letter was written to defend the central truth of the

---

[43] (18:34)
[44] (Ex 12:46; Num 9:12; Ps 34:20)
[45] (Zech 12:10)
[46] (1Jn 5:6)
[47] (1 Jn 5:8)

incarnation: that Jesus was the eternal Word of God, who became flesh and dwelt among us. So it seems that the true significance of the blood and water for John, is that it proves Jesus's humanity; He was God Incarnate, fully God - but also fully Man. But this event has been interpreted in various ways.

One common interpretation of John's later references to water and blood, is that they refer to Jesus's baptism and crucifixion. Cerinthus, an early heretic, taught that Jesus was an ordinary man, born by natural means. He only became Anointed/Christ/Messiah when the Holy Spirit came on Him at his baptism; and the Spirit then left him just before the crucifixion. So according to this interpretation, Cerinthus was teaching that Christ (the Anointed One) came by water alone. John's reference to blood and water would therefore have been designed to contradict that doctrine.

But John's letter seems to be aimed not at the Cerinthians but at those who didn't believe that Jesus Christ had come in the flesh[48]: in other words, that He was never truly human. If so, this would imply that John saw the water as indicating Jesus's divine nature (not His baptism) and the blood as indicating His humanity (not His crucifixion).

Jesus's burial

Joseph, a senior member of the Sanhedrin and a secret disciple, daringly went to Pilate and asked for Jesus's body. Watched by Mary's companions[49], he and Nicodemus took the body down, wrapped it in linen, and laid it in Joseph's own rock-hewn tomb. Then they sealed the entrance by rolling a large stone across it.

While Joseph gave Jesus his tomb, Nicodemus brought the traditional Jewish mixed-spice ointment. However, the amount he brought was extraordinary; roughly equal to Jesus's body weight. This was a burial fit for a King! How he obtained such a huge quantity in the short space of time, we are not told.

Mary Magdalene and 'the other Mary' (possibly the mother of James[50]) had followed the two men, and seen where Christ was buried. Presumably they

[48] (1Jn 4:2)
[49] (Mt 27:61; Lk 23:55,56)
[50] (Mk 16:1)

didn't know what had gone on inside the tomb, for once the sabbath was over, they too brought spices with which to anoint Him.[51]

Jewish law forbad convicted sinners being buried honourably, in a rich man's tomb. And yet Isaiah had prophesied 600 years earlier that exactly this would happen.[52] Jewish tombs normally held several bodies. The only reason Jesus could legally be buried there, was that it was brand new and unused.

Joseph's tomb was in a garden right next to Golgotha. Given the time constraint of the imminent Passover sabbath[53], it was one of very few sites where they could have buried him. Once they had finished their work, they would have hurried home in order to observe the feast.

And so we leave the scene, feeling the unbearable sadness of the women, the apostles scattered who-knows-where across Jerusalem, their hopes and dreams of Israel's redemption in tatters. But somewhere buried deep within each of them, was the faint memory that Jesus had said He would rise again!

---

[51] (Mk 16:1)

[52] (Isa 53:9)

[53] (19:31)

Resurrection joy (20:1-31)

En route from Hades to Heaven, Jesus spends time with His disciples, proving He has really been raised from the dead, and commissioning them

Eye-witnesses of the resurrection

Despite the tomb entrance having been sealed[1] *and* a security guard posted, when Mary Magdalene got there just before dawn she found the stone rolled away and the tomb empty. It seems she had arranged to rendezvous with Mary the mother of James, Salome[2], and others[3], to re-anoint Jesus's body. They arrived a little later, just after sunrise: but by then she had already run off to tell Peter and John that Jesus's body was missing.

John, probably younger than Peter, got to the tomb first. But having any contact with a dead body, or even touching a tomb, made one ritually unclean: and the Feast of Unleavened Bread, which follows on from Passover, was in progress. Tomb entrances sloped downwards into a hollowed-out underground space. So he stooped down in the half-light of dawn, and peered in - but did not enter. He saw the grave clothes, filled with precious spices, lying there. Whatever had happened, this was no grave robbery!

Peter then caught up, and with his usual impetuousness, brushed past and entered the tomb. From inside, he could now see not only the cloths that had shrouded Jesus's body, but also the burial turban. It was neatly folded just where Jesus's head had been, separate from the grave clothes. This resurrection was not like Lazarus, where others had had to loose him from the grave clothes. This was more like a butterfly leaving its cocoon, with the clothes exactly where they had been when the body was inside them.

John uses three different Greek words to distinguish Peter's 'seeing' from John's. John initially just saw with his physical eyesight, whereas Peter saw in a way that caused him to wonder what on earth had happened[4]. The Greek word is 'theorizo' - he began to theorise.

---

[1] (Mt 27:62-66)

[2] (Mk 16:1

[3] (Lk 24:1)

[4] (Lk 24:12)

Maybe he called John in to see, maybe John just couldn't *not* enter. Anyway, John too sees the neatly arranged grave clothes and turban, and now 'sees' in yet another way. The Greek word here means to see in a way which implies understanding: 'I see' - 'I get it'. He has not yet physically seen the Risen Lord, but he sees and *believes.*[5]

<u>What was it that led John to believe?</u>

At this point, neither Peter nor the author John knew the scripture, that Messiah must rise again from the dead.[6] There are many Old Testament types which hint at the resurrection: for instance, Abraham's offering of Isaac[7], or Joseph's enslavement then elevation. But from Jesus's comment to the Emmaus Road disciples[8], it seems that none of them had grasped these hints.

Perhaps the most direct prophecy is the one Peter quotes at Pentecost:-

"Therefore My heart is glad, and My glory rejoices; My flesh also will rest in hope. For You will not leave My soul in Sheol, nor will You allow Your Holy One to see corruption. You will show Me the path of life; in Your presence is fullness of joy; at Your right hand are pleasures forevermore".[9]

Isaiah had given another very clear prophecy: *"When you make His soul an offering for sin, He shall see His seed, He shall prolong His days, and the pleasure of the Lord shall prosper in His hand".*[10]

It is unlikely that the disciples had never heard or read these scriptures. They were aware of them, but hadn't grasped their significance. Peter's Pentecost sermon shows just how powerfully Jesus taught them, during the forty days between the resurrection and His ascension.[11] His teaching was all based on the Old Testament scriptures, opening their minds through the Holy Spirit.

So how *did* John come to suddenly believe?

---

[5] (20:8)
[6] (20:9)
[7] (Gen 22:9-14 & Heb 11:17-19)
[8] (Lk 24:25-27)
[9] (Ps 16:9-11, Acts 2:24-32)
[10] (Isa 53:10)
[11] (Acts 1:1-3)

Of course, Jesus had repeatedly told them He would be crucified then rise on the third day. But the crucifixion seems to have temporarily destroyed their faith. Faced with the evidence of a tomb which was open, empty and neat, John knew there could be no other explanation. It had to be true!

The evidence for the resurrection

Over the centuries, numerous people have tried to disprove the resurrection. More than one have been trained lawyers, who knew how to sift truth from deception. And yet far from disproving it, they have ended up believing, just as John did, *because of the evidence*.

The rest of the chapter gives us examples of how the disciples came to recognise the risen Christ in different ways. Mary, whose eyes were clouded with tears, recognised the sound of His voice. That evening Jesus invites the disciples in the Upper Room to see, to touch, to handle Him; and to observe Him eating fish and honeycomb. A week later, Thomas the ultimate realist, realises that Jesus had heard his earlier scepticism: and he does a u-turn into total faith, declaring Jesus to be 'My Lord and my God!'

Jesus knows exactly what will convince each individual: for some it is evidence, for others it's emotional, for some it's experiencing Jesus's omniscience, and so on. But the practical evidence is powerful:-

- The authorities were never able to produce the body, despite having taken precautions to prevent its theft. Their cover story, that the disciples had stolen the body, never stuck.
- The dramatic change in the disciples, from cowering behind closed doors to boldly preaching to the Pentecost crowds, speaks volumes.
- Had the story been an urban myth, there is no way it would have featured a woman as the first eye-witness, for women's testimony was discounted in Jewish legal affairs.
- An eyewitness says blood and water flowed from His side. There is no chance that He just fainted before being buried.
- And there were so many Old Testament prophecies that were precisely fulfilled in the manner of His death.

Why is the resurrection so important?

The different gospel accounts record many eye-witness encounters with the risen Christ. After *Mary*, the *other women* also encounter Christ. Sometime that day, Jesus appears to *Peter* individually. That afternoon *two disciples* meet Jesus on the Emmaus Road. That evening, as *the apostles* are having supper, Jesus gatecrashes and rebukes them for not believing the women, then invites them to see His wounds and touch Him, even watch Him eat, to prove that He is no ghost! A week later, He repeats this so that *Thomas* isn't left out.

Then the action moves to Galilee. *Seven of them* go fishing, and Jesus repeats the miracle he'd used for their original calling. All *eleven of them* meet Him on a mountaintop, reminiscent of when he first called them as His team. Paul tells us *five hundred disciples* met Him on a single occasion, many of whom were still alive to be cross-examined at the time of his writing.[12] Finally *James*, Jesus's brother, also met Him.[13]

Altogether there was a forty-day period in which He *'showed Himself alive to them by many infallible proofs'*[14] and taught them intensively about the Kingdom of God. It culminated with Him leading them out of Jerusalem on the Bethany Road, and ascending to heaven from the Mount of Olives.

The fact that some of the Eleven were still having doubts when they met Jesus in Galilee[15], suggests that heart knowledge of Jesus's living Presence doesn't necessarily come from just knowing the evidence. There has to be an experiential 'knowing', which He promised us in the Upper Room discourse.[16] The way He physically manifested Himself to the Eleven, was to lay the foundation on which the church has subsequently been built.

"These things are written that you may know that Jesus is the Christ, the Son of God, and that believing you may have life in His name".[17]

---

[12] (1Cor 15:6)
[13] (1Cor 15:7)
[14] (Acts 1:3)
[15] (Mt 28:17)
[16] (14:19-21)
[17] (20:31)

It is heart awareness of Jesus's living Presence that gives us assurance of our salvation, and our union with Him. Every time we see prayer answered, or experience a 'God-incidence', or become aware of His Presence as we meet in twos or threes, He is manifesting Himself to us.

If your awareness of Christ's Presence has faded compared to the days of your 'first love', ask Him to reveal Himself to you afresh & to help you recognise the myriad daily signs He is here, with you.

The resurrection is the very foundation of our faith:[18]

- It is God's declaration that Jesus is the Son of God with power[19]
- We're justified & reconciled by Christ's death, but saved by His life[20]
- Our union with Him in resurrection, gives victory over sin and death[21]
- Its the source of our hope for our own resurrection[22]

Mary's revelation (20:11-16)

By the time Mary Magdalene had followed Peter and John back to the tomb, they'd already left. The initial adrenaline rush of alerting them had passed; they were not there; and the tomb was still empty. Her grief could be contained no longer - she wept and wept and wept, thinking she was alone.

Like John, she was wary of entering the grave: but astonishingly, there were two angels sitting guarding the grave-clothes, one at the head and one at the foot of where Jesus had lain. Whether she knew at the time that they were angels, seems unclear: they were clothed in white, but angels in a place of the dead would be hard to get your head around! She responds to them as if it was a perfectly ordinary encounter.

Their question *'Why are you weeping?'* must have seemed a little tactless, to say the least. But from their point of view, there was no reason to cry: the tomb was empty because the Lord of Glory had risen from the dead! She explains that those who inflicted such awful humiliation and suffering on the

---

[18] (1 Cor 15:12-20)
[19] (Rom 1:4)
[20] (Rom 5:9,10)
[21] (Rom 6:1-11)
[22] (1Pet 1:3)

One she loved, must have removed His body; perhaps to prevent the tomb becoming a place of pilgrimage.

As she answers them, she senses someone behind her, and turns. Through her tears she sees a man whom she doesn't recognise: and he asks her the same silly question! She assumes he's a gardener employed to look after Joseph's posh tomb. If so, he would have been involved in removing Jesus's body, and would know where it had been taken. Surely he'd be glad for someone to take it off his hands?

Then came a single word that utterly changed everything, for Mary. The Master spoke her name with infinite tenderness and pity. In an instant, her grief turned into astonished joy! *'Rabboni!'*

Three days earlier, Jesus had said *"A little while, and you will not see Me; and again a little while, and you will see Me. Most assuredly, I say to you that you will weep and lament, but the world will rejoice; and you will be sorrowful, but your sorrow will be turned into joy. A woman, when she is in labour, has sorrow because her hour has come; but as soon as she has given birth to the child, she no longer remembers the anguish, for joy that a human being has been born into the world. Therefore you now have sorrow; but I will see you again and your heart will rejoice, and no one will take your joy from you".*[23]

What would *you* do, if you thought someone you loved had died a terrible death, and then suddenly there they were in front of your very eyes? My guess is that you'd hug them and hug them and hug them, until the tears of joy and relief gradually subsided. That's what Mary did.

After a while, Jesus gently disengaged, telling her not to cling to Him.

Why did He do this, when

- He had allowed other women to hold His feet, and worship Him?[24]

- He later invited the disciples to touch and handle Him?[25], and

- He invited Thomas to touch His scars and put his hand into His side?

---

[23] (15:19-22)

[24] (Matt 28:9)

[25] (Lk 24:39)

Mary's bond with Jesus seems to have been closer than the other women. She loved Him especially deeply, because He had cast seven demons out of her. She is the first person to visit the tomb, the first to see Jesus, and the one to break the marvellous news. She has the star role in John's account of the resurrection.

The reason Jesus gave for not clinging to Him, was that He was going to the Father. It was not that He was a disembodied spirit, or that her touch would in some way defile Him from entering the Father's Presence. Rather, He is saying her relationship with Him has to change from physical to spiritual.

Jesus's message for the disciples (20:16,17)

Why does Jesus instruct Mary to tell the disciples that though He hasn't *yet* ascended, He *is ascending* to His Father and their Father, His God and their God? After all, He'll see them in person only a few hours later?

Some suggest that Jesus did in fact ascend to the Father, between meeting Mary and His visit to the Upper Room that evening. The thought is that He needed to ascend in order to present His blood sacrifice in the heavenly Temple. That would explain His use of the present tense, *'I am ascending'.* However with the exception of one verse in Hebrews[26], there is nothing else to support this in scripture.

A simpler explanation is that Jesus sees Himself as mid-journey. When He died, He descended into the depths of the earth.[27] He is en route from Hades to Heaven, but with a stop-over on Earth. He is breaking His journey, to give the apostles the personal encounter needed for them to be His eye-witnesses.

Mary Magdalene knew that Jesus's message was for His disciples, not His siblings. Jesus had previously redefined His family as being those who did the will of His Father in heaven.[28] His siblings didn't believe in Him and don't seem to have been present at His crucifixion to support their mother.

---

[26] (Heb 9:11-12)

[27] (Eph 4:9)

[28] (Matt 12:46-50)

Christ's message to the apostles focussed on the huge change in their relationship with Him and with God. Having previously referred to them as disciples, then servants, then friends[29], He now calls them His brothers.

His message prepared their hearts for His meeting with them that evening.

Jesus, who they had been ashamed of so recently, was telling them He was not ashamed to call them His brothers! He had borne all their shame, on the cross - as He hung there, naked, derided and scorned. They need not be ashamed to meet Him in person, risen from the dead: for His Father, His God was also their Father, their God!

Jesus is not ashamed to call His disciples His brothers, even though they have so recently deserted Him, because they (and we) are one with Him.[30] It was His union with us that cost Him His death on the cross; and it is our union with Him that means we share His resurrection life. Our life is hidden with Christ in God: we are seated in the heavenlies, at God's right hand, in Christ.[31] Just as we have been baptised into His death and resurrection, so too we are in Him in His ascension, and in Him as He sits at the Father's right hand, the throne of all authority.

With these words, Jesus declares the fulfilment of His earlier prophecy: *"At that day, you will know that I am in My Father, and you in Me, and I in you".*[32] *"The Father Himself loves you, because you have loved Me, and have believed that I came forth from God. I came forth from the Father and have come into the world. Again, I leave the world and go to the Father".*[33]

But when Mary relays the message, despite Peter and John's findings at the tomb, no-one believed her.[34]

<u>You are My witnesses</u> (20:19-23)

Later that day, as the disciples were gathered for supper, Jesus gatecrashed the meal. They had locked and barred the doors, for fear that the Jewish

---

29 (15:15)
30 (Heb 2:11)
31 (Col 3:1-3)
32 (14:20)
33 (16:27-28)
34 (Mk 16:14)

authorities would try and arrest them on the pretext they had stolen Jesus's body.[35] But despite these security precautions, Jesus simply appeared among them in the room: we are not given any further details as to how.

This event is central to the gospel, being recorded in detail by three of the four evangelists. Each writes with a different perspective and selects different elements; but only Matthew skips it completely, fast-forwarding to Jesus's appearance in Galilee. All four gospels (and Acts too) record Jesus's 'Great Commission' to the disciples, which happened first at this meeting.

At first the disciples were terrified, thinking that they were seeing His ghost.[36] But Jesus reassured them, firstly by speaking *'Shalom!'* to them. Then He invited them to inspect His nail-marks and gashed loin, and touch Him.[37] He wanted them to know that He was really human; He was flesh and blood.

Despite their joy, the disciples still couldn't believe: it just seemed too good to be true. So Jesus ate some of the broiled fish and honeycomb they had prepared, to prove He was no ghost.[38]

It is hard for us to grasp how earth-shattering this would have been for them.

Years later, when John came to write his first letter, he expresses the wonder of it all: *"That which was from the beginning, which we have heard, which we have seen with our eyes, which we have looked at, and our hands have handled, concerning the Word of life – the life was manifested, and we have seen, and bear witness, and declared to you that eternal life which was with the Father and was manifested to us – that which we have seen and heard we declare to you, that you also may have fellowship with us; and truly our fellowship is with the Father and with His Son Jesus Christ. And these things we write to you that your joy may be full".*[39]

They were physically hearing, seeing and touching the eternal Logos of God; experiencing fellowship with the Father and the Son as they did so. They understood that the resurrection was God's declaration that Jesus was His

---

35 (Mt 28:11-15)
36 (Lk 24:37)
37 (Lk 24:38-40)
38 (Lk 24:41-43)
39 (1Jn 1:1-4)

Son, and had all His power and authority.[40] It finally proved the reality of the incarnation, that Jesus was (and is) both fully Man and fully God,

Having established His tangible presence, it seems from Luke's account that Jesus now repeated His Emmaus Road teaching, opening the scriptures to corroborate what their senses were telling them.[41] From there on, Luke's account parallels John's. Jesus goes on to commission the apostles as His witnesses to preach repentance and forgiveness of sins to all nations, starting in Jerusalem. But first they must receive the Holy Spirit.

Each gospel author focusses on different aspects of the Commission:

- *Matthew* emphasises Jesus's supreme authority, given Him by the Father as reward for His self-sacrifice. They are to make disciples, baptise them and teach them all Jesus's commandments.[42]
- *Mark* emphasises that the hearers' response to the gospel will determine whether they're saved or condemned. New believers will have the same gifts as the apostles, to cast out demons, heal the sick, speak in tongues etc.
- *Luke* emphasises preaching repentance and forgiveness of sins, and the apostles' roles as witnesses of the crucifixion and resurrection.[43] They are instructed to wait for the promised power of the Holy Spirit.
- *John* echoes Luke on this, recording how Jesus symbolically breathed on them whilst telling them they must receive His Holy Spirit. And he echoes Matthew in recording Jesus's gift of authority to forgive or retain sins.

John Stott calls this gift of authority *'the authority of a preacher, not a priest'*. It has to do with mission, and we see Peter using it in his preaching on the Day of Pentecost.[44] You'll recall how Jesus used this same authority in His own ministry, shaking the dust of Capernaum off His feet[45] but telling the paralysed man his sins were forgiven.

---

[40] (Rom 1:4)
[41] (Lk 24:44-49)
[42] (Mt 28:18-20; Phil 2:9-11)
[43] (Lk 24:46-49)
[44] (Acts 2:40)
[45] (Mt 11:20-24)

Mission and incarnation

Whilst aligning with the synoptics, John adds his own unique take on the nature of our commission, connecting it with his theme of the incarnation:

'As the Father has sent Me, I also send you.'

Of course, the Father had equipped Jesus with His authority[46], and given Him the Holy Spirit[47], just as Jesus now did to the disciples. But Jesus's words imply much more!

- Jesus was sent by the Father: *He* was the first missionary. He is our role model for all our mission work. He came in obedience to the Father; and He only spoke what He heard the Father saying, and only did what He saw the Father do. All mission must start with listening, followed by obedience.
- Jesus left the glory and peace of eternity, to dwell amongst us. We are called likewise to incarnate the gospel, living *in* the world, though not *of* it. That means identifying with the people we are sent to: living in the same circumstances, not preaching at them from some offshore haven.
- Like Him, we are sent to sinners, not to those who think they are righteous. He ate and drank with 'publicans and sinners' such as Zacchaeus. Whilst holding to the moral law, we should be known as loving and accepting, not hypocritically self-righteous.
- He did not just preach but also manifested God's Name, in His works of healing and grace. The social gospel is not enough without preaching; but preaching is ineffective unless we manifest God's heart.
- Just as Jesus was hated for telling the truth about God, we shall experience the same - often from our own family and relatives. We are to share *'the fellowship of His sufferings'* as well as *'the power of His resurrection'*.
- We are one with Christ just as much in His calling, as in His death, resurrection and ascension. His calling was to bring men back to the Father through the gospel, which is *'the power of God unto salvation for everyone who believes'*[48].

---

[46] (5:26,27)
[47] (3:34)
[48] (Rom 1:16)

It is when we count everything loss for Jesus's sake and the gospel, when our identification with Him and His mission is complete, that we fully experience what it is to *'know Him, and the power of His resurrection, and the fellowship of His sufferings'.*[49]

Thomas's scepticism is blown to pieces

For some reason Thomas missed out on that first reunion between Christ and His disciples. He is known as 'doubting Thomas' but I see him as the supreme realist amongst them. It was he who realistically faced up to the prospect of dying with Christ if they went back to Bethany.[50] And it was he who expressed the team's bewilderment about Jesus 'going to the Father'.[51] He was courageous and honest. But once bitten, twice shy. *"It's all very well for you lot - you've seen the Lord. How can you expect me to believe unless I see Him too?"*

Any resurrected crucifixion victim would have the nail marks; but only Jesus would have the additional wound in His side. Thomas demanded more than just sight or touch: to put his hand right into the wound, and touch Jesus's pierced heart!

A week later Jesus gatecrashes the Sunday evening team meal once again. Once again, the doors are locked: despite Jesus breathing on them, the disciples haven't yet received the holy boldness they had after Pentecost. He greets them, then straightaway invites Thomas to do exactly what he had stipulated. Christ's words proved that He had been present and listening, when Thomas had expressed his scepticism!

We don't read of Thomas actually touching Jesus. The realisation that Jesus knew every word he'd said, proved to him that Christ was omnipresent and all-knowing. Just like Nathanael[52], it was the knowledge that he was known inside out by Christ that undermined his scepticism.

---

[49] (Phil 3:10)
[50] (11:8,16)
[51] (14:5)
[52] (1:45-49)

His immediate response was total capitulation. Mary had called Jesus *'My Lord'*: Thomas goes a huge step further in adding, *'My God!'* He acknowledges that he is dealing with Deity Incarnate; that from now on, he will worship this Man with every fibre of his being.

> *Tradition has it that Thomas took the gospel to India, where he eventually died as a martyr.*

Jesus accepts Thomas's worship, but declares a blessing on those who believe without seeing. Like the other disciples, Thomas had seen many other signs pointing to Jesus's deity, prior to the crucifixion. But the ones John has chosen to record, along with the resurrection evidence, should enable anyone to believe that Jesus is the Christ, the Son of God. And then through believing, to enter that spiritual communion with the Father and His Son which is the essence of eternal life.

It is thought that John's gospel originally ended at this point, and that what follows in John 21 is a postscript, perhaps added by a different author.[53]

---

[53] (21:24)

En route to the Father (20:17)

Having taken flesh as the Son of God,
Jesus returns to His Father as the Son of Man,
opening heaven to us, to sit with Him.

"Jesus said to her, "Do not cling to Me, for I have not yet ascended to My Father; but go to My brethren and say to them, 'I am ascending to My Father and your Father, and to My God and your God.' ""

Prophecies about the Ascension

Some liberal theologians hold that since the Ascension is only actually described by Luke[1], it can't have really happened and must be something he made up. But there are many other references to it throughout the Old and New Testaments, especially here in John's Gospel as we shall see.

The Jews expected that Messiah would ascend to God: after all, Daniel had prophesied exactly that. He foresaw *'One like the Son of Man, coming with the clouds of heaven to the Ancient of Days'*, and being given an everlasting, worldwide Kingdom[2].

King David had also prophesied extensively about the event. After he and his people brought the Ark of God up to Jerusalem with celebrations and dancing[3], the Holy Spirit showed him that this was just a foreshadowing of a day when a Messiah King much more glorious than he would 'ascend unto the hill of the Lord'. But it would come after Messiah had suffered horribly.

Psalms 22-24, written by David a thousand years before Christ, are thought to be a trilogy. The first psalm describes the crucifixion in incredibly accurate detail, as we have seen previously. The second describes the blessings of Messiah's care for His people. But the third (psalm twenty-four) is all about Messiah arriving at the gate of Heaven, and demanding entry.

---

[1] (Lk 24:50-53, Acts 1:9)
[2] (Dan 7:13,14)
[3] (2Sam 6:12-19)

"Who may ascend into the hill of the Lord? Or who may stand in His holy place? He who has clean hands and a pure heart, who has not lifted up his soul to an idol, nor sworn deceitfully. He shall receive blessing from the Lord, and righteousness from the God of his salvation. This is Jacob, the generation of those who seek Him, who seek Your face."

"Lift up your heads, O you gates! And be lifted up, you everlasting doors!
And the King of glory shall come in."

"Who is this King of glory?"

"The Lord strong and mighty, The Lord mighty in battle.
Lift up your heads, O you gates! Lift up, you everlasting doors!
And the King of glory shall come in."

"Who is this King of glory?"

"The Lord of hosts, He is the King of glory."[4]

Later, David was shown more about it. *"You have ascended on high, You have led captivity captive; You have received gifts among men, even from the rebellious, that the Lord God might dwell there."*[5]

And later still, *"The Lord said to my Lord, 'Sit at My right hand, till I make Your enemies Your footstool.' The Lord shall send the rod of Your strength out of Zion. Rule in the midst of Your enemies!"*[6]

Jesus makes aliyah

The Hebrew word for ascent is *aliyah*. Going up to Jerusalem to attend the feasts, is called 'making Aliyah'. Jews returning to Israel, are said to 'make aliyah'. David wrote a whole liturgy of 'Psalms of Ascent'[7], to help Jews arriving in Jerusalem to prepare their hearts for the Presence of God. The word has come to have built-in undertones of joy and celebration at coming to the place where God dwells. But its full meaning is only seen, in the *aliyah* of our Lord Jesus Christ!

---

[4] (Ps 24:3–10)
[5] (Ps 68:17)
[6] (Ps 110:1–2)
[7] (Ps 120-134)

Jesus had spoken about His impending departure, prior to His death. The Upper Room discourse[8] revolves around Him trying to help His disciples understand what was about to happen. Like their fellow Jews, they had really struggled to grasp the fact that He had come from God. He talks repeatedly about 'going to the Father' as being the second half of a return journey, eventually saying bluntly,

> *"I came forth from the Father, and have come into the world.*
> *Again, I leave the world and go to the Father"*[9].

At last they seem to finally grasp that He had 'come forth from God'[10]. But that's as far as they could go. The return journey was still a mystery to them.

After the resurrection, the first thing Jesus wanted them to know, the only message that He wanted Mary to bring, was that He was *'ascending to My Father and your Father, My God and your God'*. Why did He wanted her to convey this, when He Himself would see Peter later that day, and then meet the Eleven that evening?

I believe it was to prepare their hearts: they would be feeling deeply ashamed that they had deserted Him at Calvary, and had not believed His promise that He would be raised from the dead. Mary's message conveys that He is still fully committed to them: He has not rejected them because of their failings.

We'll first deal with an apparent paradox, then pick out eight themes about the Ascension.

<u>En route to the Father</u>

Jesus says *"I have not yet ascended to My Father"* and then in the next breath, *"I am ascending to My Father"*. How can these both be true?

Imagine you are flying home from Australia to UK, but you have a few days' stopover in Dubai. You have started your journey, but not yet arrived in London. You have many friends in Dubai, and you happen to bump into one

---

[8] (John 14-17)
[9] (16:28)
[10] (16:30)

of them in the airport. You ask him or her to tell the others, *"I'm in Dubai just for a few days, but I'm en route to London"*. That was the situation here.

Christ's ascension started not from earth, but from Hell (Hades). Peter says, *"For Christ also suffered once for sins, the just for the unjust, that He might bring us to God, being put to death in the flesh but made alive by the Spirit, by whom also He went and preached to the spirits in prison, who formerly were disobedient"*. From there He *"has gone into heaven and is at the right hand of God, angels and authorities and powers having been made subject to Him"*.[11]

Paul quotes King David, to back this up: "*But to each one of us grace was given according to the measure of Christ's gift. Therefore He says: 'When He ascended on high, He led captivity captive, And gave gifts to men'. (Now this, 'He ascended' - what does it mean but that He also first descended into the lower parts of the earth? He who descended is also the One who ascended far above all the heavens, that He might fill all things.)"*[12]

The Resurrection was merely Part One of the Ascension. When Jesus met Mary, He was already en route to the Father!

Nine implications of the Ascension

1. The Incarnation and Ascension are matching bookends of the gospel

Jesus clearly saw His ascension as *returning home*. He speaks of returning *'to the One who sent Me'*, or of having come down from heaven and ascending back there, or of returning to the Father.[13]

When facing His detractors, He usually expresses this as returning 'to Him who sent Me'; whereas with His followers and disciples, He talks of returning to the Father. He knows that the Jewish leaders, rather than being Abraham's children are actually Satan's, and do not know the Father. They are from beneath, but He is from above - they are of the world, He is not. They therefore cannot conceive of where He is going.

---

[11] (1Pet 3:22)
[12] (Eph 4:7–10)
[13] (3:12-13; 6:33,38-39; 7:33-34; 8:21-23; 14:28; 16:28 etc etc)

We will not be able to grasp the meaning of the ascension, until we have believed that Christ is God Incarnate. If we find it impossible to believe He is the bread of life, sent by the Father, we would not believe it even if we saw Him actually ascending![14]

His incarnation and His ascension are the bookends of the gospel. If we preach that Jesus was born of the Virgin Mary, we must also preach that He has returned to the Father.

2. <u>The Ascension creates an open Heaven</u>

When Jacob set off to His uncle Laban's place as a naive 'mummy's boy', unaccompanied and unused to the rigours of trekking, God appeared to him in a dream. The Lord was standing at the top of a ladder from heaven to earth, and there were angels (spirits whose job is to look after those who are to inherit salvation) going up and down.

God told Jacob he would inherit the covenant promises made to his father and grandfather. Furthermore He, the Lord God, would shadow Jacob as he travelled, never leaving him until he returned home safely.[15]

Jacob's reaction was one of misplaced awe: he attributed his experience to the place, rather than the Person. But as well as renaming it Beth-El, *'the House of God'*, he also recognised it as *'the gate of heaven'*.

Fast forward to Jesus's calling of His first disciples, just after He'd been baptised and spent forty days in the wilderness. Philip talks his sceptical friend Nathanael into meeting Jesus: Nathanael is then blown away by Jesus's 'word of knowledge' about his character. Having previously said, *"Can anything good come out of Nazareth?"*, Nathanael instantly recognises Jesus as the Son of God, and King of Israel[16].

This is an astonishing revelation, but (Jesus says) it pales into insignificance compared to what he will later see: the ascended Son of God, acting as the bridge between heaven and earth! He Himself is the ladder for the angels.
He is our open Heaven.

---

[14] (6:58-64)
[15] (Gen 28:10-17)
[16] (1:45-51)

In the Upper Room, Jesus says that as well as giving them another Comforter, He Himself will not abandon them. The world will not be able to sense His presence, but they will. Not only so, but both He and the Father will dwell with anyone who loves Him: they will be permanently in residence.[17]

When He commissions His disciples to make disciples of every nation, He promises them *'Lo. I am with you always, even to the end of the age'.*[18] He will be present with each of us, wherever we are. *'He has said, "I will never leave you nor forsake you"'.*[19]

3. <u>He came as Son of God, but ascends as Son of Man</u>

When Jesus came from the Father, He came as the incarnate Son of God. *'The Word became flesh, and tabernacled among us, and we beheld His glory, glory as of the only begotten of the Father'.*[20] In Mary's womb, He took the body that the Father had prepared for Him, and experienced everything a human being can experience, from conception to the grave. He was born into a working-class family in a country under occupation; and whilst still a toddler, became a refugee. He had no privilege, no silver spoon in His mouth.

He identified totally with us, even being baptised when He had no sin to confess or repent of. Eventually He *'became sin for us, though He knew no sin'*. He bore our griefs, carried our sorrows, was wounded for our transgressions, beaten up for our iniquities, flayed alive so that we might be healed.[21] He became our fall-guy, offering His own blood in place of ours.

His total identification with us did not end when He returned to heaven. In our text[22] Jesus emphasises His continued identification with His people, saying He is returning to *'My Father and your Father, My God and your God'*. But though the Ascension is the bookend to the Incarnation, things do not go back to how they were before Christ came. Christ received a Kingdom, and a new ministry as our heavenly Advocate. But He does not shed His humanity.

---

[17] (14:15-23)
[18] (Mt 28:18-20
[19] (Heb 13:5,6)
[20] (1:14)
[21] (Isa 53:4,5)
[22] (20:17)

It is Jesus's continuing manhood, His oneness with our humanity, that qualifies Him to be our heavenly High Priest. *"Both He who sanctifies and those who are being sanctified are all of one, for which reason He is not ashamed to call them brethren, saying: "I will declare Your name to My brethren" ...In all things He had to be made like His brethren, that He might be a merciful and faithful High Priest in things pertaining to God, to make propitiation for the sins of the people."*[23]

Daniel saw Christ approaching the Father as '*One like the Son of Man*'. And John, on Patmos, says *"Having turned I saw ... One like the Son of Man"*[24], clothed in priestly robes. Just as in His earthly ministry, Jesus remains fully God and fully Man.

"We have a great High Priest who has passed through the heavens, Jesus the Son of God ... we do not have a High Priest who cannot sympathise with our weaknesses, but was in all points tempted as we are, yet without sin. Let us therefore come boldly to the throne of grace, that we may obtain mercy and find grace to help in time of need".[25]

4. **The Ascension brings us into the heavenlies**

Not only is He one with us despite His ascension, but *we are one with Him in His ascension*.

Anyone who has been baptised by immersion, knows that it symbolises our union with Christ in His death and resurrection. But the resurrection was merely part one of the ascension. How many realise that we are also 'in Him' in His ascension?

Jesus had prayed for His disciples *'that they may be with Me where I am, to behold My glory'.*[26] Now, in fulfilment of His prayer, He describes God as *'My Father and your Father, My God and your God'*. His ascension '*brought many sons to glory*'.

Paul makes this explicit in his letters to the Ephesians & Colossians:

---

[23] (Heb 2:10–18)
[24] (Rev 1:12–17)
[25] (Heb 4:14–16)
[26] (17:24)

"God ... made us alive together with Christ .., and raised us up together, and made us sit together in the heavenly places in Christ Jesus, that in the ages to come He might show the exceeding riches of His grace in His kindness toward us in Christ Jesus."[27]

As Christ was hidden from view as He ascended, our resurrection life is hidden with Him, in God: *"If then you were raised with Christ, seek those things which are above, where Christ is, sitting at the right hand of God. Set your mind on things above, not on things on the earth. For you died, and your life is hidden with Christ in God. When Christ who is our life appears, then you also will appear with Him in glory."*[28]

This 'setting our mind on things which are above' is not some mystical 'centring down' process. Paul goes on to explain that it involves putting off a fleshly mindset of *"fornication, uncleanness, passion, evil desire, and covetousness"*. And in their place, putting on *"tender mercies, kindness, humility, meekness, long-suffering; ...and love, which is the bond of perfection"*[29]. These all come from spending time seated with Christ in the heavenly realms.

Being seated with Christ in the heavenlies, gives us a totally different perspective on life: what you might call a helicopter view, watching the battle from above. It is the view Moses had, as he prayed for Joshua during the battle with Amalek.[30] It reminds us that '*the battle belongs to the Lord*', and that "*We do not wrestle against flesh and blood, but against principalities, against powers, against the rulers of the darkness of this age, against spiritual hosts of wickedness in the heavenly places. Therefore take up the whole armour of God, that you may be able to withstand in the evil day, and having done all, to stand".*[31]

Because of this heavenly perspective, our hearts are kept in peace, and our spirits experience unspeakable joy in the midst of life's trials and tribulations.

---

[27] (Eph 2:4–7)
[28] (Col 2:11- 3:4)
[29] (Col 3:5,12,14)
[30] (Gen 17:8-13)
[31] (Eph 6:12–13)

5. **<u>It also brings us into restored relationship</u>**

We saw how Daniel and David focussed on the triumphal aspect of the Ascension, but that is not Jesus's focus. He says He is ascending *'to My Father and your Father, My God and your God'*. His focus is on a *restored relationship*.

As the Son of God, He could say *"He who sent Me is with Me. The Father has not left Me alone"*.[32] But as the Son of Man, He cried out *"My God, My God, why have You forsaken Me?"*[33] He had tasted death, and knew its terrible impact on our relationship with the Father.

Most of us will have experienced broken relationships where, although we have forgiven the person we have not been reconciled. Forgiveness is unilateral, whereas reconciliation is bilateral. But *"Christ also suffered once for sins, the just for the unjust, that He might bring us to God"*.[34] The purpose of the Cross goes beyond forgiveness, to reconciliation: restored relationship.

Paul saw his ministry as one of reconciliation. *"God has reconciled us to Himself through Jesus Christ, and has given us the ministry of reconciliation (that is, that God was in Christ reconciling the world to Himself, not imputing their trespasses to them), and has committed to us the word of reconciliation. Now then, we are ambassadors for Christ, as though God were pleading through us: we implore you on Christ's behalf, be reconciled to God."*[35]

When two people are reconciled, the barrier of blame and guilt between them is removed, and they start talking to each other again. This restored relationship is not just about our legal standing before God, but about sharing our day with Him. Relationship that is not limited to functional prayer, but involves reflecting on life, with Him. This is what we often see in David's psalms: as he pours out his heart to God, he regains the helicopter view of his life, as seen from the heavenlies.

---

[32] (8:29)
[33] (Mt 27:46)
[34] (1Pet 3:18)
[35] (2Cor 5:18-21)

6. **<u>It assures us of God's Father heart towards us</u>**

In our text, Jesus tells Mary to go to His *brothers*. Though He had previously redefined His family[36], this is the first time He has called them brothers.

Brotherhood comes from having the same Father. Jesus always was and will be the unique, only-begotten Son of the Father. He will always be *"the firstborn among many brethren".*[37] But to us who have believed in Him, He gave the right to become children of God, born again by the Spirit of God.[38] And it is by our union with Him through faith, that we become His brothers, and children of God.

"Behold what manner of love the Father has bestowed on us, that we should be called children of God! ... Beloved, now we are children of God; and it has not yet been revealed what we shall be, but we know that when He is revealed, we shall be like Him, for we shall see Him as He is. And everyone who has this hope in Him purifies himself, just as He is pure."[39]

We have this unfathomable privilege, not because we chose Him, but because God chose us. *"Blessed be the God and Father of our Lord Jesus Christ, who chose us in Him before the foundation of the world, that we should be holy and without blame before Him in love, having predestined us to adoption as sons by Jesus Christ to Himself'*.[40]

Children rarely appreciate their father's qualities, but they know the feeling of security when they are cuddled up against him, or the delight of being carried on his shoulders. I used to love when Dad would occasionally pick me up from school, instead of having to catch the bus home! Or during holidays, when he took us camping. Somehow, spending time with him affirmed my identity. The same is true with Father God.

---

[36] (Mt 12:48-50)
[37] (Rom 8:29)
[38] (1:12)
[39] (1Jn 3:1–3)
[40] (Eph 1:3–6)

What wealth of meaning there is in this one word, Father!

- He'll provide everything we need - clothing, food, drink[41]
- He will always take pity on us[42] - forgiving our misdemeanours, making us better, getting us out of trouble, treating us with special care[43]
- He will always respond to our prayers, and will never give us something damaging when we are trusting Him for something good[44]
- He will discipline us, not letting us run feral like a fatherless child, training us into righteousness just as the vine-dresser trains the vine to the trellis[45]

As teenagers, many of us harbour negative thoughts about our parents. Hopefully as we grow into adulthood, we become able to see our parents as people, and appreciate their qualities. But Jesus knew His Father's heart from eternity past, and spent much of His earthly ministry challenging our false beliefs about Father God:

- The enemy wants us to believe that He is absent or uncaring; but Jesus knew Him to be continually present, and called Him the *"Living Father"*[46]
- The enemy wants us to distrust His motives, like Israel during the Exodus; but Jesus knew Him to be utterly pure, calling Him the *"Holy Father"*[47]
- The enemy wants us to believe He's harsh and cruel, but Jesus knew Him to be utterly fair in all His ways, and called Him *"Righteous Father"*[48]

Let us meditate on how different our heavenly Father is from even the best of earthly fathers. He is *'the Father of our Lord Jesus Christ'*, exactly reflected in the character of Christ. And where our fathers have failed to mirror His nature (as all earthly fathers do) let's forgive them and repent of any judgement of them; but not let their character flaws block seeing Father God as *He* truly is.

---

[41] (Mt 6:25-34)
[42] (Ps 103:13)
[43] (Ps 103:3-5)
[44] (Lk 11:9-13)
[45] (Heb 12:5-11
[46] (5:26, 6:57)
[47] (17:11)
[48] (17:25)

7. **It makes us part of a brotherhood**

The brotherhood of believers is something very precious. You may have experienced visiting believers in other countries: even when there is a language barrier, there is an immediate sense of being welcomed by family members.

John says, *"We know that we have passed from death to life, because we love the brethren".*[49]

"Anyone who sees his brother in need, and shuts up his heart against him, how does the love of God abide in him?"[50]

""If someone says, "I love God," and hates his brother, he is a liar; for he who does not love his brother whom he has seen, how can he love God whom he has not seen?"[51]

8. **It makes us worshippers and witnesses**

After the eleven Apostles had seen Jesus ascend, their response was that '*they worshipped Him, returned to Jerusalem with great joy, and were continually in the Temple praising and blessing God'.*[52] This might sound like they were in a state of bliss, utterly unconcerned with anything else. But an angel told them to get on with what He had told them to do, not just stand there staring up into the sky! So they went back to the Upper Room, and spent ten days in united prayer, studying scripture and waiting for the gift of the Spirit.

Jesus calls His Father, *"My God and your God"*. What can He mean, if He is Himself God?

Before ever He was born, Christ worshipped His Father as God: *"When He came into the world, He said: "Sacrifice and offering You did not desire, But a body You have prepared for Me. In burnt offerings and sacrifices for sin You had no pleasure. Then I said, 'Behold, I have come ... to do Your will, O*

[49] (1Jn 3:14)
[50] (1Jn 3:17)
[51] (1 Jn 4:20)
[52] (Lk 24:52,53)

God.'"[53] And throughout His ministry, He could honestly say, *"I always do those things that please Him".*[54]

Paul tells us to *'offer your bodies as a living sacrifice, holy, acceptable to God, which is your reasonable worship'.*[55] Who could he possibly be thinking of, as our role model?! The essence of Jesus's worship in His earthly life was not hymns and songs; not liturgy; not observances; nor sacrifices; but *obedience*, out of a desire to please God.

In Acts, we see that the disciples' worship involved:

- Joyfully praising and blessing God, in public worship
- Waiting on God, actively seeking the baptism of the Holy Spirit
- Preaching and witnessing boldly: and baptising the converts
- Teaching, pastoring, communion and praying with new believers[56]
- Carrying the message to all four corners of the world
- Eventually becoming *martyrs*, witnessing by dying for Christ

Public worship, private waiting on God, meditating on the word, building each other up - these are all important: but carrying on Jesus's life work of bringing men to God is central to our obedience, our worship. Jesus's command to be His witnesses is costly, as it inevitably leads to ostracism and hostility from the world. But in terms of our worship, it is up there with *'Love God with all your being'*, *'Abide in Me'*, *'Love your neighbour as yourself'*, *'Love one another as I have loved you'*, and *'Forgive one another'*. It is a front-rank element of our worship.

9. **It underlines the urgency of preaching the gospel**

Jesus had told the disciples, *"It won't be long till you're filled with the Spirit, and receive power to be My witnesses"*. You can sense the excitement in the disciples as they ask, *"Will you at this time restore the kingdom to Israel?"* And then they watch in astonishment as He ascends, to rejoin His Father.

[53] (Heb 10:5–11)
[54] (8:28,29)
[55] (Rom 12:1)
[56] (Acts 2:42)

The angel's comment, *"Why are you standing around gazing at the sky?"* is followed by, *"This same Jesus, who was taken up from you into heaven, will also come in like manner as you saw him go into heaven"*[57]. The ascension should embed within our hearts, that Jesus is coming back soon; and meantime, His instruction is, *"Occupy, till I come"*[58]. There will be a day of reckoning, when we give account of what we have done with our talents and time. And Christ's second coming will stop the clock on the 'Day of Salvation'.

---

[57] (Acts 1:11)
[58] (Lk 19:13)

Carrying on Christ's mission, until He returns

(21:1-25)

The disciples are to continue Christ's work of mission, in wisdom, love and humility, until He returns

Jesus re-enacts their original calling. (21:1-14)

The women who went to the tomb first, were told to tell the disciples that Jesus would meet them in Galilee.[1] Allowing a few days for the disciples to get from Jerusalem to Galilee, it's now about a fortnight after the crucifixion.

John says this was now the third time that Jesus showed himself to his disciples[2], so it would seem that he is only counting times when Jesus appeared to the whole group, rather than individuals.

If we guess that the two unnamed disciples in the group were Philip and Andrew, it means that all except Thomas were amongst the group Jesus had first called, whilst with John the Baptist[3]. After that it seems they had returned to their usual occupations: later we hear of them being called again, this time as Jesus is walking by Lake Galilee.

As usual, Simon Peter was the leader in their decision to go fishing. Six others of the Eleven had opted to join him. Some see this as faithless in that they were reverting back to their previous occupation; but on the other hand, they did need to support themselves. And Jesus had previously revealed Himself to them whilst they were fishing.

On that earlier occasion they had spent a fruitless night fishing, and were busy repairing their nets on the shore. But Jesus asked Simon to launch out again, and despite his misgivings he did so. They caught such a huge haul of fish that the net broke, and the boats nearly sank. Peter knelt before Jesus and said, *"Depart from me, for I am a sinful man, O Lord!"* But Jesus had replied *"Do not be afraid. From now on you will catch men"*.[4]

---

[1] (Mt 28:7 Mk 16:7)
[2] (21:14)
[3] (1:37-46)
[4] (Lk 5:1-11)

Once again on this occasion, they had had a fruitless nights work: the sun had come up, and they were still trying, about a hundred yards out from the shore. It was so hot that Peter had stripped off his fisherman's cloak. A stranger called out to them from the beach, asking whether they had caught anything. Oddly, he addressed these muscular fishermen as *'children'*.

He told them to drop the net from the other side of the boat - just a few feet from where they had been trying - and they would make a catch. When they did so, a whole shoal of fish filled the net. It was so full that even seven brawny men couldn't get it over the gunwale.

Their boat was large enough to require a decent depth of water, but the landing stage was some distance away. Where they were, the shore shelved gently into the lake; so they decided to use the boat's dinghy to drag the catch to land. It would require some heavy rowing, and would take a while, but was less likely to tear the net and lose the catch than if they used the big boat over a longer distance.

Though they hadn't recognised either Jesus's face or His voice, echoes of their first encounter with Jesus by the lake came flooding back to John. He whispered to Peter, *"It's the Lord!"* Unwilling to wait to find out, Peter grabbed his outer garment, pulled it around him and jumped overboard.

Whether he expected Jesus to enable him to walk on water, or whether he swam or waded, we don't know. But by the time the others arrived, a small barbecue was alight with a single small fish and a single bread bun.

Jesus invited the disciples to bring some of the bigger fish they'd just caught. Peter dragged the net the last few feet, and they count the astonishing catch. Probably they add some of their fish to the barbecue: but when Jesus invites them to have breakfast, it's the single small fish and the single bread bun which He serves them with. This must have reminded them of the feeding of the five thousand, and the miraculous multiplication they had seen there.

They still didn't apparently recognise Him physically, because they were wanting to ask Him, *'Who are You?'*. But the miraculous catch, the re-enactment of their first calling, and the echoes of the feeding of the five thousand meant that they *knew* He was Jesus.

N.B. T*here are two different words for fish, in Greek. The usual word, 'icthus', can mean fish of any kind, but usually of a decent size. The other word, 'opsarion', means a small fish or sardine.*

There are three main types of edible fish in Lake Galilee: each type has its own preferred habitat, and requires different fishing technique:-

- *Kinneret sardines, tens of tons of which are caught daily, pickled and treated as a delicacy*
- *Tilapia (also called 'St Peter's fish') weighing 4-5 lbs, suitable for pan frying for 1-2 persons*
- *Carp, which can weigh 13-15 lbs and are used for feasts: they are line-caught, not netted.*

Tilapia feed on underwater weeds in the shallows near the shore, hence it is thought these were the 'big fish' the disciples had caught.

A hundred and fifty three of these would weigh six or seven hundredweight,

Overall, this encounter with the risen Christ seems to have been an exact replay of their first calling by Lake Galilee: *"Follow Me, and I will make you fishers of men!"* Trying to do so in their own strength, with human means and methods, would lead only to exhaustion. However counter-intuitive His instructions might seem, it is only by obeying Him that huge catches are landed; such as happened at Pentecost. Going fishing off our own bat, without the anointing of the Holy Spirit, is pointless.

<u>Peter is brought to complete reliance on Christ</u> (21:15-25)

After breakfast, Jesus took Peter aside, further along the shore.[5] Usually this is seen as when Jesus restored Peter's relationship with Him, but in fact He had already met Peter one-on-one on Resurrection Day.[6] The meaning of their conversation on *this* occasion, goes deeper than that. It takes Peter beyond regretting his own weakness but still trusting his self-knowledge, to a place where he relies utterly on Jesus's grace. Where he trusts Jesus's knowledge of his heart, more than he trusts his self-assessment.

---

[5] (21:20)

[6] (Lk 24:34)

Peter had been known to everyone as 'Simon son of Jonah', until he first met Jesus.[7] Jesus renamed him *Cephas*, the Greek word for a stone; or in Latin, *Peter*. And He explained the meaning of Peter's new name when Peter acknowledged Him as the Christ, the Son of the Living God. It signified that this God-given insight of Peter's, would be the foundation stone of the Church. And that the forces of Hell would not prevail over it.[8]

But just minutes after that, Peter had been used by the Devil to try and tempt Jesus from following the Calvary road. In Gethsemane he had tried to use force of arms to prevent Jesus's arrest. And then in Annas's palace courtyard, he had denied three times ever having known Jesus! Not a very solid rock to build on, you might think.

Three times during the evening before the crucifixion, Peter had said he was willing to die for Christ: before the Last Supper[9], as Jesus began His farewell discourse[10], and then as they approached Gethsemane[11]. On the last of these occasions, he said the others might all abandon Jesus but he never would; in effect saying, *"I love you more than any of these others do"*. But the rock-hard loyalty that he had professed, crumbled into dust under Satan's onslaught. It was only the fact that Jesus had prayed for him that his faith would not be utterly destroyed, that enabled him to strengthen his fellow disciples afterwards.

Jesus now reverts to Peter's original name, emphasising his human origins and identity. *"Simon, son of Jonah,* do *you love Me more than these?"* What a deep, probing question!

Most or us know that the English word 'love' is used to translate four different Greek words: '*eros*' meaning erotic love; '*storge*' meaning love of country; '*philio*' meaning friendship love; and '*agape*' meaning selfless love, the love that characterises Christ.

---

[7] (1:42)
[8] (Mt 16:16-19)
[9] (Mk 14:29-31, Lk 22:31-34)
[10] (13:37)
[11] (Mt 26:33-35)

Jesus is here asking Peter, *'Do you agape Me?'* Peter has learnt to distrust his own heart, and dare not claim that level of love. So he responds guardedly, *"Yes, Lord, you know that I philio You"*.

Jesus asks the same question again, and Peter gives the same answer.

Why is Jesus repeating it? God always knows the answer, before He asks a question! So for instance, when He asks Adam, *"Where are you?"*, it is not that He can't see through the trees to where Adam is hiding. When He asks men questions, it is always to help them realise where they are, spiritually.

Furthermore, this is the only place anywhere in scripture, that God asks man the same question repeatedly. What is He seeking to gain by doing so? What is the insight He wants Peter to gain? Is He wanting to rub in Peter's weakness? That wouldn't fit with what we know of His grace.

The third time Jesus asks the question differently: *"Peter, do you philio Me?"*

Peter was grieved by Jesus's questioning of even this lesser love. He had been sure that Jesus knew he at least loved Him at the friendship level. He reiterates a third time, *"You know that I philio You"*. But this time he bases his claim not on the true state of his heart, but on Jesus's divine omniscience: *"You know **all** things"*.

- Now the work in Peter's heart is complete!
- Now he trusts Jesus's knowledge of him, more than his own judgement!
- Now he can be told, that he will eventually be crucified for Christ!

"Yet not I, but Christ in me!"

Brother, sister in Christ, have you learnt that activity in your own strength brings only exhaustion? But beyond that, have you learnt to rest in His knowledge of your heart? In His *grace*?

This is the same inner journey Paul describes in Philippians[12]: abandoning any remaining shreds of self-righteousness, self-trust, heritage, education, qualifications, character. And instead, relying wholly on the righteousness of faith, the righteousness of Christ. Even when others count us mature Christians, this journey of pressing on into Him still continues.

---

[12] (Phil 3:2-14)

Peter's new commission

Each time Peter affirms his love for Christ, Jesus responds by extending Peter's calling. Don't miss the implication: the primary qualification for anyone to shepherd the flock of God, is deep love for Jesus. If pastoral work or a teaching ministry are so consuming that we have no time to spend *'in the secret place of the Most High'*, we get burnt out and are no longer qualified for ministry.

It is love for Christ, that creates love for the brethren. But it is love for the brethren, that demonstrates the heart of Christ. *"By this shall all men know, that ye are My disciples: if you have love one for another."*

Now that the dust of Peter's crushed self-confidence has been blown away, what is left is an unshakeable confidence in Christ's knowledge of him. Remember that unlike the Greek concept of knowledge (which is factual), the Hebrew concept is one of relationship - such as a man 'knowing' his wife.

Now, Christ can start to build His church on a solid foundation stone. Peter will be a fisher of men, an evangelist: but he will also be chief under-shepherd of the sheep.

Feed My lambs

Usually, if a shepherd looks after the ewes, at lambing time the ewes will look after their young. But there will be the odd one or two whose mothers have died, or are ill; and these require intensive feeding with milk from a bottle.

At Pentecost the church suddenly grew by 2500%. It went from 120 to 3120 souls, none of whom had any spiritual parents. No wonder the disciples had to give themselves to teaching and fellowshipping with these spiritual lambs![13] Feeding them spiritually took clear priority over serving them meals.[14] And the teaching was at the baby food level; about repentance, faith, baptisms, laying on of hands, resurrection and eternal judgement.[15]

---

[13] (Acts 2:42)
[14] (Acts 6:4)
[15] (Heb 5:12-6:2)

Tend My little sheep

Jesus now uses a different word meaning a *little sheep* - what we might call a yearling? And He speaks of tending them - tenderly caring for them. Feeding relates to teaching, whereas tending is more about pastoral care: individual attention and care which ensures the lamb goes on thriving into adulthood.

Feed My little sheep

As they grow, babies need to be weaned onto solids, or else they will become nutritionally deficient. Mother's milk, the ideal food for a newborn baby, doesn't contain the right blend of vitamins and minerals for a toddler or child. And lambs must move on from the ewes' milk too, to graze for themselves. The shepherd moves them to fresh pastures.

As his life nears its close, Paul can say confidently *"I am innocent of the blood of all men, for I have not shunned to declare to you the whole counsel of God. Therefore take heed to yourselves and to all the flock among which the Holy Spirit has made you overseers, to shepherd the church of God which He purchased with His own blood"*[16]

Why did John add this epilogue?

Having just been told the sobering truth that he would eventually be crucified, Peter notices John has followed them. Was there a tiny residual element of rivalry, in Peter's question, "*Lord, what about this man?*" Or was it just that Peter and John had always been close, having worked together? We will never know. The rivalry amongst the apostles had been manifest repeatedly through their three years together. We know Peter and John went on to jointly lead the early church, healing the man at the Temple[17], being arrested together[18], etc. Peter the impulsive and vocal one, John beautifully balancing his temperament with love and reflectiveness.

Jesus's response to Peter is a classic. *"What business is it of yours, Peter, whether John will also be crucified? Even if I choose for him to live until My*

[16] (Acts 20:26-28)
[17] (Acts 3:1-6)
[18] (Acts 4:1-14)

Second Coming, what's that got to do with you? Mind your own business! Keep your eyes on Me, not on other people." "Follow Me!"

The whole chapter seems to revolve around Peter: his character, his role as first under-shepherd of Christ's flock, and how he was to follow Jesus even in the manner of his death. Perhaps it was written as a posthumous tribute to Peter, who would have been martyred by the time this gospel was circulating.

John indicates that this chapter was written to dispel the myth that had grown up, that Jesus had said He would return before John died.[19] If (as I believe) John was very old, he may have been concerned that some were anticipating Christ's return much more imminently than the facts justified; becoming 'Christian survivalists' rather than engaging with the work of mission. The charge to us all, is *'Occupy till I come!'*[20]

John's Gospel seems to end naturally at the end of chapter twenty. Many have surmised that chapter twenty-one may have been written by a different author, perhaps on behalf of the Christian community that had built up around John's ministry[21]. It seems to be an epilogue of some sort.

Looking at the chapter as a whole, its themes of

- The 'fishing of men', under the guidance of the Risen Christ
- Pastoring the flock of God, out of love for Christ; relying totally on Him
- Keeping our eyes on Christ, rather than comparing our ministry with others

are all a natural extension of the great commission Jesus was giving the disciples. They were being sent by the Father in the power of the Spirit, to continue His mission to bring salvation to the world.

Though we've reached the end of John's gospel, one more task remains: to try and sum up what John was saying about Jesus's hidden identity, now that we've read the whole book. That will be the aim of our final chapter.

---

[19] (21:22-23)
[20] (Lk 19:13)
[21] (20:24)

Christ's Hidden Identity

Summarising the key truths John wanted to convey, about who Jesus really is. This chapter is quite a long read, and you may want to allow time for each portion to sink in.

Only after working our way right through the gospel, can we fully grasp what John was saying in his Prologue. Each phrase in it was pregnant with meaning, and is fleshed out in the gospel's subsequent chapters.

Jesus exists in the eternal Present: He is alive!

'In the beginning was the Word'

Jesus says He existed before John-the-Baptist, though He was born six months after him.[1] He is the One Moses wrote about.[2] He existed before Abraham.[3]

Micah prophesies about Messiah, *'But you, Bethlehem Ephrathah, though you are little among the thousands of Judah, yet out of you shall come forth to Me the One to be Ruler in Israel, whose goings forth are from of old, from everlasting'.*[4] There are numerous references in the Old Testament to the Word of the Lord (the Jewish *Memra*) appearing to men.

He also says that He came from the Father; from heaven.[5] He already existed 'in the Beginning'[6], before time began and before Creation was formed. He repeatedly says of Himself, 'I AM'[7] - claiming the eternal personal Name of God[8] as His own. He fully shared God's glory, in eternity past.[9] And He has now been restored to that glory.[10] He also says He will be there at the last day[11], granting eternal life to some, and judging others.

---

1 (1:30)
2 (5:46,47)
3 (8:58)
4 (Mic 5:2)
5 (3:13:5:43; 6:40,51;8:24)
6 (1:1)
7 (4:26;8:58)
8 (Ex 3:14,15)
9 (17:5)
10 (17:5,24)
11 (6:39)

David prophesies of Christ, *'You are a priest forever, after the order of Melchizedek',*[12] who *'had neither beginning of days nor end of life'*[13]. This eternal Priesthood guarantees He will *always* be there to intercede for us. He has said, *"I will never leave you nor forsake you": so we may boldly say, "The LORD is my helper; I will not fear; what can man do to me?"*[14]

His perspective is totally different from ours: human life is extremely ephemeral by comparison. He sees the whole sweep of history, with a single glance. It is a gross mistake to assume that because things seem to continue as they always have, that we can safely ignore the coming Judgement.[15] We should ensure every day count towards eternity.[16]

Existence is an inadequate word for Jesus's *being*. He is eternally living, eternally aware, eternally active, eternally gracious.

<u>He is the Logos: God's powerful, effectual self-expression</u>

"In the beginning was the Word"

When God said, 'Let there be light' and there was light, He spoke through Jesus. Jesus was God's first word, and now He is God's last word.

God, who at various times and in various ways spoke in time past to the fathers by the prophets, has in these last days spoken to us by His Son, whom He has appointed heir of all things, through whom also He made the worlds; who is the brightness of His glory and the express image of His person.[17]

Conveying in English, what the Greek word 'logos' would have conveyed to John's readers, is tough. We looked at how it meant the expression of God's hidden nature; how Jews called earthly manifestations of God 'the Memra', the Word; and how to a Jew, words had a life and power of their own which went on operating long after they were spoken.

---

[12] (Ps 110:4)
[13] (Heb 7:3)
[14] (Heb 13:5,6)
[15] (2 Pet 3:1-6)
[16] (Ps 90:1-17)
[17] (Heb 1:1-3)

Greek had two different terms both of which translate in English as 'word'. 'Rhema' refers specifically to the spoken or written word; 'logos' covers many different shades of meaning, or synonyms of 'word'.

Some of these synonyms may help us grasp how Jesus is the Logos of God:

- *Message:* Jesus is Himself the message that God loves the world deeply, and offers goodwill and peace to mankind. He Himself is the gospel.
- *Teaching:* Jesus is our sole eyewitness of heavenly truth, teaching us by word and example.[18] He speaks only what the Father teaches Him.[19] All His teaching came directly from God and expressed God's character and being.[20] *'In Him are hidden all the treasures of wisdom and knowledge'.*[21] Holding on to His teaching, His logos, is key to knowing truth and abiding in Him.[22] Anyone who keeps His logos will never know death, in the sense of separation from God.[23]
- *Expression:* Jesus is the exact image of the Father. As He said, *"I and the Father are One. He who has seen Me has seen the Father"*. Just as words express a person's thoughts, He is the expression of God's mind and heart.
- *Covenant:* Jesus is the fulfilment of the New Covenant. All the promises of God came and will come true in Him. God 'gives us His Word'.
- *Authority:* His word carries ultimate authority. When He speaks, demons flee; storms cease; blind eyes see; the dead are raised to life. And at the resurrection, His word will decide whether we enter the kingdom, or depart into everlasting fire.[24]
- *Agency, power:* Christ fully achieved everything God intended, such that on the Cross He could shout, "It is finished". *'So shall My word be that goes forth from My mouth; It shall not return to Me void, but it shall accomplish what I please, and it shall prosper in the thing for which I sent it'.*[25]

---

[18] (3:11-13)
[19] (8:26,28)
[20] (7:16;8:38;12:49;4:10,24;17:8,14)
[21] (Col 2:2)
[22] (8:31-32)
[23] (8:51)
[24] (Mt 25:34,41)
[25] (Isa 55:11)

He is One in Being with God, yet an individual Person

"The Word was with God, and the Word was God"

Jesus was, and always is, face-to-face with God; or as the KJV puts it, *"in the bosom of the Father"*. And yet He also *was* God. Jesus described Himself as *'the living Bread which came down from heaven'*[26] and claimed equality with God when He said, *"I and My Father are one"*[27].

The mystery of the Godhead is that one God can be three Persons, distinct, yet One in being. Three persons united in loving and honouring one another; yet also One at a deeper level, in very substance.

This was the issue over which the Jews took such offence. For over a thousand years, they had been reciting Moses's mantra: *"Hear O Israel, the LORD our God, the LORD is one"*[28]. This sentence, known as the Shema, was the first phrase a Jewish child was taught, and the last thing a man said when dying. He would repeat it many times a day; on waking and when going to sleep, when leaving for work and when coming home, at meal times and when teaching his children. It was deeply ingrained in every Jew. So because they could not conceive of One God in Three Persons, Jesus's claim to be God and to be One with God, seemed utter blasphemy.

What they missed, was that the same Hebrew word used for 'one' in the Shema, was also used for a husband and wife becoming one, and for the re-uniting of Israel and Judah. In other words, it refers to the one-ness of unity, not of singularity.

The disciples too struggled to grasp this, right up till the Last Supper.[29] Despite Peter's revelation that *"You are the Christ, the Son of the Living God"*, it was only after the Resurrection that they fully 'got' this truth[30]; once Jesus had been *'declared to be the Son of God with power, by the Holy Spirit'*[31]. The

---

[26] (6:51,61)
[27] (10:30-33)
[28] (Deut 6:4)
[29] (14:8-11)
[30] (14:20)
[31] (Rom 1:4)

truth of the Trinity is something that can only be apprehended by faith and divine revelation.

Jesus is fully God, having eternal life in Himself.[32] He has the right to judge all mankind[33], and to give eternal life to whomever He wills[34]. Therefore everyone should worship and honour Him just as they honour the Father.[35]

Jesus has authority over Creation

"All things were made through Him, and without Him nothing was made that was made" Creation was made through Him; every detail of it.[36]

A creator can do whatever they want, with their creation. They have authority over it. A lump of clay can't say to the potter, why did you make me like this? Yet our hearts rebel at the idea of Creation, demanding autonomy and freedom to be what we want to be. For a creature to rebel against its creator is utter folly. And yet, *'His own received Him not.'*

When John says that Christ *"came unto His own"*,[37] he's not just referring to the Jews, but to the whole of mankind. Our Creator entered His own creation! one of us are His creation, and owe our being to Him.

Note John says He came *to* His own, not *from* His own. Over-focus on Jesus's Jewish roots can paint Him as merely human (denying the Incarnation) and present Christianity as Judaism's junior sibling: neither of which is true.

He is *'the firstborn of all creation'*[38]: not in the sense of being the first thing God made, but in the sense of having authority over it all. He can turn water into wine[39], or multiply loaves and fish to feed five thousand[40].

The seven signs showed that Christ is continuously active in the world, sustaining His creation. He healed seven days a week, sabbaths included.[41]

---

[32] (5:26)
[33] (5:22)
[34] (5:21;10:28)
[35] (5:23)
[36] (1:3)
[37] (1:11)
[38] (Col 1:15)
[39] (Jn 2)
[40] (Jn 5)
[41] (5:17)

He could even heal a man born blind! He is no divine clockmaker, content to wind up His workmanship then leave it to run by itself. Rather, He is alive and active within His own Creation. Therefore there is *nothing* we cannot pray for.

Jesus is the wellspring of zoe life

"In Him was life"

Before ever He was incarnate, before Creation, in eternity past, Jesus had life - *zoe* life. This life is of a different order than our biological and social lives. This life is inherent in His nature[42], just as it is for Father God. Christ made this life manifest, when He came into the world: He is the Word of life.[43]

When we say that God is the *Living* God, we're not just saying that

- He is the One who breathed into Adam the breath of life; or that
- He is active in the world, unlike idols; or that
- He is the God of the living, who has already raised to life Old Testament saints such as Abraham, Isaac and Jacob.[44]

We're saying that He has an innate quality of life quite beyond our human life, body and soul. Not subject to death, but eternal: *God*-life, if you will.

We have struggled to be consistent in how we translate the word 'zoe'. 'Eternal life' mistakenly conveys that it's primarily about duration, outlasting death. 'Spiritual life' could suggest it's to do with our spirituality, rather than the life of the Holy Spirit within us. Though both are true to a degree, they don't quite do justice to the fact that *zoe* life is life in a different dimension to anything we have previously experienced.

Being 'born again' into this new form of life, doesn't happen like human conception and birth: it's not through parental genes, or sexual intercourse, and not something we can make happen by a willed decision.[45] It is entirely the gift of God. It is given in response to faith, certainly; but even that faith came first from Him.[46]

---

[42] (5:26)
[43] (1 John 1:1,2)
[44] (Lk 20:37-38)
[45] (1:13)
[46] (Eph 2:4-8)

He came that we might have this same form of life, in abundance.[47] He gives eternal life to whomever He wills.[48] But we do not have it innately, as He does: we receive a continual supply through our union with Him.[49] He - Jesus Christ - is the Bread of Life; the bread of heaven which a man may eat of, and not die.[50] He is the Resurrection and the Life.[51] He is 'the Way, the Truth, and the Life'.[52] It is as we commune with Him, Father and Son, and with those who commune with Him, that we receive this *God*-life.[53] And it is this life, His God-life within us, that causes us to bear fruit.

Christ's life blazed with God's grace and truth

"The life was the light of men". He was "the true light which, coming into the world, enlightens every man".

By coming into the world, He gave light to all men.[54] Some have misinterpreted this as meaning that He gives the light of *reason* to all men at birth. But the darkness of men's hearts means that we can't comprehend His light. Top thinkers of all ages have been unable to grasp the gospel through intellect and reason.[55] For example Nicodemus had spent his life studying the Torah, trying to reach God by his own intellect. In his lifetime, he was recognised as *the* teacher of Israel. But Jesus told him emphatically, *"Unless a man is born again, he cannot see the Kingdom of God".*[56] It's only when God shines into our hearts and shows us His glory in the Person of Jesus Christ, that we get it.[57]

Jesus said, *"I am the light of the world. He who follows Me shall not walk in darkness, but shall have the light of life".*[58] The context is the account of the

---

47 (10:10)
48 (5:21; 10:28)
49 (15:5,6)
50 (6:48-50)
51 (11:25)
52 (14:6)
53 (1 Jn 1:3)
54 (1:9)
55 (1Cor 1:18-21)
56 (3:3)
57 (2 Cor 4:6)
58 (8:12)

woman caught in adultery, and her hypocritical accusers. That episode shows clearly what the nature of this light actually is.

Jesus's handling of the issue revealed astonishing grace, along with uncompromising holiness. *"I do not condemn you. Go, and sin no more."*[59] In doing so, His light lit up both her life, and that of her accusers. She was exposed as needing grace: they were exposed as hypocritical. The light of Jesus's life includes both elements. The witness of His life held true to God's holiness, but was also *full* of grace.[60]

Being 'the light of the world' means that He demonstrates the Father's persona. Shortly after, in dealing with the man born blind, Jesus says *"I must work the works of Him who sent Me while it is yet day: the night is coming, when no man can work. As long as I am in the world, I am the light of the world"*.[61] Believing in Jesus means believing in God: and anyone who 'gets' who Jesus is, who sees His light, sees the Father.[62]

The light He gives us is not some secret inner spiritual insight such as the Gnostics and Illuminati claimed, disconnected from moral righteousness. Nor is it self-righteousness without grace. It is *'the light of the knowledge of the glory of God, in the face of Jesus Christ'*.[63]

That glory is that God is *'the LORD, the LORD God, merciful and gracious, slow to anger and abounding in steadfast love and truth, keeping mercy for thousands, forgiving iniquity and sin, but by no means clearing the guilty'*.[64]

As we spend time in God's Presence, as Moses did in the Tent of Meeting, we too come to shine with that glory.[65]

---

[59] (8:11)
[60] (1:16,17)
[61] (9:4,5)
[62] (12:44-46)
[63] (2Cor 4:6)
[64] (Ex 34:6-7)
[65] (Exod 34:29-35; 2Cor 3:18)

Christ is our *only* light-source: human nature is dark

"The light shines in the darkness, and the darkness has never overcome it"

The Jews thought heaven was a shoo-in for anyone descended from Abraham. But Jesus tells them that spiritually they are in fact children of the Devil.[66] This is 'original sin': through Adam's sin, man's nature became utterly corrupted, and subject not just to physical death but also soul death, *and* eternal death in the lake of fire.

The fact is that by nature, *'we men love darkness rather than light, because our deeds are evil'.*[67] Rejecting His light, as the Jewish leaders did, means we are already self-condemned. Jesus's incarnation forces us to make a judgement: and the way we judge Him, determines the way we will be judged by Him.[68] If we think we see, and rely on our own understanding, we become blind: whereas if we humble ourselves and accept His teaching, we start to see.[69]

But the darkness operates through political structures and social mores,[70] as well as within us. The collaboration between Jewish leaders, Pharisees and Sadducees, and the Roman authority, was evidence of what John calls 'the world'. This covert spiritual hierarchy, ultimately headed by the Prince of Darkness, hates the light of Christ. Having tried and failed to extinguish His light by crucifying Him, the world's enmity will turn against His disciples,[71] in whom His light now shines.

John later develops this thought, relating Jesus's teaching about the world's implacable hatred towards Him and His disciples.[72] Christ warns candidly that they will face intense persecution, such as Paul's repeated floggings. Christians are called to follow their Master in sharing the fellowship of His

---

[66] (8:37-44)
[67] (3:19,20)
[68] (9:39)
[69] (9:39)
[70] (Eph 6:12)
[71] (15:18-21)
[72] (15:18-16:4)

sufferings. *"In the world, you will have tribulation. But be of good cheer, for I have overcome the world".*[73]

He laid aside His majesty, and became man

"The Word became flesh"

The central truth of John's Gospel, & the acid test of Christian orthodoxy, is that 'Jesus Christ came in the flesh'[74]. He became incarnate. John's purpose in writing was 'that you may believe that Jesus is the Christ, the Son of God'[75]: both fully God and fully man.

This issue of Christ's true identity runs all the way through the gospel. Despite John-the-Baptist's ministry as His forerunner[76], *"His own received Him not"*[77]. The Jewish authorities actively and deliberately rejected His claims to be God. His disciples found it hard to conceive that He had come from the Father, and would return to Him. Only those who receive Him as who He truly is, receive authority to become children of God. *"If you do not believe that I am He, you will die in your sins".*[78]

Jesus was not just a good man, temporarily adopted by the Holy Spirit at His baptism but then abandoned to be a purely-human sacrifice. Nor was He an emanation or avatar, a temporary manifestation of God, who merely *seemed* to have human form. Rather, He was the Son of God, who identified fully with us by taking flesh, from conception to the grave - and beyond!

Thereby He became the Son of Man. We noted how in Hebrew, the word for 'man' is 'Adam'. Every time Jesus referred to Himself as 'the Son of Man' He was claiming to be the Second Adam: one who would carry the guilt of Adam's original sin, and from whom a new mankind would spring.

---

[73] (16:33)
[74] (1Jn 4:2)
[75] (20:31)
[76] (1:6,7)
[77] (1:11)
[78] (8:24)

Christ's genuine manhood was essential if He was to become our sacrifice:-

- *'The life of the flesh is in the blood, and I have given it to you upon the altar to make atonement for your souls'* [79]
- *'Without the shedding of blood there is no remission of sins'*[80]

Crucifixion didn't usually shed blood. But unlike the two thieves, whose legs were broken, Jesus's heart was pierced by a soldier's spear. The resulting flow of water and blood was eye-witnessed by John. This was critical evidence of Christ's true manhood,[81] and thus of the validity of His sacrifice.

The verb 'became' is neither active nor passive in Greek, but 'middle voice'. This means that Christ both actively chose to become flesh, and passively was made flesh. We know that Christ actively chose to accept the body that His Father had prepared for Him,[82] knowing that it would be used for sacrifice.

There has never been a greater example of obedience to the Father. And there has never and will never be, any example of greater love than this: that not just *a* man, but *the* Son of Man, should lay down His life for His friends.

All the controversies in the Early Church centred around this issue of Christ's dual identity. By the end of John's long life the battle for the truth was fierce, and centred around belief in the incarnation.[83] John's gospel laid the foundation for his future defence of this truth in his letters. *"That which was from the beginning, which we have heard, which we have seen with our own eyes, which we have looked upon, and our hands have handled, concerning the Word of life - the life was manifested, and we have seen and bear witness, and declare to you that eternal life which was with the Father and was manifested to us - that which we have seen and heard, we declare to you".*[84]

Satan hates this truth above all others, and has sent a horde of antichrist spirits into the world to twist, undermine and discredit it. He uses false religions such as the Jehovah Witnesses, Mormons and Muslims to deny this

---

79 (Lev 17:11)
80 (Heb 9:22)
81 (1Jn 5:8)
82 (Psalm 40:6; Heb 10:5)
83 (1Jn 4:1,2)
84 (1John 1:1-3)

truth. He has sent many false Christs & false Messiahs, down through the centuries. The nearer we get to Christ's return, the more he does so. He uses sects such as the Unitarians, to undermine this truth within Christendom. Even Judaism, which was intended to be His witness, became corrupt and to this day continues to deny that He came in the flesh.

If Satan can persuade us to deny this truth, all the other truths of the gospel become irrelevant. Specifically, the atonement cannot be full atonement. If Jesus was merely a man, even a sinless man, His death could only atone for one other man. But if as the Son of Adam he bore the penalty of Adam's sin, then death is defeated!

Christ is the central focus of our worship

"He tabernacled among us"

During the exodus, the Tabernacle was right at the centre of Israel's campsite. It was the place where the Shekinah glory dwelt; where the Presence of God was manifested. It was where men could worship; where man and God could meet, despite the sin of the golden calf. It was the place of blood sacrifice, of the bread of the Presence and the seven-fold lampstand; and in its innermost sanctuary, the Ark of the Covenant, and the Mercy Seat. All these things speak of Christ, and how we can approach Almighty God through Him.

Arguing whether we should worship in Jerusalem or on Mount Gerizim[85]; which church has the best worship group or liturgy; or whether happy-clappy or smells-and-bells is better, should be utterly irrelevant to those who worship in spirit and in truth. The form of worship must fade from view, leaving Christ centre stage. We approach the throne through the body of Christ.[86] He is our real Tabernacle.

The Feast of Tabernacles was a yearly reminder of the Presence of God with Israel during the Exodus, and an anticipation of future glory when Messiah will reign in Jerusalem. It also represented a plea for the autumn rains to come, after the long hot summer. It was at the culmination of this liturgical ceremony, that Jesus shouted, *"If anyone is thirsty, let him come to Me and*

---

[85] (4:19-24)

[86] (Heb 10:19-22)

drink! He who believes in Me, as the scripture has said, 'Out of his heart will flow rivers of living water'"[87]

Jesus is where we find God's gracious and glorious Presence; where our thirst for God is slaked.

Jesus displays the glory of God's character

"We beheld His glory, glory as of the only Son of the Father"

Peter James and John had seen Jesus's glory when He was transfigured.[88] And they heard the Father say, *"This is My beloved Son: listen to Him!"*[89] But this is not what John is referring to here.

Just as the Tabernacle was where God's glory was manifest, so the miracles and teachings of Christ enabled John and his fellow-apostles to see Jesus's glory. They recognised it as identical to the Father's. They *beheld* it - physically saw signs, then pondered their meaning with amazement & awe.

John selected seven miracles which particularly demonstrated Christ's glory[90], to help his readers come to belief that Jesus was the Christ.

- Changing water into wine at Cana[91]
- Healing the royal official's son in Capernaum[92]
- Healing the paralytic at Bethesda[93]
- Feeding the five thousand[94]
- Walking on water[95]
- Healing the man blind from birth[96]
- Raising Lazarus from the dead[97]

---

[87] (7:37,38)
[88] (Lk 9:28-32)
[89] (2Pet 1:16,17)
[90] (2:11;40;20:31)
[91] (2:1–11)
[92] (4:46–54)
[93] (5:1–15)
[94] (6:5–14)
[95] (6:16–24)
[96] (9:1–7)
[97] (11:1–45)

In every case, man had reached the end of his abilities. *'When we reach the end of our hoarded resources, the Father's full giving has barely begun'*.

Each of these signs demonstrates Jesus's supernatural authority over Creation, but also His incredible kindness and compassion. Shekinah hovering over Israel's campsite, or Elijah calling down the fire of God, must have been very impressive! But the true glory of God lies in His character, His attributes.

When Moses asked to see God's glory, He described Himself thus:

"The Lord, the Lord God, merciful and gracious, long-suffering, and abounding in goodness and truth, keeping mercy for thousands, forgiving iniquity and transgression and sin, by no means clearing the guilty, visiting the iniquity of the fathers upon the children and the children's children to the third and the fourth generation."[98]

All of these qualities shine out in John's account of Jesus's ministry: especially of course in the Cross. Jesus is the exact image of His Father, in character. He expresses all the perfections of His Father's glory. *"He who has seen Me, has seen the Father"*.[99]

No-one can physically see God and survive the experience.[100] But *'the only-begotten Son, who is in the bosom of the Father, He has revealed Him'*.[101]

<u>Jesus's Sonship is uniquely glorious and eternal</u>

"Glory as of the Only-begotten of the Father"

Jesus is unique, one-of-a-kind, in many ways. To name a few,

- He is the only way to the Father.[102] He is the (only) Door of the sheep: all others who came before, claiming to be that, were charlatans.[103]
- He is the good Shepherd, uniquely ready to lay down His life for the sheep when Israel's false shepherds would abandon them to predators.[104]

---

[98] (Ex 34:6,7)
[99] (14:9; Heb 1:3)
[100] (Ex 33:20)
[101] (1:18)
[102] (14:6)
[103] (10:7)
[104] (10:11-13)

• He is unique in His knowledge and care for each individual sheep.[105]

But Jesus is the 'only-*begotten* Son'.[106] Not just God's only child in a numerical sense, but 'begotten, not made'. We saw how Isaac was referred to as Abraham's only-begotten, despite having an elder brother, because he was continuously fathered by Abraham whereas Ishmael wasn't. The word 'begotten' refers not to Jesus's conception in Mary's womb, but to the continuous Father-Son relationship He had (and has) with God.

Christ was *'in the bosom of the Father'* throughout eternity past[107], and will be '*the Lamb in the midst of the Throne'*[108] throughout eternity future. His communion with His Father was not interrupted by His incarnation, but continued throughout His earthly ministry.[109] His Father continued to show Him everything He was doing.[110] And Christ continually collaborated in His Father's actions.[111]

Jesus is *eternally* begotten. He had no birthday as the Son of God. He always was and always will be the Son. Father God has been and will always be His Father. Throughout eternity, the Son honours the Father[112], and the Father honours the Son[113]. (This is why the fifth commandment requires us to 'honour our father and mother'.) This is perfect Father-Son relationship.

The quality that distinguishes the Persons of the Trinity, is not their role - for they all collaborate in all their works - but their relationships.

---

105 (10:13,14)
106 (1:14)
107 (1:1)
108 (Rev 5:6)
109 (3:13)
110 (5:20)
111 (5:19)
112 (7:18; 8:49,50; 12:28; 17:4)
113 (5:22,23; 8:54)

Christ embodied God's grace as fully as His holiness

"Full of grace and truth"

Jesus, in whom dwells all the fullness of the Godhead[114], is full of grace and truth[115]. These are not alternatives: both are fully true of Him, all the time. It is not that He shows some grace, and others He shows judgement based on truth. Every fibre of His being is grace. And every fibre of His being is truth.

The Law of Moses listed ten actions incompatible with God's holiness. But it said nothing about how God would react, when Israel then broke the first commandment by making a golden calf. Only after Moses offered himself in substitutionary atonement[116], then prayed for a deeper personal knowledge of God's glory, did the LORD gave him a revelation of His grace and truth.

The account of the woman caught in adultery is the epitome of Jesus's grace and truth, in the pages of John's gospel. She was caught bang-to-rights, 'in flagrante'. But Jesus showed an incredibly beautiful blend of grace and truth.

Grace and truth go hand in hand in John's gospel - and in the heart of God.

- We cannot receive grace, without accepting the truth about who Jesus is. *"If you do not believe that I am He, you will die in your sins".*[117]
- And we cannot receive grace, without facing the truth about ourselves: that whether we are Abraham's seed or not, or whatever our spiritual pedigree, we are by nature sons of Satan, children of the Devil.[118]
- If we deceive others, claiming fellowship with Christ whilst living in darkness, the truth hasn't yet taken hold in us.[119] But if we share honestly, our fellowship deepens; and Christ's blood thoroughly cleanses us.
- If we say we have no sin, we deceive only ourselves, not God.[120] Whereas if we face the truth and agree with God, He grants us grace and forgiveness, and removes the guilt.

---

[114] (Col 2:9)
[115] (1:14)
[116] (Ex 32:31,32)
[117] (8:24)
[118] (8:42-45)
[119] (1John 1:6,7)
[120] (1Jn 1:8,9)

- If we deny we've ever sinned, we are actually calling God a liar.[121] And Christ will not intercede; His propitiation no longer applies.

Light and darkness cannot have fellowship together.[122]

Churches which major on *truth* often engender a culture where people are afraid to be real. Respectability takes over. But churches which major on *grace* often don't face the moral truths of scripture; and people become complacent about holiness. For true, deep fellowship to exist, grace and truth must go hand-in-hand in a church's ethos, and be modelled from the top.

In Christ, we are joined to the Fullness of the Godhead

"Of His fullness we have all received"

This verse sums up Jesus's teaching in the Upper Room discourse, about the indwelling fullness of the Holy Spirit and our direct fellowship with the Father as well as His Son.

For it pleased the Father that in Him (Christ) all the fullness should dwell... For in Him dwells all the fullness of the Godhead bodily; and you are complete in Him, who is the head of all principality and power'.[123]

The fullness of which we have received, is the fullness of the Godhead! This is the fullness which makes us complete.

Christ was filled with the Holy Spirit without measure,[124] at His baptism.[125] Out of His fullness He poured out the gift of the Holy Spirit, and now the Spirit lives in us.[126] The disciples were filled with the Holy Spirit[127] and power. We too are commanded to 'be *being filled* with the Spirit'.[128]

Once we have believed into Christ, we are joined with Him; and through Him, with the Father.[129] We live, because He lives.[130] He is the vine, we are the

---

121 (1Jn 1:10f)
122 (2Cor 6:14)
123 (Col 1:19-2:10)
124 (3:34)
125 (Mt 3:16;Lk 4:1)
126 (14:16,17)
127 (Acts 2:4)
128 (Eph 5:18)
129 (14:20)
130 (14:19)

branches:[131] His life flowing into us is what makes us fruitful. This union is maintained by our actively abiding in Him,[132] and in His love.[133]

The purpose of Christian ministry is *'to edify the body of Christ, till we all come to the unity of the faith and of the knowledge of the Son of God, to a perfect man, to the measure of the stature of the fullness of Christ'.*[134]

In His final prayer to the Father, Jesus defined eternal life as being 'that they may *know* You, the only true God, and Jesus Christ whom You have sent'. Jesus's death and resurrection was 'to bring us to the Father', and it led to our being indwelt by the Holy Spirit, and in union with Christ.

His promise to the disciples, was that they would know God in all three Persons of the Trinity. They would *know* (in the Hebrew sense of intimate experiential & relational knowledge) the love of God, the grace of our Lord Jesus Christ, and the fellowship of the Holy Spirit.

In his first letter, written sixty years after the events of the gospel, John says that his fellowship is with the Father and the Son[135] and still gives him deep joy. His awareness of the Holy Spirit within, is how he knows Christ's Presence.[136] He has learnt to discern the Holy Spirit by His testimony to Jesus's incarnation; that He is both fully God and fully man.[137] Father, Son and Holy Spirit continually testify to John from heaven, that God has given him eternal life, and that this life is in God's Son.[138] Anyone who has the Son, has life: and anyone who doesn't, doesn't.

How can it be, that Almighty God who dwells in unapproachable light, and His beloved and sinless Son Jesus, would condescend to dwell with us? How can it be, that the Holy Spirit is willing to actually dwell in us?! That the thirty-year tabernacling of Christ amongst men, would become a permanent, eternity-long bond of love between us and the Father, Son and Holy Ghost?!

---

131 (15:5)
132 (15:4)
133 (15:9)
134 (Eph 4:12,13)
135 (1Jn 1:3)
136 (1Jn 3:24)
137 (1 Jn 4:1-3, 5:6)
138 (1Jn 4:7)

The aroma of Christ's Presence is ongoing grace

"Grace upon grace"

The word 'grace' has been demeaned into a transactional formula, by the trite aphorism, 'God's Riches At Christ's Expense'.

In Greek, the word for grace is 'charis', from which we get English words like charisma and charismatic. But its original meaning isn't about attractive character so much as about gifts: free gifts. So when we talk about the gifts of the Spirit, we are talking about specific 'charismata', specific *graces* given us.

When I first met Jesus, I knew I was in the presence of Someone utterly holy. I didn't dare lift my eyes to look at Him, knowing how sinful I was. But in my spirit, I knew that though He knew me inside out (far better than my parents or my then-girlfriend) He accepted me, and loved me. Knowing I was fully known and yet loved, brought tears of joy.

That is what grace is: revelatory, undeserved, freely given, engendering deep gratitude and joy, creating lasting relationship.

When that happened, I had no idea that grace had already been operating in my life for years: even before I was born. I didn't realise that God had known me since before He made the world. Or that He had chosen me even back then, to be shaped into Christ's likeness: to be holy and blameless before Him, in His love. I didn't realise that He had been drawing me towards Jesus for years: that my Christian parents and grandparents, my Sunday School teacher, the Christian college porter at University, were all part of His grace. All of this was what Wesley called, 'prevenient grace'.

Nor did I know that my developing faith was itself a gift of God's grace. Or that Christ's coming into the world, deliberately to die on the Cross as my living sacrifice, was all of the Father's doing: that He so loved the world that He gave His only-begotten Son, to do this for *me*. But that encounter with Christ led not only to faith and love, but also to understanding that He had died for me. This is what Wesley called, 'justifying grace'.

At that early stage, I didn't realise that I could not walk with God by my own strength; that some things could not be cured even by fervent prayer, and that God sometimes says, 'My grace is sufficient'. That time and again I would need to confess my sins to Him, living in the light, so that the blood of Jesus could cleanse me from all unrighteousness. Not that I should 'continue in sin that grace may abound', but that I would learn to rely utterly on Christ's all-sufficient merit: what Wesley called, 'sustaining grace'.

Christ repeatedly faces us with the uselessness of trying to earn His favour by adding our own righteousnesses of any kind, to His grace. Circumcision (Galatians), human philosophies & other 'spiritualities' (Colossians), gnostic insights (John's letters) - all have their modern-day equivalents which boast that they have Advanced Christianity, and can (they hint) make us feel better about ourselves. But Christ wants us to know the utter security of relying solely on grace:

"Behold what manner of love the Father has bestowed on us, that we should be called children of God! Therefore the world does not know us, because it did not know Him. Beloved, now we are children of God; and it has not yet been revealed what we shall be, but we know that when He is revealed, we shall be like Him, for we shall see Him as He is. And everyone who has this hope in Him purifies himself, just as He is pure".[139]

Scripture often speaks of us as 'complete'. For example, Paul addresses his letters to 'the saints in Christ Jesus', even though he then goes on to tell them to stop stealing & lying! He tells them that there is no more condemnation for those who are in Christ.[140] And in Colossians he tells them that they have been raised with Christ and are seated with Him in the heavenlies.[141] All of this can *only* be true, if our salvation is entirely of grace.

To God be all the glory!

139 (1 Jn 3:1,2)
140 (Rom 8:1)
141 (Col 3:1-3)

Hark! The herald angels sing, "Glory to the newborn King;
Peace on earth, and mercy mild, God and sinners reconciled!"
Joyful, all ye nations rise, join the triumph of the skies;
With the angelic host proclaim, "Christ is born in Bethlehem!"
Hark! The herald angels sing, "Glory to the newborn King!"

Christ, by highest Heaven adored; Christ the everlasting Lord;
Late in time, behold Him come, offspring of a virgin's womb.
Veiled in flesh the Godhead see; hail the incarnate Deity,
Pleased as man with men to dwell, Jesus our Emmanuel.
Hark! the herald angels sing, "Glory to the newborn King!"

Hail the heavenly Prince of Peace! Hail the Sun of Righteousness!
Light and life to all He brings, risen with healing in His wings.
Mild He lays His glory by, born that man no more may die.
Born to raise the sons of earth, born to give them second birth.
Hark! the herald angels sing, "Glory to the newborn King!"

Come, Desire of nations, come, Thou of beauty art the sum;
Adam's likeness, Lord, efface; stamp Thine image in its place:
Now display Thy saving power, work in me, restore this hour;
O, to me Thyself impart, visit this believing heart.
Hark! the herald angels sing, "Glory to the newborn King!"

Charles Wesley, 1739

Appendix 1: Background to John's Gospel

When, where, why, and by whom was it written?

Why is it so different from the other gospels?

Key themes.

John's gospel starts with a bang! Its first verses are awe-inspiring, redolent of Genesis. He lays out his future themes in précis format. But it's so dense and deep, that some unpacking is essential.

We'll start with some spadework, laying a foundation for understanding. We need some cultural context, and a few key concepts. The book was written over two thousand years ago, by a Jew living as an expatriate in Greece. He wrote in his second language, not his mother tongue.

So to ensure we hear him correctly, we first need to look at:

- Who wrote it, and when?
- What do we know about the author?
- How is it distinctive from the other three gospels?
- What are its central themes?
- What were the author's aims?

Once we've done that, we'll chew over some key words, to help us grasp John's thinking and the concepts behind them.

Authorship and date

None of the four gospels explicitly name the writer. But there is *external* evidence from the second century that the Apostle John was the author.

John was bishop of Ephesus, and Smyrna was one of the churches he oversaw. Later, Polycarp was appointed as bishop there. Polycarp later told Irenaeus, another second-century bishop, that he had received this gospel direct from the Apostle. This is credible, because John lived into ripe old age, dying in AD 98 or thereabouts.

Some doubt whether a Galilean fisherman could have written such excellent Greek, known the High Priest, or had detailed knowledge of Jerusalem's layout. So they postulate a separate John, 'John the Evangelist', as the author.

Others counter with arguments that

(a) John may have dictated it to an amanuensis with good Greek, possibly a disciple of his called Papias.

(b) The High Priest is known to have regularly ordered fish from Galilee. Perhaps John was Zebedee's salesman in Jerusalem for a time?

As to *internal* evidence within the gospel,

(a) It refers to the author as 'the beloved disciple': someone who worked closely with Peter, and was present at the Last Supper. This must point to him being one of the Twelve.

(b) Its author claims to have been an eye-witness of the events.[1]

(c) His account was certified as true by a community of believers.[2]

As to the gospel's date, manuscripts exist from the early second century. Opinion favours it having been written near the end of John's life, around *AD* 95. Others believe that it must have pre-dated Jerusalem's destruction in *AD* 70, since it refers to the Pool of Bethesda;[3] and also to 'the Judaeans' as distinct from Galilean Jews. A third opinion believes that parts were written early, but collated into canonical form later; perhaps by a different author.

How one views the date it was written, determines the spiritual context. If it was prior to the Fall of Jerusalem, one might expect John to have distinguished between Pharisees and Sadducees, Scribes, Herodians and Zealots, as the other gospels do. Instead he lumps them all together as *'hoi Iudaioi'*, the Judaeans. If on the other hand, it was written in 95 AD, then the context would have been Greek culture, within the Roman Empire. By then, various heresies about Christ's true nature were beginning to be expressed, such as Docetism, and Gnosticism.

<u>What do we know about the Apostle John?</u>

John and his brother James were sons of Zebedee, a Galilean fisherman. Tradition identifies their mother as Salome, who some say was Mary's sister.

---

[1] (19:35)
[2] (21:24)
[3] (5:2)

Thus they may have been Jesus's cousins. Salome was ambitious for her sons to have high honour when Jesus's Messianic kingdom came. Jesus nicknamed them 'sons of thunder': in their zeal they proposed calling down a lightning strike on an inhospitable Samaritan village! James, John's brother, was the first Christian to be martyred, in AD 44.

John is described as 'the disciple whom Jesus loved'. He was the closest to Jesus, being seated next to Him at the Last Supper. He was the only one of the Twelve who didn't desert Jesus during the crucifixion. Jesus committed His mother into John's care, rather than trusting His siblings to look after her.

At some point, John moved to Ephesus, to oversee the Seven Churches listed in Revelation 1-3. It seems that many of the early heresies about Christ's nature started in the surrounding area we now call Turkey. John wrote three letters to these churches on how to discern between true and false teachers.

Whereas all the other apostles were martyred, John somehow survived. Legend has it that he was thrown into a vat of boiling oil, but emerged unscathed. Later he was imprisoned on the nearby island of Patmos (think Alcatraz!). Jesus appeared to him there, with a series of visions about the End Times. This we now know as 'The Book of Revelation'.

Distinctives

Once the good news was published in writing, it usually consisted of the four gospels: Matthew, Mark, Luke and John. They were written on parchment, bound together in book form - what theologians call a 'codex'.

John's gospel is very different from the other three. In general it is complementary rather than parallel, though they do overlap in places (the feeding of the five thousand, the crucifixion & the resurrection).

It records different events during Jesus's ministry than the other three:-

- It mainly focusses on Jesus's ministry in Jerusalem, whereas the others focus on Galilee and the Trans-Jordan.
- His account often mentions Jewish feasts: for example, he mentions three separate Passovers, whereas the others mention only one.
- Whereas the Synoptics contain a lot of teaching about Christian ethics,

such as the Sermon on the Mount, John contains almost none. For him, all Christian ethics were subsumed in the concept of agape love.

• He barely mentions Christ's Second Coming, instead focussing on Jesus's Presence here-and-now. Matthew records Jesus teaching His disciples about the end times and His return in glory, just before He goes to the Cross. But John records Him teaching about the Holy Spirit, and the new spiritual life they will have after His resurrection. Theologians refer to this focus on fellowship with the Father and with His Son[4] as *'realised eschatology'*.

• John calls this reality of knowing Christ, eternal life. This is a specific Greek word (*zoe*), distinct from words used for mental or psychological life (*psyche*) or bodily life (*bios*).

• John often records how the disciples only grasped Jesus's sayings with hindsight. Jesus's statement, *"Destroy this Temple, and in three days I will raise it again"*, is one example. John records that the Spirit showed them its true meaning later, after the Resurrection.

• John records Jesus using lots of symbolism: for example, *"I am the Bread of Life"*. As Jesus explains to Nicodemus, this is because He is teaching heavenly truths rather than earthly ones.

Themes

Theologians in general analyse John in two halves, plus a prologue and an epilogue. The first half focusses on seven 'signs': miracles which reveal Jesus's identity as the Son of God. The second half focusses on Christ's glory, soon to be revealed in His death and resurrection.

Individual commentators focus on particular themes such as

- Jesus's heavenly origin
- His role as the living Temple
- His superiority to Jewish heroes such as Abraham, Jacob, and Moses
- His self-revelation through the 'I AM' statements
- The Judaeans' rejection of Him, & His analysis of the reasons for that
- His relationship with His Father.

---

[4] (17:3)

In my view, John's dominant theme is about *Jesus's identity*, and specifically *the incarnation*. In that sense, the prologue is an executive summary of all that is to follow.

Jesus's arguments with the Jews all have to do with His divinity, His sonship, His being sent from God. And all His final teaching to the disciples was about His oneness with the Father and the Spirit.

John's first letter then makes complete sense. Christian communities were being torn apart by false teachings: claims Jesus either was not really a man, or not really God. In the letter, John says the ultimate test of any spirit is whether it acknowledges that 'Jesus Christ is come in the flesh'.[5]

For John, *belief in the incarnation was essential if the Cross was to have any redemptive meaning.*

John's purpose in writing the gospel

There are many different theories about John's aims.

- Some see the gospel as a collection of sermons, each 'sign' illustrating a different facet of Christ's identity.
- Others say it was written for evangelism amongst the Jews, since it majors on signs. Whereas Greeks prized wisdom and eloquence, Jews expected signs to corroborate a man's ministry. An opposing view is that his account adapts the gospel to a Hellenistic culture, using many spiritual terms they would have been familiar with such as 'the Word', 'light', 'life' etc.
- Some see it as written to fill in the blanks left by the Synoptics, or to give a more 'spiritual' take on Jesus's ministry.
- Others see it as a polemic against the Jews; or a statement of the early church's relationship to the disciples of John the Baptist.

Fortunately we are not left scratching our heads, for John states clearly why he wrote it. He wasn't trying to give a comprehensive account of the facts of Jesus's life, or His works. Rather, he selected a few key episodes, with two

[5] (1John 4:1-3)

very specific purposes. *"These are written, that you may believe that Jesus is the Christ, the Son of God, and that believing you may have life in His name"*.[6]

In other words, John was concerned with two things:

1) His readers' *belief* that Jesus Christ came in the flesh - that He was God Incarnate, our anointed Saviour

2) Their *experience* of eternal life - 'fellowship with the Father and His Son'.

So his gospel is not solely evangelistic, but also about our present-day, real-life spiritual experience.

---

[6] (20:31)

Appendix 2: Key words & their symbolic meanings

John often deliberately uses words with a dual meaning: words which have a physical, real-world meaning, but can also convey symbolic or spiritual meanings. For example, when Jesus tells Nicodemus 'You must be born *again*', it can also be translated '*from above*'. Nicodemus takes it as the former, whilst Jesus intends both meanings. John's prologue is full of such words with multiple meanings; so let's explore a few:-

The Word

John calls Jesus "the Word" - which we take to mean a spoken or written word. But to the Jews, a word was "the expression of a hidden thought".

E Stanley Jones says *"We cannot know what God is like unless God communicates through a word...When you take hold of that Word, you do not take hold of something standing between you and God — that Word, Jesus, is God available... When you take hold of Jesus, you take hold of God".*

There are many Old Testament examples of God manifesting Himself to men as a Being called 'the Angel of the LORD'. Since the Jews were ultra-careful never to liken God to man, let alone any creature, they often referred to such appearances as 'The Word of the Lord'. The Hebrew for 'word' is 'Memra'.

The Jewish Encyclopaedia defines Memra as *'"The Word", in the sense of the creative or directive word or speech of God manifesting His power in the world of matter or mind; a term used especially in the Targum as a substitute for "the Lord" when an anthropomorphic expression is to be avoided.'*

Jesus reveals God to us in human form: *"No-one has seen God at any time. The only-begotten Son, who is in the bosom of the Father, He has declared Him".*[1] He is God's last word, the ultimate expression of His character and Being. He is the Memra!

Have you ever sent an email or WhatsApp in a hurry, then regretted not being able to delete it? Or said something which you wish you hadn't?

---

[1] (1:18)

Words are active and powerful. The Jews considered words to have a life of their own.

This was specially obvious at Creation; Genesis repeatedly says, *"And God said ... and it was so".* But it is true of everything God speaks: *"My Word, that proceeds from My mouth, shall not return to Me void, but out shall accomplish what I please, and prosper in the thing for which I send it".*[2]

"The Word of God is alive and active, sharper than any two-edged sword, piercing even to the dividing of soul and spirit, of joints and marrow, and is a discerner of the thoughts and intents of the heart. And there is no creature hidden from His sight, but all things are naked and open to the eyes of Him to whom we must give account."[3]

Life

John uses three different Greek words for different types of life, which are all translated into the same English word, 'life'. They are:-

- Bios - *biological* life. The only time John uses this word for life, is when he talks about 'the pride of life'.[4] Imagine a bodybuilding competition, with the contestants strutting their stuff. That's the sort of life that this word refers to.
- Psyche - *soul life* (thoughts, emotions, & choices). John says this kind of life can be loved (held onto) or hated (laid down) in this life.[5] When Jesus talks about laying down His life, this is the word He uses. And it is what He means when He talks about us *'taking up our cross and following Him'*.
- Zoe - *spiritual life,* the living reality of fellowship with the Father and the Son.[6] This life starts now. It's a present reality; and it continues beyond our bodily death into eternity.[7] John experienced this as a joyful, loving fellowship with the Father and the Son.[8] Jesus has this life within Himself, and gives it to all those who receive Him.[9]

---

[2] (Isa 55:11)
[3] (Heb 4:12-13)
[4] (1Jn 4:15,16)
[5] (12:24-25)
[6] (17:3)
[7] (17:3)
[8] (1Jn 1:1-3)
[9] (5:26, 21)

Understanding the distinction between these different forms of life, makes sense of Jesus's enigmatic statements about laying down one's life *(psyche)*, in order to keep it for eternal life *(zoe)*. It is exactly the same concept as St Paul saying that we must crucify the flesh (not fulfil its lusts), and instead, walk by the spirit.

Theologians argue over whether the Bible sees human nature as two-fold (bipartite) or three-fold (tripartite). At times it's one, and at times the other. The easiest way to convey how the Hebrew, Greek and English words map to each other, is in tabular form:

<table>
<tr><th></th><th>HEBREW</th><th colspan="2">GREEK</th><th>ENGLISH</th></tr>
<tr><td>BODY</td><td rowspan="2">Nephesh
('Living being')</td><td rowspan="2">Sarx
('Flesh')</td><td>Bios</td><td>Biology</td></tr>
<tr><td>SOUL</td><td>Psyche</td><td>Psychology</td></tr>
<tr><td>SPIRIT</td><td>Ruach</td><td colspan="2">Pneuma</td><td>?</td></tr>
</table>

N.B: Our bodily life is our 'flesh and blood' and is how we relate to the physical world through sight, sound, touch, smell Our soul is our inner life: thoughts, emotions, desires. And it determines how we relate to those around us. Our spirit is the element that enables us to worship; to hear God; and to sense when we are morally off-beam.

Paul often focusses on the distinction between our flesh (our fallen nature), and our spirit. But he, like John, recognises the distinction between soul and spirit.[10] This is really important to recognise when thinking about our union with Christ, and being indwelt by the Holy Spirit. God intends us to be led by the Holy Spirit, operating through our spirits. Understanding that spirits indwell body and soul is key to grasping our union with Christ. Just as Legion's behaviour was driven by the many demonic spirits mingling with his spirit, our human spirits can be indwelt by the Spirit of God, and thus we become one spirit with Christ.

[10] (1 Thess 5:23; Heb 4:12)

Light

This word has several connotations:-

- Light makes things visible. Sunlight shows up where we haven't dusted! And in the same way, Jesus's light exposes our darkness.
Star Wars portrays men as having two natures, one light and one dark: one can fight for goodness and truth, or flip to the Dark Side. But scripture never portrays man like this. By nature, John says, *"men loved darkness rather than light because their deeds were evil".*[11]
The darkness within us hates the light of Christ, which exposes our evil thoughts and hidden sins.

- Light destroys darkness; but darkness can never destroy light. Where there is light, there cannot be darkness. The two are completely incompatible.
John says, *"This is the message which we have heard from Him and declare to you, that God is Light, and in Him is no darkness at all"*[12]. If we habitually live in darkness, or pretend to have no sin, no need of confession and cleansing, we are deceiving ourselves and others, but not God. We cannot have loving fellowship with God unless we 'walk in the light'. *"What fellowship has light with darkness? Or what fellowship has Christ with Belial?"*[13]

- Light symbolises purity. Whilst refusing to condemn her, Jesus says to the woman caught in adultery, *"Go and sin no more". But unlike the Pharisees,* His holiness includes grace as well as truth, forgiveness as well as moral clarity. *"He who says he abides in Him, ought to walk just as He walked".*[14]. His whole life, not just His teaching, radiated light.

- Light brings life. Without sunlight there would be no vegetation, no life of any form, on Planet Earth. Jesus says, *"I am the Light of the world, He who follows Me shall not walk in darkness but have the light of life".*
John says, *"In Him was life, and the life was the light of men".* In ethical and cultural terms, His life was the single most influential life in human history. However that moral and spiritual enlightenment always operates through a

---

[11] (3:19)
[12] (1Jn 1:5)
[13] (2 Cor 6:14,15)
[14] (1Jn 2:6)

transfusion of His life into us.

When John describes Jesus as *"the true Light which gives light to every man (by) coming into the world"*[15], some see this as teaching that Christ's sacrifice restored humanity's free will from the effects of the Fall, enabling us to choose to repent. But even the greatest of spiritual teachers, such as Nicodemus, cannot grasp the wisdom of the cross unless they're first born again. Christ Himself is the Light of the world, and we can only become 'sons of light' through ongoing discipleship, once we have believed in Him[16].

Glory

In English we use the word *glory* to mean honour or distinction. For example, *"He didn't cover himself with glory, did he?"* It can also be used as a verb meaning exultation: we *'glory in the Lord'*.

But in Hebrew, the word *'kabod'* means weight, weightiness, importance. Paul talks about *'our light affliction working for us a far more exceeding and eternal weight of glory'*[17].

Of course to a Jew it also meant the physical radiance of God's Presence. His Shekinah glory had hovered over the Israelites as they journeyed through the desert at night, filling the Holy of Holies in the Tabernacle. This was the glory that caused Moses' face to become radiant, in the Tent of Meeting!

This glory of God was hidden when Jesus came to earth: He 'veiled it in flesh', He 'laid aside His majesty', 'did not count equality with God something to be held onto' and humbled Himself to become man. It was only once the Father had revealed to Peter that Jesus was the Messiah, the Son of God, that the disciples could then experience the Transfiguration.[18]

John sees Jesus's hidden glory being displayed in each of the seven miraculous signs he selects, not just in that one private revelation at the Transfiguration. After recounting the turning of water into wine in Cana, he says, *"This beginning of signs Jesus did in Cana of Galilee, and manifested His*

---

[15] (John 1:9)
[16] (John 12:35,36)
[17] (2Cor 4:17)
[18] (Matt 17:1-9)

glory; and His disciples believed in Him".[19] The healing of the nobleman's son, the lame man at the Pool of Bethesda, the feeding of the five thousand, the healing of the man born blind, raising Lazarus from the dead, and lastly, His own resurrection - they all revealed Jesus's hidden glory.

But there was a fuller revelation of His glory still to come: for as He walks to the Garden of Gethsemane, Jesus prays for His disciples, *"Father, I desire that they also whom You gave Me may be with Me where I am, that they my behold My glory which You have given Me; for You loved Me before the foundation of the world".*[20]

Just as Moses saw the glory of God, and John saw it, we too are to see it. For Paul says, *"We all, with unveiled faces, beholding as in a mirror the glory of the Lord, are being transformed into the same image from glory to glory, by the Spirit of the Lord".*[21]

My prayer for you, as you read these chapters, is that John's experience may become yours too: *"We beheld His glory, glory as of the only-begotten Son of the Father, full of grace and truth".*

The Jews

John frequently refers to opposition from 'the Jews': for example when the Pharisees excommunicate the man born blind[22]. This has led to a perception that John is antisemitic. But in fact, the Greek word refers to Judaeans as a geographic - not ethnic - group, distinct from Samaritans and Galileans.

Jesus Himself was a Judaean[23], though many Judaeans thought He was Galilean[24]. John, though Galilean, is not anti-Judaean per se; and he is certainly not anti-semitic, as some would have us believe. Rather, he sees the Judaeans' disbelief in Jesus's incarnation as being driven by an anti-Christ spirit, as he explains in his subsequent letter.[25]

---

[19] (2:11)
[20] (17:24)
[21] (2Cor 3:18)
[22] (9:19-22, 29-34)
[23] (4:43-45)
[24] (7:40-42)
[25] (1Jn 4:2-3)

Appendix 3: Questions to ponder

- How far does 'believing *into* Jesus' figure in the gospel we preach to others, if at all? And how far are we ourselves *'in the wheelbarrow'*? (See p234)
- If Jesus is active in His creation to this day, how should that affect our sense of anticipation and expectancy as we live our daily lives?
- If Jesus lives in permanent and perfect Father-Son relationship with God, how does that change the way we see our relationship with God?
- Beyond Christmas carols, how central is the incarnation in our worship? How far is it the yardstick by which we test whether what we hear is truth?
- If you died today, how would friends and family describe you? Honest? Hypocritical? Upright? Unprincipled? Or 'full of grace and truth', like Jesus?
- If Jesus is the good Shepherd, and we are His sheep - prone to wander, but tuned to His call - what should be our attitude to fellow believers?
- If the 'Upper Room discourse' describes the 'normal' Christian experience of God, how far does our own Christian experience match up?
- If Jesus was the first missionary, sent by the Father, what does 'As the Father sent Me, so send I you' mean in our daily lives?
- If the Spirit's main role is to witness to Jesus, and to strengthen us as we too witness and face blowback, have we been 'baptised in Spirit and fire'?
- If Jesus has returned to His Father and His pre-incarnate glory, and we are seated with Him in the heavenlies, how should this affect the way we pray?
- How much is 'beholding His glory' part of your spiritual walk? How easy do you find it, to enter into adoration as you pray?

About the Author

Andrew was for many years a London family doctor. Coming from Methodist roots, he came to personal faith whilst at university. Seeking to receive the Holy Spirit led to a lifelong passion for studying scripture, which was fed further by strong biblical teaching from his first pastor, and in the Christian Union.

Since taking early retirement he has been involved in church leadership roles, mission work abroad, and the Christian healing ministry. For the last decade he has been writing on various biblical topics; details of which can be supplied on request

Having to 'shield' since Covid came five years ago, has meant being shut in with God much of the time. This has been a massive blessing-in-disguise - a season of deep joy! And John's Gospel has been its primary wellspring.

He can be contacted at *reachingouttoGod@gmail.com*.